The Focke-Wulf Fw 200 Condor

The Focke-Wulf Fw 200 Condor

Jerry Scutts

Crécy Publishing

Published in 2010 by Crécy Publishing Limited, Manchester

Copyright © Jerry Scutts 2008

A CIP record for this book is available from the British Library

ISBN 9 78085 9791311

Printed and bound in Great Britain
by MPG Books Ltd

Crécy Publishing Limited
1a Ringway Trading Estate, Shadowmoss Road, Manchester M22 5LH
www.crecy.co.uk

Frontispiece:
Condors of I./KG 40 lined up at Bordeaux-Merignac, September 1941. Note the blanked out 'world in a ring' badge on the nose.
C Goss

Contents

Introduction

One of several dozen civil aircraft impressed into the Luftwaffe in the years immediately prior to the outbreak of the Second World War, the Focke-Wulf Fw 200 Condor found a unique role after Germany opened hostilities on 1 September 1939. Preoccupied with the concept of Blitzkrieg ('lightning war'), the Luftwaffe High Command became aware of several shortfalls in the aircraft inventory when the conflict widened to indicate anything but a war of limited duration. Among these were long-range maritime reconnaissance and anti-shipping attack, heavy transport, effective battlefield anti-tank capability, and so on. After the subjugation of France, Britain alone was in a position to reject any peace terms offered by Adolf Hitler's Nazi regime. For Germany, dealing militarily with a strong nation that showed every intention of fighting on was totally alien, far outside what the military forces of a largely land-locked country had yet experienced. An island enemy separated from Germany's captured French air bases by 100 miles of water was not a situation the Luftwaffe had yet faced, and when it failed to gain air superiority over the RAF early in 1940 an invasion of the British Isles was clearly indicated.

This also posed several insurmountable problems, not the least of which was that the Royal Navy remained a force to be reckoned with, as did the RAF's fighter squadrons, based mainly in southern England primarily to intercept incoming bombers. The outcome of such a campaign could not be a guaranteed German victory, despite Hermann Goering's boasts to the contrary. Germany had other war-making potential, including the imposition of a sea blockade by unrestricted submarine assault. This could ostensibly bring about the success narrowly denied Germany in the First World War – deprivation of food, arms and other vital supplies to the point of starvation of the British populace. Karl Doenitz, C-in-C of the Kriegsmarine's U-boat arm, believed that that goal could be achieved in the current war using more aggressive tactics by a greater number of advanced-design U-boats and the added dimension of large-scale air attacks on shipping, a form of warfare largely beyond the German air arm in the first war. Maritime reconnaissance and attack therefore became, largely by default, the forte of the militarised Focke-Wulf Condor, the attractive pre-war airliner that had heralded German dominance of the world's civil air routes in the last years of peace.

Denied the sound basis of an organised maritime air arm by official pontification and personal aggrandisement on the part of Hermann Goering, at a time when he was able to manipulate and persuade Hitler with seeming ease, the naval air service found itself 'making do' with a largely inshore force of flying boats and floatplanes. It did, however, enjoy an affinity with the officers who were responsible for modifying and deploying the Condor – the one aircraft type available in sufficient numbers – for the exacting role of anti-shipping strike hundreds of miles out into the North Atlantic. Things would improve once the importance of a maritime air force was proven with several new designs and new units, but in the meantime OKL – Oberkommando der Luftwaffe – concurred with the views of men such as Edgar Petersen, a highly energetic advocate of maritime warfare who had a Kriegsmarine and Luftwaffe background, that military Condors had to made available immediately.

As an emergency measure Focke-Wulf consequently turned its elegant prewar airliner into a warplane. It was far from ideally suited for the role, was never available in sufficient numbers and was dangerously susceptible to destruction by enemy aircraft, shipboard guns and other defensive devices … and yet the Condor achieved a combat record – not to mention a notorious reputation – far beyond its theoretical military limitations. Those negative aspects could be proven time and again by structural engineers, wind tunnel figures and test pilot reports. All the results were valid – except to the crews of Kampfgeschwader 40, with its striking world-encircling insignia, who steadfastly took the Condors out to fight what amounted almost to a private war. They had little choice but to get on with the job they were ordered to do and, as many an Allied seaman was only too well aware, they did it with ruthless efficiency in the harsh and dangerous Battle of the Atlantic, where no quarter was asked and all too rarely given.

Acknowledgements

In compiling this account of the development and service use of the Focke-Wulf Condor numerous individuals and organisations have helped. Alphabetically these include:

Heidi Bailey; Ian Carter; Eddie Creek; Duxford Historical Archives; Nathan Howland; Imperial War Museum Department of Documents and Photographic Archive; IWM Archive, Duxford; Philip Jarrett; Lufthansa PR, Alfred Price; Franz Selinger; Harold Thiele; Dennis Tomlinson, Steven Walden and John Weal.

Last but not least, my sincere thanks to my publisher Gill Richardson who had every right to tear her hair out but kept her cool until the manuscript was finally delivered.

My thanks to one and all.

Jerry Scutts
Blackheath
London
2008

Chapter 1

Elegant newcomer

As international airline routes expanded rapidly during the 1930s, they gave rise to a need for a new generation of aircraft with the necessary size and range to serve distant destinations on a regular, route-structured basis. Several countries competed with each other to design and construct monoplane aircraft in the multi-engine configuration that would be required, among them Germany, a country regenerated after Adolf Hitler's assumption of power in 1933. The nation's state airline, Deutsch Luft Hansa (known as Deutsche Lufthansa – DLH – from 30 June 1933), sought to secure new aircraft suited to the demands of these new routes, particularly those intended to serve locations that were growing increasingly important in the development of international trade. Air services far distant from the operator's base had been well served to some extent by flying boats, but there was an increasing move towards more permanent airports with road and rail transport links, which in turn gave rise to a new generation of landplanes to establish regular, timetabled schedules. With these new aircraft came a nucleus of passengers who would eventually open up air travel to those who had never previously had the means to fly aboard. An increase in potential air passengers was assured almost in spite of any event that may have postponed it; sooner or later the world would take wing as never before.

Given the relatively modest power output of the aero engines of the day, four would be needed to provide the necessary range and reliability to meet international safety standards. In addition, such aircraft would have to accommodate ample quantities of fuel as well as space for the maximum number of passengers and freight. Even medium-leg routes were being flown by aircraft with the safety factor of three engines, notably the Savoia Marchetti S.73, Fokker F.VII and, arguably the most famous tri-motor in history, the Junkers Ju 52/3m.

Halfway into the decade Germany fervently wished to demonstrate that it had utterly overcome the strictures imposed upon it by the Treaty of Versailles following the First World War and was ready to undertake a major, re-energised, role on the world stage. One sure way to project the prestige of a revitalised nation was to have its state airline equipped with the most modern aircraft and for them to be seen in every part of the globe.

Company profile

Focke-Wulf's own title was derived from the surnames of its co-founders, Heinrich Focke and Georg Wulf, aviation engineers who had formed a partnership prior to the First World War. This arrangement endured into the difficult postwar years and was resurrected in 1921 with a design for a two-seat monoplane. This, the A 7 Storch ('Stork'), a private venture monoplane in the 'sportsplane' category, was the first tangible result of the collaboration; it re-established the Focke and Wulf partnership, in due course as a manufacturer of reliable if not highly innovative transport and liaison aircraft.

Focke and Wulf made their association official on 1 January 1924 with the creation of the Focke-Wulf Flugzeugbau AG (FWF). Based at Bremen Airport, initially in premises shared with the airline Deutsche Aero Lloyd, FWF initiated the production of aeroplanes with the first A 7 Storch. While the sole example had concluded a successful maiden flight in November 1921, it was subsequently damaged in a storm and was not rebuilt until mid-1922. Fitted with a 55hp Siemens radial engine, the aircraft was registered and given a passenger licence. A demonstration for local businessmen in 1923 led eventually to an allocation of the funds the young company needed with which to build a sound operation. This materialised in the form of a 200,000RM contribution from the Bremen-based business group led by Dr Ludwig Roselius, owner of the Kaffee-Hag company, which enabled Focke-Wulf to establish an 'aircraft building enterprise'; on formation it included Heinrich Focke as technical director, Georg Wulf as test pilot and Dr Werner Naumann as Commercial Director.

FWF went on to build a succession of small passenger-carrying airliners and trainers until 1927 when the radical F 19a Ente ('Duck') emerged. This twin-engine machine had a canard or tail-first configuration and was based on an earlier design with which Wilhelm Focke, Heinrich's elder brother, had been associated. The Ente first flew in September 1927, with Oberingenieur (chief engineer) Georg Wulf at the controls. Fourteen more flights were made before disaster struck. On 29 September Wulf was demonstrating the aircraft's single-engine characteristics when it spun into the ground.

Wulf did not survive the crash, the cause of which was later found to be a broken control rod rather than a design flaw. Despite the huge setback of losing one of its founders, Focke's team continued development of the Ente; however, it did not manage to secure any commercial orders, even after a European demonstration and sales tour.

Up to the mid-1920s Focke-Wulf produced designs in several different categories, usually in the very small numbers typical of the period – indeed, it was not unusual for just a single example to be completed before a design revision brought about a new designation for the same little-changed airframe.

Nothing if not diverse in its approach, FWF designs of the inter-war period included the A 20/28 Habicht ('Hawk'), a three-to-four-seat passenger airliner; the A 21 Mowe ('Seagull') photographic reconnaissance aircraft; the A 26 eight-seat airliner; and the A 32 Bussard ('Buzzard') and A 33 Sperber ('Sparrowhawk'), which were six- and three-seat airliners respectively. Some 'new' aircraft that were allocated different type numbers were actually rebuilds or modifications of existing Focke-Wulf designs.

When he arrived at Focke-Wulf, Dipl Ing Kurt Waldemar Tank brought with him invaluable experience. He had worked diligently to keep himself abreast of all things aeronautical and became an avid student of the latest techniques and advances in aeronautical design. Having been project director with Bayerische Flugzeugwerke (later Messerschmitt AG) between January 1930 and December 1931, Tank joined Focke-Wulf before the end of the year as director of the design department.

Tank's fascination with the progress of aviation meant that he was virtually a self-made engineer with an intimate working knowledge of the theory and practice of flight in all its forms. And he was no armchair technician, but a skilled pilot who usually flew the aircraft his company built, combining the role of designer with that of test pilot, which was a very unusual approach. By the time the company flew the A 39, a two-seat reconnaissance aircraft of 1931, Kurt Tank was, as technical director, able to supervise some of the design work, this being primarily in the hands of Dipl Ing Wilhelm Bansemir. Tank gathered around him a highly skilled team of designers and engineers, some of whom had previously worked for the famous Albatros company, which the Bremen-based concern absorbed in 1931.

Work on the parasol-wing A 40 reconnaissance aircraft taxed Tank's skills to the limit; its inherent instability proved incurable, a drawback that removed any realistic chance of winning a production contract. It came as no surprise that the A 40 lost out in competition with the He 46, although it was one of the first aircraft to be identified as a Focke-Wulf product when it became the Fw 40 under the revised aircraft designation system introduced by the RLM, the Reichsluftfahrtministerium or German aviation ministry, in 1933.

Between the assumption of power by Hitler's National Socialists and the end of the Second World War, Focke-Wulf went on to build twenty or so aircraft types and their derivatives; numerous projects were also studied and the company additionally began the manufacture of autogiros and helicopters. Heinrich Focke became increasingly preoccupied by rotary-winged flight and left the company in 1933 to take over the new Focke-Achgelis GmbH and concentrate entirely on helicopter development. This left the parent company free to put all its expertise into fixed-wing designs, and between 1928 and 1939, when the first Fw 190 appeared, the company completed approximately 1,895 aircraft.

In 1945, in common with much of Germany's aircraft industry, Focke-Wulf's manufacturing plants lay in ruins. However, the company recovered, albeit slowly, and by 1946 was working on its first postwar jet-powered project, the vertical-take-off VAK 191B. In the interim years the company had formed a partnership with the Dutch manufacturer Fokker. Collaboration with representatives of the old-established German aviation companies, principally those who had been with Heinkel, led to the formation of Vereinigte Flugtechnische Werke (VFW), which initiated the development of the twin-jet VFW 614 airliner in 1961.

Few could accuse Condor designer Kurt Tank of being an 'armchair engineer'. White overalls, worn on numerous test and delivery flights while he was on the flight deck, became something of a trademark.

Kurt Tank left Germany after the war and established himself in Argentina, where he worked on an improved version of the Pulqui I ('Arrow') jet fighter designed by Emile Dewoitine. Tank's Pulqui II was based on the configuration of the Ta 183 jet fighter he had developed during the war, and although the result could have been a potential boost to Argentina's air arm, it was not produced in quantity.

Tank bade farewell to South America to pursue his aviation interests in India, where he designed the HF-24 Marut for Hindustan Aircraft Limited. Entering service with the Indian Air Force in June 1977, the first indigenous jet fighter on the sub-continent gave a good account of itself in the fighter-bomber role but was restricted as an interceptor by an engine of limited power. Some further development was undertaken, although the IAF soon opted to licence-build Russian equipment, primarily the MiG-21.

Kurt Tank finally returned to Germany and for a brief spell worked for the Messerschmitt-Bolkow-Blohm (MBB) consortium before ill health overtook him. He passed away on 5 June 1983.

*

When the RLM issued a request for proposals to build a fast four-engine airliner to DLH requirements on 19 January 1936, the ministry may have been aware that Focke-Wulf had production capacity to spare at Bremen. Having recently switched to producing all-metal airframes, FWF seemed well able – notwithstanding the company's lack of experience in building this class of aircraft – to undertake such a design. Having previously worked on all-metal marine aircraft with the Rohrbach company, Kurt Tank certainly thought so.

While a large airliner was a challenging new project for Focke-Wulf, in terms of technical expertise, the management believed that the company was well placed to offer the directors of

Deutsch Luft Hansa a design that promised to set new records for both manufacturer and customer. But with no previous experience of building any large aircraft, the Focke-Wulf Flugzeubau was not the obvious choice to embark on a prestigious new airliner. By hiring Kurt Tank, however, the small company had fortuitously endowed itself with a progressive engineering titan.

Focke-Wulf was probably not as well known by the general public as the larger German aeronautical concerns such as Dornier, Junkers and Messerschmitt, as they had all perpetuated the name(s) of their individual founders. As he had not been a founder of FWF, Tank's name was not initially used in the company title, although he was nevertheless granted this honour in January 1943, after which all subsequent designs were identified by his abbreviated initial 'Ta'. Any project initiated before that date carried the familiar 'Fw' company prefix, even if Tank had had a major hand in the design.

Foreign engines

A significant step in creating one of the few four-engine aircraft that took to the air in the Third Reich before the war was the 1930-34 procurement of aero engines from the United States. In the days before German industry was organised enough to produce its own engines and airframes in quantity, this agreement resulted in 569 engines arriving in the country, which was indeed fortuitous. Several prototypes, including the Heinkel He 70, He 112 and Bf 109, were consequently able to make their initial flights and begin testing powered by 'foreign' engines, whereas waiting for indigenous powerplants would have resulted in costly and unacceptable delays.

Most significant to the history of what became the Fw 200 was the fact that BMW had in 1929 obtained licenses from Pratt & Whitney to manufacture SE1-G Hornet and R-1830 Twin Wasp air-cooled radial engines. As the BMW 132 the German company would eventually manufacture Hornet derivatives to the extent of 24,000 units up to 1944. In June 1939 BMW had also acquired Siemens Flugmotorenwerk, which was then building radial engines under the name Bramo. Siemens soon relinquished its aero engine interests, by which time the Brandenburg Motor Works (Bramo) had merged with BMW in order to prevent two companies manufacturing air-cooled engines and competing unnecessarily.

The Bramo name was perpetuated by BMW in the Bramo and Bramo Fafnir engines, the company eventually supplying 4,088 examples; these were identified by various model numbers beginning with the 139, a 14-cylinder powerplant that was in turn a development of the 720hp 132L, which was to power the Condor on its flights to America and Tokyo. This engine was all but identical to that known to Bramo as the 329.

Numerous test flights were conducted with the first Fw 200, the aircraft being fitted with BMW 132 radials to replace the original Pratt & Whitney Hornet engines.

Initial steps in 1936

Following the RLM request, Tank responded with a design study for an airliner that would incorporate the latest aerodynamic and structural techniques. It would have an unusually long-span wing of 108 feet (32.97 metres), with a slim chord to provide maximum lift, and would be powered by four Pratt & Whitney SE1-G Hornet engines of 875hp, pending the availability of BMW powerplants.

Legend has it that Tank's discussions with Dr Strussel, DLH's technical director, stemmed from a chance first meeting at a railway station. In conversation, Focke-Wulf's technical director convinced Strussel that aeronautics had advanced to the point where it was perfectly feasible to build an airliner that could cross the Atlantic and operate a commercial service to the USA. Tank himself had only a vague idea of what form the layout of the 'Condor' (the name the RLM had confirmed, in line with Focke-Wulf's penchant for naming its aeroplanes after species of bird) would take, but lost no time in asking Oberingenieur Ludwig Mittelhuber to work out a design based on his ideas.

Whether or not Strussel was convinced by Tank, an engineer who wanted to dispense with the cumbersome but well-proven flying boats that had previously dominated the large civil aircraft market, he was soon poring over plans of the impressive-looking landplane that was the outcome of the conversion on a train, or so the story goes.

The broad parameters of the Condor's configuration had been specified by the RLM in a February 1936 order to proceed with an airliner operated by a flight crew of four including one cabin attendant and capable of carrying up to 25 passengers. BMW 132 G engines were specified, as was a range of 750 miles (1,200km) and a top speed of 300mph (480kmph).

FWF had started work immediately; Strussel conferred with Freiherr von Gablenz, a fellow director of Deutsch Lufthansa, and by June 1936 the airline was taking an active interest in the new aircraft. Still somewhat doubting that Focke-Wulf could deliver – von Gablenz knew that a realistic timescale for prototypes to be ready was at least two to three years – he is famously said to have bet Tank a crate of champagne that he would be unable to have a prototype flying inside twelve months. This was a remarkably short time scale for such a large project, but perhaps with their tongues firmly in their cheeks, the two men were delighted when Tank accepted the bet. He was determined to win it.

The airliner project was allocated, by permission of the RLM, the unusually high type number 200. Tank felt this to be appropriate, stating that it reflected a design that was way ahead in its class and more ambitious than anything else the company had previously built.

At that time German aeronautical companies were allocated a block of 'build numbers', Focke-Wulf's being 8-189 to 8-191. These numbers served as a progressive record of production achievement and in Focke-Wulf's case represented three projects that were more or less current or about to enter the design study stage in the immediate future. Then producing the Fw 44 Stieglitz ('Goldfinch') trainer and the twin-engined Fw 58 Weihe ('Kite') communications type, FWF had built a reputation for sound designs that possessed a high degree of reliability; few doubted that a much larger project, progressed under Tank's masterly hand, would fail to establish an equally sound reputation.

Work in progress

Projected Focke-Wulf designs had in fact almost reached the number 200, with the still-born Fw 187 Falke ('Falcon') twin-engined fighter (of 1937) and the subsequent 189 Uhu ('Eagle Owl'), which first flew in 1938 and entered service with the Luftwaffe in 1940 as a reconnaissance aircraft. In between, so to speak, was the superlative Fw 190 fighter series and the Fw 191 bomber, the latter destined not to proceed far beyond the prototype/experimental stage after its initial flight tests were completed in 1943.

At its main base in Bremen, Focke-Wulf's draughtsmen and engineers worked diligently under the able leadership of Dipl-Ing Wilhelm Bansemir's design team to produce a wooden mock-up of the new airliner in the shortest possible time. By June 1936 this had advanced far enough for DLH to make an inspection and issue a development contract, covering two prototypes and ten Fw 200A-0 production examples. This agreement for a dozen airframes appears almost certainly to have been an initial contract, with further similar aircraft subsequently added and identified as early production examples.

Airframe innovations

The Fw 200 was a conventional, low-wing monoplane with a single vertical tail unit and a three-point landing gear. Each engine drove two-bladed, fixed-pitch VDM-Hamilton propellers with spinners, a configuration detail that would be retained on all the early production examples but removed later. All four engine cowlings were remarkably smooth, with air intakes being provided only on each outboard pair to slightly compromise the pleasing lines. Otherwise the entire airframe was remarkably streamlined without excrescences to mar the flush-riveted stressed skin. Hydraulically operated split flaps were incorporated, covered with Elektron magnesium alloy. The cantilever wing, with its aspect ratio of 9.15, consisted of a horizontal centre-section that carried the engine mountings, with dihedral and tapered outer panels. Each outboard engine nacelle was canted outwards by a few degrees in order to minimise torque and dampen any tendency to swing during the take-off run. To save weight the wing was fabric-covered aft of the main spar with all control surfaces (which were also fabric-covered) being manually operated but incorporating geared tabs and electrically driven trim tabs. Overall, the effect was of a sweptback wing with a distinctly kinked trailing edge.

Unique undercarriage

Among the innovative features of the Fw 200 were forked oleo legs that carried single mainwheels on the early production examples and were made, as was the tailwheel, to fold forwards. Carried forward of the oleo legs, the wheels were attached to swing links equipped with diagonal shock struts. Both main undercarriage units were fully retractable and completely enclosed by twin doors in each inboard nacelle when retracted.

On the ground, the Condor appeared to 'kneel' as a result of the bracing struts of the main oleos being kinked at approximately the mid-point and being aligned horizontally. This was an attempt to overcome an international problem with airliners of the period whereby the main landing gear legs would usually fail to extend fully in the event of a loss of hydraulic pressure. In the Focke-Wulf design the legs were made to extend far enough for the exposed wheels to provide a cushioning effect in the event of an emergency landing. It was also envisaged that each leg would 'fall free' and be locked in position by the air flow, should they fail to lock down completely at the first attempt. Early in production (from the Fw 200B onwards) each main undercarriage unit was fitted with double mainwheels to enhance the aircraft's 'soft' landing properties.

The fully castoring tailwheel strut was made unusually long, in effect raising the tail by several inches and providing the aircraft with a ground attitude that was as 'flat' as possible to enhance passenger boarding and disembarking. These and other features would instil a degree of passenger comfort unmatched by rival air carriers and create considerable traveller loyalty to Germany's elegant Condor.

Cockpit

The cockpit of the Condor was provided with full dual controls, the main instrument dials being grouped neatly across a 'bridge' panel with a central vertical console incorporating supplementary instruments and two sets of four throttle levers. Red (port) and green (starboard) colour coding of the throttle and mixture lever knobs was provided.

A circular observation window, a distinctive design feature of all the Condors, was set into the port side in line with the pilot's seat to provide a useful downwards view of the main landing gear during take-off and landing.

A radio room for the flight engineer, containing a chart table with a moveable seat, was located on the starboard side of the forward fuselage behind the co-pilot. Banks of instruments, each with its removable console, were located in front of the engineer for ease of operation.

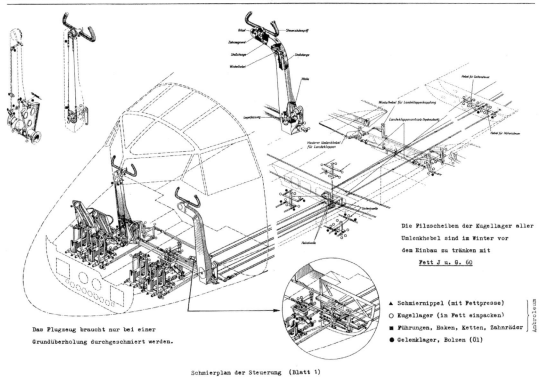

A diagram from the official Focke-Wulf handbook illustrating the flight deck controls including the control columns, rudder pedals and some of the control runs.

Seating

In original form and up to and including the Fw 200B, the civil Condor was configured to carry 23 passengers, a maximum of 26 seats being provided. Nine forward 'smoking' seats were located behind the stewards' area immediately aft of the cockpit, with fourteen 'non-smoking' seats situated in a central compartment behind the main bulkhead. Toilet/washroom facilities were provided for crew and passengers with such additional refinements as a post room, pantry and luggage stowage. A second compartment was designed to take larger items of passengers' luggage. Entry/exit doors were provided on both sides of the fuselage aft of the wing, and eighteen rectangular windows (nine per side) gave the occupants of the cabin an excellent view of the outside world.

Maiden flight

Kurt Tank's wager that the Fw 200 would make its maiden flight inside a year was lost, but only by about four weeks. In thirteen months the prototype was completed, with the American engines installed. This was a remarkable achievement and, eager to pass the milestone of the first flight, the date of 27 July was given out, possibly by the company. This was incorrect and may have stemmed from Bremen hosting what would today be termed a 'roll-out' ceremony, with industry officials and major customer representatives welcomed by the manufacturer to examine the aircraft at close quarters and celebrate a milestone achievement – which the completion of the first Fw 200 undoubtedly was. The date has been mistakenly quoted as that of the first flight, but some weeks were to pass before this significant event took place.

It was on 6 September 1937 that the Fw 200V-1 (Werke Nr 2000/D-AERE) took off on its maiden flight from Bremen-Neuenlander airfield piloted by test pilot Hans Sander with designer Kurt Tank acting as co-pilot. The initial flight was the first of many conducted to complete manufacturer's trials and verify the smooth functioning of the myriad items necessary for the issue of a commercial licence. As for the wager, although von Gablenz had technically won, he magnanimously accepted the short overrun and, when Tank's champagne duly arrived, he despatched a second crate to the designer.

Devoid of markings, the Fw 200 V-1 reached flight status in a remarkably short time. In this view it still has the original rounded-off rudder, which was subsequently increased in area. *P. Jarrett*

Kurt Tank was fully involved with monitoring the handling of the prototype Condor during its maiden flight, which reportedly went well, the V-1 proving that the Fw 200 flew as well as it looked. The company lost little time in completing a second aircraft (2484/D-AETA) by 27 October, and both the V-1 and V-2 were shown publicly at Berlin-Tempelhof on 27 November 1937. By that date about ninety flights had been made by the first Condor and sixty by the second.

In comparison with the original Fw 200 drawings, some airframe modifications had been necessary during construction and flight tests. Stability had been enhanced by the addition of adjustable end-plate finlets attached to each horizontal stabiliser, although the flight crew found that the elevators had actually been overbalanced to the point where the pilot had some difficulty in holding the aircraft on course. During the first flight Tank solicited the aid of a mechanic, the third occupant of the aircraft on that occasion, to help him to hold the control column steady. This was a problem that was easily rectified by adjusting the balance of the elevators.

Wind tunnel testing of models at Rechlin had also revealed that the original wing design, given a pronounced kink at the trailing edge, caused some adverse effect on the centre of gravity; the outer wing panels were revised to overcome the problem. Also, some redesign of the vertical tail surfaces had been found necessary. More rudder area was added, the distinct curvature at the top of the trailing edge, an original feature of the prototype, being squared off.

Although the first flights of the Condor were made with fixed-pitch Hamilton airscrews fitted to the Hornet engines, these were eventually replaced by three-bladed variable-pitch VDM/Hamilton Standard propellers, which were fully feathering. Spinners were fitted over each propeller hub to enhance streamlining, although these too were subsequently dispensed with. Each engine delivered 760hp, providing a total of 3,040hp.

The first Condor had an empty weight of 2,030lb (9,200kg); adding the weight of the crew, a payload of 5,500lb (2,480kg), together with fuel and oil, brought the maximum permissible load to 10,580lb (4,800kg).

The take-off weight for the Fw 200V-1 was established at 30,870lb (14,000kg), making D-AERE, and D-AETA (which was also powered by the S-1 E-G), the lightest Condors of the entire early series. This was far from unusual for most prototypes, prior to the addition of operational equipment, be it passenger seating, navigational aids and radio sets or additional internal fuel cells, invariably possessed a lighter all-up weight, a factor reflected in control pressures. Numerous pilot reports confirm that the first examples of the new aircraft type were the most pleasant to fly in this respect.

Few observers could deny that Focke-Wulf had produced a fine-looking aeroplane with graceful, unspoiled lines, making the Condor one of the most striking potential airliners of its day. Equally, it was inevitable that, by the time of its debut, rivals had emerged to share in the vast expansion of airline travel that was anticipated for the 1940s.

At a time of unprecedented expansion of international air routes and concurrent industry competition to sell aircraft to operate them, the Condor had by late 1937 been joined in the international design stakes by other nations with industries able to develop multi-engine airliners.

Four engines became the yardstick that aviation authorities sought for safety and reliability in airliners that were serving a fast-changing world in terms of new destinations. Countries outside Germany that saw the revenue-earning potential of long-distance services included the United States, which produced the advanced Boeing Model 307 (247) Stratoliner; among its modern features was cabin pressurisation, used for the first time in a commercial airliner and offering unprecedented 'above the weather' high-altitude flight in undreamed-of comfort for the occupants. Other companies appreciated the potential, notably Douglas with the DC-4E. The 'E' denoted experimental status and the subsequent airliner-cum-military-transport incorporated several significant changes when it flew in reconfigured form as the DC-4 in 1942.

Work on four-engine designs in France was centred on the products of Marcel Bloch. Although the company designed the Model 160, this did not enter service before the war but was revamped in 1945. The world-renowned Fokker company, with its sound background in commercial aircraft, likewise temporarily suspended the design and manufacture of large civil airliners after completing but a single example of the F.XXXVI with its characteristic fixed landing gear.

In Great Britain de Havilland produced the very essence of aeronautical streamlining in the DH 91 Albatross, which made extensive use of wood in its construction. Armstrong Whitworth built the high-wing AW 27 Ensign and this, together with its contemporaries, enjoyed a degree of success in airline service. The number of passengers needing to fly over lengthy routes on a regular basis was then relatively small, enabling manufacturers to limit the number of seats and provide ample leg room for the occupants and good ease of movement for the stewards. Production contracts for the big airliners were also tiny compared to how large they would become after the war. Some of these international designs that flew in prototype form in the last years of peace would have been potential rivals to the Focke-Wulf 200 had civil air travel not been interrupted by the Second World War. The main contenders are listed in Table 1.

Table 1: First flight dates of multi-engine airliners

Type	First flight	Country of origin
Fokker F.XXXVI	circa 1935	The Netherlands
De Havilland Albatross	May 1937	Great Britain
Fw 200 Condor	Sept 1937	Germany
Armstrong Whitworth AW 27	Jan 1938	Great Britain
Douglas DC-4E	June 1938	USA
Boeing Model 307 (247)	Dec 1938	USA
Bloch Model 160	circa 1938/9	France

That the world was shrinking as far as international air travel was concerned was highlighted in a number of ways. Not the least of these was the epic flight by a Russian Tupolev design, the single-engined Ant-25 (RD-2) during June and July 1937. It seemed that everyone who could do so was out to establish an aviation 'first', and in June the same Russian machine claimed a world distance record and followed this up with a record flight to the USA – so it was not as if the Condor was without rivals. With the right aircraft, any number of new records were waiting to be established and claimed officially as such under Federation Aeronautic Internationale (FAI) rules.

German's own industry had also produced a potential close rival to the Condor when Junkers unveiled the Junkers Ju 90 in August 1937, this being a development of the Ju 89 that had first flown in December 1936. An aircraft that was considerably larger than the Fw 200, the Ju 90A emerged from the Junkers plant at Dessau even more slowly than did the Fw 200 from Bremen, but it eventually became a second long-range Luftwaffe maritime reconnaissance type based on the developed Ju 290, which flew in August 1942. The Ju 290 was to initially complement the Condor and take over some of its reconnaissance duties in late 1943-44.

Well aware of strides being made with the new generation of airliners around the world, DLH lost no time in informing FWF on 5 April 1937 to stockpile material to complete three more Fw 200s (2893-2895). Procurement of a completely new aircraft could not realistically be speeded up; the state airline had to await satisfactory performance figures obtained from tests with the prototypes before placing further firm orders. Armed with these figures DLH was able to confirm the order for the next three Condors on 9 December 1937.

It was well known that DLH's intention was to introduce the Condor into service by the summer of 1938, a goal that was met. For its part Focke-Wulf beat any potential rivals to provide aircraft for such a service to begin, although to save time it was obliged to make any modifications resulting from evaluation data while airframe assembly progressed. DLH wanted to begin a Condor service with the refined Fw 200S1 (A-0), and the first example (2893/D-ADHR) incorporated the aforementioned wing and vertical tail modifications. These latter changes were also made to the V-1 and V-2, although the manufacturer did not allow this work to delay any of the 'new build' examples.

Earlier in the year the necessary airframe changes were made to the Fw 200V-1, which had, under the name *Brandenburg*, commenced its 200-hour evaluation on 6 February. Within the month, on the 28th, the aircraft was returned to FWF for modification. The V-2 then took over route-proving, beginning on 6 May.

Political chess

A number of significant events in 1938 brought Europe to the brink of war. In March Germany annexed Austria, another move by Hitler to ostensibly bring all German nationals within the protectorate of the Greater Reich. Other nations did not view the Austrian Anschluss in quite the same light but no direct action was taken and the expansionist Nazi agenda continued with the occupation of the Sudetenland area of Czechoslovakia. Overlooking the fact that they were witnessing steps along the slow road to another war, representatives of Britain, France and Italy met in Munich and agreed to the occupation, while in September British Prime Minister Neville Chamberlain returned home after talks with Hitler to make his famous 'Peace in our time' speech.

These events mobilised the Luftwaffe units based in Germany while the Legion Condor was completing a combat demonstration by some of its new aircraft over Spain in support of Franco's Nationalists. What the world witnessed in Spain held grim portents if such actions were applied in other countries.

By the end of 1938 Britain had gained vital time to build up her air defences, Republican Spain had all but fallen to Franco, and Germany had secured as much territory as was practical, short of war. Some of the events of the year had indirectly affected the Fw 200 insofar as individual aircraft were selected as military transports straight off the drawing board as and when they might be needed for future Luftwaffe operations.

Much of the aeronautical calendar of 1938 was, however, taken up with civil operations and continual expansion of new routes. Early demonstration flights by the prototype Fw 200s impressed observers who noted that the German giant attained a top speed of 200mph (375kmph), faster than any of its rivals by a significant margin. Lufthansa had, they agreed, purchased an elegant new aircraft pleasing to the eye and capable of reaching destinations much more quickly than before. Neither was the comfortable seating overlooked by appreciative potential passengers. Even making allowance for the atmosphere of the times, the German national carrier's 'seal of approval' reflected confidence in German design and official support for the industry. In financial circles the potential to earn valuable foreign currency when the aircraft was offered for sale abroad showed sound business acumen.

Some three years beforehand, Germany had finally relinquished all restrictions imposed by the terms of the Treaty of Versailles and an unprecedented period of growth, already under way, took on a new impetus. No field reflected this situation more than the aviation industry, with DLH at the forefront of the expansion of civil flying; German manufacturers expanded and supplied modern aircraft equal to if not better than the world's best. Pilots and crews could openly be trained in large numbers to operate the airliners – some of which were little more than military types in civilian clothing – that would form the core of the Luftwaffe's bomber and transport force. The Fw 200 would similarly become part of this transition from peace to war, whereby the national airline was able to maintain services (albeit limited) over several routes without undue interference by a state of war.

It goes without saying that DLH did not cease operations on the day war broke out, pass all its aircraft to the Luftwaffe and pay off all its pilots and crews. Such a process did inevitably take place, but over a lengthy period of time, as airline crews and aircraft were transferred to boost Luftwaffe crew complements. And the prestigious Condor was destined to serve in a special unit dedicated to flying Hitler and his inner circle in considerable comfort, a valuable approval rating for what was becoming a well-regarded aircraft. As far as the civilian Condors were concerned, Lufthansa retained enough aircraft to continue air services at least for the first years of the war. With production numbers remaining modest, some of the early Condors were, as an expedient measure, to see both civil and military service.

Table 2: German four-engine aircraft types, 1936-42

Type	First flight
Junkers Ju 89	Dec 1936
Junkers Ju 90	Aug 1937
Heinkel He 116	mid-1937
Blohm & Voss Bv 142	Oct 1938
Heinkel He 177	Nov 1939
Messerschmitt Me 264	Dec 1941
Junkers Ju 290	Aug 1942

NB: With the exception of the He 177, with its coupled engines in twin cowlings, all of the above types had their engines in four separate cowlings.

As a matter of historic record it is worth noting that Blohm und Voss, renowned for its seaplanes and flying boats, created the Bv 142, one of the company's few landplane designs, by adapting the Ha 139 float seaplane to take a wheeled landing gear. Intended to meet a requirement for a transatlantic mail carrier, four examples were tested by DLH before the war but no orders materialised. The aircraft subsequently saw limited Luftwaffe service in the transport role.

Junkers, which had established its tri-motor Ju 52/3m as the Luftwaffe's premier transport, also led the field in terms of production and military service of its larger designs, even though the total produced remained quite small.

Flying boats sidelined

While the 1930s saw many of the world's long-distance air routes served by seaplanes, the advent of a new generation of faster, more efficient landplanes would lead to the quite rapid demise of this enjoyable form of travel in the late 1940s and 1950s. Seaplanes and flying boats would, however, play a significant part in the impending war, Germany having developed two-, three- and four-engine types, to culminate in the mighty Bv 222, one of the largest in this class of aircraft to see action.

Had the war not intervened it is almost certain that DLH would, using the Condor, have successfully negotiated an agreement for a transatlantic service from Germany to the USA. For a European carrier, such a route was seen not only as highly prestigious but a revenue-earner with enormous potential. Although such a service could not begin before Europe was once again plunged into war, Focke-Wulf was able to prove that the Condor was quite capable of flying the Atlantic and to operate across the Pacific via the 'great circle route' with its well-established waypoints.

Flight tests

The Fw 200V-1 was delivered to DLH at Berlin-Staaken on 4 February 1938 for the mandatory 200 flying hours test. This was completed by 28 February and the aircraft was returned to Focke-Wulf for conversion to Fw 200V-1/U standard, which mainly involved the fitting of extra fuel tanks for a proposed round-the-world flight. As such this did not take place and the aircraft, allocated the registration D-AERE and named *Brandenburg*, (later *Saarland*) was returned to DLH and was based at Berlin-Tempelhof by 27 November 1938. By that time the civil registration had been changed to D-ACON, under which marks the first Condor would undertake a number of headline-making flights.

Bremen, meanwhile, was busy working through the batch of twelve Fw 200A-0 pre-production aircraft (Werke Nummern 2484, 2892-2895, 2993-2996, 3098-3099 and 3324). Construction of the first of these began at Bremen in the spring of 1938; to give an idea of the time it then took to finish large aircraft that had to be virtually hand-built, the last example of the A-0 series would not be completed until early in 1939. By that time the early Condors had put Focke-Wulf's elegant new airliner firmly in the minds of the public through its well-reported appearances around the world.

Corporate colours

DLH chose a striking black and silver colour scheme for its Fw 200s at a time when international airliner plumage was generally sober and understated. The German carrier had historically used silver and black but, with a larger 'canvas' to work with, the airline used the Condor very skilfully to the point where it dominated all other types in DLH service. Many of the world's national airlines stuck to a conservative livery, short on colour trim and bearing the regulation international registration markings on an unpainted 'natural aluminium' finish. There were exceptions, with coloured fuselage cheat lines highlighting the name of the carrier – but Luft Hansa's livery managed to embrace the entire airframe and could hardly be mistaken for its bold, innovative approach.

State airline service

Between 1937 and 1939 Luft Hansa took delivery of five Condors, these being the only aircraft covered by the original contract. Outwardly they did not differ from a further four delivered to the airline but seconded to the Luftwaffe for logistics support during the invasion of Norway in 1940; two more went directly to the RLM. Excluding the prototype and the four foreign airline deliveries, this list accounted for all the prewar civil Condors originally built as such.

Germany's prewar airline route network was comprehensive; many of the well-established regional destinations within the borders of the expanded Third Reich were served by twin- and tri-motor aircraft such as the Ju 52. Several hundred examples of the 'Tante Ju' had been ordered from Junkers and the unmistakable lines of the aircraft, with its 'corrugated' skin, put not only DLH but German civil aviation in general on the map. Focke-Wulf's interests in Berlin were handled by Heinz Junge, who frequently conferred with Major Carganico, then military commander of Berlin-Tempelhof Airport.

For the passenger the introduction of the Fw 200 added an exciting new dimension to international air travel when major world cities began to be served by four-engine aircraft for the first time. On 25 June 1939 DLH inaugurated a Condor service to London from Berlin, this being flown by D-AETA *Westfalen*.

The Condor's potential was not lost on other airlines, and the Focke-Wulf order book was healthy as the 1930s dwindled. *Jutlandia* was one of two examples acquired by the Danish carrier DDL. *P. Jarrett*

Fast-moving events on the world stage dictated that the Fw 200 would see a relatively short period of airline service in Europe as gradually, with the annexation of Austria and the re-occupation of the Rhineland, the burgeoning influence of Germany moved inexorably towards confrontation and war. In the remaining months of peace, however, the Fw 200 began to operate DLH domestic services during the summer of 1938 on the Berlin-Vienna run (beginning that June), the aircraft also serving Frankfurt and Munich from the state capital.

Flying the mail

Carrying mail was a secondary, if highly important and lucrative service to that of flying passengers, and Lufthansa planned several routes where the output from the postal authorities took precedence. One route where the airline enjoyed something of a monopoly was that crossing the South Atlantic and linking continental Europe with the African continent for the first time. Established in February 1934 with flying boats and amphibious aircraft, the service was soon recognised as a pioneering operation in the history of commercial aviation. It served primarily the destinations of Lisbon and Natal, and towards the end of the decade before the outbreak of war the Focke-Wulf Condor was introduced, its impressive range proving to be a boon. There was not time, however, to develop the route structure much further before hostilities commenced, and the use of the Condor was in any event limited by the few aircraft that were available in 1938-39.

Understandably the war prevented fuller expansion of the planned DLH route network to several overseas destinations, but, as stated previously, the Condor in both civil and military guise would continue to be flown on diplomatic and quasi-military schedules for most of the impending conflict.

Prestige in the air

In prewar days record flights, particularly those of an 'intercontinental' nature, did much to put an aircraft type, its manufacturer and its country of origin to the forefront. The attendant publicity boosted the company order books, as well as international prestige. Germany did not fail to grasp the propaganda value of such flights and the long-range Condor proved the ideal aircraft to 'show the flag'.

The Fw 200V-1 (S-1) initiated the first of several inaugural flights on 27 June 1938 – which did not always go exactly according to plan. A flight to Cairo with members of the international press corps occupying most of the seats was arranged at Kurt Tank's behest. The Condor's designer wanted to complete a Berlin-Cairo-Berlin flight in 24 hours and herald it as a distance record under FAI rules. Using D-ADHR *Saarland*, the outbound leg of the flight was completed without incident but on the return from Cairo the Condor had to stop in Salonika and await repairs to a damaged tailwheel.

The flight had to be curtailed, leaving DLH to initiate what today would be called a 'damage limitation exercise' to ward off any bad publicity. Fortunately the degree of criticism that newspaper editors and proprietors took it upon themselves to print in the 1930s was a mere shadow of 21st-century scandal-mongering, and the airline's reputation emerged practically unblemished.

First to New York

Being in a position to operate regular services from Europe to the United States remained an immensely profitable prize for the major carriers, including Lufthansa. In the late 1930s only a select few airlines then operated suitable aircraft for a transatlantic service, and with the Focke-Wulf Condor the German flag-carrier looked well placed to steal a march on its competitors. Such an important service usually began with one or more proving flights, and D-ACON, alias *Brandenburg*, was made ready to fly to New York on 11 August 1938. The aircraft took off from Berlin-Staaken Airport in the hands of Flug Kapitän Dipl-Ing Alfred Henke.

This was in fact a less ambitious flight, as DLH had previously planned to circumnavigate the globe by flying onwards from the US West Coast to Honolulu and Tokyo, returning through South East Asia. Then the US authorities stepped in and, for political and diplomatic reasons, denied DLH overflying and landing rights. The German carrier was nevertheless given permission to fly to New York.

By following the great east-west circle route via Glasgow, Iceland, Greenland, Newfoundland and the eastern seaboard of the US, the Condor arrived over New York on 10/11 August 1938 after a flight time totalling 24 hours and 36 minutes, having logged 4,000 miles (6,371km) in that time. In America much was made of the visit of an aircraft from Europe – still a relatively rare event in those days – and hundreds of people turned up at Floyd Bennett Field to witness *Brandenburg* land and taxi in. Newsreel cameras made the most of the visit despite rain bringing out the umbrellas and doing its best to dampen the event. Floyd Bennett was used as it was the only New York air terminal with adequate concrete runways.

DLH had initiated the flight with the transatlantic record very much in mind – and to achieve its goal a little subterfuge was adopted. To ensure confirmation of the flight by the FAI and to avoid any foreseeable technical malfunction, a few modifications were made, not the least of which was to transform the Fw 200V-1 (D-AERE) into D-ACON. Inside, the Condor had an extra fuel tank

Luft Hansa was well aware that a service to America was the key to airline expansion, and although the German carrier faced much official opposition, the flag-waving flight from Berlin to New York in August 1938 was a very welcome and prestigious 'first'. *Lufthansa*

Rain could not dampen Germany's prestige the day the mighty Focke-Wulf Condor turned up at Floyd Bennett Field. *Lufthansa*

rather than full passenger seating to increase its range and provide a margin of safety should a mishap occur. To save weight even the interior cabin panelling was removed, and to ensure that nothing had been left to chance the aircraft was test flown from Staaken on several occasions between 4 and 18 July 1938. Ownership of the aircraft had meanwhile passed from DLH to the RLM, which had ordered the modifications for the flight to New York.

On their return to Germany Henke and his crew were given a royal welcome, with ecstatic people lining the route from the airport to the RLM building. The Condor crew were required to make a comprehensive report for the ministry officials and what they said doubtless reached the highest circles.

Lufthansa duly claimed the record but was thwarted in its original intention, as mentioned above. As the planned flight to Tokyo also coincided with Germany's occupation of the Sudetenland and the Munich agreement with Britain, the flight was delayed until both those events had passed without armed conflict breaking out.

In any event the American authorities did not look kindly on the political direction that Hitler's Germany had chosen, and had made moves to all but veto airline expansion by a nation that had been deprived of all its overseas territories after the First World War. The prevailing view in Washington was that even by the 1930s Germany still had no sovereignty and therefore no

There was no denying the effort that DLH had put into making the Condor instantly recognisable wherever it went by the simple application of one of the most striking liveries ever worn by an airliner in the 1930s. *Lufthansa*

territorial bargaining power. Neither did she hold privileges to overfly, land or carry traffic, although these rights were reluctantly granted on a limited basis, for without them DLH would have been unable to operate outside Germany at all.

By imposing a restriction whereby Luft Hansa was allowed only 28 North Atlantic crossings in 1938, the US Government killed all hopes of a regular, scheduled passenger service between the two countries. This prohibitive ruling applied to other German aviation interests, not only those of DLH. As a further setback the stipulated number of crossings was to be in the nature of non-commercial 'evaluation flights'.

The US steadfastly continued to deny the German carrier landing rights, a decision conveyed to Berlin by DLH representative Martin Wronsky, a prewar director of the airline and a man who worked tirelessly to establish a transatlantic service between Germany and North America.

Even when this ambition was pursued after the war, it was to no avail. By then many Americans had witnessed first hand the horrors of the Third Reich's racial policies and they not only held out on the main issue but played up Wronsky's National Socialist links (which, probably unwisely, he attempted to minimise). His efforts were blocked to the point that the unfortunate individual committed suicide in 1946.

As far as the general public was concerned, the Condor's transatlantic flight was a great success and no doubt there were those in the crowd who wondered when America and Germany would be linked by a regular air service. The Condor flew back to Germany on 13/14 August, the log-book recording an improved time of 19 hours 55 minutes, a saving of some five hours. Retracing much the same route as on the outward leg, Henke's crew consisted of Hptm Rudolf Freiherr von Moreau, Walter Kober and Paul Dierberg. After D-ACON returned to Germany it was for a short period deployed as a transport with the Luftwaffe training unit based at Juterborg. This was believed to have been in the nature of an exercise designed to confirm the advantage of large transport aircraft in situations demanding a substantial tonnage of materiel to be delivered to troops in the field.

Tokyo record

Inaugurating a service to the Far East was an equally attractive prospect for DLH, and an even more ambitious record was in the making on 28 November 1938 when *Brandenburg* lifted off from Berlin-Tempelhof for its postponed trip to Tokyo and set course for Japan. The flight plan was via Basra, Karachi, Hanoi and thence to Tokyo-Tachikawa Airport, where the Condor touched down on 30 November at 14.13 CET (Central European Time). In Germany much interest was generated by this flight, orders to equip Japan's national airline (Dai Nippon kk) with five Condors being taken up with a contract issued on 17 December 1938. Had events turned out differently these aircraft would probably have been operated by Manchurian Airlines from the spring of 1940. This reference to a second Japanese carrier is interesting and may have strongly hinted at follow-on orders after the principal customer, Dai Nippon, had established the Condor on routes out of its main base in Tokyo.

The Japan flight was also the last by the Condor prototype, for en route back to Germany on 6 December it suffered fuel starvation. Incorrect operation of the fuel cross-feed and premature deployment of the flaps caused it to enter a low-speed stall, apparently giving the pilot no option but to ditch in shallow waters off Rosario Point in the Philippines. All the flight crew, including Georg Kohne of Focke-Wulf, were rescued. The wrecked Condor was retrieved but not before salt water corrosion and the effects of a typhoon had inflicted further damage. Rough handling by a salvage crew left the badly damaged airliner to be hauled aboard the Hapag vessel SS *Kulmerland*, which docked at Hamburg on 1 February 1939. There the first of the Condors was declared to have been damaged beyond repair. Photographs taken on the dockside left no doubt as to the severe structural strains to which the Fw 200 had been subjected during its immersion in the waters of the Pacific Ocean, although examination of the wreckage may have proved of value in the Condor's future development.

Having questioned the flight crew on the Japanese flight, Kurt Tank was said to have been livid; nobody who knew the man had seen him so furious before or since when it transpired that the loss of *Brandenburg* was avoidable and due solely to inexperience on the part of the flight engineer/co-pilot. Had this individual paid more attention to the fuel system he would have realised that the engines had been temporarily starved of fuel at a point where the auxiliary overload tanks should have been switched in, the internal tanks having run dry. Remedial action would have quickly reconnected the flow of fuel and the aircraft would, everyone believed, have come through without any mishap. Instead, Tank's beautiful airliner was dropped into the South China Sea to be pounded into wreckage by unforgiving ocean breakers.

Chapter 2

Last months of peace

Reconnaissance and transport

Although the crash of the prototype Condor was a setback for Focke-Wulf, the event did little to damage the aircraft's already good reputation, and the fact that nobody had lost their life clearly brought a great sense of relief. Also, having a very impressive new airliner introduced by the country's national airline and setting records was a 'stamp of approval' that did no harm at all to the type's export potential, and so it was to be with the Fw 200. No fewer than forty-six examples of the improved Fw 200B had been ordered by the summer of 1939. In the meantime several airlines, among them the Danish carrier Det Danske Luftfartselskab (DDL), took an early interest and placed orders for two examples of the early Fw 200A-0 production aircraft without waiting for the Fw 200B model. Identified as Fw 200KA-1 export models, on 28 July 1939 the first Condor in the colours of DDL touched down at Croydon when OY-DAM's flight from Copenhagen became the first Danish airliner to fly into a UK airport.

In Finland, the Finnish airline Aero OY, or Finnish Aero as it was popularly known, required new aircraft to enable it to build up its service between Finland and England. Increasing trade between the two countries was a first priority, although a welcome boost in passenger revenues was anticipated by the Olympic Games, which were scheduled to be held in Helsinki in 1940.

A degree of re-registering took place with the early Condors, and D-ACON was originally identified as D-AERE, the Fw 200 V1. As *Brandenburg* it completed the New York run in August 1938 but was lost that December en route back from Japan. *P. Jarrett*

In August 1938 Focke-Wulf had offered the Nordic airline a pre-production Fw 200A-0 for delivery the following year, but by October 1939 this had been changed to an Fw 200B, for delivery in September or October 1940. Although this latter aircraft was to have been powered by BMW 132H engines of 850hp and with three-bladed propellers, Aero opted for P&W Hornet engines and signed an order for two such examples on 27 January 1939. These airframes (0009 and 0010), based on the Fw 200B, were known by Aero OY as Fw 200KB-1s, the former being the V5 identified as OH-CLA; the second machine was similar and was allocated the registration OH-CLB.

Kurt Tank himself was apparently the driving force behind a publicity campaign linking the Condor with the Helsinki Games, with Aero allocating the names *Karjala* and *Petsamo*, two of the main event venues of the games, to the new airliners. Naming airliners had been a common practice in Germany for some years and had become popular with other airlines. In the event neither of the Danish Condors had their names taken up for reasons beyond their control.

In May 1939 Aero amended its order to stipulate more powerful P&W S1E-G engines for its Condors, a move believed to have been necessary to increase the safety factor when operating the aircraft from icy runways. An option for a third Condor was also placed at that time, this also being designated as an Fw 200KB-1 but based on an Fw 200C-3 airframe (0046/OH-CLC).

Table 3: The first transport Condors

Variant	W Nr	Registration	Name	Remarks
Fw 200V-1	2000	D-AERE	*Brandenburg*	Later re-registered D-ACON
Fw 200V-2	2484	D-AETA	*Westfalen*	
Fw 200	2891*			
Fw 200A-0/S1	2893	D-ADHR	*Saarland*	
Fw 200A-0/S2/KA-1	2894	OY-DAM	*Dania*	Later G-AGAY *Wolf*
Fw 200A-0 (S-3)	2895	D-AMHC	*Nordmark*	
Fw 200A-0 (S-4)	2993	OY-DEM	*Jutlandia*	
Fw 200A-0 (S-5)	2994	D-ARHW	*Friesland*	
Fw 200A-0 (S-6)	2995	D-ASBK	*Holstein*	Later PP-CBJ *Arumani*
Fw 200A-0 (S-7)	2996	D-AXFO	*Pommern*	Later PP-CBI *Abaitara*
Fw 200A-0 (S-8)	3098	D-ACVH	*Grenzmark*	
Fw 200V-3 (S-9)	3099	D-ARHU	*Ostmark* *Immelmann III*	Later D-2600, WL-2600 and 26-00
Fw 200A-0 (S-10)	3324	D-ABOD	*Kurmark*	
Fw 200B-1 (V4)	0001	D-ACWG		Not delivered. As V10 to Rowehl as BS+AF
Fw 200C-4	0111	D-ASVX	*Thuringen*	Captured at war's end by RAF
Fw 200KB-1 (V5)	0009	OH-CLA	*Kurmark*	Not delivered. Later D-AEQP
Fw 200KB-1	0010	OH-CLB	*Westfalen*	Not delivered. Later D-AFST
Fw 200KC-1 (V6)	0017			Ordered By Dai-Nippon. Not delivered To Luftwaffe as NA+WJ
Fw 200KC-1	0018			Ordered By Dai-Nippon. Not delivered To Luftwaffe as NA+WK
Fw 200KC-1	0019		*Rheinland*	Ordered By Dai-Nippon. Not delivered To DLH as D-AWSK
Fw 200KC-1	0020		*Holstein*	Ordered By Dai-Nippon. Not delivered To DLH as D-ACWG To Luftwaffe as NA+WM
Fw 200KC -1	0021		*Pommern*	Ordered By Dai-Nippon. Not delivered To DLH as D-AMHL To Luftwaffe as NA+WN

The first twelve Fw 200s were those allocated original Focke-Wulf Werke Nummern and all were assembled at Bremen/Neuenlander airfield. When series production for the Luftwaffe began, the RLM issued a set of numbers covering 268 aircraft – 200 0001 to 0268. They were assembled by FWF at Bremen and also at Cottbuss. Blohm & Voss was brought into the Condor programme at a later date to undertake manufacture at Finkenwerder and other subcontractors and their locations (where known) are listed in the main text.

* W Nr 2891 is identified in some references as the sole Fw 200A (without any suffix) and was possibly intended only as a static test airframe. These tests are believed to have been completed during the winter of 1937/38.

An early draftee into the Luftwaffe, *Saarland*, alias Fw 200A-01, became GF+GF. It was flown to several destinations before the war including Moscow, when it carried von Ribbentrop for high-level talks. Lacking a full suite of flame dampers for the engine exhausts, early Condors were also fitted with two-blade propellers for their Hornet-derived engines. *MAP*

The saga of Dania

Soon after OY-DAM *Dania* was completed, Kurt Tank himself took the controls and flew it to Copenhagen/Kastrup on 14 July 1939 – delivery by the company test pilot was another unusual approach by FWF. Later that month the aircraft initiated DDL international flights to London. A scant two months later Europe was at war and there was a touch of irony in the fact that the first Danish Condor was the first (and almost the only) Fw 200 to visit England; certainly no other example of Kurt Tank's elegant airliner was to spend most of the war on the other side of the Channel, albeit by accident rather than design.

DDL's service to London continued until the spring of 1940 when, on 9 April, *Dania* landed at Shoreham Airport. The British and Danish civil aviation authorities agreed that they had little choice but to impound the Condor – as Denmark had been invaded by the Germans that day. There was no going back and the Condor was impressed onto the British civil register as G-AGAY and given the name *Wolf*. On 15 May 1940, the day the Dutch finally capitulated, it was decided to repaint the aircraft in the wartime camouflage colours of the British Overseas Airways Corporation. The subsequent flying career of Britain's Condor was very brief; when the aircraft had landed it had sustained some damage to the tailwheel oleo and was flown to Whitchurch near Bristol for repair. While there the tail had to be supported by sandbags, due to the risk of further damage from local high winds.

An aircraft type rarely seen in England, Fw 200 A-02 was given the UK registration G-AGAY when OY-DAM, one of the Danish Condors, flew in on the day Denmark was attacked by Germany. Impressed by the RAF and allocated the serial number DX177, the aircraft served as an instructional airframe for the ATA in the UK for several years before being broken up.

Briefly resplendent in its original bright orange overall livery, OY-DAM created considerable interest, not least among BOAC staff, who cast a professional eye over what 'the other side' was doing. They noted the ease of maintenance afforded by the BMW engine cowlings with their access panels resembling a petal arrangement. These also afforded some protection from rain if work had to carried out in the open. Positive comments were also made on the quality of the passenger seats as well as the instrument panel layout with its colour-coded left- and right-hand controls.

This particular Condor suffered further damage on 12 July 1940 when it swung during a landing approach at White Waltham airfield and collided with a grass-cutting machine, causing some damage to its undercarriage. Although it was not repaired and was declared a write-off, on 9 January 1941 it was allocated the RAF serial number DX177. As a single foreign design with no spares support, it was impractical to fly the Condor further and it was finally passed to the Air Transport Auxiliary for testing emergency escape procedures. The ex-Danish Condor served in this capacity for the duration of the war before apparently being badly damaged at Northolt in 1946 and subsequently scrapped.

Other early Condors of note included the Fw 200V-2 (2484/D-AETA) *Westfalen*. Allocated out-of-sequence Werke Nummern, most of the early aircraft had varied careers in civil and military service. A much-travelled machine, the V-2 carried out route-proving flights for DLH, toured the Baltic states in June 1938 and was passed to the Luftwaffe the following August. Modified with cameras for high-altitude photo reconnaissance after it was painted in Luftwaffe camouflage, the aircraft was drafted into the front line in Norway where it was destroyed on 25 May 1940 by Gloster Gladiator fighters of No 263 Squadron operating from Norwegian mudflats. These outmoded fighters posed something of a threat as they were the only enemy aircraft based on Norwegian soil at that time.

VIP transport

A far more exotic operational career awaited some Condors, including the Fw 200V-3 (2892/D-2600/26-00) *Immelmann III*. Becoming one of Adolf Hitler's personal transports, the Condor's name followed on in sequence from his two personal Ju 52/3ms, *Immelmann I* and *II*, perpetuating the name of Max Immelmann, one of Germany's most famous First World War fighter aces. Further details of these and the other VIP Condors may be found in the final chapter.

As noted in the somewhat haphazard constructor's number sequence above, Condor 2891 is something of a mystery as it was not included in the Werke Nummer blocks covering the twelve original Fw 200s built at the main Focke-Wulf plant at Bremen/Neuenlander airfield. It can be seen from Table 3 how the Versuch (prototype) machines not only had several alternative designations (with the identity Fw 200A-0 being taken up from airframe 2893), but they appeared to be built way out of any logical sequence. This was in fact fairly common German practice; when prototypes were modified to test new systems their original Versuch number was either retained or allocated a different number. In the latter case the revised number did not automatically indicate a new airframe but more often than not a fairly extensive modification.

Last year of peace

If world events has been fast-moving in 1938, they gathered even more pace in 1939. Following the end of the Spanish Civil War on 28 March, Hitler finalised plans for the subjugation of north-western Europe to provide Germany with *Lebensraum* ('living space'), a goal that could only be achieved by military conquest. To safeguard his plans the German dictator had entered into a non-aggression pact with Stalin and followed this with a similar agreement with France. The Franco-German pact of 6 December 1937 achieved the object of lulling Hitler's nearest potential adversary into a false sense of security to the point where border transgressions by France were kept to a minimum – there was little wish to antagonise the Germans and precipitate conflict before the country's defences had been built up. As much as possible was done to mobilise the French, Belgian and Dutch air arms and put them on a war footing, although events were soon to reveal just how much national defence had been neglected in the decades following the end of the First World War.

Seemingly daunted by international developments, the Dutch Government suspended work on long-range airliners such as the Fokker F 36, one of which was photographed in September 1934. *P. Jarrett*

The Second World War begins

When Germany invaded Poland on 1 September 1939 numerous German civil aviation projects were affected either directly or indirectly. Requisitions by the Luftwaffe of transport aircraft were now more likely, which meant that some civil contracts would be difficult if not impossible to fulfil. FWF's production of the Condor was still modest even as Britain and France declared war on Germany on the 3rd. By that date FWF had delivered a second Condor after the original record-breaking D-AERE *Brandenburg* (subsequently re-registered as D-ACON), this being D-AETA, the V-2.

A typically busy schedule was planned for this aircraft, which had first flown in late 1937. It had begun proving flights on 6 May 1938 and was at Berlin-Tempelhof on 27 November that year. *Westfalen* had begun a tour of Scandinavian countries in June and was noted at Saloniki on one of its early stops and at Schipol during the summer. The flight, in the hands of Captain Siegfried Graf Schack von Wittenau, was primarily for the benefit of DDL, the overseas launch customer for the type.

To widespread relief elsewhere, the German attack on Poland brought no immediate sign that Armageddon was about to overtake all of north-western Europe; the change from peace manifested itself in subtle ways as the first weeks of the Second World War unfolded. Poland succumbed to overwhelming military force and other countries rattled their sabres but made no moves against Germany. As the borders of Poland were redefined by Hitler and Stalin under the auspices of their non-aggression pact, the weather began to worsen. Within weeks, in deference to the bitter weather of the late autumn and winter months, life in many parts of the continent went on almost as usual as 1939 passed into history.

Confusion

An unreal feeling that the conflict, the 'Phoney War' as an American journalist was to immortalise it, was a long way away prevailed even in Germany. There were no mass air raids as predicted in some quarters and in many areas of commerce it was business as usual. At Bremen, FWF organised a Condor to obtain a new type certificate for Aero OY's Fw 200KB-1s due to the fact that their engines had been changed. The Fw 200V-5 (0009) was the aircraft used for certification purposes but it appears that some pressure was put on the company not to release any more export Fw 200s that could be used in Germany.

In talks with the Finns, Focke-Wulf cited the required revisions as a reason for a delayed delivery date, from November 1939 to early 1940. In Germany both OKL and the RLM studied modifications that would fully exploit the Condor's 1,000-mile (1,600km) range in a reconnaissance role. It was a time of great change – not to say confusion – as existing civil airliners were seconded into military transport duties while aircraft intended to fulfil orders from airlines (which had paid at least some of the costs) were still being built at Bremen. As the qualified merits of the Fw 200 dawned on the Luftwaffe High Command, it was obvious that the most pressing problem it faced was the fact that FWF had only built a very small number of them, irrespective of the intended customers.

Surprise requirement

The need for such an aircraft as the Condor came as a surprise in most official quarters; the fact that all heavy bomber development had been cancelled apart from the Heinkel He 177 (the prototype of which was to make its maiden fight on 19 November 1939) suited the military hierarchy. With investment in four-engine aircraft not entirely prohibited but cut to the bone, more medium-sized twin-engine bombers could be built to swell the ranks of the Kampfgeschwader making Germany strong enough to win the predicted short war. The intriguing He 177 could perhaps be useful at a later date, and in 1939 it was not eating into precious resources to a degree that was in any way prohibitive. The sudden need to militarise the Fw 200 as a stop-gap measure led to numerous questions with few definite answers.

There would be unavoidable delays in certifying a militarised Condor: any new aircraft type scheduled to see service with the Luftwaffe also had to pass flight and acceptance tests by the Erpobungsstelle Rechlin, Germany's central testing establishment on the shores of Lake Müritz. Since its founding in the 1920s the E-Stelle, as it was commonly known, had grown both in size and importance to the point that nothing was allowed to be used by the air force without Rechlin's official stamp.

With the rate that the Luftwaffe was expanded in the late 1930s, the E-Stelle's workload was massive and concentrated almost entirely on new aircraft types. The decision to test the Focke-Wulf Condor as a military transport represented an additional workload to the staff at Rechlin, as the aircraft had not previously been included in any of their schedules. Despite having obtained civil certification, military testing was required and to this end Fw 200KC-1 (0002) was delivered to Rechlin on 1 February 1940.

Owing to the urgency to get the armed Condor cleared for Luftwaffe service, the E-Stelle agreed to an accelerated test programme that included a routine number of flights before an airworthiness certificate could be issued. That it was possible to complete the work more quickly than would usually have been the case was due partly to E-Stelle staff members being sent to Bremen to work with FWF. Wind tunnel tests and associated data were closely scrutinised, presumably to the satisfaction of the government officials. By April 1940 the Condor was issued with the necessary certification for Luftwaffe service: this was almost certainly achieved by using only the aircraft identified above, which had previously logged Luftwaffe flight time with Kurierstaffel Petersen to which it had been assigned before its first flight, on 1 October 1939.

This was another German practice that saved time on Condor deliveries; working from order specifications, FWF fitted equipment that tailored individual aircraft to a transport or military role during production rather than waiting until the aircraft in question was completed.

Before the war an Fw 200 built to civil or military specification differed little in overall configuration and the early series examples were powered by similar engines under almost identical cowlings. Where the machines clearly were different was in the location of machine-gun armament and/or camera ports. Even then a transport role did not always specify the fitting of machine-gun positions as not all of the Condors were armed. Once they had served in a given role for a required period it was not uncommon for the early-production Condors to be returned to Focke-Wulf for further modification.

Events tended almost to overtake any lengthy delay in putting the Condor into military hands, as by the spring of 1940 the Luftwaffe had formulated plans to attack its neighbours in Western Europe in a similar fashion to the Blitzkrieg in Poland. Where necessary the Condor would be deployed in a transport and photographic reconnaissance role, although the latter was not so important, there being numerous other aircraft types that could be used, provided that long range was not a requirement. As mentioned elsewhere, several individual aircraft were modified as PR aircraft at Rechlin. Delay in E-Stelle certification did not prevent the aircraft being used for training sorties, these becoming increasingly important to student crews who were unlikely to have flown (or even flown in) such a large machine.

The Luftwaffe's requirement for every Condor completed or under construction led to a cessation of work on the Aero examples by February 1940. In March of that year Finland was obliged to go to war with the Soviet Union, a country then allied to Germany; this development appears not to have caused any major upheaval, although Aero did contact Focke-Wulf to advise that the names selected for its Condors should not be used as both Karjala (Karelia) and Petsamo, located respectively in the eastern and northern parts of Finland, had taken on a heightened political sensitivity when the Russians had made territorial demands on both areas.

Then, on 11 April 1940, the RLM officially confiscated both aircraft. The Finns appear to have accepted this move as almost inevitable, although their immediate concern was over the deposits they had previously paid for them. These sums were repaid in due course, but Aero management harboured considerable regret that one of Germany's main allies could not now inaugurate a planned long-distance passenger service, a situation not eased by the knowledge that DLH and the Luftwaffe were putting the aircraft to similar use despite the war.

DLH lost few opportunities to show the flag for its Condor service, D-AMHC *Nordmark* being well to the fore in this respect, shortly before military service beckoned. *Lufthansa*

Aero had a further regret that a little-publicised aspect of ordering the Condor – indeed, a major reason for doing so – was the proposed establishment of a transatlantic route to the United States. This goal, one that was eagerly sought by several airlines once aircraft such as the Focke-Wulf Condor were available to achieve it, was the subject of a January 1939 meeting of the heads of all four Nordic carriers in Oslo. It was proposed that a strong case should be made for such a service and that approaches should be made to the Americans as a first step towards the granting of traffic rights. In the event a joint Scandinavian consortium to fly the Atlantic had to wait some six years for peace in Europe.

Condors in Brazil

One of the few countries that did manage to introduce the striking new Focke-Wulf airliner into service in time to set fresh flight records before the war was Brazil. Few people were aware of the imminence of the conflict when Cruzeiro do Sul, a Luft Hansa subsidiary set up as Sindicato Condor Ltda, took delivery of two Fw 200A-0s on 29 June 1939. These machines, 2996/PP-CBI and 2995/PP-CBJ, were registered on 21 July and 14 August respectively. Named *Abaitara* (ex-D-AXFO) and *Arumani* (D-ASBK), they were destined to rank among the longest-lived examples.

With its new registration PP-CBI, the former D-AXFO *Pommern* promised an unprecedented service into the Brazilian hinterland for as long as Servicos Aeros Condor could maintain the Fw 200 German support being withdrawn when Brazil declared war on the Axis.

FOCKE-WULF FW 200 CONDOR

During their delivery flight from Germany to South America the Condors established a new record for the ocean crossing from Bathurst to Natal of 9 hours 47 minutes, and by so doing became the first Luft Hansa landplanes to cross the South Atlantic.

Without delay the Condors were put onto the Rio-Sao Paulo-Oporto Alegre-Buenos Aires route. Shortly afterwards war intervened to gradually erode this service, due mainly to strained relations with the Nazi regime and fuel restrictions imposed after the United States entered the war in December 1941. Condor operations were suspended that same month.

Siding with the Allied cause during the Second World War, Brazil dispensed with her previous reliance on German personnel to run the national airline and changed the carrier's name to Servicos Aereos Condor Ltda on 19 August 1941. The two Fw 200s were a major part of the fleet, which was otherwise composed mainly of Ju 52/3ms when operations were restarted in April 1942; later the airline was nationalised and given the new name Servicos Aereos Cruzeiro do Sul Ltda, which was formally adopted on 16 January 1943.

The Focke-Wulf Condors continued to serve the airline, more popularly known as Southern Cross (Cruzeiro do Sul) after the constellation observed in the night sky in the southern hemisphere. The carrier maintained an operating schedule throughout the remaining war years, during which both of the Condors were re-engined with Pratt & Whitney radials, both as a result of a shortage of spares for the original BMW powerplants and the availability of those of American origin supplied under Lend Lease.

Operating a quasi-military service during the war, Southern Cross aircraft were employed to patrol the country's thousands of miles of coastline as well as transporting troops and supplies between Recife and the island of Fernando de Noronha.

Both the Brazilian Fw 200s survived the war years and served until 1950, when they were unceremoniously broken up between 2 May and 30 August of that year, bringing to an end one of the longest operating records for the type.

Japan's contribution

When Imperial Japan's war on China began in July 1937 the country's leaders found themselves in a position similar to that of Germany insofar as the country's industrial base was not really large enough to construct four-engine military aircraft on a 'mass-production' basis. This fact was highlighted when Tokyo went shopping for suitable types to manufacture under licence and turned initially to its major Axis partner. Japan could reduce development time by buying aircraft or adapting existing designs and several German projects were examined.

Mitsubishi was the apparent driving force behind the so-called Ki 90, a project based on the Ju 90. This proved to carry a manufacturing agreement that was far too complex for the delegation to countenance, and the six-man negotiating team, which included Jiro Takeda, Business Department Chief, and engineer Yyunojo Ozawa of Mitsubishi, then talked with Focke-Wulf.

The main point of these meetings was to explore the feasibility of Japan ordering military aircraft or developing armed versions of existing civil types such as the Condor. For several years prior to the Second World War Japan had been importing examples of German aircraft for test and comparison purposes with indigenous designs. But time was not on the side of the Japanese delegation and, maybe because of this, the Imperial Army apparently vetoed any agreement with Focke-Wulf. Another reason may have been that, having dealt almost exclusively with Junkers in the field of large transports, the Japanese did not wish to become involved in another set of working practices, construction methods and management structures. Somewhat ironically in view of the events that lay ahead, the Japanese then turned to the United States.

When Dai Nippon kk placed its order for the Fw 200, the military saw that a significant gap in inventory could perhaps be filled by an armed version of the Condor. There was no equivalent four-engine design of Japanese origin in the planning stage at that time, hence the desire to acquire such aircraft from abroad. The single indigenous type in this class, the Nakajima G8N1, only appeared in late 1944, far too late for the Navy to train enough crews or to form a single Sentai before the war ended.

Had the war not intervened the commercial Condors would have faced competition from Europe and the USA. A significant challenge would probably have come from Boeing's pressurised Stratoliner. *P. Jarrett*

One of Britain's contenders in the prewar 'four-engine' airline stakes was the beautiful de Havilland DH 91 Albatross. *P. Jarrett*

Britain's Imperial Airways flew the Armstrong Whitworth AW Ensign, another potential rival to the Fw 200. *P. Jarrett*

Condor rivals in Germany were few, but the Junkers concern came closest with the Ju 90. The developed Ju 290 transport eventually saw service in a role similar to that of the Fw 200. *P. Jarrett*

Despite the negative outcome of the talks with FWF, Kurt Tank was enthusiastic about the Japanese idea and engineering drawings of the Fw 200 were adapted to show a version incorporating armament including a dorsal turret positioned in line with the rear of the ventral gondola. This latter design addition is more or less attributable to the Japanese, whose plans specified up to three 7.9mm machine-guns to arm its Fw 200B.

An ingenious approach to increasing the Condor's military capability without compromising its light structure, the gondola probably housed a third machine-gun firing aft.

Most importantly, some valuable data emerged when the increased weight of bombs, machine-guns, ammunition, armour and extra crew seating was calculated. And although the configuration of a Japanese military version of the Fw 200KC is open to some speculation, such an aircraft would undoubtedly have undergone some significant changes from the civil version and been not dissimilar to the aircraft that entered service with the Luftwaffe. According to Focke-Wulf records, the Japanese Navy would have taken up options on six armed aircraft had the German embargo not prevented any further exports in 1939.

The outbreak of the Pacific War in December 1941 did not sever all connections with the Focke-Wulf concern, which delivered at least one example of the Fw 190A fighter to Japan for evaluation. But the sheer distance between the two Axis countries was to prove all but crippling for U-boats, and IJN submarines embarked on a two-way trade. Numerous visits by German crews to Japanese ports and vice versa saw the Yanagi system accomplish what it could given the limited space aboard submarines. Although the Japanese boats were much larger than their German counterparts, they could comfortably accommodate only blueprints, plans, documents and other items such as machine tools and so on – items that were small enough to be packed into a submarine's internal spaces. Surface freighters delivered tons of materiel until such time as the Allies cottoned onto the trade and set out to sink as many transport ships as possible. In this they largely succeeded, so that neither Germany nor Japan was able to benefit fully from the other's technological development. That said, the Japanese received from Germany much more than they were able to send, as their European ally's giant strides in many fields, particularly that of aeronautics, dominated any other comparable achievements in the rest of the world at least for the first half of the war. Japan could hardly keep pace.

Stillborn 'Trudy'

Not that the 'Japanese Fw 200' was entirely forgotten, even after the chance to operate the type had passed. In 1942 Allied intelligence officers drew up a simple recognition code, listing Japanese aircraft types in the belief that the actual manufacturers' names would be too garbled in radio transmissions – and taxing on pilots' memories in the heat of combat. They gave every known Nipponese design a code based on male and female names, identifying fighters and bombers respectively.

This all-embracing system extended to several foreign aircraft that the Japanese tested but never operated, and even to projected designs that might (or might not) have entered the Army or Navy inventories. Thus the Western world came to believe (albeit briefly) that the Messerschmitt Bf 109 bearing the blood red hinomaru marking flew operationally and had even been met in combat under the code name 'Mike', that the Focke-Wulf Fw 190 saw service as the 'Fred' – and that the Fw 200 might eventually be encountered under the reporting name 'Trudy'. Issuing a mere paper project with a code name could be seen as diligence at its best, but inclusions of aircraft that did not exist as far as the IJA/IJN were concerned certainly caused some confusion; not, it should be said, that it was easy to obtain reliable information from Japanese sources. Eventually, when no armed prototype of the Fw 200B materialised, the code name 'Trudy' was shelved and not reallocated. In addition, the fighters named 'Mike' and 'Fred' were quietly forgotten.

Japan's requirement for long-range aircraft was obvious considering the country's geographical location and, although a few practical steps could be taken to redress the situation by buying 'off the shelf' in Europe and America, the fact remains that it appears to have been Germany's oriental ally that helped drive the idea of arming the Fw 200. Unfortunately no original plans of how a Japanese Condor would have been configured appear to have survived, but modern side-view drawings provide a fair idea of the changes made to the fuselage and the size and shape of the weapons gondola with its modest defensive/offensive armament of a trio of light machine-guns (as apparently stipulated in the original 'order'). The armament, typical of the immediate prewar period, would have undoubtedly have been increased at a later date as a result of combat experience.

One can only speculate that the Japanese intended the Condor's gondola to incorporate a bomb bay as well one or two guns, in similar fashion to that fitted to the aircraft used by the Luftwaffe. In general, heavier armament, particularly large-calibre cannon, as adopted by the Germans would likely have been copied by the Japanese.

Drawings have surfaced showing a very short gondola fitted to the Fw 200V-10, otherwise known as an 'A' model. As other references appear to relegate the Fw 200A to a single testbed, the implied existence of more examples poses a not untypical problem.

In any event, Kurt Tank was reportedly enthusiastic about arming the Condor and, whoever was responsible for the original concept, he had little difficulty in selling the idea to the RLM. It became standard procedure to arm aircraft that had been designed to carry passengers or mail with a token defensive gun or two when they were drafted into the Luftwaffe, a process that very few avoided. Dozens of aircraft in numerous categories that had their origins in civil contracts would be utilised for a variety of military tasks – indeed, several had been designed with a military role uppermost – as long as the war lasted.

In the case of the Condor a requirement for the elegant airliner to don camouflage paint went hand-in-hand with a need to be armed when reconnaissance was broadened out into a maritime attack role. Under the policy of attacking British assets in whatever form, it made economic sense for an aircraft able to patrol far out into the Atlantic to find ships and prevent them from reaching port.

Naval air arm – the background

Germany's war footing also raised several questions that had few definitive or immediate answers, including where maritime reconnaissance aircraft would be based to be most effective. If the Wehrmacht appeared supremely confident in its air support and was ready to embark on campaigns that would restore Germany's honour after the shame of Versailles, there was one element in the armed forces' order of battle that was not so confident of immediate victory over its potential adversaries, namely the Kriegsmarine, the German Navy.

While the Nazis had embarked upon an impressive shipbuilding programme and launched some of the most modern and capable warships the world had yet seen, and Admiral Doenitz concentrated on building U-boats at an unprecedented rate, the establishment of a supplemental fleet air arm had not been properly addressed.

Despite the well-founded interwar arguments that had been put forward by the Kriegsmarine for a separate naval air arm independent of the air force, the officers of which would understand the often unique requirements of such a force, Hermann Goering, Commander in Chief of the Luftwaffe, had gradually overruled anyone who challenged his assumed right to control everything that flew in Germany, preferably under the aegis of 'his' air force. This unfortunate and ultimately damaging commandeering of what might have become a larger and more effective maritime air force did not in the long run hamper long-range reconnaissance to any great extent.

Hitler's belief that any future military campaigns against Germany's neighbouring countries could be conducted with great speed unfolded after 10 May 1940. Modern aircraft and tanks were again deployed in a Blitzkrieg assault against France, Belgium and the Low Countries, and within weeks the impossible had happened: the French Army, saddled with outmoded equipment and lacking sound tactical warfare plans, was being defeated.

As far as the land campaign in Europe was concerned, Hitler could afford to bide his time, sit out the 1939/40 winter and strike when his forces were ready. This he did, preparing his masterstroke with infinite care; with the support of a highly professional cadre of Army Generals, the campaign had the added element of a powerful Luftwaffe, which most significantly had developed dive-bombing to a degree that materially and psychologically was unmatched by any of the opposing air forces. Against weak defences the much-vaunted Stukas spread terror and destruction among those who had the added misfortune of seeing the Panzers following up.

Blitzkrieg elements – bombers, Stukas, fighters and PR aircraft – proved briefly to be unbeatable, but when objectives, areas and countries were firmly in German hands, the wider war posed an immense challenge. It was almost as though the High Command believed that the conflict need not extend beyond the coast at all. Britain's steadfast position was but the first step to ruining Hitler's plan to dominate the entire European land mass by military force. At first this was seen as a minor setback that could be overcome; gaining utter domination of the sea lanes around the British Isles would be of paramount importance. Karl Doenitz believed that his U-boats could achieve that desired state backed by aircraft to deal with any vessels his undersea fleet might have overlooked.

The main problem was that when the Fw 200 was found to be the only type with any practical application to the maritime role, the Luftwaffe was obliged to concentrate crews and aircraft into a single Geschwader, whereas it would normally have formed several anti-shipping units based on the experience gained from the early deployment of KG 40. And in common with other branches of the Luftwaffe, much could have been learned in the last years of peace.

A bird in the hand…

At the same time it is difficult to counter the fact that, lacking a purpose-built design that should have left the drawing board in 1938 at the latest, even a fully functioning maritime air arm would still have been obliged to await output of either the Fw 200 to build up or to turn to another aircraft entirely. This was to have been the He 177, but because this new bomber was not ready to fulfil any one of a number of roles it had designed to undertake, expedient measures had to be taken.

To sum up the background to the military use of the Fw 200, maritime operations using purpose-built long-range aircraft was one of several areas for which the Luftwaffe High Command failed to plan. In addition, training a five- or six-man crew to the point where they could navigate with confidence over vast stretches of ocean proved to be something of a problem. Such individuals would ideally have had a naval/nautical background, and although a percentage of the men who entered the flying training schools did have such experience, they were relatively few and in many cases older in relation to the number of cadets the Luftwaffe was training.

Being able to call on Luft Hansa crews saved the day initially, although the Germans did not plan for a very large pool of trained crews to fill the shoes of those who were lost in combat. Had the war indeed been 'short', such a need would not have arisen and there would have been little requirement for specialised units such as KG 40. It was when the war showed no sign of ending on German terms (ie unassailable military victory) in 1940 that the cracks in strategy began to show; fortunately for the Germans, the experienced, mainly ex-airline crews able to navigate accurately over great distances and thereby carry out maritime reconnaissance effectively, were initially well able to handle combat sorties into the Bay of Biscay and the wider sweep of the Atlantic Ocean.

But it cannot have been overlooked in all quarters that some difficulties might arise if the conflict lasted longer than the military lifespan of the nucleus of ex-airline crews. Some of them would undoubtedly succumb to the attrition rate over a period of time. In 1940 the trick was to anticipate what that time period would be – nobody in Germany or Britain could answer that question.

Chapter 3

Condor military variants

In respect of arming the Fw 200 to turn it into an effective combat aircraft for Luftwaffe use, Kurt Tank – who, incidentally, retained great personal enthusiasm for the Condor – delegated much of the early design work to construction engineer Wilhelm Bansemir. Transforming an airliner into a military weapon was a virtually unique exercise at that time and a challenge that would otherwise have required a complete rebuild. But there was no time to carry out such extensive work and Focke-Wulf was contracted to build what amounted to a compromise, but in far less time than it would have taken to develop a new aircraft.

The production time span of the Fw 200 was from 1937 to 1944, the bulk of the Luftwaffe deliveries taking place between 1940 and 1943. In that period Focke-Wulf managed to develop the basic design and produce eight variants based on the Fw 200C-3. Production ended early in 1944, and all Condors had been delivered by the late summer of that year.

Although the early military Condors lacked some of the refinements that came later, particularly the Lofte 7D bombsight, aircraft were otherwise fitted with a Goetz GV 219 bombsight. A modified Revi reflector sight similar to that used in other German aircraft, the Goetz at least provided the pilot with aiming reference points during low-level shipping attacks, but was unable to compute more sophisticated data including drift, angle of attack and overwater speed, which the Lofte could do – but without it Fw 200 shipping strikes would have been far less accurate. Accurately estimating the height of an aircraft over water was often difficult in less than crystal-clear conditions, but the Echolot height-finding apparatus assisted the Condor crew in this important respect. Used in conjunction with the Lofte sight, it invariably gave accurate readings. In the unlikely event of all his sighting aids being inoperable, the Condor captain could use the time-honoured ring-and-bead sight, which was provided ahead of the cockpit windscreen.

Gradually the Condor evolved to accommodate additional military equipment including the Lofte bombsight, wing racks and a more complex gondola forward section, but the tall dorsal turret was not necessarily fitted at the same time. The phased changes are well illustrated by this Fw 200C-3. *MAP*

From the various published references and official documentation the researcher will find a substantial number of Focke-Wulf Condor variants, some of which may have been revised and/or 'found' to boost any existing list artificially; this may well give the impression that there were more than was actually the case. On occasion, if designations that should have been corrected in written form were left to be perpetuated in the next book on the aircraft, the confusion was destined to continue. To meet this challenge the author has listed below every known sub-type associated with the Condor found in numerous references. However, the list should be treated with caution as in some instances two different designations, particularly those carrying the 'U' series of suffixes denoting equipment changes, may not have been as extensive as indicated. Most first-line Luftwaffe aircraft designations carried these role qualifications, which in most cases are a handy aide-memoire to different configurations, armament modifications and equipment changes – but the opposite can be true if the sub-variant did not exist as such, the technical changes did not merit any qualification, or they were duplications. After all, these designations were for the benefit of air and ground crews, neither of whom would want to be confused by expecting differences to aircraft that were technically exactly the same.

Certain key features identified most of the Condors that served with the Luftwaffe, including the pilot's round viewing window, the prominent external bracing strips above the fuselage door frame, the pronounced kink to the wing trailing edge and the design of the landing gear.

The known/quoted military variants of the Fw 200 were as follows:

Focke-Wulf Fw 200A

A single airframe without any suffix is believed to have been completed as a static test vehicle with Werke Nummer 2891. (The original Japanese armed version has also been identified as an Fw 200A).

Fw 200A-0

Fitted with 720hp BMW 132G-1 engines, the ten initial Fw 200A-0s were followed by a further batch of aircraft variously identified, but, as noted in Table 3, the initial production run of Condors also included several individual aircraft that were considered by FWF as Versuch (prototype) aircraft. Others originally built as airliners were destined for varied careers in both civil and military service.

Lacking the under-fuselage gondola that carried the main armament in later models, the Fw 200A-0s were not generally armed for their transport and PR roles. Externally the early Condors could also be identified by the two-blade propellers fitted to the BMW 132 series of engines.

Focke-Wulf Fw 200B-1

This designation was supposedly reserved for the fourteen Condors that were built for German service, whereas the KB-1s were intended for export. They were powered by the BMW 132H engine of 830hp, which provided 110hp more than the BMW G-1's 720hp. However, in 1939 FWF allegedly made a 'paper' allocation of four Fw 200s to the Sino-German airline known as Eurasia, before the German Government cancelled all potential orders and/or options by foreign buyers.

Fw 200B-2

Also fitted with the BMW 132H engine with a power reduction of 20hp, the B-2 was deployed mainly as a transport.

Focke-Wulf Fw 200KA-1

This designation had been reserved for the aircraft ordered as airliners by Danske Luftfartselskab.

Fw 200KB-1/D-1

The KB suffix identified an export order in company records, the KB-1 having been allocated to the two aircraft in airliner configuration ordered by aero OY. No Condors with the KB suffix were delivered to their foreign customers but were acquired by the Luftwaffe and completed as Fw 200D-1 unarmed transports.

Fw 200KC-1/D-2

FWF identified five aircraft with the KC-1 designation as those that were ordered by Dai Nippon (W Nr 0017 to 0021), these being based on the Fw 200V-4, but eventually being delivered to the Luftwaffe as D-2 transport variants.

Focke-Wulf Fw 200C-0

As with the Fw 200B-2, the C-0 was powered by BMW 132H engines of 830hp.

Basically equipped to undertake a military transport role, the Fw 200C-0 had provision for three 7.9mm MG 15 machine-guns. These weapons were grouped in the fuselage and the new 'short' ventral gondola, which featured a tapered aft section that was fully glazed to provide a good view for a gunner. Positioned in A Stand (nose), B Stand (aft gondola) and C Stand (dorsal fuselage) positions, this arrangement set a general standard for the light armament layout of the early military Condors.

Abb. 2   A-Stand, Ansicht von innen in Flugrichtung

Abb. 6   C-Stand, Ansicht von außen, Gefechtsstellung

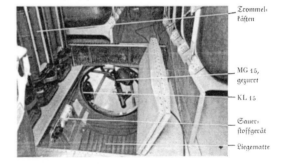

Abb. 5   C-Stand, Ansicht von innen, Reiseflugstellung

Above left: The A Stand machine gun position, looking towards the flight deck. *Official*

Above right: To operate an MG 15 machine-gun from the C Stand position in the aft gondola, a rotating ring mounting was provided, as was a lengthwise opening in the lower Perspex section. The gun was stowed when it was not in use. *Official*

Right: Access to the forward dorsal machine gun in the LLG 'bubble' provided the early-model Condors with a degree of defence against enemy aircraft, although flexible guns were mainly used against ships. *Official*

In addition to guns, the gondola was equipped with racks, release gear and lengthwise double access doors (opening along the centre line) to accommodate, typically, up to twelve 220lb (100kg) bombs internally. Racks and shackles for four 550lb (250kg) bombs were provided below each outboard engine nacelle and on single wing racks incorporating aerodynamic fairings fitted with standard ETC release gear. This unusual approach to bomb carriage was necessary to avoid grouping the additional weight close together in a more conventional fuselage bay, thus overstressing the structure and adversely affecting the aircraft's centre of gravity.

Hinged panels and inspection hatches enabled easy access to the Condor's ventral gondola, which was the primary weapons bay. The low contours of the KL 16 rear gun position with an MG 15 in place is evident. *Official*

Führungs-rolle   Führungs-rolle

Abb. 29
ETC 500/IX b in Rumpfwanne, von unten gesehen.

A view of the gondola bay showing a standard ETC 600 rack in place. *Official*

Schloß 50/X in Belade-stellung

Abb. 35 Beladen von Gerüst 4 Schloß 50/X von Hand.

It was sometimes quicker to manhandle smaller bombs without the aid of mechanical equipment. In this view an SC 50 is being located. *Official*

Abb. 25 Abnehmen des Kaliberbandes und der Rollenböcke nach dem Beladen.

Its substantial size enabled the Condor to carry a range of standard Luftwaffe bombs up to the SC 250, one of which is in position in this view. *Official*

Gabel zum Aufsetzen der Lade-apparate

Abb. 24 Aufsetzen der Ladeapparate.

As loading was in progress a crew member could observe the location of the bomb load through one of the many inspection hatches provided in the Condor's gondola. *Official*

Although tests had confirmed that the Fw 200C could safely lift 3970lb (SC 1,800kg) bombs, the aircraft was more usually loaded with SC 250, SC 500 or PC 500kg bombs.

Several (exact number unknown) Fw200C-0s were fitted with one or more fixed cameras set into the forward fuselage floor. The type was almost certainly the standard Zeiss Rb 50/30, which weighed 160lb (72.5kg).

The Fw 200V2 was the earliest known variant to have cameras installed, but others followed suit. Some local strengthening of the airframe was carried out to absorb the additional weight of military equipment.

Pulley assistance quickly hoisted bombs into the Condor's gondola bay and, depending on the model, the wing and nacelle racks. *Thiele*

Abb. 44 *Heißen einer LMA III unter die Fläche.*

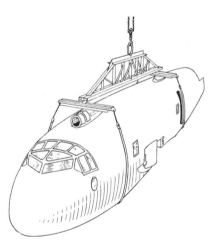

Rumpf in Heißvorrichtung
Spant 4 u. 6

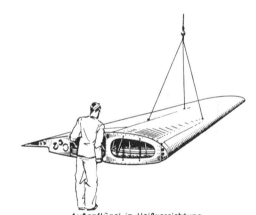

Außenflügel in Heißvorrichtung

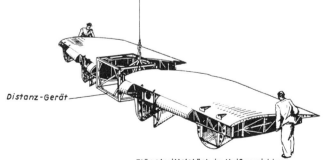

Distanz-Gerät

Flügelmittelstück in Heißvorrichtung

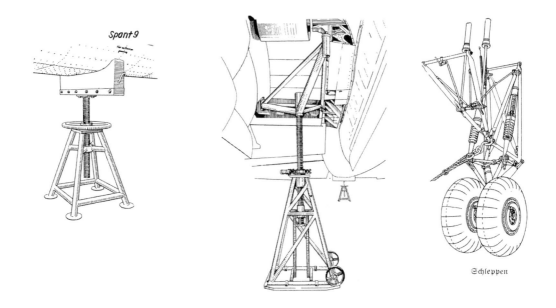

Spant 9

Schleppen

Aufbocken des Flugzeuges

Anlage 11

Fw 200C-1

Also fitted with 850hp BMW 132H engines driving two-blade propellers, the early production Fw 200C series (designated C-1 and C-2) represented the first of the true military variants. Fixed armament was now boosted by the installation of a single 20mm MG FF cannon in the nose and an MG 15 machine-gun in respective fore and aft positions in a lengthened gondola. In addition, one MG 15 was fitted into a forward teardrop-shaped dorsal position with a fourth MG 15 forming the aft dorsal defence.

For PR purposes two Rb 50/30 cameras could be fitted into a forward ventral position in the fuselage floor for vertical photography. The camera bodies and lenses, with variable focal lengths, were located behind shutters and braced to prevent vibration. Oblique photographic coverage of shipping targets was an integral part of every sortie, a task that invariably fell to the dorsal gunner with his excellent vantage point and room to pan the camera as required.

The range of the C-1 was increased by giving over some fuselage cabin space to fuel cells and the necessary feed lines. Incidentally, the C-1 was also identified for a time as the Fw 200C-1-XA.

An interior view of the radio operator's position in the early Fw 200C-1/C-2s. A degree of revision to the bank of 'black boxes' was necessary when a radar power unit and controls had to be located in that position. *Official*

Einschalten

Vor dem Start

An der Hauptschalttafel im Führerraum:

| 1 | Selbstschalter „Verbrauchergruppe V FT" einschalten (schwarzer Knopf). |

Am Schaltkasten SchK. 13 am Funkerplatz:

| 2 | ZFF/LFF-Schalter im Feld „Funker" und „Besatzung" auf „Aus". |

Am Fern-Bedienungs-Gerät FBG. 3:

| 3 | Schlepp-Antennen-Schalter auf Mittelstellung. |

Kurz nach dem Start

Selbstschalter am Funkerplatz in nachstehender Reihenfolge einschalten! (schwarze Knöpfe drücken)

4	Selbstschalter F 42 — 10 A — RH-F. (Röhrenheizung - Funk).
5	Selbstschalter F 46 — 6 A — RH-Nav. (Röhrenheizung - Navigation).
6	Selbstschalter F 48 — 6 A — RH-E-DLH. (Röhrenheizung - DLH-Empfänger).

1 Minute warten.

7	Selbstschalter F 44 — 6 A — U 10/E (Empfänger-Umformer).
8	Selbstschalter F 43 — 20 A — U 10/S (Sender-Umformer).
9	Selbstschalter F 45 — 6 A — AH/10 (Antennenhaspel).
10	Selbstschalter F 49 — 6 A — U 8 (Navigations-Umformer).
10 a	Selbstschalter F 47 — 10 A — U DLH. (DLH-Umformer).

Anm. zu 5, 6, 10 und 10a: Nur bei Bedarf einschalten

Halterung

Handfurbel

Abb. 3 Kurbelgetriebe zum Schließen der Klappen der Rumpfwanne und der Motorgondeln.

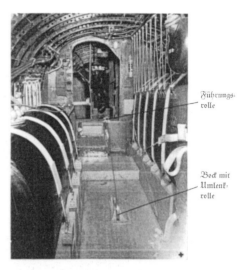

Führungs-
rolle

Bock mit
Umlenk-
rolle

Abb. 34 Rollenanordnung im Rumpf.

Abb. 30 Befestigung der hinteren Flasche des Flaz 10 b am C-Stand — Stuhl.

Above left: Extending the range was a wartime requirement for many military aircraft and the Condor's role made it a virtual necessity. Fortunately there was ample cabin space for fuel bladders and their associated feed valves once all the passenger seats had been removed. *Official*

Above right: A general view of the cabin of an Fw 200C-1/2 reveals the full range-extension fuel load. Although vital for its role, the Condor's volatile cargo made it terribly vulnerable to attack, particularly by enemy aircraft. *Official*

Left: The utilitarian approach to locating fuel bladders in the empty interior of the Condor nonetheless shows the ease with which the bladders could be anchored. *Official*

Fw 200C-2

According to available records only eight C-2s were built, although the sub-type was significant as it introduced the recessed outboard engine nacelle configuration. This shallow space aft of the engine firewall was fitted with a rack to enable the carriage of a single 550lb (250kg) bomb, an LMA III or LMB III mine, a supply container or a 66-imperial-gallon (300-litre) drop tank. In order to minimise drag, the fuel tank was in effect mounted backwards, ie. with its slimmer section towards the front of the aircraft rather than the other way round as was normal on a fighter. This method ensured that as little of the tank as possible protruded below the nacelle and was a further attempt to distribute the Condor's payload evenly over the airframe to avoid over-stressing and drag.

Among the ordnance loads the Condor could carry were LMA III (PVC 1006L) mines. These utilised the standard suspension lugs otherwise occupied by bombs, and on deployment a parachute was used to slow down the mine. *Official*

Abb. 45 LMB III auf dem Beladewagen.

A groundcrewman keeps a wary eye on the hoisting procedure for an LMA III, mainly to ensure that the mine does not swing out of line or adopts too steep a fore or aft angle while being firmly attached to the Condor's racks. *Official*

Fw 200C-3

By November 1940 Focke-Wulf had addressed the shortcomings of the Fw 200's light airliner structure when pressed into military service and, beginning with W Nr 0025, produced the Fw 200C-3, a variant incorporating as much airframe strengthening compared with previous sub-types as the company could accomplish without a major redesign or compromising safety through adding too much extra weight.

The Bramo 323 R-2 Fafnir engines of the Fw 200C-3 onwards were rated at 900hp with two-speed superchargers designed to automatically cut in at 3,000 revolutions. Three-blade propellers became standard with this powerplant and for all subsequent aircraft. Water-methanol injection increased available power to 1,200hp, this figure usually being quoted as standard for the C series.

Under normal flight conditions the engines were set at 1,750 to 1,800rpm on .9 to .95 boost, each of the four Bramo units developing 500hp. Airscrews were set between 1015 and 1045. At these settings an IAS flight of 170mph (270kmph) could be maintained for a patrol period of between twelve and thirteen hours with all engines using 110-116 gallons (500-530 litres) of fuel per hour. The rate of climb of a standard Fw 200C was 6.5-10ft/min (2-3m/sec) with the high-altitude supercharger (boost) designed to cut in at 10,000 feet (3,000 metres). All four engines rotated in the same direction, which occasionally made the aircraft something of a handful on take-off.

The Fw 200C-3 could be identified by redesigned engine cowlings incorporating multi-branch exhaust pipes and separately grouped cooling flaps in four sections. The cowlings were also more 'rounded' at the front and lengthened. Additional cowling fairings visible forward of each exhaust branch also marked out the C series. Each manifold, in multiple branches, exhausted via a cut-out section in the cowling flaps; alternatively, single pipes sufficed if flame damping was not required.

The cowlings were divided into hinged 'petal' sections for ease of access, and complete engines were designed for easy removal from the wing bulkhead, supported by standard-issue workstands, and wheeling clear of the aircraft for servicing or replacement.

The Fw 200C-3 series, of which there were at least 82 examples, were initially built by FWF at Cottbus, although Blohm und Voss subsequently took over production. Eight sub-variants have been identified, as listed below.

The unfaired outer wing bomb racks are obvious on this Fw 200C-3, which has the distinctive framed cupola aft of the cockpit for a single machine-gun. *MAP*

Fw 200C-3/U1

The C-3/U1 introduced a dorsal turret housing a single 15mm MG 151 cannon, a weapon that was also fitted in the front of the ventral gondola in place of the 20mm MG FF cannon, although in some cases the lighter cannon was retained until such time as the aircraft underwent inspection and major servicing. The C-3 also had the 'long' under-fuselage gondola that extended beyond the wing trailing edge.

Introduction of a forward dorsal hydraulic HDL 131 turret armed with a single 15mm MG 151 cannon warranted a new suffix. Provision was made for 75 cannon rounds; the aft dorsal position was retained, as it was on virtually every example of the military Condor.

Fw 200C-3/U2

An acute need for an automatic or 'computing' bombsight was met by the Fw 200C-3/U2, which had the gondola cannon raised slightly from its original mounting for a physically smaller machine-gun to be substituted, initially to allow room for a Lofte 7D sight, the mechanism of which was set into a well in the gondola floor; externally the sight body was faired in and protruded below the gondola just aft of the glazed area as a 'teardrop' to the starboard side of the floor. The bracing to support the transparent glazing adjacent to the cannon was revised to incorporate a flat, 'square' vision panel compared to the circular panel of preceding variants.

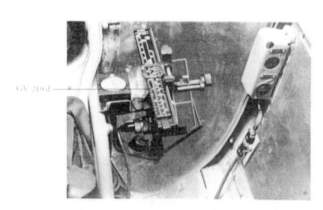

A GV 219d sight was fitted to early Condors to enable a crewman to compute the size of the target vessel. The Lofte 7D was a significant improvement, however, being compared to the famed American Norden sight in terms of accuracy. *Official*

The top turret armament briefly reverted to the lighter Fw Type 19 'blister' position (fitted with a single machine-gun) to save some weight before operational necessity resulted in the powered HDL 151 turret becoming an almost universal fitting on all subsequent Condors, including transports.

Fw 200C-3/U4

This variant was identified in company records as an extra-long-range reconnaissance bomber, with a normal fuel capacity of 7,810 litres (five 1,000-litre tanks in the rear fuselage and four 390-litre tanks in mid-fuselage) to be boosted by two 625-litre auxiliary tanks located in cells in the outboard engine nacelles.

The C-3 also introduced provision for two further MG 15s in 'manual' beam positions on either side of the fuselage, and examples of this variant usually carried an additional gunner; some aircraft also had the MG 15 machine-guns replaced by heavier MG 131s. The side guns were usually stowed and only mounted to fire from side hatches if the situation warranted their use. In operation a bar fitted across each window aperture supported the gun, which was operated manually.

Fw 200C-3/U7

This designation was apparently adopted for several aircraft equipped with the necessary guidance systems to test-launch the Hs 293A air-to-ground missile. This almost certainly meant that the aircraft carried a version of the FuG 203/230 Kehl-Strassburg radio control transmitter. An important guidance system used to control either the Hs 293 or, potentially, the SD 1400 X, the Kehl IV produced by Telefunkel and Opta was probably that installed in this version of the Condor. Alternatively the aircraft may have been utilised for flight trials of the Kehl I and III transmitters, neither of which entered production.

Fw 200C-4

Together with the Fw 200C-3, Focke-Wulf built between 105 and 115 Fw 200C-4s, making it the most prolific of the series: two main sub-variants were intended primarily as reconnaissance bombers and two as transports. All four were given the usual letter-numeral suffix to denote the fitting of the Gema Rostock ASV radar, later the FuG 200 Hohentweil blind bombing radar, and an MG 151/20 cannon or MG 131 machine-gun installed in the gondola nose, depending on whether or not a Lofte 7D bombsight was fitted. The early Rostock radar required two transmitting antennas (two horizontal dipoles and reflectors) mounted on the nose, and two similar arrays fitted on both the Condor's wing leading edges. Canted outwards for enhanced reception, Rostock gave bearings via an alternating capacity switch that coupled the receiver to each wing array in turn to give echoes in selected sectors over a 60km range.

A familiar view of the Fw 200C-4 showing the full antennae array for Rostock ASV radar. As an aircraft engaged on tests, it has had its fuselage code reduced to the single letter 'N'. *IWM*

Fw 200C-4/U1

This was a single example (W Nr 0137) of an intended high-speed transport that retained the Fw 19 forward dorsal turret and a single MG 15; the shorter ventral gondola had provision for a single MG 15 fore and aft, while an Fw 20 rear dorsal position was provided with a single MG 15 machine-gun. The aircraft actually served as an eleven-seat airliner for Adolf Hitler and was on the strength of the Fliegerstaffel des Führers from 1942. It appears that this machine differed from other Condors in that the aft end of the ventral gondola was widened and provided with a revised window arrangement.

Fw 200C-4/U2

A second one-off example (0138) of a high-speed transport variant with all armament removed, this Condor had fourteen seats. It served with KG 40, the Fl des Führers and DLH as a crew trainer.

Fw 200C-4/U3

The second of the C-4 reconnaissance bombers, the C-4/U3 was almost certainly fitted with standard armament, there being no indication of any other special equipment apart from radar.

Fw 200C-4/U4

The two examples of the C-4/U4 (0152 and 0153) were used by KG 40 as crew trainers.

Fw 200C-5

Condor development continued with the Fw 200C-5 transport, at least fifteen of which were completed and delivered in 1943. These may well have been the aircraft selected for Rostock installation for a thorough operational trial over the Atlantic; the same number of aircraft were involved in the programme, which was designed to prove that ASV radar gave a significant advantage. Few of the results obtained appear to have survived, although the quality of German airborne radar had gradually matured.

Fw 200C-5/FK

No examples of the C-5/FK have been identified by Werke Nummer and the reason (if any) for the FK suffix remains obscure.

Fw 200C-5/U1

A single C-5/U1 (0201) has been identified as such. It was identified as TA+MB before serving with KG 40 as F8+DT.

Fw 200C-5/U2

An unknown number of Condors were known as C-5/U2s, which probably differed mainly in the type and calibre of armament fitted.

Fw 200C-6

Otherwise similar to the C-4, the fourteen Fw 200C-6s completed were modified to carry two Hs 293A missiles and FuG 203b Kehl III missile control equipment. Racks for the Hs 293 radio-controlled bomb were incorporated into re-profiled outboard engine nacelles; these were metal fairings that covered the recesses for the previous carriage of bombs, supply canisters or drop tanks and restored the horizontal profile. This ensured that the bulky Henschel missile had a level launch attitude while the carrier aircraft maintained straight and level flight.

Further revision of the forward sighting station in the ventral gondola restored a circular sighting panel with additional bracing, sections of which were external. The round sighting panel was of smaller diameter than that previously fitted to Fw 200C variants.

Fw 200C-6/U2

The only known sub-variant of the C-6 was the aircraft used by Albert Speer; how extensive its interior fittings were is unknown

Fw 200C-7

Only a handful of C-7 transport conversions (?) are believed to have been completed before FWF concentrated on a final production programme to produce the Fw 200C-8 reconnaissance bomber; there is some doubt that such a variant existed as a separate sub-type in company or Luftwaffe records.

Fw 200C-8

As the final Condor variant to appear, the C-8 reconnaissance bomber was initially understood to have been a conversion of existing airframes based on the C-6 and intended mainly as a refined Hs 293A carrier, again with deepened outer engine nacelles re-contoured as missile carriers. If this was indeed the case, the C-8s were all given new Werke Nummern, strongly indicating that they were in fact 'new build' examples.

Although externally of similar configuration to previous variants, the C-8 had the distinctive Condor long ventral gondola extended further forward and stripped of internal bomb racks and equipment to save weight. Also, the lengthways bomb doors were usually sealed.

Although provision for a forward-firing machine-gun or cannon was retained, these weapons were not always fitted as a further weight-saving measure.

The forward part of the C-8's gondola lined up on a vertical axis with the cockpit windscreen, whereas all previous versions terminated on a line through the rear cockpit windows. This almost certainly enabled an extra bay in the gondola to house additional electronics equipment associated with 'command and control' of the Hs 293 and, speculatively, an operator's seat. Externally the forward section of the gondola was more pronounced due to some revision of the sighting 'bubble' for a cannon or machine-gun compared to earlier variants and was similar to that first introduced on the C-6, although there were detail differences.

External bracing was in evidence below the bubble, as was a ducting section for the ejection of spent cartridge cases with a 'pen nib' opening at its lower, open end. A 'teardrop' fairing also appeared on the starboard side behind the V-shaped window and forward of the twin windows that had been standard on all aircraft fitted with the 'long' gondola. The purpose of the fairing is not known with certainty.

Fw 200C-8 0256, among the last Condors built as production tailed off during 1943, has all the late war refinements including FuG 200 radar and the gondola extension, but lacks flame dampers on the exhausts.

Focke-Wulf was contracted to build twenty-two Fw 200C-8s and as far as is known all examples were completed and provided with the deeper outer engine nacelles to support the Hs 293A missile and the nose aerial array for an FuG 200 Hohentweil radar, which could be fitted as standard.

Fw 200C-8/U10

A further variant linked to the last version of the Condor, there are few records of how the U10 differed from a standard C-8.

Fw 200C-10

The very last sub-type of the Fw 200 to be identified in available records, the C-10 was intended to fulfil a long-range reconnaissance role at a lighter all-up weight to enhance performance and endurance; most variants actually included aircraft that were used in this role, for which any superfluous equipment, including some of the armament, would be removed to save weight, depending on the operational patrol area. It is known that as well as the refuelling lines installed in the original passenger cabin to accommodate six additional fuel cells, there was enough space in the bomb bay area above the gondola to fit five or six additional fuel cells for purely reconnaissance sorties. This configuration may well have applied mainly (or solely) to the Fw 200C-10.

A full radar antennae, flame damper exhausts and the much-revised gondola area tended to indicate a late-model Fw 200C-6 or C-8 (coded +AD in this case), but these changes were not a foolproof guide to a variant. *Author's collection*

Production totals

Various production figures for the Fw 200 are quoted by reference sources, but 262 and 'about 276 examples' appear to be as reliable as these sources get! Others quote a figure of 268 military examples. A final, accurate figure appears elusive and difficult to determine from available records due possibly to a degree of re-manufacture and updating of existing airframes. Of these, 252 aircraft are known to have been accepted by the Luftwaffe as follows:

Year	Number accepted
1940	26
1941	58
1942	84
1943	76
1944	8

This total of 252 aircraft would need perhaps to have fourteen (or twenty-two) pre-production or Versuch machines added to obtain the higher figure of 276, although 'accepted by the Luftwaffe' has to be qualified for some of the early aircraft that served in both civil and military roles and were not owned by the air force under the more normal procurement system.

Chapter 4

1939: An eventful year

Even as Germany launched the opening campaign of the Second World War, some seemingly insignificant cracks were beginning to show in the Luftwaffe order of battle – or rather in the lessons learned from results obtained by the actual deployment of the Luftwaffe. For example, photographic reconnaissance had been given a much higher priority than the wider world might have assumed. To outsiders the Luftwaffe seemed only to exist to wage war: commentators of newsreels stressed only the strong points of an air offensive with massed use of bombers and fighters. This was of course exactly what the Nazi hierarchy wanted the world to believe, but such displays of military might hid some important aspects of aerial warfare, without which the front-line Geschwader would have been far less effective.

Photographic reconnaissance was one of the most important behind-the-scenes activities and some time before Hitler moved against Poland the Luftwaffe had formed a substantial number of long-range (Fernaufklarungstaffeln or Aufklarungsstaffeln) and short-range (Nahaufklarungstaffeln) reconnaissance units.

Oberkommando der Wehrmacht (OKW) had laid the groundwork for a comprehensive system of photo intelligence and interpretation during the 1930s and much was achieved before the war. To hide the fact that files were being compiled on potential targets, much of the aerial surveillance work was of a clandestine nature, carried out by sports flying clubs, commercial flights and even by the crew of the airship *Graf Zeppelin*.

Much of this valuable work failed to be fully exploited, however, when in 1935 the system was decentralised and no officer of high enough rank was put in charge of what had expanded into an excellent service. Numerous overflights had resulted in comprehensive dossiers containing superb high-resolution prints from Zeiss cameras, world-renowned for their quality. Prints covering major installations of use to Germany's potential enemies in time of war were amassed and used for operational purposes, although the results of front-line PR sorties soon began to vary. Units left much to their own devices had to arrange, interpret and use intelligence material as the situation dictated, but many of them lacked enough skilled photographic interpreters at local, unit level.

OKW continued to base its operations on the intelligence gathered, often via mobile darkrooms that developed the films and prepared visual sighting reports backed by up-to-the-minute overflights of battle lines by field commanders. But there were occasions when no further coverage of a given area was deemed necessary, especially in terms of short-range tactical target areas. This patchy approach to PR was revealed during the Battle of Britain when Luftwaffe bomber crews repeatedly hit non-strategic targets as a result of faulty intelligence and photo coverage. There was nothing wrong with the prints the crews were using – quite the reverse – but the images often indicated the 'wrong' targets, which was a direct fault of overall strategic planning by the Luftwaffe High Command.

The Condor's PR role

When the war began individual Staffeln were undertaking long-range reconnaissance sorties at the behest of either the field army to which they were attached or in response to requests made at Fliegerkorps or Luftflotten level, to which most first-line units were subordinated. The composition of reconnaissance units varied to a significant degree, the convenient division of short or long range (depending on the aircraft type deployed) often overlapping.

As far as the Fw 200 was concerned, long-range, often weather-related, sorties were usually flown by aircraft of the staff reconnaissance flight. Also, the data obtained was specific to the Condor unit, for the converted Focke-Wulf airliner was generally flying further than other types and briefing officers and aircrews alike wanted a clear picture of the conditions they and often they alone were likely to encounter hundreds of miles from base. Any useful information on enemy activity that the Condor crews could concurrently gather on such sorties went into the files for future operations.

Although Germany was at war, the unit that would deploy the Condor in its most effective role continued to train aircrew through the winter of 1939/40. PR flights had the dual advantage of providing excellent flight training and gathering intelligence data by flying to specific areas, while the High Command pondered its next move. As far as the U-boat arm was concerned it appears that integrating long-range attacks by Condors in cooperation with the submarine fleet had not yet been formulated.

Improved aircraft

Focke-Wulf's modification programme for the Condor resulted in the C series, which was to endure in several sub-variants until the end of production in 1943. Following the Fw 200C-0 came the improved C-1, both these variants being used for training, transport, reconnaissance and early maritime operations in the hands of both training units and the forerunners of the new Kampfgeschwader 40, which before its formation flew a variety of aircraft including the Fw 200B, which lacked the familiar under-fuselage gondola incorporating a weapons bay that hallmarked the C series.

Cleaner lines in keeping with its airliner origins were evident on the Fw 200C-0 series before military requirements demanded the installation of gun turrets. With its engines running up to full power, the risk of fire increased – hence the four extinguishers carefully placed for immediate use. *MAP*

The fitting of the extended and deepened outer engine nacelles that boosted the Condor's bomb load is seen to advantage on Fw 200C BS+AJ, which also shows the high contrast of the upper-surface green camouflage colours.

Details abound in this view of an early-production Condor (named *Vega*), including the engine cowling intakes, oil cooler fairings, an open gondola hatch and the nacelle bomb rack.

The Fw 200C had accommodation for a crew of five for standard operational sorties. The complement usually consisted of a pilot and co-pilot, a navigator/radio operator/gunner, a flight engineer/gunner and a second (rear) gunner. On certain flights the Condor would carry six men, the extra individual invariably being a meteorologist, or 'weather frog', in Luftwaffe slang.

Colourful journalese

Alternatively, newspaper reporters charged with capturing the exploits of Luftwaffe units in print for newspapers or the Luftwaffe house magazine *Signal* would join the crew. Many early war operations were the subject of dozens of propaganda tracts aimed at the general public and, more specifically, at well-educated young men who would be most likely to join the Luftwaffe and train as aircrew. Often highly colourful in their approach, these booklets painted a glowing picture of a near-invincible force sweeping all opposition before it.

In the case of the Condor, few other nations could match the deployment of a very elegant former passenger airliner that had been modified for one or more wartime roles, and the Luftwaffe High Command was not slow in publicising what must have come across as a bold and daring concept. Numerous photographs, some of them in colour, were published by *Signal* at a time when colour film stock was not widely available.

Although he had only a few aircraft even as the winter of 1939 approached, Edgar Petersen managed to pool slim resources and oversee the training of enough crews to form the basis for KG 40. With the active assistance of Oberstleutnant Martin Harlinghausen, Petersen established his course at Oldenburg and was made chief instructor. He was quite enthusiastic over the potential represented by the Fw 200 and was not to be daunted even when he became aware of the pessimistic contents of Technical Office (C-Amt) Building Programme report No 16 dated 25 October 1939.

The C-Amt report projected a total of only forty-six new Fw 200s being built before production ceased, only one of which had been delivered by 31 August. It stated that a further example being built in September 1939 would be completed by December. These reports, prepared with good intentions, were designed to show where the RLM could cut programmes and save money. They changed frequently in terms of actual and projected build numbers, totals of aircraft in production and termination dates.

During the early winter of 1939 Edgar Petersen continued to work towards an operational debut for his anti-shipping unit, dividing his time between keeping things running smoothly at Oldenburg and establishing a Blindflugschule (Instrument-Flying Training School) at Celle. This was the school, established in 1934 where Petersen had previously held a staff position and some key members of KG 40 were his ex-colleagues from Celle. Designation changes made later created BS 6, which remained active until the end of the war.

If the C-Amt's production forecast was a little sobering, it is easy to see that Petersen had little choice but to gloss over any problems that might have been caused by FWF's production rate for the Condor. From his unique position he was confident that, if necessary, the transfer of several Condors from DLH would provide enough aircraft to enable his initial training courses to be completed. Individual Condors, irrespective of their civil or military origins, would give numerous crews the all-important 'feel' of handling a four-engine aircraft (as against the tri-motor Ju 52) when little else in that category was available.

Both Harlinghausen and Petersen knew the value of specialist training for the type of war flying that KG 40 would be called upon to undertake. Both officers were experienced pilots, Petersen himself having many hours of airline flight time in his log-book, recording visits to such destinations as Seville, Las Palmas and Tripoli. Petersen also had the undoubted advantage of having seen combat in the Spanish Civil War with the Legion Condor's AS./88, the maritime force attached to the German air order of battle. He was thus able to impart certain occurrences that work perfectly under peacetime conditions but have a habit of taking on a different slant under the impetus of war – items that no textbook or classroom lecture can cover in quite the same way.

At Oldenburg trainees regularly practised navigation by flying the Condor out over the North Sea or the Baltic to additionally hone their skills in ship recognition and carry out various methods of low-altitude shipping attack. For overwater patrols a system of basic 'race track' flight patterns was established, with a long outward leg followed by a wide turn and return on a parallel long leg. An alternative was a series of wide, circular flight paths, each of which covered an area wide enough for the aircrew to log any shipping activity inside it over a considerable distance. Crews became proficient at detecting a potential quarry with the aid of powerful binoculars for, apart from the Condor's instruments, dead reckoning-type navigation and time-expired flight duration logs, there were no other aids available. Each circle or race track could be varied as to flight duration, fuel load and prevailing weather conditions. This element of training was particularly important as it would be duplicated almost exactly when the new crews were posted to KG 40.

Gradually each trainee crew reached a reasonable standard of competence and was expected to be able to navigate accurately. In regard to the intricacies of navigation, officers with a naval background had some advantage over those who did not, as the maritime challenges in guiding aircraft and ships across miles of featureless ocean had many similarities in common.

Inevitably the singular new long-range unit formed at Bremen in October 1939 was soon widely referred to as the 'Kurier' or 'Condor' Staffel, which had something of a ring to it. It was bound to attract young crews who wanted to accept the challenge of being part of a unit unique in the Luftwaffe. Edgar Petersen soon had a full complement of seasoned pilots and crewmen to act as instructors and pass on their experience to the younger men. He himself travelled throughout the Reich to recruit suitable candidates for his maritime flying courses; many individuals were rejected at a time when the standards could afford to be high, a situation that would change in due course.

Although the primary wartime Condor combat unit is noted here as having its origins established in 1939, it stemmed directly from the Fernaufklarungsstaffel Ob.d.l. created at the behest of Luftwaffe Chief of Staff Hans Jeschonneck. I./Gruppe KG 40 would not formally be made operational for another few months, but it was to receive a small number of Fw 200C-1s before the first war patrol was undertaken in 1940. In addition, the Condor had yet to complete a series of E-Stelle tests to confirm its suitability as a combat aircraft for the Luftwaffe. In short, the process of providing the Luftwaffe with a potent maritime air element took place over several months, until the degree that it would actually be needed was dictated largely by the progress of the war in Western Europe.

Adding low-altitude shipping attack (with few sighting aids to hone the techniques) to an expanding training curriculum, Petersen's unit took delivery of six Fw 200C-0s in November 1939. These machines were quite capable of carrying out combat flights despite lacking the full airframe strengthening that FWF was incorporating into the subsequent Condors. Availability of several C-0s did, however, enable training to be as realistic as possible.

Promotion was also relatively rapid in KG 40's forerunner unit. The Luftwaffe did not generally bestow high rank on individuals despite instances of considerable experience, but it announced that most officers who transferred would be made up to the rank of Oberleutnant. One proviso was that each individual had to hold current flying certificates for the third and fourth quarters of 1939 before making the transition to a four-engine type.

Table 4: Early dates of KG 40 and its forerunner unit (various sources)

1939	
January	Formation of Versuchsstelle fur Hohenflug (VfH – Experimental Station for High Altitude Flying) under Theodore Rowehl
25/29 July	Condor Berlin-Siam flight with ten stops en route
1 August	Fliegerkorps X formed with Martin Harlinghausen in command; Edgar Petersen becomes Navigation Officer (Stab./Fl K X)
3 September	Britain declares war on Germany
12 September	Erhard Milch backs continued production/modification of Fw 200 for maritime role
23 September	I./KG 40 officially formed
1 October	Fernaufklarungstaffel Ob.d.l. formed at Bremen (later nucleus of I./KG 40) with Petersen in command
1 October	Petersen promoted to Major
25 October	C-Amt report No 16 on Condor production status
November	Six Fw 200C-0s delivered to KG 40
1940	
8 April	First KG 40 wartime sortie
21 April	First Condor loss and first sinking
18 April	Formation of I./Gruppe
26 October	Attack on *Empress of Britain*
18 November	First magnetic mines laid in British coastal waters by Luftwaffe aircraft
1941	
January	Führer's order places KG 40 under command of German Navy

As already noted, there was still some official opposition to the Luftwaffe operating a four-engine aircraft when all such programmes were supposed to have been cancelled. This view reflected a general lack of appreciation that if a maritime reconnaissance requirement existed it had to be fulfilled immediately – not until such time as the Heinkel He 177 might be ready for service. One can, however, understand the great anticipation – indeed, faith is not putting it too strongly – for the He 177 to be a success; as one of the few four-engine bomber programmes that the RLM had allowed to proceed, it was expected to be a maid of all work and master of all. Early indications that the Heinkel design would require a lengthy test period, mainly to overcome problems with its complex engine arrangement, added weight to Petersen's argument that the Condor was the only immediate choice.

To back his argument Petersen was fortunate in obtaining the support of Reich Air Minister Erhard Milch, and as a result the company settled into a steady building programme much as before. There was little or no alternative without OKL/RLM giving the Condor top priority status, and this was never forthcoming.

Clandestine PR role

As early as January 1939 the Luftwaffe had formed part of what became a vast research and development organisation, much of it intended to remain secret. Several aspects of this clandestine work involved the high-altitude and long-range capability of the Fw 200, including the Versuchsstelle fur Hohenflug (VfH, or Experimental Station for High Altitude Flying). Formed under the command of Theodor Rowehl within the Versuchsverband OKL, this was just one of several units that were commonly referred to by the name of the commanding officer. Rowehl was instrumental in establishing – or perhaps re-establishing – the vital need for aerial reconnaissance in war, a discipline that the Luftwaffe had, as mentioned earlier, planned well but not maintained to the original high standards.

Few unarmed, special-purpose aircraft entered Luftwaffe service, although several designs were put forward and flown. Officially the view was that PR was an essential part of offensive combat operations and workhorse types such as the Ju 88 were consequently flown by numerous units. Some of these aircraft were unarmed to save weight, but they were first and foremost considered to be ready for combat if the need arose. In contrast there was the remarkable if obsolete Junkers Ju 86, perhaps the best-known German reconnaissance aircraft and one of the exceptions that proved the rule insofar as it was much modified but never armed for ultra-high-altitude PR sorties.

Rowehl's unit tested new types that could be adapted for the reconnaissance role, among them the Fw 200V-10 (200-0001/BS+AF). Before it crashed on 23 November 1939 after taking off from Jever, the aircraft had been delivered to the VfH to have cameras fitted. At the same time the Condor was modified to enable it to carry additional fuel, which boosted its range to 3,100 miles (5,000km). When it came down, the V-10 was pronounced a write-off as it had suffered a broken back in the crash-landing, which had also wrenched the starboard outer engine away from its mountings.

Kommando Rowehl had other Condors on its strength, however, the earliest production example being the V-2 2484/WL+AETA. This machine was delivered to Rechlin in August 1939, also for conversion to a camera platform, before passing to the VfH.

A third Condor, Fw 200A-0 (S-3) 2895/WL-AMHC, ex-*Nordmark*, was also converted to carry two Rb 30/50 cameras for high-altitude photography after delivery to Rechlin on 29 August 1939, and was flown by the VfH in September 1939 as a PR trainer. On 28 November 1939 it was transferred to I./KG 40 in Germany to become F8+HH – which begs the question as to exactly how early elements of KG 40 appeared on Luftwaffe rolls. It would appear in the case of this particular Condor that the 'paper establishment' preceded actual deployment for some months. Loaned to 4./KGrzbV 107 on 7 April 1940, 2895 was later re-coded TK+BS.

Lacking wing bomb racks, Fw 200C BS+AG runs up its engines on a snow-covered airfield. Despite the low temperature a fire extinguisher stands by. *MAP*

The low-key operations of Petersen's long-range Staffel continued throughout the winter of 1939/40, when the weather threatened to curtail anything more than high-priority flying. Cadet crews did, however, need to keep up their stipulated number of flying hours and this they did with remarkably few incidents. Condors continued to be delivered to the Staffel, including B-1s 0012 and 0013, consecutive aircraft off the FWF production line. As in other instances, both Condors were assigned to Petersen's unit before they had been completed, on 1 October 1939,and in both cases this date was before either example had made its maiden flight. Subsequently the two aircraft would be delivered to I./KG 40 on the same day, 17 April 1940.

It was fortunate that the embryo KG 40 had enough ex-Luft Hansa pilots and crewmen who were generally well experienced in long-distance flying, a skill that was to prove invaluable. The unit's early complement included Oberleutnants Rudolf Mayr, Bernard Jope, Edmund Daser and Fritz Fliegel, together with Leutnant Hans Buchholz, Heinrich Schlosser and Konrad Verlohr. After he was promoted to Hauptmann, Verlohr distinguished himself by sinking two ships totalling 10,857grt (gross registered tons) on 16 January 1941.

Hauptmann Daser's crew are caught by a photographer shortly after their return from a sortie over Norway in 1942. Once again KG 40's code appears in front of a neatly rendered fuselage Balkenkreuz, which, if the aircraft remained in service long, would soon exhibit signs of wear and tear from hours of over-water flying. *F. Selinger*

Well bolstered from the Arctic weather they frequently encountered, Edmund Daser's Condor crew leave their aircraft after a sortie. Fur hats seemed to be quite popular flying wear in KG 40. *F. Selinger*

Daser was to became Staffel Kapitän of I./KG 40 in April 1941 and flew, among other examples, Fw 200C F8+CH during 1940. It was, however, difficult, given the complexity of the large aircraft with which his unit was equipped, for pilots – even those with the skill of Daser and others – to fly a personal aircraft as frequently as they might have liked. By contrast, fighter pilots could enjoy this advantage for many months, whereas Condor crews were often obliged to fly the aircraft that was available. And advantage it certainly was, as pilots were emphatic in their belief that no two military aircraft were exactly the same. Different machines seemed to handle better than their contemporaries, accelerate more quickly and generally fly free of small technical defects – those small idiosyncrasies that would mark out one aircraft from another, although of course they looked identical. Nobody could really say why this was, but every air force was to record much the same type of experience. In the case of the Condor, therefore, pilots such as Daser could claim no priority – all they could expect was to fly a favourite example when it was serviceable.

No provocation

Fortunately for the Germans, and the men of the air arms opposing them on the new Western Front, the 'Phoney War' seemed to be just that for a few precious months. Neither side wished to provoke the other – which did not mean to say that a basic state of readiness for the next move was overlooked. It became increasingly clear that Hitler would attack in western Europe, but the direction and form the offensive would take were open to speculation. As a precaution the RAF moved a portion of its fighter and light bomber force to France, a move begun on 2 September, becoming in the process the Advanced Air Striking Force.

Activity at sea was almost entirely centred on the actions of Germany's U-boat arm, with numerous crews starting to find easy pickings around Britain's shores and out into the Western Approaches. Coastal Command's riposte to this growing threat to the country's lifelines was limited by suitable aircraft in adequate numbers, and the picture in general terms was of the two sides groping in the dark while 'getting their eye in', analysing what results they gained from early war sorties and trying to estimate how the threat would grow and how quickly. Britain's service chiefs had to juggle a triple threat from the Germans – aircraft, capital ships and U-boats.

With an inventory of too few modern aircraft, Coastal Command had begun the war with two first-line Groups with fourteen squadrons of flying boats and landplanes. A third group of five squadrons flew obsolete and largely ineffectual types that would be replaced as soon as possible. Included in the order of battle on 3 September 1939 were two types that would become part of the Focke-Wulf Condor story, namely the Short Sunderland and Lockheed Hudson. Both had origins in civil designs, not so dissimilar from that of the Condor itself.

As a military flying boat, the Sunderland was a tough and capable aircraft, well liked by its crews. With four engines bestowing a radius of action of some 1,700 miles (which translated into an endurance of more than twelve hours), the Sunderland could encroach upon the Condor's patrol territory with relative ease. Luftwaffe and German crews would later clash on several occasions. As far as long-range air cover of convoys was concerned, the early months of the war recorded many Sunderland sorties. Far better equipped than its German opposite number in terms of crew comfort and cooking facilities, the Short flying boat was reasonably well-armed and able to absorb damage. The singular four-engined type available to Coastal Command in 1940, the Sunderland was able to carry out numerous patrols that served to boost morale among merchant ship sailors at a difficult time.

Of all the Allied aircraft the Condor met in combat, the Short Sunderland was one of the first. Able to match the German aircraft in terms of range, the big flying boat, represented here by a Mk I (W3984) of No 10 Squadron, RAAF, caused the loss of several Condors. *IWM*

Coastal's bombers

One of the most welcome types to join the Coastal force was the Hudson. The first American aircraft to cross the Atlantic for service with the RAF, this twin-engine patrol bomber was an airliner derivative that met with outstanding success in the military role. Able to stay airborne for six hours, the Hudson had a very useful radius of action of just under 1,000 miles and it too would later cross swords with the Condor.

An early antagonist to the Luftwaffe over the Atlantic, the Lockheed Hudson was the first American aircraft to equip Coastal Command. Hudsons had a useful range and several clashed with Condors resulted in losses for the Germans. A Mk I of No 224 Squadron is seen departing on a patrol. *IWM*

Starved of enough suitable maritime aircraft (in much the same way as the Luftwaffe), Coastal had to 'make do and mend' if Britain was to have any cover for its increasingly important merchant shipping fleet as German's blockade began to bite in the winter of 1940/41. Not that there were many bombers suitable for sustained convoy protection patrols; Bomber Command jealously guarded its assets in this respect, with only limited support being granted for naval operations.

The bombing of German capital ships if they were caught in ports had high priority but only a limited effect in practice, and attacking U-boats resulted in few successes for months on end. Halifaxes were used on several such operations but no spectacular sinkings were recorded, although it was felt in Whitehall that the raids were keeping the German warships 'bottled up' and at anchor where they could do little harm.

Two of the other bombers with which Britain went to war were the twin-engine Armstrong Whitworth Whitley and the Vickers Wellington. Both were drafted into Coastal Command for Atlantic patrols and anti-submarine warfare, although only the much-loved and capable 'Wimpey' was to stay the course until the end. Modified to accommodate successively efficient anti-submarine depth charges and bombs, together with sea-search radars and such nasty surprises for U-boat crews as the Leigh Light, the Wellington was a much-changed aircraft when the Vickers engineers had adapted it specifically for anti-submarine and sea patrol operations. Coastal was consequently issued with an aircraft that proved lethal to a number of unfortunate U-boats crews.

The Whitley also did its bit to combat the U-boat menace, but its performance was such that its 1935 design vintage did not lend itself to much modification for the Coastal role. In due course the Whitley was also replaced by other types, but in 1940 what was needed most urgently was the range obtainable from four engines. The Short Stirling was ruled out – which left the Halifax.

None of the Handley Page bombers were actually diverted to Coastal Command until the end of 1942, by which time the first Consolidated B-24 Liberators and B-17 Fortresses were re-equipping several Coastal squadrons. Even with four-engined aircraft at their disposal the Allies had to contend with a 300-mile (485km) 'Atlantic Gap' between Europe and Canada, which the American bombers were deployed to close, but this they did only gradually as airfields in locations such as those in the Azores were utilised.

Untroubled

Before Lend-Lease US aircraft began arriving in England in substantial numbers, Sunderlands alone had the range to maintain a watch on U-boat operations, German surface ships – and the activities of KG 40. There were so few of them, however, that Condor crews were little troubled by the relatively rare sight of the Short flying boat.

A few early war skirmishes involving Sunderlands had resulted in the destruction of several Ju 88s; the British flying boat had turned in an impressive performance, giving rise to the nickname 'Flying Porcupine'. This the Sunderland could not always live up to as its seven Browning 0.303in machine-guns could have little deadly effect against a cannon-armed fighter-bomber of the calibre of the Ju 88, as some later combats were to show. Ironically the Ju 88s often encountered in combat over the Atlantic were part of V./KG 40's fighter force. Nevertheless, the Sunderland's armament remained one of its assets in the eyes of the Germans, and a patrolling Condor crew searching for seaborne targets would generally try to avoid contact. In any event, shooting down enemy flying boats would result in only an indirect advantage to their own sorties and those of the U-boat fleet.

Massive advantage

One undeniable advantage the Allied air forces enjoyed was the fact that positive moves were made to improve Coastal Command's inventory as the war progressed and production picked up; thus the Beaufighter and Mosquito, modified for specialised anti-shipping, maritime patrol and attack roles, gave the Command examples of two of the most successful aircraft of the war. This was in marked contrast to the Germans, who were obliged to modify a handful of aircraft to the very limit of (and in many cases arguably well beyond) their ability to be effective warplanes.

Awaiting spring

As the 'Phoney War' months of inactivity continued to bring with them weather that was ever more prohibitive to safe flying, the Condor Staffel undertook low-key reconnaissance and transport flights, in effect marking time until the conditions improved with the spring. Additional flying hours were, however, to stand the Condor crews in good stead when the war in western Europe began in earnest; a glance at the map quickly revealed a need for support and supply flights for German's ground forces if they repeated the Blitzkrieg-type campaign that had brought success in Poland.

Aircraft were despatched to the Condor Staffel immediately they were completed by FWF at Bremen. The Luftwaffe unit, located conveniently close by at the airfield at Neulanderfeld, checked over each aircraft before logging its Stammkenzeichen, or radio code, which was used for air-to-air/air-to-ground identification generally before an aircraft joined a military unit. These codes were, however, retained on individual Condors for some time, even when they were officially on charge to KG 40 – indeed, some were never repainted in the unit code 'F8'. This was generally speaking because the aircraft in question was on the unit's strength but serving in a second-line role – training, courier work, test flying and so forth. Every Condor was allocated the familiar four-letter radio code, in line with standard Luftwaffe practice.

August 1939: quick off the mark

If the land war was at a very low key for seven months after Hitler invaded Poland, the conflict at sea was quite the opposite. It could be said with some justification that Admiral Karl Doenitz launched the first U-boat campaign even before war began. On 19 and 25 August 1939, fourteen and sixteen boats respectively were positioned in the North Atlantic to await the order to attack Allied shipping. Within days the *Graf Spee* and *Deutschland* also set sail. The British Admiralty, collectively horrified at the ease with which the German capital ships had begun their war patrols undetected by aircraft or Royal Navy warships, made the erroneous assumption that it was Hitler's battleships and cruisers that posed the main threat to seaborne commerce. This arguably gave Doenitz a slim advantage in a slightly unreal situation insofar as, had his boats been systematically attacked by the RAF, the latter would not have posed a very real threat as the prewar bombs carried by Coastal aircraft were shown to be less than effective against U-boats, particularly if they were submerged. Thus, when Doenitz opened his offensive on 3 September by sinking the passenger ship *Athenia*, British freighters began to go down with terrifying regularity. There were then thirty-nine U-boats (out of total of fifty-eight extant) on patrol in the Atlantic, and in September 1939 alone they sent forty-one ships totalling 153,800grt to the bottom.

Preoccupied with deploying his U-boats most effectively, Karl Doenitz had undertaken a huge responsibility. A fervent believer in the ability of his underwater fleet to be instrumental in strangling Britain's seaborne lifeline, Doenitz had studied the record of U-boats in the First World War and had seen how close the boats of the Kaiser's Navy had come to achieving a similar goal. In terms of U-boat support, the earlier war had little or no aviation dimension, but it became clear that in the present conflict aerial reconnaissance would be valuable in locating shipping targets and passing details to U-boat headquarters for onward transmission to submarine captains. Prior knowledge of the location, speed and course of ships would give fleet U-boats greater freedom of action by reducing patrol times and curtailing fruitless searches that burned precious fuel oil. Doenitz and his command officers realised that there was not a great deal of choice as regards the aircraft types that could be used for such operations – only the Fw 200 and Junkers Ju 90 had seen some service with Luft Hansa and were capable of covering considerable distances.

In the case of the Ju 90, production was so modest that all dozen or so existing aircraft retained Versuch designations. The V-5 had been the first example to briefly bear Luft Hansa colours in 1939, and several others intended for South African Airways were not delivered before there were inducted into the Luftwaffe. Four Ju 90B-1s were then completed, but not all of them operated with the German airline due to the outbreak of war. Doenitz was therefore obliged to 'adopt' the Fw 200 on several counts, not the least of which was that there were a few more of them than the Junkers design. By the outbreak of war, despite the fact that the number of Condors was barely enough to equip a single Luftwaffe Staffel, Harlinghausen and Petersen persuaded Doenitz that the Focke-Wulf airliner was equal to the task in hand.

Not that as a transport the Ju 90 was entirely overlooked; a robust design, and well thought of in military circles, it had a loaded weight of 50,706lb (23,000kg) and a range of 775 miles (1,247km), and although the all-up weight was very close to that of the Condor, numbers were often what counted most, and the Ju 90 gave a valuable boost to early airlift and supply operations flown over long distances. Lacking heavy transports after the general cancellation of four-engine designs, the Luftwaffe

Type VII and IX U-boats are being replenished for sea at one of the pens built to protect them from Allied bombs at Trondheim in Norway. Thus almost immune from attack while in port, Admiral Doenitz's submarines had months of combat in the open sea, ably assisted by the Condors. *IWM*

was forced to rely on a disproportionately large number of Ju 52/3ms. The older Junkers design could only carry loads suited to its configuration, which is where the larger types came into their own. Ironically, the Junkers concern enjoyed a certain long-term advantage in having built fewer Ju 90s; given time to develop the original design as the Ju 290, the company produced an aircraft that was strengthened and armed to better suit it to the rigours of a maritime role than was the Condor.

Wartime transport flights

Before the Fw 200 became Germany's principal maritime reconnaissance bomber, it made its combat debut deployed, together with the Ju 90, as a transport. Beginning in April 1940, each type carried out the first wartime flights during the Norwegian campaign. Larger transport aircraft were issued to the unit, which had its origins in Fernaufklarungstaffel Ob.d.l. 107; retaining the same unit number it became KGrzbV 107 (Kampfgeschwader zur besonderen Verwendung – Bomber Unit on Special Duties) for the Norwegian campaign. In the meantime, part of I./KG 40 was organised and equipped with Fw 200C-1s, individual Staffeln being intended to undertake a reconnaissance rather than a transport role.

An ice-covered runway and bad weather resulted in this landing accident when an Fw 200D-1 (then marked as VB+UA and serving with 2./KGrzbV 108) demolished its port wing and most of a wooden hanger at Gardermoen in Norway on 14 December 1940. The damage to the aircraft was put at 70 per cent. *J. V. Crow*

It was planned that the Condors would back up a force of several hundred Ju 52s by handling and airlifting heavy equipment and undertaking casualty evacuation among more routine troop transport flights. That part of Scandinavia lay at the limit of the range of numerous combat aircraft, a fact that hampered Allied air operations in support of friendly ground forces. Luftwaffe units based in Germany set several new distance records when they had initially to operate from their home airfields before Norwegian airfields were captured. Such sorties enabled individual Condor crews to quickly accumulate flying hours following their combat debut.

Radio communications played a highly significant part in early Condor operations, irrespective of whether the aircraft was directly supporting the U-boat campaign or carrying out independent transport and reconnaissance flights. The routine use of radio signals represented the Condor's main passive weapon, and an integral part of its effectiveness when it brought U-boats into action – and radio was also a vital aid to navigation. Transmitting single vessel and convoy locations to U-boats resulted in numerous indirect shipping 'kills' for the Luftwaffe crews, even though they had not launched anything more lethal than signals into the ether. It was this capability, once it was realised by the British Admiralty, that gave the Fw 200 a fearsome reputation among Allied seamen.

During the early war years the awareness of KG 40's modus operandi engendered the feeling among Allied sailors that if the aircraft did not sink you, its crew would soon find a U-boat that would. This was no comfort to men doing their bit to supply Great Britain with the vital materials she needed to continue the fight. Psychologically the big and quite intimidating Condors held all the cards above the grey, unforgiving waters of the Atlantic. This reaction might sound irrational now, but in 1940-41 it came into the realm of fear of the unknown, reflecting the fact that only very few people would have seen any four-engine aeroplane before.

Navigation was something of a bone of contention with several 'old hares' who swore by Naval doctrine rather than that taught by the Luftwaffe. It was quite common for individual members of Condor crews to wear the uniform of the Kriegsmarine and to hold Naval rank, such was the ostensibly separate status of German maritime aviation during the years immediately preceding the war. Goering, however, only reluctantly vested command of such units in Naval hands and gradually brought virtually all flying formations under Luftwaffe rather than Kriegsmarine control. There remained a considerable (and vitally important) Naval input to such units as KG 40, however, the nature of the unit's role making this a virtual necessity. Areas such as navigation, weather conditions, ship recognition, map-reading and a working knowledge of those coastal areas over which the unit was likely to operate took on a far greater importance than they would have in a standard bomber Geschwader.

When KG 40 began operations, long-range aircraft such as the Fw 200 would rarely be used for short-range sorties but were reserved for use by a Stab Staffel (staff reconnaissance flight) within the Kampfgeschwader. These aircraft would gather data – primarily weather-related – for specific use by the parent Kampfgeschwader. Wartime conditions later made it necessary for weather data to be logged on all operational flights and to be disseminated to all commands and units engaged in anti-shipping sorties.

Despite the maritime requirement, the work of converting existing civil Condors to military configuration could not therefore be given the urgency that would have been the case had the aircraft been required as a conventional bomber. But with a specialised role there was no question of it being cancelled or downgraded if such a need was to be fulfilled, although a lack of understanding of a maritime role in some circles did make this a distinct possibility.

It never hurts, as the saying goes, to have 'friends in high places', and fortunately, as previously noted, the Condor numbered Erhard Milch among its heavyweight champions, and it was he who managed to order the Fw 200 conversion programme to continue. This decision assured that the Luftwaffe at least had some long-range maritime capability.

Chapter 5

1940: Military operations

Having not been called upon to participate in the opening rounds of the war on the Western Front, the embryo KG 40 continued to concentrate on its mixed transport, reconnaissance and training programme. While the weather remained bad, with fog, rain and snow keeping aircraft grounded, Edgar Petersen built up a comprehensive set of operational requirements with which to fulfil the maritime reconnaissance role in conjunction with the U-boat arm as and when the time came. One of his main concerns was that, despite the Condor Staffel taking delivery of most new aircraft built by Focke-Wulf, serviceability and availability remained a challenge. Each aircraft engaged on a lengthy flight, be it of a second-line operational, training or transport nature, taxed the Condor's delicate airframe to the point where the aircraft were spending a disproportionate time on the ground, either being maintained or repaired. There were rarely more than a dozen aircraft available for operations at any given period. This would have been a problem in other first-line Geschwader, but as Petersen's unit was rarely called upon to send out more than two aircraft at a time, low availability was not usually critical. Condor serviceability remained a constant worry, however, as did the technical changes being made to improve succeeding models of the C series. Some of these were proving to be time-consuming.

Numerous Condors led seemingly charmed lives throughout the war. Fw 200C-4/U2 CE+IC was no exception, and lasted until the night of 26/27 April 1945, when it was shot down.

January

Anti-shipping attacks by the Luftwaffe were not intended to be the sole province of the Fw 200, as units equipped with the Heinkel He 111 and Ju 88 had been deployed against seaborne targets right from the beginning of the war. Every vessel arriving in a British port assisted the enemy's war effort, and the German air offensive was gradually extended to take advantage of the low level of retaliation that could be mustered against air attack. Accordingly between 7 and 13 January Britain's fishing fleet was singled out. This offensive was further broadened to include general shipping found off the east coast of the British Isles, the first attacks being carried out on 29-30 January. Few if any of these are believed to have involved Condors, but those surveillance sorties that were flown produced valuable sighting reports on shipping movements, were passed to Luftwaffe headquarters.

February

No action apart from routine reconnaissance sorties had materialised by the second month of 1940. Appalling weather still mitigated against maritime operations to a significant degree, obliging both sides to await an improvement in the conditions. Continent-wide blankets of snow, ice and fog kept flying to a minimum.

March

When the German High Command issued its plan for Operation 'Weserubung' ('Weser Exercise') on 1 March 1940, British forces moved across the Channel to help their European allies organise in the event of an attack on France and the Low Countries. In addition, the Germans planned to secure Norway by initially capturing the main airfields at Oslo and Stavanger.

KGrzbV 105, one of several transport units established before the invasion to train crews, was the only one operating four-engine aircraft. The substantial internal freight capacity of both the Fw 200 and Ju 90 was to prove useful in the weeks following the invasion of Norway, the heavy transport unit retaining its temporary title for the duration of the campaign.

April

Having signed one of several non-aggression treaties to remove impediments to his next military move, Hitler was all but ready to make exactly such a move by the first week of April. The assault began on 9 April with German troops landing at Narvik, Trondheim, Bergen and Stavanger. Concurrently Oslo and Kristiansund were bombed.

A fourth VfH Focke-Wulf Condor was made available for a PR/support role, this being a Fw 200B-1 (0003/BS+AH). Among the operations flown were several to the Trondheim area, mainly to ascertain if the prevailing weather was suitable to land groundcrews of KuFlGr 506. Conditions were indeed seen to be favourable, and in the afternoon of the first day these men were ferried in by five Condors and a single 1929-vintage Junkers G-38.

In the Luftwaffe order of battle for hostilities against Scandinavia, the Fw 200 was included as a transport type, initially based at Keil/Holtenau. Eight were under the command of a Major Dannenberg, who headed Kampfgruppe KGrzbV 105, the inventory of which also included eleven Ju 90s, Ju 53/3ms and the Junkers G 38. The unit, part of KGrzbV 172, moved to Hamburg-Fuhlsbuttel and was the only transport Gruppe to operate the Fw 200 in the Norwegian campaign. Most of the flying was of a reinforcement nature, but many sorties were hampered by the appalling weather.

The ground fighting abated after ten days but several ground units were encircled and in urgent need of air supply – particularly fresh troops. Accordingly KGrzbV 107 and 108 had long-range tanks fitted to their aircraft and were ordered to fly one thousand paratroops of Parachute Rifle Regiment 2 together with mountain infantry for a jump over Narvik. The troops were picked up in Holland, made their jump and managed to extricate the besieged German forces.

It might seem typical of the aggressive stance of the entire Luftwaffe that the above transport abbreviation stood for Kampfgeschwader zur besonderen Verwendung – literally 'Bomber Unit on Special Duties'. Whoever it was who came up with this designation wished (or so it seemed) to demonstrate that nothing so mundane as transport or training flights needed to be undertaken by Goering's mighty air force! In reality the Norwegian campaign was costly for the Luftwaffe: of 617 transport aircraft (mainly Ju 52s) deployed, a third were lost to various causes.

Warship watch

It was also vital for the Germans to ascertain the position and strength of British warships, and to ascertain the disposition of the Royal Navy's Home Fleet at its base at Scapa Flow, for the Germans shared the apprehension of their British opposite numbers as to the activities of capital ships.

Historically, the Royal Navy's might at sea was well known to the German High Command, and the Kriegsmarine was as anxious to know the whereabouts of the home fleet as the Admiralty was to pinpoint the very capable enemy ships, particularly the 'pocket battleships' and armoured cruisers.

One VfH Condor operated out of Konisberg for the initial flights over northern Norway before it was transferred to Stavanger. Flown by Cornelius 'Conny' Noell, the aircraft was an undeniably large target for enemy fighters and the first sortie into Stavanger proved to be highly dangerous as it arrived just as the RAF was strafing and bombing the airfield. Noell loitered over a fjord and landed only when the British aircraft had left the area. His surveillance of Scapa Flow verified that the enemy fleet was still in port, this and other flights initiating a period of attacks against the Scottish anchorage by the Luftwaffe medium bomber force, all of which were largely abortive. Hitler's edict not to damage civilian dwellings in the process of bombing enemy fleet anchorages was as short-lived as that imposed by the British, who initially placed similar restrictions on Bomber Command aircraft sent to attack the German fleet.

Having proven over Norway that the Fw 200's impressive range could be utilised in future PR sorties, the VfH appears to have concentrated on using other aircraft, little more data on the unit's Condors having come to light. As noted, the Condors that were fitted with cameras were modified at Rechlin but, as also mentioned elsewhere, not all aircraft were affected by the PR change.

Devoid of much of their passenger seating and with extra fuel tanks occupying the cabin space, the Condors proved more than adequate for supply flights into Norwegian airfields from Germany. Air transport was a service in which the Luftwaffe was to excel in every one of the early, significant land campaigns, and it was maintained for as long as vulnerable transport aircraft could survive against the opposition.

A typical early sortie to Norway was carried out by a single I./Gruppe Condor on 11 April. Flying over the Trondheim area, the crew reported little enemy naval activity but the following day promised some lively action when a single Condor crew observed four British destroyers off Narvik. Although the subsequent attack carried out by the German aircraft met with no success, it was recorded as the only Luftwaffe sorties in that area for the day.

Able Luftwaffe air support helped the rapid capture of strategic points in Norway including Oslo and Stavanger; on 12 April KGrzbV 105 used eighteen aircraft to ferry aviation supplies into Trondheim-Vaernes airfield.

British troops launched a counter-attack after landing at Narvik on 14 April, the Royal Navy providing what support it could under the threat of Luftwaffe air attack. Being caught by enemy bombers in the confines of the Norwegian fjords was not a prospect the Navy relished, there being a vital need not to waste valuable ships if the gains were not worthwhile. Nevertheless the Navy committed a sizeable force to the campaign.

A few days later, on 18 April, with British warships still much in evidence, Fliegerkorps X was ordered to attack vessels located in Vaagsfjord, Tromso and Harstad. Both the Condors of I./KG 40 and the He 111s of II./KG 26 were involved in the Luftwaffe response, three Fw 200Cs taking off at midday. Some two hours later a force of sixteen British ships – one carrier, three battleships, three cruisers, eight destroyers and a large freighter – was observed. Contemporary photographs suggest that the Condors deployed were considered to be reconnaissance machines (almost certainly Fw 200C-1s).

This overhead view shows several salient details of an Fw 200C including the basic but effective 'interrupter gear' behind the cockpit to prevent gunfire damage to the airframe, the cut-outs in the engine cooling gills for the exhaust pipes, and the foremost of two ventilators or air extractors for the main cabin located along the Condor's dorsal spine. *Thiele*

The battleship *Warspite* was the first enemy vessel to be attacked (probably by the Heinkels) before the bombers turned their attention to the carrier, HMS *Furious*. One Condor crew dropped its bombs and claimed a near miss that, although reportedly causing some damage to the ship's propellers, appeared not to have impeded her progress.

Considering the risk they ran, these assaults by bomber crews were daring indeed: British warships were in general less heavily armed at that stage of the war than they were subsequently, but a chance hit by the AA guns they did carry could cause considerable damage. Confusion over exactly which Condor sub-type was involved in the above action by I./Gruppe KG 40 would strongly suggest that offensive action was mostly restricted to 'surveillance and reporting'.

The campaign in Norway ground on during the spring weeks of 1940, with the Wehrmacht and Luftwaffe gradually gaining the upper hand. A single Fw 200C flown by Oblt Beckhaus of 1./Staffel KG 40 failed to return on 21 April, the aircraft having taken off for an evening reconnaissance of the Narvik area. Bad weather was the most likely cause of the loss, one of the first – if not the first – suffered by the Staffel during a maritime (as against transport) operation.

May

Both Stab. and 2./Staffel of I./KG 40 were established on 1 May 1940, while 1./Staffel continued to fly reconnaissance sorties over Scandinavia, as it did for the duration of the Norwegian campaign. By early May the struggle for Norway was entering its final phase as the British forces' brave but futile effort increasingly suffered from the lack of a cohesive plan of action – and enough troops and supplies. There had been so little time to launch a response to the German invasion that a decisive result on the ground in contrast to the Wehrmacht's sounder tactics – with excellent air support from the Luftwaffe – was highly optimistic at best. Over the two days 1-2 May British ground forces began to evacuate from Andalsnes and Namsos, although it would be several weeks before units allied to the small Norwegian resistance effort were forced to abandon the country completely.

Royal Navy activity was considerable, however, and on 5 May a single Fw 200 of 1./Staffel reported units of the British Home Fleet in Ototfjord. As was common practice, other Luftwaffe units were then sent to attack the ships.

Throughout the abortive attempt by British forces to hold on to some Norwegian territory, troop movements and disposition could hardly be kept secret from German surveillance flights. I./KG 40's aerial reporting service was appreciated by the Luftwaffe medium bomber crews, whose attacks could be planned against a known – or fairly well-estimated – target strength in terms of AA guns and even small arms fire. That said, the bombers met with only mixed success.

On 17 May, while German armour scythed through central Europe, a single Condor bombed the Norwegian steamer *Torgtind*, which sank in Aldrasundet, Helgeland. Radio messages confirmed the presence of other shipping targets to the north, and KG 26 and 30 were sent to deal with them. The Condors flew regularly to maintain a presence over Norway, sorties taking them to Narvik, Namsos and Trondheim.

Although the Norwegian campaign had demonstrated that KG 40's Condors could provide a valuable support service and the unit's combat debut had resulted in few crew or aircraft casualties to date, the fighting was marked by considerable enemy air opposition. Both the RAF and Fleet Air Arm offered what support they could to hard-pressed and ill-equipped ground forces. Relatively few Luftwaffe aircraft were destroyed as air combat was spread over considerable areas of land and sea. Types unlikely to survive determined fighter attack certainly included the Condor, crews of KG 40 realising that they might on occasion be caught in 'the wrong place at the wrong time'.

Sure enough, on 29 May the Fw 200C flown by Lt Otto Freytag was intercepted as it was bombing targets at Tromso. A Hurricane of No 46 Squadron flown by P/O N. L. Banks closed in and shot down the Condor, the crew of six – including the Kommandeur, Oblt Gunther Thiel – being killed. The Condor did not fall into the sea but came to rest on Dyroy Island and the bodies of all members of the crew were later recovered.

June

Almost inevitably the remaining British troops in Norway were increasingly isolated in a country that, by its very nature, mitigated against cohesive land operations. Supported ably by Norwegian patriots who knew the terrain and could melt away if the Germans became a threat, regular Army personnel remained exposed to enemy action. Determined to secure all of Norway, Hitler pressed for a decisive end to the short campaign and this duly came about as the end of May approached.

With Norway about to fall completely under German control, I./KG 40 flew its final sorties in that theatre of war – at least as far as those in direct support of the troops fighting ashore were concerned. On 3 June the British began to evacuate, using Narvik to embark troops. On 9 June Norway surrendered.

That same day Condors attacked the 13,241grt freighter *Vandyck*, located 30 miles north of Andoy Island, west of Narvik. The single Fw 200C responsible set the British-registered vessel on fire to the extent that it had to be abandoned by its crew; seven men were killed and 161 reached the shore to be captured. This action, one of the first recorded incidents of a merchant ship being attacked by a Condor during the Second World War, did not result in the vessel sinking, but it passed into German hands as a war prize.

With Norway out of the war as a combatant the Germans were able to bring the war with France to another triumphant conclusion, an armistice being signed on 22 June 1940. This incredible defeat of one of the largest armies in existence stunned the outside world, but on closer examination it was clear that none of the western European nations had been in any way prepared for the kind of modern warfare Germany had unleashed on her adversaries. Even if they had not been totally taken by surprise, the Belgian and Dutch forces had little to counter such rapid advances by tanks and troops. In the air they had all put up a gallant fight, but superior German tactics, combined with combat experience, had won the day.

Pending Britain's response to Hitler's peace overtures, the Luftwaffe moved up to occupy former Armée de l'Air bases in preparation for a cross-Channel assault. Together with the medium bomber Kampfgeschwader, KG 40 received orders to change its location. As part of the build-up in France for operations against the British Isles, I./Gruppe consequently moved forward to Brest-Guipavas airfield in Brittany.

There were no realistic plans to deploy a handful of Focke-Wulf Condors in daylight bombing raids on England in company with their twin-engine counterparts, but that probably did not stop some misgivings among the maritime aircrew. Yet, given that the mood was one of yet another easy victory for the Luftwaffe, the Condor crewmen could be forgiven for believing the widely held notion that Britain could not hold out for long and they would soon sally forth simply to add their bombs to the rubble of half a dozen blitzed British cities.

For the time being wiser councils prevailed; they decided that Brest was not after all an ideal location for the Condors as the facilities were inadequate for handling heavy, multi-engine aircraft and the airfield was also judged to be too close to England. In the event of a bombing raid by the RAF, the Condors would have been vulnerable. Another move was consequently made to Bordeaux-Merignac, the location most associated with KG 40's Condor operations.

New airfields

When the airfields along the Atlantic coast of France were taken over by the Germans they indicated a significant expansion of operations into the Bay of Biscay and the eastern Atlantic, both by aircraft and submarines. The availability of the one aircraft capable of exploiting locations such as Bordeaux-Merignac and Brest-Guipavas (considered now as a supplementary airfield to Bordeaux), together with those in Norway and Holland, to conduct long-range maritime reconnaissance sorties, would, it was believed, yield positive results in the Atlantic war.

Weather search

June 1940 also saw three Condors taking off from Luneberg for a seventeen-hour non-stop flight, some elements of the new I./Gruppe having previously transferred from Bremen-Neulanderfeld for this specific purpose. The Condor trio completed their mission and returned safely. Advance data in weather conditions was vital in the Far North, and Condors carried meteorologists as far west as East Greenland and north to Svalbard to compile information on cloud build-up, the likelihood of aerial icing, wind speed and direction. These sorties were alternatively flown from Gardermoen in Norway, an airfield situated far enough north to be subjected to conditions harsh enough to ground aircraft completely and/or force diversions. The fact that returning crews apparently had nowhere to land added an urgency to the adverse weather data and emphasised the need for blind-landing aids. A good case was thus made for the siting of the Lorenz blind-landing system on the more remote airfields in Scandinavia to make them safer and provide KG 40's aircraft with greater operational flexibility. Lorenz landing aids were installed without delay.

Fully shrouded to protect it from the elements, a Condor shares the apron of an airfield in the Far North with a Bf 109F possibly belonging to JG 5. Several such locations were used by the Condors to extend their reach, including Gardermoen in Norway. *BA*

Shorter-range landplanes, seaplanes and flying boats under the direction of the German Navy would continue to provide shorter-range support, and the Luftwaffe and Kriegsmarine lost no time in using their new bases to attack Allied shipping to supplement ultra-long-range sorties well up into the Arctic Circle. The airfields were strategically located right down the Atlantic coast of Europe from Bordeaux to Kirkenes in Norway. For Condor and U-boat crews alike these bases, particularly those in France, represented a significantly reduced patrol time compared with sailings from German ports and a greater coverage of an area of sea hitherto the almost exclusive province of Allied shipping and aircraft. The Battle of the Atlantic was about to enter a new phase.

July

With the Battle of Britain raging, RAF fighter squadrons were preoccupied almost entirely with defending the country against Luftwaffe bombing raids, and from July KG 40 was able to patrol the waters around Britain without undue risk of interception. These sorties were flown with the aim of sinking any ship useful to the enemy, irrespective of tonnage. From trawlers to tankers, all were fair game for attack, as supplies of all kinds were vital to Britain's ability to feed her population and prosecute the war. The first vessel to suffer the attentions of KG 40's Condors was the *Volante*, which was attacked on 12 July south-west of Iceland.

Irish patrol line

When commencing their patrols the Condors usually flew westwards from French bases and out across the Bay of Biscay before a turn northwards enabled them to skirt the west coast of Ireland. In order to reduce crew fatigue, aircraft would often land at Trondheim or Stavanger in Norway before returning to France after completing a second patrol. Crews generally adopted the established 'race track' patterns that overlapped at certain points and broadened the coverage if two or more aircraft were airborne at the same time.

The outward flight towards Ireland became a regular route for the Condor crews with some variation depending on operational requirements. As the British convoys increased in size and frequency, pro-German agents in Portugal and Gibraltar kept watch and passed their sighting reports to Germany; as a result KG 40's patrol area was extended and it became common for the big Focke-Wulfs to be seen off the coast of neutral Portugal, Spain and Gibraltar.

Portugal became something of a haven for crews of damaged aircraft, and several were to put down there during the course of the war. Surviving crewmen could also be reassured that they would eventually be returned to their unit even if their aircraft was impounded by the Portuguese authorities. Spain's policy was similar insofar as the crews were returned, but their aircraft were invariably impounded.

Inclement weather, which was frequently prevalent around Ireland, while representing some hazard to the German crews also shielded their presence from Allied aircraft. The nature of the relationship between the Irish and English governments also meant that only the six northern counties were in sympathy with the Allied cause to the point that RAF aircraft were stationed on several land bases with additional coastal flying boat facilities.

Southern Ireland (Eire) was to all intents and purposes neutral, with a small Irish Air Corps (IAC) defence force liable to intercept any aircraft of the combatants that transgressed her borders. If the aircraft in question was obliged to land – occasionally persuaded by bursts from several Irish Army AA batteries – the crew risked internment for the duration of hostilities.

For the Luftwaffe Condor crews, much the same situation prevailed in southern Ireland as in Portugal and Spain, although those who force-landed in Ireland often found they were among friends rather than enemies. In reality Condors flew across Eire almost with impunity in the first months of the war, the IAC being weak in terms of modern fighters able enough to catch them.

For the Germans, however, there were hazards enough without fighters that may or may not have fired on them; the structural weakness of the Condor manifested itself in the inexplicable loss of several KG 40 aircraft by early 1941. A lack of enough internal bulkheads was the suspected cause of a weak tail unit, which failed under extreme stress. This problem continued until a remedial programme of tail-strengthening was introduced on the Fw 200C-3. Even then, the problem was never entirely eradicated. Structural weakness inherent in a civil airliner impressed into military service was well known to the men who flew Condors and, despite such a flaw being well-publicised by enemy propaganda, the actual number of aircraft lost as a direct result of this problem appears to have been smaller than might be imagined. A further contributory factor in Condor losses was engine fire: normally very reliable, the BMW powerplants did on occasion fail with disastrous results. Another manifestation of the stresses imposed on 'civil-rated' powerplants, fire in vulnerable areas such as fuel and oil lines was invariably lethal to numerous aircraft, and the Condor was no exception.

This Condor has probably force-landed in a field in Spain. The pattern of wreckage, including the undamaged propellers, indicates that the aircraft was destroyed by the crew activating a self-destruct device. Note the uniforms worn by the men on the right. *MAP*

Taking delivery of all ten Fw 200C-1s in June 1940, I./KG 40 adopted the famous 'world in a ring' emblem, which was painted on both sides of the nose of most aircraft belonging to the Gruppe. The badge was 'handed', ie. the outline map of the world behind the 'Saturn ring' appeared with appropriate changes to indicate an aircraft traversing the globe in opposite directions.

In July 1940 I./KG 40 was subordinated to Marine Gruppe West for U-boat support duties, and during the month 1./ and 2./Staffeln transferred to Bordeaux-Merignac, while III./KG 40 moved its aircraft into Cognac.

Forecast

By the time the C-Amt had issued a further Condor production programme on 1 July 1940, sixteen examples of the Fw 200C-0 (sic) had been delivered to the Luftwaffe. This bulletin, in similar fashion to those issued previously to cover most of the aircraft being built in Germany, projected production from the date of issue and quoted a figure of fifty-four Condors that would have been delivered by October 1941. Not for the last time the C-Amt production office's estimation of Condor construction totals would prove erroneous, as would the cut-off date (as above). Apart from the aircraft actually delivered, the projected figures were notoriously unreliable insofar as they were changed almost on a daily basis, with certain types reinstated in production while the building of others was suspended and/or increased. Clearly, neither the Condor's usefulness as a combat aircraft nor the numbers required were fully appreciated – a situation it seems to have shared with other aircraft in the Luftwaffe's inventory designed for 'special' roles.

This was partly because the High Command remained optimistic that the fighting in western Europe and Scandinavia could be contained and result in a German 'short war' victory; events such as the successful completion of the campaign in Norway, then the Balkans, forced such figures to be continually revised. Moreover, the state of the industry made accurate accounting very difficult. The problem was that Germany's supply of raw materials was being stretched; with the country at war, aircraft attrition began to bite early and, while replacements of the most important types continued to be supplied to the front-line units, it became obvious that the industry was simply building too many aircraft in too many categories, several of which were obsolete. Drastic cutbacks were ordered to redress this anomaly, but in reality the picture changed little.

Maritime background

When Hermann Goering took over control of the Luftwaffe, officers of the Kriegsmarine assumed that a strong Naval element would have been concurrently established to undertake a number of specialised maritime sorties, particularly those of torpedo attack. Germany's first aircraft carrier, the *Graf Zeppelin*, had been laid down and there was every indication that a fleet air arm would soon operate under a German flag. Delays plagued the completion of the carrier and, despite constant assurances from Adolf Hitler that a force of Naval Ju 87s and Me 109s would soon be in a position to take on the carriers of the Royal Navy, nothing of the kind took place. Goering, exercising his influence over the Führer while placating the admirals with constant promises, managed to stall the carrier to the point where its development was halted and eventually abandoned. This left the Kriegsmarine to operate a coastal force mainly composed of floatplanes, which undertook several maritime-related duties with relatively minor success. Alternatively the Navy could borrow aircraft from the Luftwaffe, and was obliged to rely on twin-engine bombers to undertake every task from reconnaissance to bombing, and from torpedo attack to transport. But these aircraft simply did not have the trained crews or the range to traverse hundreds of miles of sea when the 'short war' envisaged in 1939 broadened out to encompass three war fronts. A fourth front was the ocean waters around the expanded territories of the Third Reich – which demanded coverage by four-engine aircraft. The Fw 200 was available to fill the breach – only just, but it proved to be enough.

July mining

In mid-1940 KG 40's airmen were well aware of the risks they ran if they ventured too close to the British Isles, particularly at that stage of the war with fighter defences on full alert. Guns were also part of the defences. Losses on mining sorties added up to a slow but inexorable war of attrition and, however necessary it was, Petersen feared that losing any of his Fw 200s to a cause other than direct attack on enemy shipping was a waste of resources. Replacements would also be more difficult to come by if he lost the cream of his original crews.

Mining continued, however, to reach something of a peak towards the end of 1940, but at least the enemy appeared not to have determined the full details of the type of mine(s) the Luftwaffe was generally using. In this the Germans were wrong, as would be revealed a few months later.

With Luftwaffe bomber operations against England taking top priority in Luftwaffe planning during the summer months, few noticed a tiny proportion of the Kampfgeschwader's effort diversifying into the role of mine-laying, principally twelve early sorties from Brest by KG 40. Laying up to four 2,200lb (1,000kg) magnetic mines per aircraft proved disproportionately costly and, horrified at losing any of his specialised force, Petersen managed to persuade Luftwaffe Chief of Staff Jeschonneck to return the Condors to reconnaissance work at the end of July. Among KG 40's losses from mine-laying sorties were two Fw 200C-1s flown respectively by Hptm Roman Steszyn (F8+EH) and Hptm Volkmar Zenker (F8+BH). Steszyn was drowned when his Condor was shot down into the sea off Hartlepool by British AA fire on the night of 19/20 July. Actually a member of KG 51, Steszyn's fate was shared by Feldwebel Meier and Zraunig. The two other members of the crew, Feldwebel Kulken and Nicolai, became PoWs. Steszyn was Staffel Kapitän of I./KG 40 at the time of his loss.

The aircraft captained by Hptm Volkmar Zenker was forced to ditch off Belfast on the 24th after the crew had trouble releasing the last of four magnetic mines. When Zenker took the aircraft down to jettison the mine he was as low as 15 metres; opening the throttles brought both port engines to a stop and the aircraft banked steeply. To avoid the wingtip ploughing into the water, Zenker feathered the starboard engines to counter the swing and prepared to ditch. It was a difficult decision, as the Condor still had fuel, but there was a blockage in the fuel lines caused, he suspected, by the long dive with the engines throttled back. With no altitude, even full revolutions may not have lifted the aircraft in time, and Zenker put the Condor into the sea at as level an attitude as he could manage.

Despite frantic efforts to inflate a dinghy after the ditching (the interior quickly filled with water), Bordfunker Uffz Heinz Hocker finally managed to do so after swimming away. Zenker was soon exhausted but he and Gefr Hohmann climbed into the dinghy, where the German airmen awaited their fate. This materialised in the form of an Irish patrol boat, which hauled them aboard and headed into Belfast harbour. Nothing was heard from two other members of the Condor's crew. Petersen had consequently lost two Staffel Kapitän (Zenker was in command of II./KG 40 at that time) in less than a week. Wastage of experienced pilots supported Petersen's case for leaving mine-laying to other units.

Weather conditions in the North Atlantic were rarely neutral as the autumn months heralded winter; both sides gained or lost in the heaving turbulence of the ocean surface, the endless grey overcast, the wind and, in due course, snowfall. Figures for shipping losses to air attack typically showed a slackening-off in activity during these months. Up to late September 1940 six small freighters and fishing boats were sunk, the largest being the 5,152grt Greek vessel *Kalliopi*. Believed damaged by Condor attack off Tory Island, the ship went aground in Sheephaven Bay.

As well as hostile enemy reaction to their aggressive actions, Condor crews plying the Atlantic airways had to cope with often highly unpredictable and dangerous weather conditions – their major adversary at certain times of the year. Combat damage and loss of navigational aids could set them on a devious course, en route for an eventual landfall in hostile or neutral territory. Good navigational skills were, however, an asset that many of the ex-Luft Hansa and Navy crews had brought with them to Kampfgeschwader 40, and becoming lost or disorientated on an operational sortie was not the hazard it might have been in other units; it did happen, but not often enough to be a problem. Those same ex- civilian aircrews were obliged to allow for the sudden loss of en-route radio beacons and markers that were routine prewar aids to assist navigation of civil airliners. This gap was not allowed to remain for long, however; once the Germans had secured suitable locations in France and Norway, a network of beacons was established and used by KG 40 and other units for the duration of the war.

Had the weather not intervened, the air and ground crews of KG 40 would have had a great deal more to contend with if a proposed British carrier raid on Bordeaux had taken place. Planned to be carried out by no less than Force H, the Royal Navy's principal strike element, between 23 and 27 July, the attack would have comprised the carrier *Ark Royal*, the cruiser *Enterprise* and four destroyers. Other ships would have provided additional gunfire support as necessary – but the attack was thwarted by mist and had to be called off. Force H headed back to Gibraltar and no further attacks on the French coastal base were planned as far as it is known. Certainly none was carried out.

August

Kampfgeschwader 40's first reconnaissance operation from Bordeaux-Merignac took place on 8 August and the unit was (almost literally!) instrumental – although it took no direct part – in the planning for 'Adler Tag' on 13 August. Goering's final grand strike against Britain's defences needed the right conditions and meteorological data filed by crews of KG 40 and Wettererkundsstaffeln 1 and 161 confirmed that a spell of good weather lay ahead as a result of a ridge of high pressure building up to the north-east from the Azores. Thus the scene was set for the Luftwaffe's 'knock-out blow' to the RAF.

Diversions

Although KG 40's Fw 200s were almost entirely utilised for maritime patrol and attack, another diversion came late in August when, with the Battle of Britain at its height, aircraft of I./Gruppe were ordered to bomb the city and port of Liverpool, thereby boosting the number of Luftwaffe aircraft on one of several large-scale bombing raids against industrial targets in the British Isles. As well as KG 40, several specialist units, including Epr 210, LG 1, KGr 100 and KGr 126, were included in the order of battle, and each operation was planned with great attention to detail.

To carry out a conventional bombing raid on an important British port such as Liverpool, an operation that could be sanctioned at that time only by Goering himself, Condor crews relied on tried and tested dead reckoning, or Koppelnavigation, backed by radio and visual fixes. The rest of the force was guided to the target(s) by pathfinder units, the line crews in the bomber Gruppen getting used to utilising radio signals to check their coordinates. Despite the detailed planning, KG

40 could contribute little to the impact of strategic bombing. The unit had, for example, seven serviceable aircraft on 18 August, the day the Luftwaffe lost one hundred. No Condors were among the casualties that day, and in several August raids little was achieved by the bomber force as a whole. Not that KG 40 was able to contribute much in terms of bomb tonnage against land targets, crews also being well aware that their poorly protected machines were very vulnerable to AA fire, although the British defences do not appear to have caused many casualties among the participating crews. It was a considerable morale booster for the civilian population to hear the AA guns pounding away, sending thousands of shells into the sky and, in close company with searchlights, obtaining an occasional success by hitting and bringing down enemy aircraft.

Attacks on Merseyside began in August 1940 and were to continue until the summer of 1941 as part of the nocturnal blitz of strategic targets throughout the British Isles; most sorties were undertaken by the standard Luftwaffe twin-engined types, although a single KG 40 aircraft did become a casualty when returning from one of the early raids on Liverpool. On 29 August 1940 an Fw 200C-2 of I./Gruppe force-landed at Bordeaux, short of fuel.

During this period KG 40's Condors also carried out sorties against the Scottish city of Glasgow. This token contribution to the night assault on the British Isles was limited in scope and relatively short-lived – as indeed was the participation of some of the front-line bomber units, which, by the middle of 1941, were about to exchange their forward French bases for airfields in Eastern Europe to support the assault on the Soviet Union.

Two Condors were reported by an RAF pilot over the Portsmouth area on 1 October, but no combat took place. KG 40 was hardly in a position to contribute significantly to raids that were often wide-ranging and too modestly sized to achieve a concentrated bomb pattern. Condors would, however, continue their forays over the British Isles.

Even though KG 40 was nearly always under strength, Admiral Doenitz appreciated the value of long-range air support in helping his U-boats to detect shipping targets, via D/F radio link messages to headquarters and onward transmission to boats at sea. The main problem with this system was the inevitable time delay between the first sighting by the aircrew, transmission (in code) to headquarters, decoding and onward transmission to U-boats in position to carry out an effective attack.

Electronic aids were of little use to KG 40, and the unit continued to use its own system to find ships. Attacks by individual aircraft became standard operational procedure although, after the convoy system was introduced by the British in 1939, almost immediately hostilities began, there was more emphasis on aircrews reporting their location to U-boat radio operators via D/F signal.

This system brought about potentially more numerous targets, particularly when Doenitz could deploy his U-boats as multi-group 'wolf packs'. Sighting reports from aircraft were sent to Bordeaux using coded tables, Bordeaux then passing the information to Befehlshaber der U-Boote (BdU) Headquarters then instructed aircraft to send a D/F signal to the U-boat in the best position to attack the convoy. Signals on 400 to 450k/cs consisted on long dashes of up to thirty seconds duration with a two-second pause between dashes. Transmissions were to be completed in a period of eight minutes, with twenty minutes set as the maximum. There was no other direct communication with U-boats, and transmissions received from aircraft were not acknowledged for security reasons. Although this system had its drawbacks, mainly in the time it required, both Petersen and Harlinghausen appreciated the realities of the situation. They welcomed the Condor in its new supporting role, as any time lost in cooperating with U-boats did not mean that Allied ships were any safer; should they be caught by KG 40's aircraft the vulnerable freighters faced a tough fight to prevent them from being sunk.

Traditional navigation

Position fixing was aided in the case of KG 40 as the Fw 200's equipment invariably included a sextant. Thus able to plot the position of stars and other heavenly bodies by marking position lines on charts with the help of special tables, the maritime crews were working with a early form of astro-navigation. They had the advantage of navigators well trained in this discipline and were

To reach distant targets, many of KG 40's Condors were fitted with extra fuel cells installed in the cabin. Accurate navigation was a standard requirement, and here a crewman checks his maps, oblivious of the enormous risk to the aircraft if enemy fire penetrated the fuselage and the flimsy fuel cells.

virtually unique in the Luftwaffe, which generally did not favour this method of navigation. For their part, ex-Naval crews did not think much of the Luftwaffe-issue charts, which they believed generally attempted to cover too wide an area. Their own charts, neatly divided off in squares on a basic grid, proved far more readable and accurate for their purposes.

During this early phase of the Battle of the Atlantic, Condor crews carried out numerous independent attacks on shipping, which were often more direct and effective than calling in submarines. This was another phase of KG 40's operations that crews found to be preferable to utilising the main Luftwaffe bomber force, as Goering had envisaged. Despite the obvious risk of attacking heavily armed merchantmen (of which there were few at that time), the Condor crews were generally assured of some success, in contrast to the results obtained by the Kampfflieger. The Navy had long advised that when merchant ships were located they should be attacked first rather than have the bombers go after any escorts, thus alerting the freighters.

The result was that the neat groupings of merchant ships would break ranks, necessitating individual attacks by the bombers, which usually obtained limited results. Such tactics also brought into play the firepower of any escort ships accompanying the freighters – another development that had a detrimental effect on the Luftwaffe's efforts. There is, however, little evidence that anyone in the High Command with enough rank to persuade Goering to change doctrine appeared to listen to this sound advice, despite continual efforts by Naval staff.

As well as the new French bases, KG 40 additionally utilised the captured Norwegian airfields at Stavanger-Sola and Trondheim-Vaernes. By so doing Condor crews could sweep much of the Bay of Biscay and North Atlantic out to 20 degrees West between Gibraltar and Finisterre, and north up to the Arctic Circle, flying their 'race track' and 'circular' pattern sea searches. These often involved I./KG 40's aircraft in flights lasting up to fourteen hours.

The subsequent establishment of Fliegerführer Nord, with its headquarters at Stavanger under Luftflotte 5, further stressed the important war role that KG 40 was undertaking. The bases used by KG 40 became a network, an integral part of the unit's operations for more than two years.

Although the actual date when the Battle of the Atlantic began can rightly be said to have been 3 September 1939, the conflict was quite one-sided as U-boat attacks on Allied shipping climbed steadily in number. By the following summer RAF and Royal Navy retaliation and counter-measures were of necessity of an ad hoc nature while Britain remained under threat of invasion and her skies were dominated by the Luftwaffe.

This plan was in terms of W/T traffic between air reconnaissance and specific U-boats, a tightening up of procedure already being followed. Otherwise it did admit the possibility that U-boat ciphers might eventually be read by British intelligence, just as the B-Dienst service personnel were reading the BAMS code.

Attack plan

As the early Condors lacked a modern bombsight, Petersen's Staffel worked out tactics that compensated and utilised the Condor appropriately. He and his crews found that a shallow dive followed by a very low, 100-150-foot (30-46-metre) run parallel to the target ship's centre line would almost guarantee a hit with one or more bombs. The resulting explosions would often sink or disable the unarmed merchant vessels that KG 40 was sent against in the first months of the war. Even if the bombs missed, strafing with machine-guns invariably started fires that could prove disastrous to the target. Volatile cargoes such as wood, foodstuffs and fuel oil would ignite readily if the attacking aircraft could get off a few well-aimed cannon and machine-gun rounds during the run-in. The only drawback to this tactic for the German aircrews was their exposure to any form of anti-aircraft defence the ships carried.

To raise the bombs high enough to fit the Condor's nacelle racks the lifting gear sometimes required a little help from a pile of wooden blocks. Such expediency seems to have met with the approval of the watching Luftwaffe officers.

Although it was of 'low-profile' design, the HD 131 forward dorsal (A Stand) gun position first fitted to the early-model Fw 200Cs could only withstand the recoil of a machine-gun, when a cannon was really needed.

There were two versions of the tall HDL 151 hydraulic dorsal turret, which, installed in the A Stand position, became an unmistakeable feature of the mid-to-late-war Condors. Bracing was necessary to house an MG 151/20 cannon without any detrimental effects from recoil. *A. Price*

Fitting a cannon into an HDL dorsal turret doubled the Condor's heavy-calibre firepower to give much greater destructive capability. In addition, up to four machine-guns enabled all quarters to be covered. *Author's collection*

Experienced seamen gunners could provide a hot reception for a comparatively large aircraft if conditions were clear. And the Condor, with its 107-foot (32.6-metre) wingspan represented a substantial aiming point, particularly at its generally low-level target run-in at modest airspeeds. Armour plating 10mm thick was, as many crews had commented, quite modest and unprotected crew stations, especially in the rear fuselage, led to fatalities or injuries if the fire from surface vessels struck the Condor in those areas – indeed, there were occasions when the only serious casualties were sustained by crewmen wielding the demountable machine-guns otherwise stowed in the rear fuselage. These guns were, however, provided with a more than adequate supply of ammunition, several of the characteristic 'saddle' magazines being clipped to the fuselage walls.

Turret guns added substantially to the weight of fire a Condor was able to bring to bear on its target, the German propensity for mounting a single cannon ensuring that the aircraft did not become nose heavy. Ammunition supply to the MG FF cannon was limited so the onus was on the gunner to shoot accurately, and even when heavier armament raised the all-up weight of the aircraft, the cannon turret was retained on most examples from the Fw 200C-3 onwards. Incidentally, the C-3 was able to lift a maximum war load of 11,900lb (5,400kg), this figure including the internal load in the ventral gondola and addition fuel cells in the fuselage cabin space.

The forward section of the Fw 200's gondola accommodated a 20mm MG FF cannon with minimum alteration to the framing of the early D Stand position, even when a Lofte 7D bombsight was squeezed in behind it.

Later production Condors exhibited a significantly revised gondola front area with the machine-gun or cannon positioned higher in a circular sighting 'bubble'. The gondola was also extended forward and a section of metal tubing provided a conduit for the empty shell casings.

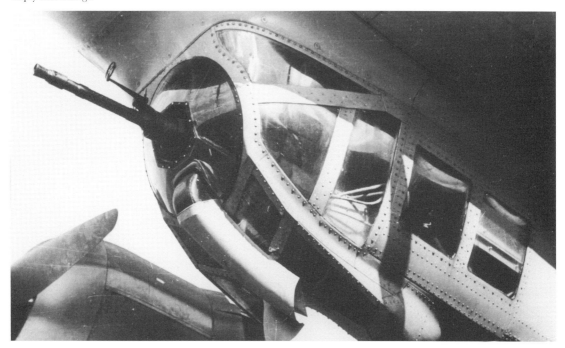

In general terms the Focke-Wulf Condor had been turned into an effective warplane, well armed for the role it was to undertake. Details of the weaponry carried by the various sub-variants can to found in Chapter 3.

Allied counter-measures

To deter the Condors, some of the ships vital to Britain's survival were progressively armed with guns of various calibres, although these were generally in short supply. Arming merchant vessels had not, understandably enough, been a high prewar priority. To give the hard-pressed sailors something to fight back with, a variety of ad hoc weapons were developed – if that is not too grand a description. These included simple ejectors designed to fire coils of wire to entangle parts of aircraft, particularly airscrews, in streamers that fanned out after they were discharged. Alternatively, there was a rocket-propelled, mortar-like weapon that consisted of a rudimentary 'stove pipe' fitted with a spring that could propel flares skywards at high speed. There was no method of aiming and the detonation of the rocket had little more advantage than an element of surprise.

Less lethal than a fighter, Allied ships nevertheless tried out a number of ad hoc explosive devices designed to cripple or bring down a Condor. Parachute mines on long cables were tried, designed to wrap themselves around flying surfaces in the hope that they would jam something vital – but if the cable trailed too far behind, the aircraft could land without much danger. *F. Selinger*

On the other hand, if the flare hit something considerable damage could be inflicted on an aircraft, particularly at close range. At the very least it was hoped that the weapon would persuade the German aircrews to seek less aggressive targets, and the psychological feeling that at least there was something with which to deter the raiders should not be underestimated. However, the difficulties in timing the discharge to the point that the aircraft passed close enough can be appreciated; the sailors had mere seconds to make that calculation. On 14 August 1940 Oberlt Vuellers of 3./Staffel came up against this weapon when he attacked a freighter. Running in at typical low altitude, the Condor is known to have been met by a barrage of the wire-streaming rockets, although whether the ship or the Focke-Wulf came off worst is unknown.

FOCKE-WULF FW 200 CONDOR

New directive

On 17 August a slight reduction in the hitherto steady rise in sinkings by submarines prompted Hitler to issue a directive to implement the 'Doenitz Plan'. This had three separate elements:

1   Individual U-boats were to receive direct information of intelligence material derived from air reconnaissance and B-Dienst sources including reading BAMS – British and Allied Merchant Ship – code information.

2   One or more U-boats were to shadow convoys on the surface in daylight.

3   Only on receipt of instructions from German Naval HQ were combined night attacks (either submerged or on the surface) to be carried out by U-boat wolf packs in the vicinity of convoys.

This and other official directives worked through to increase losses of Allied merchant shipping, which had risen steadily since 1939. KG 40's Condors had made a significant contribution to the figures, which caused alarm in the Admiralty and the office of the Prime Minister, Winston Churchill. He considered winning the Battle of the Atlantic to be as vital as any pivotal land campaign.

Internment

Inevitably damaged German aircraft did have to land in the wrong place as a matter of expediency and the first internment casualty suffered by KG 40 occurred on 20 August 1940 when an Fw 200C, Werk Nr 0015, F8+KH, was obliged to make a crash landing in Country Kerry, Ireland. The aircraft, which had taken off from Abbeville in France, was flying a meteorological sortie but was, as per standard operating procedure, armed in case any targets of opportunity presented themselves. Der Nebel, as the Met men were nicknamed by the Luftwaffe crews, took readings for some three hours before the captain, Oberlt Kurt Mollenhauer, climbed to 5,000 feet (1,525 metres) and set course for France. Overcast cloud that broke up at that point showed that the aircraft was actually over the Irish county of Kerry rather than the sea.

It proved impossible for the radio operator to obtain an accurate bearing, so the Condor turned back out to sea. Suddenly the aircraft shook alarmingly and the crew realised that they were experiencing turbulence as a result of proximity to the ground – which meant that they were far too low. It was fortunate for its occupants that the Condor was flying almost straight and level with a slight nose-up attitude, parallel to the rising ground of Faha Ridge. It was then only seconds away from making contact with Mount Brandon, which rises to more than 3,000 feet (953 metres) in that part of the county. The Condor struck a large rock and began to break up, spilling its crew from the shattered fuselage. Only two men suffered minor injuries, one had an injured back and Mollenhauer nursed a broken ankle. They were doubly lucky that the remains of their aircraft did not slide off the ridge where it came to rest on the edge of a sheer drop to a lake. Local people were soon on the scene and the German airmen were revived with brandy and chocolate. They were helped down to the village of Faha, the Republican population of which were quite pro-German and generally hostile to their own government.

Ultimately the Condor crew ended up in No 2 Internment Camp at the Curragh in County Kildare, where Kurt Mollenhauer reportedly gave his captors a hard time. In any event he was able to return to Ireland in 1988 for a reunion with some of the villagers who had helped him and his crewmen all those years ago.

September

At the height of the Battle of Britain a set of circumstances enabled RAF Fighter Command to regroup when the Luftwaffe bomber force suddenly abandoned its daylight assault on vital airfields and switched its effort to London. In the meantime KG 40 continued its anti-shipping sorties but at a time when, to the British, seaborne losses seemed somewhat insignificant while a greater threat loomed.

October

Through the early autumn weeks the RAF gradually redressed the situation after the Luftwaffe's switch in targets, and 'Adler Tag' did not bring the results anticipated by Berlin. Instead the months of September and October recorded not the final demise of the defending fighter force but heavy losses by the Kampfgeschwader. Once the Battle of Britain turned into a campaign of strategic bombing at night, the RAF's fighter force was able to reinforce but deploy only sporadically, preferably in clear moonlight conditions; the German bomber crews suffered far fewer losses and found that their aircraft were almost immune from interception. It was a situation with many ironies, with the civilian populations of London, Liverpool, Coventry and other cities being the losers.

New command structure

A period of long-overdue rationalisation of Luftwaffe maritime strength began on 16 October 1940 when Lt Gen Coeler's 9th Flieger Division, which had since the spring directed mining operations against UK ports, became IX Fliegerkorps, with a new base in Holland. Meanwhile X Fliegerkorps was posted away to Sicily to be replaced in Europe by two new subordinate commands, created somewhat belatedly under Luftflotte 5, to take over all anti-shipping operations. Consequently Fliegerführer Nord (which was later split to form Nord and Nord-Ost sub-commands) and Fliegerführer Lofoten were made responsible for reconnaissance and bombing operations north of latitude 58 degrees North. The North Sea area from Latitude 52 degrees West to 58 degrees North remained the responsibility of Führer der Seeluftstreitkräfte, with flying boats and seaplanes based mainly on the west coast of Jutland.

With mine-laying operations in British waters now the responsibility of IX Fliegerkorps (much to the relief of Edgar Petersen!), it was clear that further rationalisation was necessary to bring long-range reconnaissance under a more logical command structure in closer cooperation with the headquarters of the U-boat arm. Planning for an integrated command was put in hand without delay.

Semi-permanently based in France, KG 40 was by the late summer of 1940 in a position to intensify its commerce raiding campaign against Allied convoys and reconnaissance sorties to log shipping movements in support of the U-boat arm. The latter duty was now a major part of KG 40's operations.

There was a plethora of surface targets, as the crews of the big bombers noted on their patrols around the British Isles. Few ships were immune from attack by the Condors although those flying the flags of neutral countries enjoyed some protection. This was not guaranteed, however; diplomatic pressure on Germany and adverse press reports that followed incidents when such vessels were bombed, either deliberately or in error, tended to keep neutral losses to a minimum. In the adverse weather conditions they often encountered, the Condor crews made errors in ship recognition. Considering the diversity of vessels that plied the waters around Britain's coast, such errors were all but inevitable and a number of genuine mistakes were made. Whatever the reason, legitimate denial of enemy supplies or not, the Focke-Wulf Condor was soon labelled as a pariah of the high seas, with a bad reputation that grew worse with every ship KG 40's aircraft damaged or sent to the bottom.

Fighter!

Lacking enough of her own long-range maritime aircraft and naval escort vessels, Britain had limited options when it came to combating U-boats, German Naval vessels or the Condors. An Admiralty conference convened on 12 November 1940 discussed the urgent need for some form of fighter defence for the convoys, and as a stop-gap measure their Lordships conceived the Fighter Catapult Ship programme. Based initially around five merchant vessels and the former seaplane tender *Pegasus*, which would act as a trials ship, the concept was simple and could be initiated without delay. Rigging a catapult on the bow of a freighter and mounting a fighter that could be launched at short notice to scare off and/or destroy a German commerce raider was an expedient measure that was implemented when the first CAM – Catapult Aircraft Merchantman – ship put to sea.

Attrition continues

Condors continued to be sent against the occasional land target and on 15 October two of KG 40's aircraft attempted to make a precision raid on the Rolls-Royce works at Hillingdon in Middlesex. However, the crews of both aircraft apparently failed to locate the target. On 20 October Irish waters claimed the lives of the entire crew of an Fw 200 (F8+OK), which went into the sea off Galway. The circumstances are unknown, although another weather- related loss certainly cannot be ruled out.

In a further demonstration of their superior range, the Condors also attacked the city of Glasgow, but their limited bomb capacity caused little damage. It was not seriously suggested that KG 40's maritime force be switched to such unproductive sorties on any great scale, even under the cover of darkness, but the ability of the Condor to penetrate far inland was a tempting experiment that OKL wished to prove.

October 1940 had not brought very positive war results for KG 40, and on the 22nd the unit had to record the loss of Oblt Erich Adam and his 2./Staffel crew when their Fw 200C-2 (0024/F8+DK) went missing off the west coast of Ireland. This loss may in fact have been confused with that of Oblt Theodor Schuldt and crew, who were also listed as missing off the Irish coast on that day.

Bigger fish

On 26 October Bernard Jope of 2./Staffel found himself in position to attack what was KG 40's largest shipping target to date, the 42,348grt liner *Empress of Britain*, sailing off the coast of Ireland. Bombs and gunfire succeeded in setting the vessel on fire and she was abandoned by all but a skeleton crew, only to be finished off later by U-32 (ObltzS Hans Jenisch) at a point north-west of Bloody Foreland. Jope himself was surprised at the singular lack of defensive armament carried by such a large ship, a fact he commented on in radio and press interviews shortly after his successful sortie – a stark illustration of how poor Britain's Merchant Navy then was in this respect. Ships sailing unescorted were clearly at great risk but they continued to do so, despite the fact that the convoy system had been in force for nearly a year.

Bernard Jope (centre), the pilot responsible for crippling the liner *Empress of Britain* in October 1940, is seen with two fellow officers of KG 40 including Lt Thayer (left). As the largest ship attacked by Condors up that date, the *Empress* incident received much publicity and was long remembered, as was Jope's part in its eventual sinking by a U-boat. *F. Selinger*

November

Despite this grouping of ships offering some mutual protection against air attack, sailing in convoy was in itself no protection to individual vessels if they were singled out. And although the system clearly made the risk to the attacking aircraft marginally greater than before, due to the assumed presence of escorts ships, each vessel had enough space between it and the next in line for an alert aircrew to dash in and pick one off before escaping from the area unscathed. It took mere minutes for a seasoned Condor crew to carry out their bombing and strafing run(s).

How much protection ships in convoy could expect was limited to their own armament and that of a handful of Royal Navy escort vessels, there being scarcely enough of the latter to cover adequately the columns of slow freighters until new construction could make good the early war losses. Several freighters were lucky enough to pack their own protection in the form of Vickers or Lewis machine-guns and/or a four-pounder howitzer plus flares. But defensive weapons, even small arms, were far from available in the numbers required by the huge numbers of ships that constituted the British Merchant Navy.

In addition to (or in place of) guns, a few ingenious devices that were 'guaranteed' to bring down the marauding German bombers – or at the very least dissuade them from pressing home their attack – were installed in individual ships, but the military value of these rarely rose above the level of morale-booster for the ship's company. There was of course nothing wrong with boosting morale and the level of confidence in a sorely-pressed crew labouring under the natural rigours of a wartime sea voyage with the not insignificant threat of attack by a Condor. Even with something very modest with which to hit back, the seamen did not feel quite so naked when a four-engined aircraft loomed out of the mist or came their way at a great height to be identified as the German commerce raider. The Luftwaffe's propaganda, plus British press reports, turned the Focke-Wulf 200 into a spectre to haunt even the most hard-bitten sea captain. To the horror of Winston Churchill and their Lordships at the Admiralty, not to mention the seamen who had to face them, KG 40's aircraft were anything but ghosts, as the winter of 1940/41 was to prove.

Scores of merchant ship crews, made up by individual seamen from all over the globe, were about to face a terrifying four months of carnage as the Germans brought their Condors, U-boats, surface raiders, capital ships and E-boats into almost continual action with the aim of bringing Britain to her knees.

Added to the hazards faced by British and Allied merchant ships were the magnetic and acoustic mines, a surprisingly high number of which were laid around the British Isles, some of them by the Condors of KG 40. By the time the *Empress of Britain* was sunk by air attack and the torpedoes of U-38 in October 1940, the Battle of the Atlantic had claimed 471 vessels to U-boat attack alone. This represented a loss of a highly significant five million tons of vital goods. Britain was estimated to need forty-three million tons to maintain her people and continue to resist Germany – and the ship losses to submarines did not take into account those vessels sunk by air attack and mines.

Luftwaffe successes against shipping continued to rise steadily, proof that Petersen's faith in the Fw 200 had been justified. However, his crews were sometimes alarmed at the weakness of the early-model Condors. As airliners saddled with military loads they knew that their machines required careful handling, but operational emergencies could easily override such dictates; a Condor returning from a sortie with combat damage and obliged to make a heavy landing, probably low on fuel, could induce an ominous rending on touch down, a sound that heralded the impending failure of the wing spar. If that occurred and the weakened spar indeed cracked, it would invariably break the aircraft's back, resulting in a virtual write-off, good only for spare parts.

Photographs indicate that Condors tended to break in two distinct areas: spar failures would drop the wing down at the trailing edge, jacking the nose up, while a weakened fuselage would result in the fuselage snapping in two aft of the wing. Both resulted in a sometimes welcome influx of spares and items from salvaged components such as engines and propellers, as in many instances neither suffered any damage.

An Fw 200 C-4 (0141/F8+FW) has broken its back after a heavy landing at Bordeaux on 27 July 1943; its aft fuselage band indicates former duty as a transport in Russia or the Mediterranean. *J. V. Crow*

Loss of the *Apapa*

By November 1940 the sea war had rapidly spread further east as U-boats sought out enemy ships far beyond the range of KG 40's aircraft, although that did not reduce the tonnage sent to the bottom by the Condors. The toll for November included the liners *Windsor Castle* and *Empress of Japan*, both of which were then serving as troopships. The Condors inflicted damage on both ships, although neither of them were sunk as a direct result of the attacks.

It was relatively unusual for more than one Condor to attack a ship, primarily because KG 40's utilisation of available aircraft had to be spread evenly across the Geschwader. A disproportionately high number of sorties imposed undue strain on individual airframes and a close check on operating hours was maintained to ensure that in general this did not reach a critical stage. As with all first-line Luftwaffe units, KG 40's aircrews had a small army of specialists to back them up. These ground staff personnel handled everything from the vital servicing and refuelling of the aircraft to ensuring that signals, transport and stores always met established standards of efficiency.

When a Condor attacked the *Apapa* (9,333grt) on 15 November, the vessel was 200 miles west of Achill Head in County Mayo, proceeding at eight knots. Thick low cloud was penetrated by the Condor, which dropped to 150 feet (46 metres) and released two delayed-action bombs. One of them wrecked the vessel's engines and fire broke out in adjacent areas. Thick black smoke poured out of the ship, which also had a large hole torn in her port side. The order to abandon was given as the *Apapa* took on a heavy list to port, with the fire spreading. Most of the complement of 261 persons was rescued, although eighteen members of the crew and six passengers perished; the *Apapa* gained the unfortunate distinction of becoming the first vessel to go down as a result of air attack by a Condor while sailing under the optimistic protection of a convoy. This was a clear demonstration of how easy a single Condor attack could prove disastrous to an individual freighter; the ease with which the big Focke-Wulf could disable and sink a merchant ship probably surprised the Germans as much as the British. The *Apapa* had been part of the twenty-three-ship convoy SL.53 out of Freetown, and the combat report of German aircrew credited with sinking her must have made interesting reading. She would not be the last vessel to be plucked from a convoy.

Despite the British authorities having with all speed instigated a convoy system for merchant ships, this did not guarantee invulnerability. It had nevertheless been proven that merchant ships in convoy under a naval escort had a better chance at survival simply because the U-boat or aircraft was presented with multiple targets. A single ship on the open sea had far less chance of out-running or indeed out-gunning such well-armed adversaries. Any protection, however passive, was welcome by the British Merchant Navy as the German submarine offensive stretched British resources to the limit. It was the period when the top U-boat 'aces' built their scores, some at an incredible rate, with multiple sinkings in a single day or night during the first 'happy time'.

Bombs on Merignac

In direct response to Condor attacks on shipping, the RAF's most effective counter at that time was to bomb KG 40's airfields. On the night of 22/23 November 1940 Bomber Command despatched a sizeable force of around one hundred aircraft; most headed for various targets in the Ruhr, while a percentage of the crews were briefed to attack Bordeaux/Merignac. This they did, and two Condors (0009/ex-D-AEQP, the former *Kurmark*), and a C-3 (0027) were destroyed on the ground. The former aircraft, then serving in a transport role, was quite harmless to Allied shipping but the distinction was hardly of major interest to the RAF crews, who almost certainly failed to note the subtle difference in configuration!

Mine confirmation

Any questions posed by the type of mines the Luftwaffe was using were answered on the night of 23/24 November 1940 when British observers saw an object drop from an aircraft (type unknown) into the mud flats near Shoeburyness. This incident occurred three nights after several German aircraft were chased away from the Thames Estuary after having dropped mines attached to parachutes. This had become a regular practice during night bombing raids, and there is ample evidence that the Luftwaffe did not or could not always release the mines over water. Also on 22 November, something exploded in the vicinity of the *Rerukuni Maru*, one of Japan's finest liners. On the following day the RN destroyer HMS *Gypsy* succumbed to a mine detonation in much the same location. The British authorities were now almost totally convinced that the Germans were sowing magnetic mines, but before introducing effective counter-measures they had to know the exact type and characteristics of the weapon. The object lying in the mud at Shoeburyness provided the answers.

Any German advantage in the technology of mine warfare was soon eroded; by beginning the campaign early, mines laid by submarines had tended to be largely ineffectual. With the magnetic type the stakes were raised, and in August 1940 the Luftwaffe began to deploy acoustic mines. Both types were familiar to Royal Navy experts as Britain had actually invented both for her own use.

Sweeping mines was a highly skilled and dangerous business and at the start of the war there were not enough ships that could be spared for conversion to specialised mine-hunters. Aircraft losses tended to reduce the number of Luftwaffe mine-laying sorties and, although they did not stop, KG 40 flew few of them after the end of 1940.

Highly relieved to be released from the burden of an exacting and dangerous aspect of aerial warfare, Petersen realised that, although losses of Condors directly or indirectly attributable to mine-laying operations had been small, personnel and aircraft losses on maritime operations in general had worked through to the point that by late 1940/1941 the aircrew selection process for KG 40 had to change. It was hampered by the fact that, in replacing a number of the highly respected 'old heads' who had been lost on operations, a significant proportion of the officers Petersen interviewed were certainly mature and 'steady' individuals but were really too old for the kind of flying his unit was undertaking on virtually a daily basis. As time went on, the age limit had to be extended pending younger men completing their flying training, and although this was a far from ideal situation, a seat on the flight deck of a Focke-Wulf Condor imposed less of a physical strain on older men than other branches of the service might have done.

Staffel personnel came from training units (many from the Grosskampffliegerschule, located at Soesterberg, Holland) during 1940, or as transferees from regular bomber Geschwader as well as the school at Celle.

December

In targeting Bordeaux the RAF ostensibly had a dual purpose in that an Italian submarine base known as Betasom was located at Bacalan to the north of the city and had become active after the fall of France. Several squadrons of Wellington Mks III and V, Whitley IIIs and Vs and Hampdens were available to 3, 4 and 5 Group squadrons based on airfields in East Anglia, Yorkshire and Lincolnshire. The Gironde area of northern France was within range of these bases and on the night of 8/9 December 1940 a force of forty-four aircraft was despatched to Bordeaux. Among the units participating were Nos 49, 115 and 149 Squadrons. Little damage was done to the submarines or their base, but the city and some shipping in the port were badly bombed.

When British Intelligence became aware that KG 40 had moved into Bordeaux, the reaction in military terms was remarkably low-key. Winston Churchill's fears about the effectiveness of the U-boat campaign (and the threat posed by the Condors) were well known, at least at cabinet level, yet the singular static target at Bordeaux and its nest of Focke-Wulfs was never subjected to a precision bombing attack to rival many of the spectacular Lancaster and Mosquito strikes. Even if these latter had come a little later in the war than the heyday of KG 40's marauders, there was no reason why a raid in late 1942 and/or early 1943 could not have devastated the home of KG 40, destroyed or badly damaged the relatively few aircraft the unit had ready for operations, wrecked hangars and workshops, and generally made life difficult for one of the most dangerous formations the Luftwaffe ever established. As it was, intruder-type operations against Bordeaux were officially stated by British Intelligence to be 'difficult' and little more was done.

For some time BI maintained little more than a watching brief on German anti-shipping operations, Bomber Command's several attempts at evening the odds notwithstanding. The fact that the brilliant team of code-breakers stationed at Bletchley Park became fully aware of the operations of individual U-boats and the W/T support given to them by the Condors was a vital if passive tool, and counter-measures to help protect merchant ships were developed with all speed – which is not to say that every possible means of hitting back should perhaps have been implemented earlier. Bombing a vulnerable airfield – as against submarine pens, which proved impervious to hundreds of HE bombs of any size for most of the war – might be assumed to have been the easiest option for the RAF. In general, however, the Condors were spared enemy air attack and continued to cause havoc.

Irish hunting ground

KG 40 actively responded to the increasing number of shipping targets plying the waters around Britain, although its aircraft availability rate remained low. This situation could not be blamed on any one factor apart perhaps from a slow production rate for new aircraft. When they received them the KG 40 groundcrews, as ever, did their best to check over and 'sign off' enough aircraft as fit to operate on each day that sorties were required.

There were several areas where seaborne targets were almost certain to be found, one being the waters off the east and south coasts of Ireland. Condor patrols were sent out on most days, aircraft serviceability generally permitting two or three to be used. This normal utilisation figure was increased to five if a particularly lucrative target presented itself – and if the aircraft were available. There was little point in an experienced crew setting out in a machine that had defects likely to cause its loss as a result of battle damage or structural failure under the stress of combat. Invariably minor malfunctions had to be overlooked, as was normal in any intense operational situation, but in general a high level of serviceability was maintained by the groundcrews on each individual Fw 200.

Taking off from Bordeaux the Condor crews chose either to head straight for Ireland to search for shipping 'targets of opportunity' or they would take a bearing of about 310 degrees, which would place them well west of Ireland. Aircraft hunting prey on the waters surrounding the Emerald Isle usually crossed the Irish coast over the south-western counties of Cork or Kerry at an altitude of 2,000 feet (610 metres). They would then climb to 10,000 ft (3,050 metres) and exit Irish territory over Mayo or Donegal. On 18 December aircraft of I./Gruppe carried out three patrols in this area, the first taking off at 0555 (German time). No shipping was found and a second patrol was launched at 0610. After four an a half hours of steady flying, with the crew scanning the seas with their powerful binoculars, a potential target – a vessel of 3,000grt – was observed. This was attacked, only for the crew to watch the one bomb that hit the ship bounce off into the sea. Whether or not the attack was pressed home was not recorded, nor apparently was the name of ship.

A second Condor had taken off from Bordeaux eight minutes earlier on the 18th and this aircraft also set course for the Irish Sea. Around 0900 local time the crew came upon the 1,010grt British tanker *Osage* when it was some six miles off the Arklow Light Vessel. The Condor put four SC 250 bombs into the ship, which sank, all twenty-one crewmen being rescued by the British collier *Crownhill*.

Resuming his patrol, the captain of this second Condor set a northerly course to pass Dublin on the port side when he spotted the 2,691grt freighter *Tweed* at 0931 off the Rockabill light. Initiating an attack, the Condor apparently inflicted some damage on the vessel. Then, for reasons unknown, the Condor crew suddenly switched their attention to the mail boat *Cambria* (3,462grt) sailing east of Howth Head, Dublin. This vessel was subjected to a bombing and strafing run at about 1000 local time, although all four of the bombs released by the Condor missed. The aircraft's gunners sprayed the ship's upper works, injuring the *Cambria*'s third officer and a passenger and causing some damage. Again the Condor abruptly turned away, this time heading west to pass over neutral territory; Dublin airport and part of the city passed below as the pilot initiated a climb. A southerly heading took the aircraft over East Leinster, and Irish territory passed astern of it at a point between Wexford and Waterford.

Such sorties by German aircraft were usually seen and reported by the Irish Coast Watching Service, which had its headquarters located at Howth. The service received data from a series of lookout posts located on prominent headlands and passed it to the appropriate authorities for further action, as necessary.

On 19 December at 0554 local time, a single Condor again left Bordeaux for an Irish Sea patrol, being logged by the coast watchers at 1015 local time heading south. About an hour later the Condor had reached the South Wexford coast and dived to an altitude of some 50 feet (15 metres) as it passed Rosslare Bay. The crew spotted two ships, one of which was the Irish vessel *Lanarhone*, sailing under the appropriate colours and clearly marked with the word 'Eire' on its sides. The Condor circled the ship twice, rocked its wings as it passed overhead and flew off to investigate the second vessel. This, the Irish-registered lights tender *Isolda*, was flying the red ensign and was on its way to relieve the crew of the Coningbeg Light Vessel. The Condor dropped a quartet of SC 250 bombs, which caused an explosion and fire. Six of the ship's crew were killed and there were twenty-nine survivors from the stricken vessel.

The above series of actions fought by KG 40 were typical of an area where enemy shipping targets proved plentiful and there were little or no defences. In general terms in-shore patrols were for the period more fruitful for the Luftwaffe crews and, although things would not remain the same for long, the tally of enemy vessels attacked and/or sunk could sometimes be higher than those found on a long-range Atlantic patrol.

For KG 40 personnel stationed at Bordeaux the RAF raid earlier in the month must have indicated that others would follow, and on two consecutive nights, 25/26 and 27/28 December, Bomber Command indeed appeared again over that part of France. On both nights the target was Merignac aerodrome, which lay west of the city. Although the RAF effort was substantial, with more than seventy aircraft participating, little damage was apparently done to the base facilities or KG 40's aircraft. Thereafter things remained quiet in terms of this form of enemy retaliation until the spring of 1941. As indicated earlier, this delay appears strange considering the top priority afforded to the Battle of the Atlantic by British Intelligence, the Admiralty and Coastal Command.

Coastal may have requested greater support from Bomber Command to the point of transferring far more heavy bombers than it ever received and for more raids to be made against important targets, but these pleas were generally resisted as the area bombing of German cities gradually become firm-set British policy.

For the first two years or so the only means of taking the war to the enemy was Britain's medium bomber force; ineffective as it was later proved to have been, this striking power had to be built up – most diversions, even to specific and important Coastal Command targets, were viewed as hindering this goal. Bordeaux-Merignac therefore enjoyed a relatively peaceful existence without the mess and disruption faced by German bomber and fighter airfields in France, despite Winston Churchill's famous quote that the U-boat and the Condor had become the 'Scourge of the Atlantic'.

Chapter 6

1941: Changing fortunes

January

At the start of 1941 the composition of KG 40 remained almost unchanged, and the training and replacement Staffel, as with the main formation, remained under the direction of Fliegerkorps IV with its headquarters at Rennes. Use was made during the year of a secondary base at Amiens by (E)./KG 40, equipped mainly with Condors but also having a number of He 111s on strength. With the autumn and winter months of 1940/41 bringing a greater emphasis on night operations against targets in England, this indicated to the regular Kampfgeschwader crews that, with Hitler's postponement rather than complete cancellation of Operation 'Seelowe', the Kanalkampf was far from over. Moreover, for some months to come the Luftwaffe would be the instrument of the Führer's plan to return to the offensive against Britain once the Soviet Union had been defeated in an optimistically short period of time.

The bomber unit order of battle for the night offensive hardly affected KG 40 as the Condor had settled into its own operational deployment, which was unquestionably bringing results. Bombing ships in convoy and the many 'independents' that continued to sail alone and unescorted, the Condor crews were arguably inflicting as great a degree of damage as their Kampfgeschwader colleagues. As the four-engine bombers sought and often found worthwhile targets for their offensive payload, so vital supplies failed to reach the British Isles. The 250kg bomb, backed up by 20mm cannon and 7.9mm machine-gun rounds, usually proved more than adequate to cripple and sink poorly defended merchant ships, which had generally been constructed to meet peacetime maritime standards rather then the challenges of war. Many freighters were ancient and more than a few had seen service in 1914-18, which is not to imply that they were unseaworthy but perhaps a little less resilient to air attack compared to more modern vessels.

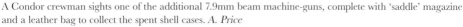

A Condor crewman sights one of the additional 7.9mm beam machine-guns, complete with 'saddle' magazine and a leather bag to collect the spent shell cases. *A. Price*

It has to be said that KG 40's crews attacked ships quite indiscriminately, no vessel being considered too small for attack. Numerous eye-witnesses also cite the fact that the big bombers often strafed without dropping bombs and immediately flew away when they could easily have made sure that the vessel they singled out went to the bottom. This meant that numerous ships suffered only superficial damage, perhaps also causing a few crew casualties. Nobody could quite understand the strategy behind such attacks and the question was never fully answered satisfactorily from the Allied point of view.

In contrast to the 'probing' attacks mentioned above, there were numerous demonstrations of how effective an aggressive attack by a single Condor could be, such as on 6 January 1941 when the 6,273grt freighter *Clytoneus* became another victim of KG 40. The ship was in convoy en route from the Dutch East Indies, carrying a general cargo that included tea, sugar and flour. When the Condor spotted her she was 280 miles (450km) north-west of Ireland's aptly named Bloody Foreland in County Donegal. At approximately 0800 the Condor ran in over the ship's stern and dropped two bombs, both of which were 'near misses' but fell close enough amidships for the aftershocks from the explosions to bring down the vessel's foremast and radio aerial and fracture the propeller shaft. As per the strict instructions that stragglers had to fend for themselves if they could not keep up with the slowest ship in the convoy, the *Clytoneus* was left behind and the crew braced themselves for a repeat attack. This materialised as a beam run, starboard to port, the Condor maintaining a height of 250 feet (76 metres) to release two more bombs. These struck the foredeck abaft No 2 hatch but, despite heavy damage forward of the bridge and a fire breaking out in the hold, the ship's crew let fly with a 12-pounder AA gun. This display of gallant defiance proved ineffectual and the Condor carried out a third run, dropped more bombs – all of which missed – and strafed the length of the vessel, which was taking water in the engine room and blazing furiously. It had taken the Condor crew just eight minutes to deny the enemy another precious cargo, but mercifully not more seamen. All hands got away safely when the *Clytoneus* was abandoned, the men being rescued the following day by naval ships.

As for the German aircrew, their aircraft had taken hits from the ship's AA gun. This was later confirmed when the Condor made for France by flying across Ireland, where, at some point in the flight, it crashed.

KG 40 continued its daylight war on shipping throughout January, although sometimes low visibility made that term only relative at best, the crews often having to cope with the dense fog that prevailed over Atlantic waters during the winter months, creating a hazard to flight operations and in some areas hiding ships that were potential targets. Beneath the fog, Allied seamen maintained a watch on the skies and, equally importantly, listened for the sound of aero engines. Aircraft recognition was not a strong point among seamen and precious minutes were wasted while the finer points of the Whitley, Wellington and Sunderland were debated. A degree of optimism that Coastal Command had many aircraft and was able to be everywhere was as gratifying as it was naive, and the confirmation that the four-engined aeroplane coming in fast on the ship's bow at low level was actually German came as a nasty shock.

Menacing enough to seamen, some of whom had never seen so large an aircraft even in peacetime, the Focke-Wulf Condor forged a fearsome reputation for efficient destruction of Allied ships in wartime. *F. Selinger*

Individual crews opted to paint their shipping successes on the fin or rudder of their Condors, including that of I./Gruppe's K8+CH, which has two ships together with a record of sorties over Norway. The tall wooden structures to shield the aircraft against shrapnel are noteworthy. *J. V. Crow*

Such low-visibility sorties were not without risk or casualties to the German aircrews themselves, and on 10 January an Fw 200C-3 (0035/F8+AB) of I./KG 40 flown by Oblt F. Burmeister attacked the ocean-going tug SS *Seaman* some 200 miles (322km) north-west of Ireland at 1350. Making the now usual bow-to-stern run along the length of the vessel, and on this occasion dropping two bombs, both of which missed, Burmeister would still have considered the tug an easy victim.

The reason for this standard attack was that, if the target ship was armed, the gun was almost always positioned on the stern and could not easily be brought to bear forward. Even if it was able to do so, the field of fire was limited by numerous deck fittings. By the time the Condor had cleared the stern of the vessel the German gunners were on the point of opening strafing fire, even if they had not already done so.

On this occasion, to show that the exception often proved the rule, rounds from a Lewis gun, manned by the ship's mate, one Mr Reilly, hit the Condor squarely. It sheered off and promptly plunged into the sea with one of its engines on fire. Burmeister and two of his crew (identified in the records only as B. Gumbert and R. Steimeyer) were rescued by the *Seaman*'s crew and taken prisoner, although three other occupants of the aircraft perished. A replacement for Burmeister had to be quickly found, as he was due to be posted to Doenitz's headquarters as Special Liaison Officer.

In a month marked by even more appalling weather than normal, German aircraft sank eleven British ships with a combined tonnage of 46,395grt. Eight vessels were the victims of Condors in the Western Approaches, among them the freighter *Langleegorse* (4,524grt), which became another statistic of the Atlantic war when she was bombed and sunk on the 23rd. Part of convoy SL.61, the vessel was homeward bound from Durban when she was attacked.

The last day of January recorded the demise of the *Rowanbank* (5,159grt), intercepted and bombed at a position about 1,100 miles (1,770km) from Merignac. In convoy SL.62 out of Freetown en route from Lourenço Marques to Oban, the ship nevertheless succumbed to bomb damage and went down with all sixty-eight members of her crew.

Advanced picture

Interception of radio transmissions enabled the German 'B' service to build a comprehensive picture of the sea traffic to and from Britain and even to anticipate the type of cargo the ships in a typical convoy were likely to be carrying, depending on the port of origin. The convoy identification was a simple enough system, as Table 5 indicates. It was unfortunate that, despite the ships' cargoes often being of a general nature, the exit port became readily identifiable with certain foodstuffs, raw materials, manufactured articles and so on. This made it relatively easy for agents to transmit the information to Germany where analysis was rapid and usually in time to position one or more U-boat wolf packs to intercept.

When the Allies began dispatching JW- and PQ-coded convoys to Russia, it was simple enough to deduce that, if the ships' holds were fully utilising all available space for food and other passive war material, deck cargoes would be accommodating aircraft, tanks and motor vehicles, all of which the Soviets were able to put to good use as the German war machine swept towards Moscow and Leningrad.

Table 5: Convoy codes

Outbound from Great Britain		Inbound to Great Britain	
OB	Liverpool to Halifax, Nova Scotia	CU	New York-Curacao to GB
ON	GB to Halifax	HX	Halifax to GB
SC	GB to the USA	HG	Gibraltar to GB
OG	GB to Gibraltar	MK	Gibraltar to GB (after 26 October 1942)
KM	GB to Gibraltar (after 26 October 1942)	MKF	Mediterranean-North Africa to GB (fast)
KMF	GB to North Africa-Port Said (fast)	MKS	Mediterranean-North Africa to GB (slow)
KMS	GB to North Africa-Port Said (slow)	SC	Halifax to GB (slow)
KX	GB to Gibraltar (special)	SL	West Africa to GB (slow)
OG	GB to Gibraltar	SLS	West Africa to GB (fast)
ONS	GB to North America	QP	Russia to GB
ON	GB to North America	UT	USA to GB (military)
OS	GB to West Africa	XK	Gibraltar to GB (special)
JW	GB to Russia		
PQ	GB to Russia		
WS	GB to Middle East and India (military)	**Others**	
		UG	US to North Africa
		UGF	US to North Africa
		UGS	US to North Africa

Armed with the appropriate code, it was a simple enough matter for pro-German agents in Gibraltar, Portugal and other neutral locations to confirm and transmit convoy details to U-boat command. With advance knowledge of the number and class of vessel in the convoy, Doenitz could despatch submarines and aircraft to rendezvous with the ships on a simple directional/time-elapsed basis. While this was not an exact science, the U-boat C-in-C was right more often than not – but as the few instances quoted here show, a potentially lethal gathering of submarines was not a foregone guarantee of many successful sinkings.

Allied measures to thwart the combined threat were still few, but the re-routing of convoys played its part in minimising losses. The convoys from Freetown were more vulnerable to air attack as they were not, unlike the OB, HX and SC convoys from North American ports, routed to the north of Scotland. The more northerly passage stretched the range of the Condors from their bases in southern France and brought them into the radius of action flown by the aircraft of RAF Coastal Command. At that time the most dangerous of these remained the Sunderland, which was well able not only to sink U-boats but also to defend itself in an air-to-air engagement.

Sunderland patrols into the Bay of Biscay brought about the occasional clash with KG 40's Condors, one such taking place at 1254 on 11 January 1941 about 300 miles (483km) west of Bloody Foreland. The result of the combat was inconclusive, although Flt Lt Lindsay's gunners believed that they had damaged the enemy machine. It seemed that they were right, as a British monitoring unit picked up the Condor's message: 'SOS. Coast reached.' A short time later the German crew sent: 'SOS. Forced to alight on sea near coast.'

Two Fw 200s actually crashed that day, but neither was the direct result of aerial combat, according to Luftwaffe records. One was Fw 200C-3 0028/F8+??, which force-landed in the sea off the Ile de Re, a small island lying off the coast of France at La Rochelle. All the crew were rescued, although their aircraft was lost through damage that was officially attributed to German flak. This may well have been the aircraft attacked by the Sunderland.

The second loss to inventory was Fw 200C-3 0037/F8+GL of 3./Staffel KG 40, which crashed at Merignac in bad visibility, resulting in 25 per cent damage. An RAF reconnaissance photograph of Bordeaux taken the following day showed a stricken Condor on the SW/NE runway with a severed port wing lying nearby. This might also have been the aircraft involved in aerial combat. After repair this particular Condor was passed to 7./Staffel, only to sustain 20 per cent damage to its undercarriage on 14 February 1942 on a ferry flight to Staaken. Passed to (B)./26, it took part in the relief airlift operation at Demyansk, Russia early in 1942.

An inherent main spar weakness was a drawback the Luftwaffe had to accept when the Condor was drafted into an anti-shipping role. Seemingly the spar has failed shortly after this aircraft had started its take-off run, the external bomb load shaking loose in the process.

Another KG 40 Condor has come to grief, probably after a very heavy landing and battle damage. Condor write-offs seemed to have two patterns, and although this aircraft's break point was the centre of the fuselage rather than the wing spar, the result was much the same.

U-boat scores soar

Even though January 1941 was an early waypoint in the long Battle of the Atlantic, individual U-boats were emerging as high scorers in terms of Allied shipping sunk. One Type VIIB boat, U-48, had, since commissioning in April 1939 and completing her first war cruise beginning on 19 August that year, sunk forty-five ships. The period was also marked with several home leaves and complaints by German submariners about the reliability of their LTF 5 torpedoes. Had this latter weapon been able to achieve anywhere near the desired 90-100 per cent effectiveness, U-48's captain believed he would have undoubtedly achieved an even higher score. U-boat skippers were reporting a frustratingly high level of dud torpedo launches, a problem that was addressed by the Kriegsmarine but not entirely eradicated.

February

Ships from various nations, some not at war with the combatants, were liable to run foul of the Condors despite their neutrality flags, and on 5 February one of these 'independents', the Greek vessel *Ioannis M. Embiricos*, became a target for Oblt Paul Gommert's crew. Flying Fw 200C-3 0042/F8+AH, Gommert, then Staffel Kapitän of I./KG 40, flew a wide-ranging patrol, firstly to seek out ships sailing off the coast of Scotland. Nothing was found and the Condor set a new course southwards to cover the coast of Ireland. There Gommert came upon the freighter SS *Merchant C* in Irish waters off County Cork. Sailing in convoy, the ship was singled out for attack by the Condor – which was incidentally a replacement for an earlier 'F8+AH' – but it proved not to be as vulnerable as the German airmen might have assumed. Return fire from the ship's guns set the Condor alight, the aircraft probably being further damaged by fire from a freighter named *Major C*.

Limping away from the scene of action, the stricken aircraft was at an altitude of 850 feet (260 metres) when it plunged into a belt of fog obscuring much of the west of Ireland – and the mountains of Cork and Kerry. The Condor struck the side of Cashelfeane or Cashelane Hill and disintegrated in a ball of fire. Paul Gommert, the sole survivor, was dragged from the flames by Mary Nugent, a veteran of the old Irish Republican Army's female contingent, Cumann na mBan, whose members, among other talents, were experienced in first aid.

As Mary tended his wounds the German airman asked his rescuer where he was and when she confirmed that he was in Ireland he replied, 'Good. Good.'

The rest of the Condor crew were buried in the grounds of Bantry Abbey with full military honours (as afforded to all airmen, Allied or Axis), which included an army band. Among the mourners was Henning Thomsen, First Secretary of the German Legation in Dublin. An Irish ordnance detachment destroyed the Condor's bomb load, which had been scattered in the crash, with some of the missiles rolling down the mountain slopes. The German aircrew survivor was given intensive medical treatment before convalescing at a seaside resort; rather ironically, Mary Nugent received the Reich Civilian Merit Medal for her brave rescue, accompanied by a letter from Adolf Hitler.

In the meantime the damaged Greek freighter did not go down until the day after the Condor crashed, a not unusual occurrence and one that made confirmation of some sinkings claimed by KG 40 (and other Luftwaffe units) difficult to verify.

The final destruction of several damaged ships was often carried out by U-boats while others would be abandoned to drift for hours, if not days, before finally going down. German aircrews could rarely wait around to photograph the final demise of crippled targets, and some claims could not be verified insofar as a given ship that eventually slipped beneath the waves could not definitely be proven to have succumbed solely to air attack by KG 40, although the location of the stricken vessel was a reliable clue. Moreover, a sortie by other aircraft some hours later to the stricken ship's last reported position would not necessarily find anything. Had the vessel been abandoned by her crew in an area patrolled by friendly naval units, it would not be allowed to drift but would be sunk to prevent it becoming a hazard to navigation. Merchant shipping crews were also under instruction to scuttle their ship for the same reason, provided there was time to do so.

Five down

Cooperation between KG 40's maritime aircraft and U-boats increased in the first weeks of 1941. On 9 February five Condors of 2./Staffel, which was then led by the Staffel Kapitän Hptm Fritz Fliegel – who was once again at the controls of Fw 200C-3/U2 0043/F8+AB – were vectored by U-37 (Leutnant zur See Nicolaus Clausen) onto ships of convoy HG.53 south-west of Lisbon, homeward bound from Gibraltar to Liverpool.

In what constituted a major operation by KG 40, sorties by no fewer than six Condors in several separate actions brought spectacular results for the German airmen. Five ships from HG.53 were attacked and sunk by five Condors on the 9th. Then on the 19th Edgar Petersen himself attacked two vessels from convoy OB.287, one more on the 21st and five on the 26th. Responding to bearings passed by U-47 (Gunther Prien's boat), the Condors involved in the latter action thus accounted for shipping totalling 20,755grt, which was to be the greatest single wartime success recorded by the Geschwader.

Condors captained by Fliegel, Adam, Buchholz, Jope (then Staffel Kapitän of IV./KG 40) and Schlosser had attacked and destroyed four British and one Norwegian ship, totalling 9,201grt. This multiple success was rarely repeated as circumstances forced the unit to deploy fewer aircraft with less risk of losing the precious Condors and their crews.

Fritz Fliegel's machine enjoyed the flexibility of having been fitted with extra-long-range fuel tanks. Five months on, the same aircraft was on the strength of Stab./KG 40 and had become something of a personal favourite of Fliegel, one of the unit's most experienced pilots. Condors were, as related elsewhere, subject to rotation between different Staffeln of KG 40, and part of an inevitable practice that managed to maintain a balance of available aircraft throughout I./Gruppe while it was the single operator of the Fw 200.

Oberstleutnant Edgar Petersen (centre) with Edmund Daser, Bernhard Jope, Hans Buchholz and Rudolf Mayr. White cap covers were retained by those officers of KG 40 who had previously served in the Navy. *F. Selinger*

Lone wolves

It goes without saying that U-boats frequently sent ships to the bottom without any direct assistance from KG 40's Condors, but in February 1941 Herbert Schultze's boat was operating west of the North Channel and Ireland, and having some difficulty in locating convoy OB.287, which he had been ordered to attack on the 19th. Schultze then received a sighting report from a Condor, which proved to be inexact and no targets were found. KG 40's aircraft again attempted to assist U-48 on 25 March, a homeward-bound convoy south of Iceland being the intended quarry. Once again the outcome of this cooperation proved inconclusive.

Worsening weather during the quite grim winter of 1940-41 was a double-edged sword for the crews of maritime aircraft such as the Condor. On the one hand, if they took off safely they could assume that their targets would to be less alert to the possibility of attack in such poor visibility – but if KG 40's crack navigators could guide their pilots through the murk to home in on shipping, there was an even chance of success with reduced fear of retaliation. It was a little ironic, but a mark perhaps of the threat posed by KG 40's bombers, that RAF Coastal Command mounted several 'anti-Focke-Wulf' patrols into the Bay of Biscay in 1941. Deploying the Beaufighter, the most potent fighter then in the inventory, these sorties generally failed to deplete KG 40 by a significant amount, as a successful interception remained a matter of luck, spot-on navigation and clear visibility.

Irrespective of the German aircraft type they hoped to intercept, the RAF aircrews invariably came upon the more numerous He 111s, Ju 88s or shorter-ranged maritime machines such as the Bv 138 rather than Condors, the operational numbers of which remained quite low and were therefore rarely encountered by RAF aircraft – a situation exploited fully by KG 40 at every possible opportunity. The German crews had no desire to test their aircraft against the RAF, for they could anticipate the outcome of a combat with anything more agile (and that meant virtually every type the British possessed!) with a fair degree of accuracy, not to say pessimism!

Such a sanguine view of air combat did not mean that Condor crews would always duck a fight and, when another brush with a Sunderland had materialised on 29 January, it had been the Germans who had opened the proceedings. Flying Officer Aikman of No 210 Squadron sighted his adversary south of Eire at 1127. The German crew (believed to have been that of Alfred Wintersamt flying an Fw 200C-3) reacted with a diving port-quarter attack on the British flying boat, opening fire at a range of 500 yards (457 metres). Rounds struck the Sunderland's rear turret and wounded the gunner, but the Condor was itself damaged by return fire, hits being observed by the RAF aircrew in the port engines and cockpit area. The Sunderland crew later stated that the Condor 'retired hurt' with the propeller of its port inner engine windmilling. It would appear, however, that the German captain managed to put his aircraft down safely, no Condor being recorded by the Luftwaffe's daily summary of aircraft accidents and losses.

Edgar Petersen himself flew on operations whenever possible, and during February 1941 his crews continued to enjoy success, as already noted. By then, ships in the British convoys were doing their best to fight back; several stop-gap ideas were developed to hinder a Condor attack, even if not being quite lethal enough to bring down the offending aircraft. A variation on the abovementioned rocket-and-wire-cables device was a parachute and cable device armed with a bomb. The principle of the cable attaching itself to the aircraft was similar, the difference being that the bomb would then detonate against the airframe. Wrapping the cable around a propeller, which would drag the bomb in against a wing or fuselage surface, was understandably a method that required a fair degree of skill, not to mention luck, on the part of the operator. It did happen that the cable entangled the tail surface of the attacking Condor, which was then obliged to head for home; if the coils of wire did not jam the flying surfaces to the point of endangering the aircraft, the crew had no choice but to drag the small 'chute all the way back to base.

The entwined cable was next to impossible to jettison in flight and more than one lucky crew touched down with the bomb and parachute bouncing down the runway behind the aircraft. There was little danger if the explosive device came to rest several feet behind the Condor before detonating, and more than one crew walked away from an aircraft festooned with fine wire dragging a dud round. Even if it proved to be live, if the cable was too long the aircraft was not in any great danger. Fortunately for KG 40's complement, this particular anti-aircraft weapon was not in vogue for very long.

March

To better co-ordinate attacks by air and submarine units a more or less independent Luftwaffe sub-command known as Fliegerführer Atlantik was formed in March 1941 under Luftflotte 3 and established its headquarters near Lorient. A comprehensive plotting system was established to chart the passage of Kriegsmarine U-boats, surface ships and aircraft into areas through which British shipping was known to pass. Martin Harlinghausen was appointed to head the new command. At about the same time KG 40's Condors were provided with some back-up through a general expansion of the Geschwader; the unit was enlarged by adding a third Gruppe, 4./Staffel being issued with He 111s to begin operations at the end of April as part of II./KG 40. The other units of II./Gruppe (V. and VI./KG 40) operated the Do 217. A third full Gruppe was also planned by OKL to fly the Fw 200 at such time as sufficient aircraft were available, but in the event this did not come about until the end of 1941.

Of the 115 aircraft then available to Fliegerführer Atlantik, I./KG 40 had twenty-nine Fw 200s, arguably the most effective maritime type; as before, virtually the entire current Condor output had to be allocated to this single Gruppe to maintain the Fw 200 fleet at nominal strength.

On 2 March I./KG 40 lost Fw 200C-3 0031/F8+BT when it strayed at little too close to the coast of Scotland early that afternoon. At 1435, when the Condor was off Sumburgh in the Shetland Islands, the crew spotted fighters and made off with all speed. In pursuit were Hurricanes of No 3 Squadron led by P/Os Robertson and Gabb. Either or both of the RAF pilots succeeded in hitting the Condor, which was able to land at Stavanger-Sola with one crew member having been wounded in an exchange of fire.

An Fw 200C-3 of I./KG 40 at Bordeaux in March 1941. With a dozen men on hand to check the aircraft over, all that could be done to send the crew safely on their way was done. *J. V. Crow*

A week later Fw 200C-3 0040/SG+KP crashed on take-off at Bordeaux-Merignac and suffered 40 per cent damage. The exact cause of the accident is unknown but one crewman was killed and the captain, Oblt Wilhelm Claussen, and two other crewmen were injured.

Aerial combat

To Allied seamen, KG 40's distinctive 'world in a ring' insignia had become synonymous with a deadly foe, whose activities were about to be expanded, although the number of Condors ranged against them remained modest. The big Focke-Wulfs operating in the area did locate single ships, these often being directly attacked by the aircraft that tracked them down rather than submarines. Boats with a crack crew such as Schultze's U-48 also worked independently and found their own targets without the aid of air reconnaissance.

This and subsequent war patrols resulted in the sinking of a grand total of fifty-seven ships (including a Royal Navy sloop), making U-48 the most successful German submarine of the war. The small part played by KG 40's Condors in this impressive total was not untypical: the majority of U-boat kills were achieved by crew sighting and patiently tracking contacts, backed up by headquarters (Y-service) data. Having broken the Allied code that identified both outward and inward convoys, it was relatively easily for Karl Doenitz to direct the German boats to the right area. For their part, the Condor crews were well aware that the time-lag between transmitting their coded sighting reports to U-boat HQ and one or more submarines actually attacking the vessel they had located could prove prohibitive. Alternatively KG 40's bombs could despatch the ship without this delay, and on numerous occasions that is what happened. Denying the enemy his vital supplies was the whole point of the exercise, irrespective of the means by which it was achieved. Therefore the independent, 'parallel' war of the Condors and the U-boats continued, with the two elements crossing over when expedient.

Another accident on 18 March resulted in five personnel fatalities when Lt Hans Winkler and four of his crew were unable to prevent their Fw 200C-3 (0041/SG+KQ) going down. The Condor, believed to have been coded F8+AH of I./KG 40, crashed in flames about 30 miles (50 km) south of Brest. One member of the crew who had suffered injuries is known to have survived.

In the half light of dawn on 25 March a single Condor made an attack run on the Canadian Pacific freighter *Beaverbrae* (9,956grt). Flying at 300 feet (92 metres) above the waves, the German machine bombed and strafed the vessel, setting it on fire. So intense did the flames become that the ship had to be abandoned.

On 24 March Fritz Fliegel's anti-shipping prowess was officially marked by presentation of the Ritterkreuz (RK), the citation noting that his unit had then been credited with sinking a total of thirty-nine ships. Jope, Buchholz and Daser had also become Ritterkreuztrager by that date. Their awards were presented, as was then normal practice, by Adolf Hitler in person; for many of the recipients who were decorated only once, such a ceremony was the one and only time they were able to meet their leader in the flesh.

A skirmish on 28 March put an anonymous Condor and a Ju 88 in contact with a Sunderland of No 201 Squadron. The big German bomber, apparently preoccupied in attacking a merchant ship, was engaged head-on by the British flying boat. Hits were claimed by the RAF gunners and, although the action of the opposing escort fighter is unrecorded, the Sunderland emerged unscathed in a not untypical meeting between the two four-engine types where the outcome of the combat was inconclusive. The presence of a fighter was a little unusual as the Ju 88, almost certainly from V./KG 40, did not fly Condor escort sorties on a regular basis.

April

Frustrated in their necessarily limited air and seaborne response to the carnage in the North Atlantic, the British again hit back at KG 40 by bombing Merignac and Lorient on the night of 12/13 April 1941. Having decided in March that the Condors based at Merignac posed more of an immediate threat than the Italian submarines based at nearby Bacalan, the RAF made further attempts to damage the German anti-shipping unit on the ground. This raid on the former French base by a force of eleven Wellingtons did succeed in destroying Fw 200D-2 0020, one of the aircraft that had originally been allocated for delivery to Japan and had previously served with Lufthansa as D-ACWG *Holstein*.

At the time of its demise 0020 was serving as F8+GL with III./KG 40, having previously operated as a transport with 2./KGrzbV upon delivery to the Luftwaffe in August 1940. On 27 March 1941 the aircraft, which was one of the Condors modified to carry Rb 30 cameras and extra fuel to boost its range to 3,100 miles (5,000km), had, in the hands of Oblt Bernard Jope and Kapitän Polletin of the E-Stelle, completed an epic seventeen-hour flight from Stavanger-Sola to the eastern area of Iceland and Scoresby Sound in east Greenland before returning to Trondheim-Vaernes. It would appear that the British raid did little to deter KG 40's operations by, for example, destroying workshop facilities or fuel storage, and the unit's operations carried on without an appreciable break.

On 18 April another Condor crew, that of Oblt Ernst Muller, were forced to take to their dinghies when their Fw 200C-3 (0053/F8+GL) of III./KG 40 came under AA fire from convoy escorts and ditched off Schull, County Cork. Muller and all six of his crewmen were rescued by an Irish vessel.

The other side of the operational coin proved unlucky for Oblt Hermann Richter of I./KG 40, who was attacked by a Beaufighter while flying Fw 200C-3 0039/F8+AH. At the controls of the British fighter (T3237/PN-K) was Flt Lt Bill Riley of No 252 Squadron, which was temporarily based at Aldergrove in Northern Ireland specifically to hunt enemy aircraft over the Western Approaches. Riley and his observer, W/O Donaldson, spotted the Condor at 1420 flying a course of 210 degrees. Riley made his opening attack from 275 metres (300 yards) on the Condor's beam, firing toward the tail. Short bursts at point-blank range proved fatal and, despite Richter's rear gunner firing back at the Beaufighter, fire soon took hold in the port wing root. Riley noted that the Condor swung left at a downwards angle then straightened out before diving straight into the sea in flames at a 45-degree angle. No survivors and hardy any wreckage were observed by the RAF crew.

Oblt Roland Schelcher of 1./Staffel went down on 29 April. Flying Fw 200C-3 0054/F8+HH, he was killed when his aircraft was intercepted and shot down by Fleet Air Arm fighters while on patrol off the Shetland Islands.

While Allied shipping losses to U-boats continued to climb steadily, success eluded the Condor crews on numerous sorties, many hours being spent fruitlessly searching for an elusive quarry, often in less than ideal flying weather. Planned rendezvous with U-boats were occasionally missed and, even when the aircrews attacked independently, the results could not always be verified due to poor visibility or damage to the aircraft from enemy fire. Under such circumstances it was almost inevitable that some of the highly experienced members of the prewar airline crews who formed the original cadre of KG 40 would be lost.

Sunlight reflecting off the fuselage finish could partially obscure the code letters of individual Condors, including F8+EH of 1./Staffel, seen here. *MAP*

A KG 40 crew receives last-minute briefing on the prevailing maritime situation as it prepares for another sortie.

Early Condors lacked any form of sea search or weather mapping radar, but this equipment was fitted to variants as and when it became available. ASV sets for reconnaissance were the victim of a slow building rate – but British Intelligence wanted proof that the Germans had not yet achieved an airborne set reliable enough to be installed quickly.

Armed with the basic knowledge of where the Condors of KG 40 were based, where and when they generally operated and the small numbers of aircraft deployed, BI officers had from the autumn of 1940 been unable to confirm if airborne sea-search radar was assisting the crack German unit in achieving its deadly purpose. With every successive sinking attributed to KG 40 this question was a vexed one: if the Condors did have radar installed it would confirm the enemy's rapid progress in this area, which in itself was worrying because comparable British ASV was not quite ready for service. But the frustration of not knowing either way was greater when no solution offered itself. Direct, low-level PR coverage of Bordeaux was ruled out in deference to the defences and the weather; neither could any personnel of KG 40 be pressed to tell what he knew about radar – because at that time none had fallen into British hands.

Portugal snaps

A chance remark by an Irish WAAF from Dublin brought about the answer. She knew that Condor crews returning from patrols tended to photograph anything that caught their eye around the coast. This included Portuguese fishing vessels, the crews of which also had cameras and regularly photographed Luftwaffe and Portuguese aircraft that dipped low over them for a photo run. As the story goes it was suggested that prizes be offered to the fishermen who took the best shots; they had to make no distinction in favour of Condors to avoid arousing any suspicion, and by April 1941 the required confirmation was to hand – no radar aerials had been observed on any Fw 200s. This in itself was a satisfactory answer, but one not entirely reassuring to the British authorities as it meant that KG 40 was achieving its remarkable record of merchant ship sinkings without any electronic aids. It only served to reinforce the view that the German crews of this singular Luftwaffe unit were highly trained and very proficient.

May

Combat attrition was a grim reality to KG 40, as it was to most operational units irrespective of nationality or, indeed, the skill of the airmen involved. Even so, it came as a shock when highly experienced pilots appeared to have been deserted by 'flyer's luck' for whatever reason. On 19 May 1941 Kampfgeschwader 40's entire air and ground crew compliment were stunned by the news that Oberlt Hans Buchholz had failed to return from a war patrol.

Flying his Fw 200C-3 (0060/F8+DH, or F8 +AH according to intelligence reports), Buchholz had taken off from Bordeaux at 0001 that morning; the Condor carried four 250kg bombs and the crew had orders to patrol the Western Approaches. They found the 8,000-ton freighter SS *Umgeni* sailing some 250 miles (400km) west of Donegal Bay on the coast of Northern Ireland.

Buchholz attacked. The Condor ran in on the ship, which responded with return fire from its 12-pounder gun and, in something of a freak lucky shot, a single round penetrated the cockpit and hit the pilot's seat. Fire broke out in the nose area of the aircraft and Buchholz and first radio operator, Oberfw Paul Schmidt, were wounded. A single bomb was dropped after the incident although the Condor clearly became uncontrollable as it crashed into the sea off Hollywood, about 350 miles (560km) due west of Bloody Foreland shortly afterwards. The five remaining members of the crew were rescued from the stricken aircraft, but the two wounded men drowned before they could be picked up. The surviving German airmen were taken to Belfast and into captivity.

Overleaf: Obviously pleased with a recent sortie, the members of this Condor crew commanded by Hauptmann Hans Buchholz (centre) wear the Iron Cross almost as a standard accoutrement to their uniforms. *F. Selinger*

Buchholz was a grievous loss to KG 40. At thirty-two years of age he had been credited with sinking ten merchant ships totalling 60,800grt by April 1941, and had been awarded the RK on 19 May. His score had by that time risen to include a further eight ships of 48,000grt damaged, some of them so badly that the British authorities considered them to have been lost. British Intelligence reports, not known for their sentimentality, nevertheless acknowledged the passing of a worthy adversary and a highly skilled and experienced pilot.

As the gruelling Battle of the Atlantic ground on with little or no relief from the intense pressure experienced by both sides, already exhausted by the sheer effort of simple survival, the British were finally able to interview members of KG 40 who had been rescued. More than a few RAF and RN officers were extremely interested in what these men had to say.

Condor and other Luftwaffe aircrew survivors were interrogated for information under the usual, well-established system. In many cases, individuals were remarkably candid about the merits or demerits of their aircraft and did not attempt to gloss over shortcomings in operational procedures. These valuable verbatim comments helped to build up a picture of the morale of KG 40, a unit reckoned by the British to be of great danger to their shipping. Conversations were carefully analysed for information, especially details of any new equipment that had been issued to Luftwaffe units, and compared with the data generated by previous PoW interrogations. They were then typed up and distributed to various interested parties, eventually being published in précised form, as Air Ministry Weekly Intelligence Summaries.

Without realising the fact, the captured KG 40 crews enabled the British to build up a remarkably clear picture of the unit's operations. The details published in the reports extended to comprehensive vignettes of such items as the layouts of the different airfields used by the unit, the system of blind approach in inclement weather conditions, the typical wavelengths of radio transmissions to U-boats and land bases, the number of personnel and aircraft strengths at different periods, and an ongoing general view of, what was to those on the opposing side, one of the most dangerous units in the Luftwaffe.

June

During the month Bruno Mussolini, son of the Italian dictator, visited KG 40 at Bordeaux. On a short sortie he briefly took the controls of a Condor, but the duty pilot felt it wise to restrict the flight to no further than the three-mile limit of the aerodrome. Understandably his German host was surely preoccupied with the likely repercussions the loss of a member of a friendly head of state's family in a routine accident might bring forth.

Below and overleaf: The spectre of fire haunted wartime aircraft just as it always had at other times. This KG 40 Fw 200A-0 (S-1) was soon consumed following an engine start incident at Aalborg-West in Denmark on 15 June 1941. The aircraft was then on the strength of X./(Erg) KG 40, indicating that the fire started in No 3 engine. *J. V. Crow*

Losses continue

Operating lone aircraft at a great distance from base put KG 40 at some disadvantage in determining the exact causes if aircraft failed to return. While radio signals were not expected to be sent even by a crew in dire straits – such was not an advisable option in airspace where the enemy might well intercept – and the aircraft in question was not observed, it would to all intents and purposes be lost without trace. Only later, perhaps even years after the end of the war, might the circumstances of the loss be revealed. One such mysterious incident occurred on 15 June 1941 when an Fw 200C-3 (0061/F8+KL) of III./KG 40, captained by Oblt Erich Westermann and six crewmen, did not return to Bordeaux.

Having taken off for a patrol at 0214 to find convoy HG.65, reported to be south-west of Gibraltar, Westermann's flight path would have taken him over Spain. He never arrived at that point as the Condor exploded and crashed in flames at 0530 about 2.5 miles (4km) east of Amarelja in Portugal with no survivors. There is some indication that the crew did in this instance send a message to report 'technical difficulties' beforehand and, although the aircraft had suffered 20 per cent damage during a take-off on 21 May, there is no indication that this was in any way related to the Condor's ultimate loss.

In a separate incident on the same day Fw 200C-1 0008/F8+FH fell victim to problems serious enough for the 1./Staffel crew under Lt Otto Gose to steer a course for Spain. Putting down in a field at Navia in the Asturas area, the crew included Obgfr Oskar Meissner (position in the aircraft unknown). All airmen returned to France three days later after their Condor had been repaired.

Reportedly a third Condor from I./KG 40 coded F8+DH was shot down into the sea 350 miles (560km) due west of Bloody Foreland on 19 June, although the circumstances surrounding this loss are unknown.

21 June

Another momentous event in the turbulent history of the Second World War thundered into the world's headlines on 21 June when Operation 'Barbarossa' began. Having perpetrated a sudden, brutal stab in the back against a former ally, Hitler had taken the greatest gamble of his doubtful career as a military strategist. Much of the Luftwaffe bomber, ground-attack and fighter forces were committed to the new Eastern Front to support a three-pronged ground offensive towards the Russian capital, the historic city of Leningrad and the Caucasus oilfields; the loss of any or all of these locations would, it was estimated, bring the Soviet state to its knees. Time would prove that the German dictator's timetable of self-destruction had many more ambitious and ultimately futile steps to take. Meanwhile KG 40's personnel, who might have watched the newsreels, read their newspapers and shrugged at a new phase of the war that seemed unlikely to concern them directly, went about their business as usual.

July

Such was the scope of German victories against the new Russian enemy that little could detract from the sheer scale of the advance. As July came in, a sour note clouded KG 40's horizon when Condor F8+EL flown by Hptm Rudolf Mayr, with Oblt Dostlebe among his crew, failed to return to base after a sortie. A unit that could ill afford another run of combat losses due to the slow replacement rate of its aircraft, KG 40 had nevertheless to continue to meet its operational commitments with the aircraft it had. But the attrition rate was unlikely to accommodate such worries and the next crew to become a statistic in the Luftwaffe Quartermaster General's accounting was the Condor flown by one of KG 40's most respected pilots, none other than Hptm Fritz Fliegel.

Then part of Stab./I Gruppe and the 2./ Staffel Kapitän, Fliegel had undertaken a patrol on 18 July, flying Fw 200 C-3/U2 0043/F8+AB, another example of the C series fitted with long-range tanks. The crew found a target in the form of the ships of the convoy OB.346 when it was about 340 miles (550km) west of Donegal Bay. The highly experienced Fliegel made his run on the *Pilar de Larrinaga*, a 7,046grt freighter. What he may not have been aware of was that a Hurricane from HMS *Maplin* was about to intercept the Condor and attack it head-on. Pilot Lt Everett in W9227 was still closing the range to be sure of a kill when a drama unfolded below him. Fliegel's starboard-to-port beam approach to the freighter drew fire from the ship's four machine-guns and a 12-pounder HA, the German crew responding with cannon and machine-gun rounds and a bomb, which hit the vessel's saloon area. Meanwhile Lt Everett was about to open fire when the Condor's port wing broke away. It had, eye-witnesses reported, been hit by enough machine-gun rounds and a shell from the larger gun to fatally weaken the root structure at that point. No member of Fliegel's crew is known to have survived.

Arguably the most famous Fw 200 of them all was this C-3/U2 (0043/SG+KS/F8+AB), the subject of a series of photos that appeared in numerous Axis and Allied publications, with an advertisement for paint! Today it still turns up as a representative view of the type.
Author's collection

Hudson handiwork brought down an Fw 200C shadowing an Atlantic convoy on 25 July 1941. Going in at full throttle, the RAF crew fired at point blank range and set the Condor on fire whereupon it turned steeply and went into the sea. The German skipper nevertheless brought off a level ditching allowing all but one of the crew to escape and be picked up. *IWM*

It was not only the pilot of this particular aircraft who was widely known; in a former guise, the Condor itself had enjoyed almost a life of its own. Painted with the Stammkirchen SG+KS, it was photographed and the print(s) widely published in Germany and abroad to became the representative type-recognition image, appearing in numerous periodicals and as postcards. It even became the main focus of a poster advertising paint sold by a Berlin supplier! Unwitting fame continues to follow this particular Condor to the present day as even the briefest mention of the type in books, articles and so forth, if accompanied by a single representative photo, will invariably show SG+KS/F8+AB!

Clash

As RAF Coastal Command's squadrons increased, so KG 40's Condors could expect to encounter more enemy aircraft, and although the Germans preferred to avoid combat, that proved impossible for one crew on 23 July 1941. Having taken off from Bordeaux at 0230 the crew of Fw 200 C-3 0069/F8+BB had been briefed for a meteorological/armed reconnaissance sortie for which it carried four 1,000lb (450kg) bombs. Having detected convoy HG.69, the Condor pilot, Obfw Heinrich Bleichert, dropped to 300 feet (90 metres) to initiate an attack. Before he could do so he encountered a Hudson V of No 233 Squadron (AM536/ZS-J) from Aldergrove piloted by P/O Ron O. H. Down, which was engaged on convoy protection duty. The German crew (from the Stab of I./KG 40) exchanged fire before turning away, but the faster Hudson gave chase, caught up and pumped shells into the Fw 200, which sustained fatal damage. Keeping very low to avoid enemy fire striking the underside of his aircraft, Bleichert executed a textbook ditching 250 miles (400km) north-west of Ireland, the Condor alighting on an even keel and floating long enough for the crew to abandon the aircraft in good order without undue risk of being trapped as it gradually filled with water.

A ditching well recorded on film, the abandoning of F8+BB at just after 0800 was covered by the Hudson that had shot it down and subsequently by a Wellington (DF-S) of No 221 Squadron. Taking to their rubber dinghies without delay resulted in seven men being rescued by the British corvette HMS *Begonia*, the only fatality among the Condor crew being August Dollinger, a meteorological officer who had been killed by machine-gun fire from the Hudson.

Of the six men aboard the Condor the pilot and co-pilot, Josef Raczak, sustained wounds, believed not to have been serious, while radio operator Fw Karl Kebelhoer, second radio operator Gefr Josef Weid and B/M Obfw Heinrich Grube were reported to have come through their ordeal unscathed. The story of this Condor versus Hudson clash was given extensive coverage in the book *Coastal Command*, one of a number published by HMSO during the war years to provide the general public with an insight into the work of the British armed services.

The Luftwaffe did much the same with a series of booklets covering most aspects of the German military services, although it has to be said that as a recruiting tool the books appear to have been aimed at the more gullible German youngster; they were much shorter on hard facts than their British counterparts and full of flag-waving propaganda laced with deeds of daring in which the Germans invariably emerged triumphant. At least one of the books purported to cover a typical Focke-Wulf Condor sortie, with the German crew sallying forth to fight the good fight, never mind some important details that always seem to get in the way of a good story!

The 23 July clash highlighted the risks that a passive meteorological officer ran when occupying a seat in an operational aircraft engaged on a war flight. The gathering of weather data was vital to all aerial operations, but particularly to KG 40 and the Condor crews who regularly made room for an additional crew member on their operational rosters. Being injured or killed while simply taking atmospheric samples and other weather-related activities was cruel luck, and aircrews came to fully appreciate the high price that accurate forecasts could exact. The weather service assisted them in their daily duty of navigating around hostile storm fronts while seeking out enemy shipping in remote regions; without them the crews might face long hours of ploughing through hostile and dangerous fog, rain and low cloud. Equally, an inclement front could be used to their advantage if they knew its extent – information possibly denied to the crews of enemy vessels who may not have had access to similar up-to-the minute forecasts.

KG 40's airborne reconnaissance service took on great importance in the Battle of the Atlantic, as the unit's aircraft were able to seek out weather changes within the huge patrol arcs they were capable of covering. Few other aircraft in the Luftwaffe could match the Condor's endurance, and the weather forecasting service became part of KG 40's raison d'être.

Atlas and Rostock

If there was one item of equipment the Fw 200 could use to advantage as KG 40's patrol area widened to take in hundreds of square miles of featureless ocean, it was a radar that could detect ships with a fair degree of accuracy. Pin-pointing potential seaborne targets would curtail the time spent on what might have been an otherwise fruitless patrol, and would create the chance of sending more Allied war materiel to the bottom.

Early in July 1941 a test model of a 136 MHz Air-to-Surface Vessel (ASV) radar known as FuG Atlas-Echolot was installed in an Fw 200C-3/U3 (0064/F8+HH), which served as a prototype. However, early results were disappointing insofar as the equipment did not give sufficiently long-range detection. A second radar, FuG 216 Neptun-S, showed little significant improvement. Installed in Fw 200C-4 0106/NT+BF, which may have additionally carried the KG 40 code F8+BH, Neptun was also judged not to be the answer to the ASV requirement.

The Gema company's ASV set known as FuG 217 Rostock (without any further classification) followed, the development of this 120 MHz set having benefited from the examination of a British H2S radar from a wrecked bomber. Available for testing in a Fw 200C-4/U3 (0130/VY+OD) by the end of 1941, the Rostock set had its detection range boosted to 37 miles (60km). Externally, the elegant nose of the Focke-Wulf Condor now sprouted several dipoles supported by long horizontal bracing struts to position them in front of the aircraft. Additional transmit-receive antennae were positioned above and below the Condor's wing surface outboard of the engines.

An azimuth antennae array for the FuG 216 Neptun-S ASV – air to surface vessel – radar had to be located on the fuselage, as this Condor shows. The aircraft (F8+BH) is jacked up in a flying attitude for swinging the compasses, probably to obtain a more representative test reading from the radar scope. A. Price

It is not known how many flights were needed to thoroughly test FuG 217, but the above Condor, which retained the code VY+OD when on the strength of III./KG 40, was probably still carrying out radar-related test flights when it was badly damaged in a crash on 2 November 1943. The subsequent accident report stated that the pilot was responsible for the 30 per cent damage sustained by the aircraft. Incidentally, the records state that the aircraft was 'non-operational' at Doberitz when the accident occurred. Its subsequent fate is unknown, but in any event these test flights appear to have satisfied the technical staff that ordering Rostock sets for the ASV role would be advantageous to Condor operations.

The radar engineers were pleased to have several Condors at their disposal for test purposes as, although their industry tried to make electronic equipment as compact as possible, cramming such items into limited space was not ideal. Test aircraft such as the otherwise reliable Ju 88 had not always proved to be satisfactory, and a number of crashes had occurred.

With Rostock sets installed in a small number of their Fw 200C-4s, KG 40's crews were able to practise detecting ships at a greater range than previously. The electronic aid was an undoubted asset to the tracking of surface targets although the early radars required a high degree of concentration on the part of the operator and a familiarity with the behaviour of radio waves to correctly interpret exactly what the radar beam was transmitting back to a small screen in the aircraft. Only time would give the operators the ability to sort genuine targets from the confusing sea of 'clutter' that plagued almost all of the early airborne radars.

'Night-fighter' radar

More refined was the high-resolution FuG 200 Hohentweil, a major step forward in the development and reliability of German airborne radar. Operating on a 54cm wavelength, this set transmitted a concentrated beam of energy over a range of 50 miles (80km), which enabled clear-definition images of ships to be 'read', and, if necessary, assistance could be given to blind bombing attacks carried out from high altitude.

Adapted to air-to-surface search, Hohentweil was first installed in a Condor during late 1941. Thereafter aircraft were equipped as the sets became available, although the output rate was quite slow and it might be months before an individual aircraft could have the necessary aerial array, power generator and 'scope' fitted, tested and cleared for operational use. Inside the Fw 200 a radar operator shared the position formerly the sole domain of the crew's radio operator.

As FuG 200 sets were virtually 'hand built', initially for use by the Nachtjagd, it took almost a year for III./KG 40 to get it installed in sixteen of the twenty-six Condors it then had on strength. Coming into service when it did, the improved radar more or less coincided with the decline of the Condor as a maritime search-and-combat aircraft. Not all of KG 40's aircraft were equipped with radar and the number of successful sinkings as a direct result of electronic detection is believed to have been quite modest, due mainly to the changing nature of the Atlantic battle.

Torpedo revival

Diversion of specialised aircraft for supplementary roles was a challenge faced by numerous wartime commanders, and KG 40 was no exception. The Fw 200's valuable cargo capacity had been utilised on several occasions earlier in the conflict and the aircraft's size led to it being the centre of several experiments, not all of which were put into practice for various reasons. A further development of the Condor's ability to haul substantial loads led in August 1941 to another new idea. KG 40 was obliged to loan six Fw 200s for a proposed torpedo attack role in the Mediterranean. These were aircraft of 9./Staffel, a unit that had only existed since April 1941, having been formed from a nucleus of personnel of 3./KG 1.

Having begun war operations with very few modern aircraft that were capable of launching torpedoes, the Luftwaffe had since initiated low-priority training of selected bomber crews to deliver the weapon. The primary types chosen for this demanding role were the He 111 and Ju 88 and, having perfected the launching technique, the Germans suddenly became enthusiastic and put considerable faith in the torpedo as the primary anti-shipping weapon. This philosophy, undoubtedly influenced by the fame garnered by the Regia Aeronautica with its SM 79-equipped units, continued to be adhered to despite evidence to the contrary. The growing strength of the opposition had reached the point that, when KG 26 and other units began an anti-shipping offensive with torpedoes, it was found – as with so many aspects of aerial warfare – that the German response was 'too little and too late'. Moreover, in the case of the Condor, 'wrong aircraft' could well be added. It was left to He 111s and Ju 88/188s to execute Luftwaffe torpedo attacks by converted bombers, which their crews carried out with efficiency and courage. They were of course limited by the range of their twin-engine aircraft, hence the interest in bringing the Condor into the picture, even though it was quite unsuited to the role.

Trying to overcome the conundrum of equipping an aircraft with the necessary range to seek out shipping far from land bases, an Fw 200 torpedo-carrier may, however, have had some merit. Several drawbacks were conveniently put aside and the Luftwaffe pressed ahead with crew training and tests to the point of mounting a trial operation.

Much of the enthusiasm for torpedo bombing using the Condor stemmed from Martin Harlinghausen, who, it will be recalled, was the driving force behind the establishment of KG 40 as a long-range maritime force. Harlinghausen had looked closely at the options open to the Luftwaffe quite soon after Fl K X arrived in Tripoli. Of these, crippling the Suez Canal and thus denying passage to Allied vessels was a clear priority, despite the difficulties involved. Not the least of these was the distance of the canal from the main base for the aircraft that would be used in such an operation, at Benghazi.

White-jacketed Major Martin Harlinghausen with Hauptmann Daser (far left) and Major Petersen (centre) with other members of KG 40 at Bordeaux. Harlinghausen, an officer dedicated to anti-shipping work, had a long and distinguished career in Luftwaffe maritime aviation and rose in rank after the war. *F. Selinger*

Under imminent threat of capture by British forces, Benghazi was some 700 miles (1,125km) from Suez. Flying from the island of Rhodes would have been a safer option, but the Germans had not as yet stocked the local airfield with fuel. Harlinghausen therefore launched the operation – which was aimed at sinking numerous ships of a reported British convoy and blocking the canal – from Benghazi, leading the He 111 force himself with Hptm Robert Kowalewski piloting his aircraft. Various factors combined to turn the raid into a minor disaster; starved of fuel, all the Heinkels were on their return scattered over several desert landing grounds – in a few instances the wrong landing grounds – leading to the capture of their crews. Only one made it back to base.

Despite this setback, Harlinghausen's bold plan, which for a time became known as the Suez Kommando, expanded to the point that X./KG 40 despatched Fw 200A-0 S-5 F8+EU to Athens-Eleusis during the year to undertake a support (transport) role. This venerable machine retained its original engines, complete with two-bladed propellers, at that time. Although the Condor is not widely associated with operations in the Mediterranean, the presence of Harlinghausen's small unit probably lent impetus to the torpedo Condor idea, which was pushed ahead. A brief experimental programme appeared to confirm that a Condor was capable of launching a pair of standard LT 5 torpedoes from its outer wing racks, provided that the flap area immediately in line with the racks was modified by a cut-out to enable the fins of the weapon, which was 15 feet (4.5 metres) long, to clear the aircraft cleanly.

Operational testing soon highlighted the difficulties: torpedo-bombing required precision flying of a high order, and was beset with numerous possibilities of malfunction if the speed and altitude of the carrier aircraft did not meet tight parameters. If the aircraft released the weapon at too high an altitude the attack was as good as doomed as the torpedo would nose dive. In short, the torpedo was not really a viable weapon for the Condor, an aircraft that had no special sighting equipment to align it on the target and had never possessed the acceleration or rate of climb to get well clear of the intended target before it reacted with AA fire. Also, flying low over water at the heights necessary for accurate torpedo release could create buffeting that threatened to overstress the airframe.

Training of crews (using the six 9./Staffel machines, which included F8+GH) soon revealed the Condor's unsuitability as a torpedo bomber, an initial operation on 30 December proving abortive. Soon afterwards a need to utilise the aircraft, based mainly at Catania in Sicily, on transport duties ended the initial attempt at turning the Fw 200 into a torpedo bomber, much to the relief of the 'pioneers' who were handed the considerable responsibility of proving that a large, structurally weak aircraft could effectively meet that task!

A small but significant confirmation of the temporary nature of the Mediterranean secondment was the fact that the Condors appeared to have received no modification to their original paintwork. Usually Luftwaffe aircraft operating in the Mediterranean area had a white fuselage band applied together with white outer panels on the undersides of the wings, but there is little or no photographic proof of these markings being applied to the Condors.

A representative view of an Fw 200C-3, in this case F8+GH, with open cowling flaps, the Fw 19 dorsal turret and 'regulation' treatment of the aircraft's individual letter below the port wing, which in this case is white, denoting 1./Staffel.

Harlinghausen was not, however, about to let the matter drop. For some time torpedo training continued for selected KG 40 crews. The manufacturers of the Condor were brought into the programme insofar as modifications for torpedo carriage resulted in a small batch of twenty-five C-3/U4s being fitted with racks and the necessary wiring and so forth to enable them to launch two torpedoes. There were enough doubts as to whether the Condor could be turned into an effective anti-shipping weapon – not the least of which were those voiced by the crews – but Petersen's enthusiasm drove the concept forward. This was despite mounting evidence that the superiority of the torpedo was losing credibility as the nature of maritime warfare changed and German guided weapons became a reality. These latter seemed to represent a much more viable and safer method of attacking enemy ships – but it had to be taken into account that not all war theatres had decisive numbers of escorts for vulnerable merchant ships or air cover from carriers. German bombers could still strike effectively given weak opposition in areas such as the far northern latitudes that included the Russian ports for convoys from Britain.

The airborne torpedo itself was the subject of a lengthy international programme to make the basic weapon more effective – specifically to overcome the tendency of all torpedoes to nose dive if they were released at too high an altitude – by the addition of wing and tail surfaces. This came to fruition in the LT 950, which was not proceeded with and did not enter operational service.

Some German aerial torpedoes were fitted with a wooden 'air tail' similar to that found necessary on similar British weapons carried by RAF strike aircraft. This detachable wooden tail bestowed the necessary stability immediately the torpedo was released from a carrier aircraft such as the He 111 and Ju 88. Using standard aerial torpedoes, both types met with some success but, as related, this did not appear to extend to the aircraft of IX./KG 40. While the prospect of the Fw 200 carrying torpedoes was not entirely ruled out, the war situation changed yet again to the point that the Mediterranean area was quite unsafe for numerous Luftwaffe transport aircraft – and that in effect included the Condor.

Further attrition

Another Condor was lost to KG 40's inventory on or about 9 July when the aircraft piloted by Oberlt Rohrbach went down into the North Sea of the north-western coast of Holland. Some losses – not necessarily the one mentioned above – were reportedly the result of the German crews being confused by signals from British directional beacons that operated on the same frequency as those situated in France and used regularly by the Luftwaffe. Using the Elektra system, KG 40 received an excellent directional service by several ground stations including that at the big naval base at Norddeich.

Operational attrition suffered by KG 40 varied due to a number of factors – and the vagaries of weather and/or enemy activity made no concessions to pilot experience. This was demonstrated forcibly on 16 July when a Condor with Oberfw Rowald at the controls failed to return. With more than one hundred war flights behind him, men like Rowald were the backbone of KG 40 and under different circumstances his experience would have been spread widely among younger crew members via the unit's training organisation. This latter continued to function until 1944, the Fw 200 then being grouped in 12./Staffel prior to its disbandment at Lechfeld on 11-12 April.

On 24 July the waters off Ireland claimed the life of Hptm Konrad Verlohr and his five-man crew when their Fw 200C-3 (0026/F8+CH) of I./Gruppe went into the sea west of Ireland. Verlohr was then the Kapitän of 1./Staffel.

New threat

In the Atlantic, improved Allied counter-measures to KG 40's long-range patrols were gradually coming into operational use. One was nearly revealed on (18 July 1941) 8 August 1941 when an Fw 200C-3 (0066/KF+QF) suddenly took fire in the starboard wing and promptly crashed into the sea. Having attacked a freighter and set it on fire, the Condor had been about to deliver the coup de grâce when gunners on an accompanying vessel found its range. Apparently unseen by the Germans, their aircraft, with Uffz Hansek in command of a five-man crew, was also on the point of coming under attack from a single-engine fighter, far from any shore base. This was Fleet Air Arm Hurricane W2977 of 804 Squadron, which had been carried by the Naval Auxiliary Vessel *Maplin*

On this occasion the pilot, Lt (A) R. W. H. 'Bob' Everett, RNVR, never had a chance to use his guns before the Condor went down. Everett headed for home, stretching his fuel enough to reach St Angelo on the shores of Lough Erne in Ireland. Before the month was out he would get a real crack at a Condor.

Before that, on 23 July, KG 40 lost Fw 200C F8+BB, another victim of the unforgiving ocean. The aircraft went down some 150 miles (240km) off the west coast of Ireland.

First blood to a 'catafighter'

On 31 July *Maplin* sailed to meet a convoy outbound from Sierra Leone, and on 3 August Everett was the duty pilot when a Condor was sighted to the south of the ship. Having launched, Everett cursed the poor acceleration of the Hurricane Mk IA he was flying. When he did overhaul the Condor, the German crew put up a spirited defence, ultimately to no avail as the Hurricane's machine-gun fire found its mark. The Condor went into the sea, as did Everett's Hurricane. In line with standing orders for pilots of the catapulted fighters, he ditched as near as possible to a naval escort and, after some anxious moments extricating himself from the cockpit under water, was rescued by the destroyer HMS *Wanderer*.

There were further isolated skirmishes between Fw 200s and single Hurricanes, although U-boats took a toll of the latter's parent ships. Not until 25 October 1942 was another Condor lost to this cause. Flown by Oblt Arno Gross, Fw 200C-3/U4 0070/F8+DS and its six-man crew was attacked during an anti-shipping sortie and destroyed by a Hurricane flown by F/O Norman Taylor, who had launched from the bow catapult of the SS *Empire Heath* while escorting convoy HG.91 to Gibraltar. The combat occurred some 300 miles (480km) off the coast of Portugal.

Although the Focke-Wulf 200 had played a very minor part in the attack on the British Isles the previous summer, Fliegerführer Atlantik's bomber and seaplane force was, one year on from its formation, handed the responsibility of patrolling the English Channel and the Western Approaches to reduce the movement of British coastal convoys. These aircraft, together with a number of Kampfgruppen that remained in France when Hitler attacked Russia, could only maintain a very limited cross-Channel offensive until such time as the bulk of the Kampfgeschwader returned from the Eastern Front. Once Russia had been defeated Hitler made it known that he fully intended to resume the attack and force Britain into submission. In the meantime the following units were to continue a war of attrition against coastal shipping and the vessels comprising ocean-going convoys into and out of British ports:

I./KG 40 (Fw 200)

II./KG 40 (Do 217)

III./KG 40 (He 111)

KGr 606 (Ju 88)

KuFlGr 106 (Ju 88)

2./506 (Ju 88)

1./906 (He 115)

5./906 (Ar 196/He 114)

Early in August 1941 these units represented a force of 151 aircraft and, added to those of KG 2 with Do 217s and KG 30's Ju 88s, which had been retained in France to undertake strategic attacks on British targets, the force seemed impressive enough. But by mid-month the number of serviceable aircraft at the disposal of Fliegerführer Atlantik was put at only sixty-eight machines. This total would fluctuate and be boosted significantly by the 'heavyweight' Dorniers and Ju 88s, but the number of important targets in the UK was enormous, far too numerous for such a force to cause any lasting damage, given the Luftwaffe's general tactics of spreading its bombing effort thinly over several of them. With the seaplanes covering the inshore shipping lanes – operations that ran an increased risk from the defences – the Condors were better employed plying their trade at longer range and continuing very much as an independent force by dint of the aircraft's unique and (for the time being) unchallenged capabilities. At least Fliegerführer Atlantik was able to retain enough aircraft to mount requisite operational sorties from mid-1941, for most of the Kampfgeschwader had been posted to the East to participate in Operation 'Barbarossa' beginning on 22 June.

Changing fortunes

Throughout 1941 KG 40 crews participated in the independent sinking of several more Allied ships and the directing of groups of U-boats onto others, not always successfully. On 21 August the Condor aircrews sighted a convoy and reported the fact to Befehlshaber der U-boote (B.d.U), which reacted in the usual fashion, but the submarines failed to locate any of the ships. An attempt to home an eight-strong U-boat wolf pack onto convoy OG.72 on 1 September also failed. On 18 September another RK went to a member of KG 40 when Austrian-born Oberlt Rudolf Mons of I./Gruppe was decorated; at that time his unit was stated to have sunk 63,000grt of Allied shipping.

Oblt Rudolf Mons was one of KG 40's outstanding pilots who led many shipping attacks and quickly ran up his own personal score. His prowess at the controls of a Focke-Wulf Condor was recognised with the award of the Ritterkreuz on 18 September 1941. *F. Selinger*

Battling the Martlets

While single fighters carried aboard the CAM ships were an irritation to the German aircrews, several of whom flew off when confronted by an enemy fighter where one was quite unexpected, the effectiveness of their main offensive weapon was limited as, after a launch, the aircraft could not 'land on' but had to ditch. Also, the elderly Hurricane Mk IAs (which also lacked folding wings) used for the purpose were armed only with 0.303-inch machine-guns, which were not nearly as effective as cannon. But the mere presence of a fighter in mid-Atlantic served as a deterrent, one that made the Condor crews wary of an enemy response that was 100 per cent more dangerous than AA fire from ships.

As well as Hurricanes the freighters with bow catapults mounted the Fairey Fulmar. Similarly armed with eight Brownings, the Fulmar was well liked by its two-man crew and the aircraft was quite manoeuvrable, despite being larger than a Hurricane. Several Condors were chased away from their intended targets by the British fighters, although the limitations of the 'one-way' catapult scheme were clear, particularly if trained pilots could not be picked up and were lost.

More conventional Allied fighter cover for shipping was being increased by the provision of small escort carriers (so small and cheap that they were jokingly said to be purchased in Woolworths!). So for a time 'Woolworth carrier' it was. In addition, more warships were being built in British yards and these would eventually prove overwhelming to German aircraft and U-boats alike.

But it was the potency of the escort carrier that would give most concern to the Condor crews, as was demonstrated forcibly on 21 September 1941 when an Fw 200C-3/U4 (0078/F8+EL) flown by Lt Georg Schaffranek was intercepted and shot down by three Grumman Wildcats of 802 Squadron from the first Royal Navy escort carrier, HMS *Audacity*. Having taken off from Cognac at 0655, the Condor crew had been briefed to detect a convoy reported by a U-boat near PLQ 35W/3056. Whether or not the German aircrew came across any Allied ships is unknown, but their fate was sealed when *Audacity*'s aircraft intercepted their Condor.

In terms of fighters that effectively combated long-range German bombers, the true answer was the Merchant Aircraft Carrier and the Grumman F4F Wildcat. Initially known by the FAA as the Martlet, this tough little American fighter was sent to sea on equally tiny aircraft carriers ensuring that pilots at least had a place to land after combat. The example seen here (BJ513) is a Martlet I allocated to the Royal Navy. *Author's collection*

The modest size of the escort carriers based on the hulls of merchant ships meant they had limited aircraft capacity – but they could be built quickly and, with a complement of Wildcat fighters, they proved lethal to several Condor crews. HMS *Alexia* has a typical 'Woolworth carrier' configuration. *IWM*

By an odd coincidence *Audacity* had not been built in a British shipyard. She had gone down a German slipway as the freighter *Hannover*, and had since become a British 'war prize' and converted by fixing a flight deck over the cut-down merchant ship superstructure. As a freighter she was originally re-named *Empire Audacity* until commissioning as a naval vessel as HMS *Audacity*. The little carrier was well named: there was no conventional island to control operations as in a fleet carrier, and embarked aircraft had no hangarage. All servicing had to be carried out on the open with aircraft ranged down the centre of the flight deck. It was a wet, cold and dangerous business for everyone aboard, irrespective of rank or function. But as the pioneers of a war-winning concept, the individuals who manned the 'Jeep carriers', as the Americans called them, proved their worth against the German raiders at a time when the Royal Navy's air strike capability was thinly stretched.

The experiences of a CAM ship pilot were quite different from those on an escort carrier, however small it was. Taking off from a postage-stamp-sized flight deck in an Atlantic swell could bring about moments of high drama for the pilots, who at least had a place to return to after a sortie. This was in stark contrast to their catapult fighter colleagues whose 'airfield' was any location in RAF or RN hands. But the reality was often that airfields were quite out of range, in which case the fighter pilot chose any 'flat' area of ocean, hopefully with a friendly vessel nearby.

One of the first American aircraft to benefit Britain under the Lend-Lease agreement, the Grumman F4F (initially named Martlet Mk I or II under British nomenclature) was a sturdy little fighter armed with a mixture of 0.30 and 0.50-inch machine-guns. The latter weapon was standard on most US wartime fighters and proved a very reliable weapon in combat, its weight of fire effectively bridging the gap between the rifle-calibre .30 and the 20mm cannon.

Selected to be the Fleet Air Arm fighter type embarked on the first of the 'Woolworth carriers', Martlets provided the Navy pilots with valuable experience in carrier operations, often under less than ideal conditions. The small carriers pitched and rolled on their merchant ship hulls and many a 'hairy' incident alerted pilots and handlers alike to the drawbacks of deploying such vessels. But at the time nothing else was available. Fleet carriers, almost worth their weight in gold, simply could not be spared to undertake convoy escort work. In the meantime the men of the 'Woolworth/Jeep carriers' bravely filled the gap.

On 21 September *Audacity*'s shipborne fighter element was six Martlet IIs of 802 Squadron, FAA. Protecting convoy OG.74 outbound from Britain (see Table 5 for the codes allocated to convoys sailing to and from the UK) by searching for U-boats threatening the Allied ships, Sub Lieutenants N. H. Patterson and G. R. P. Fletcher instead came upon Hptm de la Franck's Condor from III./KG 40. Intent on bombing several ships that had previously been torpedoed, the German crew tried in vain to evade fire from the American fighters. The FAA pilots poured a combined 320 rounds of 0.50-inch or (in American parlance) 'fifty caliber' ammunition into the Condor and reportedly completely severed its tail. All six members of the Condor crew perished.

Five ships were lost from the convoy, although this 'raising of the stakes' in Allied convoy protection posed a potentially serious threat to the Condor force, and on 8 November this was highlighted by the loss of an Fw 200C-3/U4 (0083/F8+EL). Flying his second sortie of the day, Oblt Karl Kruger's 3./Staffel crew gave a good account of themselves and shot down the Martlet I (BJ516) flown by 802's CO, Lt Cdr John Wintour. Having set the enemy aircraft alight, Wintour was probably the victim of an accurate burst by one of the German gunners who sent it down. A second Martlet, flown by Sub Lt Hutchinson, attacked and destroyed the Condor, but the loss of Wintour with his experience and enthusiasm was widely felt at a difficult time. All members of Kruger's crew of five perished when their aircraft fell into the sea off the west coast of Portugal. They too would be mourned and their operational experience missed.

December

Five days into the final month of what had been a highly successful year for KG 40, the attrition rate took another upward notch when Fw Ludwig Kogel crashed near Cognac airfield while flying Fw 200C-3/U4 0085 KE+II (or KE+IJ). All six members of the crew perished.

A large-scale assault on convoy HG.76 by the Seerauber U-boat group began on 14 December. Faced with a target comprising thirty-two ships and the 36th Escort Group, the five-strong U-boat group bided it time; one of the Condors sighted the convoy at midday on the 16th and the U-boats struck. Mixed success followed, with the escort group scoring hits on submarines, they in their turn sending a number of vessels to the bottom. Not untypically the action went on for several days.

On 19 December 1941 two more Condors were shot down by *Audacity*'s Martlets, these being Fw 200C-3/U4s 0086/F8+IH and 0073/F8+IH, flown respectively by Oberleutnants Hans Hase and Herbert Schreyer. KG 40 thus lost more valuable crewmen; all six aboard Schreyer's aircraft perished, but there may have been survivors when the Condor flown by Hase of 3./Staffel came down off the west coast of Portugal. Oblt Schreyer, a member of 1./Staffel, attempted a crash-landing at Ramales in the Santander area of Spain but all the crew were killed in the subsequent crash. *Audacity*'s tally of Condors got no higher than an impressive five, as she was sunk by U-751 (Lt Cdr Bigalk) on the night of 21/22 December as part of the operation to protect the ships of HG.76.

By then the Americans were combatants in the Battle of the Atlantic; following the attack on Pearl Harbor on 7 December the ocean dividing the US and Europe would no longer be a hunting ground for German U-boats and aircraft to sink US or neutral vessels at will. Within months the war would for Germany take on a deadly turn that would eventually prove fatal.

By February 1941 I./KG 40's tally of Allied ships sunk had risen to a total of eighty-five since the first vessel had been sent to the bottom on 1 August 1940. From the original twelve aircraft per Staffel, the total complement of the three component Staffeln had not increased at all, but had during the intervening months been maintained at a nominal thirty-six. And despite the gradually increasing strength of the opposition towards the end of this period, the sole maritime Kampfgeschwader soldiered on; a second Gruppe (III./KG 40) equipped with He 111s was added to the Geschwader in April 1941 with a third (II./KG 40) being formed to go operational that May.

By mid-1941, IV./, V./ and VI./KG 40 were operational with Condors, although the misfortunes of war meant that III./Gruppe only deployed the type in the anti-shipping role from mid-1943, following reorganisation after nine aircraft were lost to inventory flying transport sorties at Stalingrad.

The expansion of KG 40 in 1941 had resulted in a significant increase in utilisation of the Condors, their crews marking out the year as a whole as the unit's most successful to date with a steady rise in the experience of replacement crews. Available figures recorded that, in March, fifty-five sorties were flown, with seventy-four in April and sixty-two in November.

The end result of these operations hardly made comfortable reading in the Whitehall corridors of power, yet the British Government failed to find an effective counter to KG 40 for many months.

For the Germans, using their own fighters to protect bombers and transports was the least favourable duty for many a fighter pilot. The Condors chugged along at 123mph (198kmph) while the fighters' engines overheated and the Jagdflieger watched the featureless ocean with rising apprehension. It took little imagination to realise just how long a man would last if he had the misfortune to ditch and to take to his rubber dinghy. Even if the Seenotdienst was alerted to his plight without delay, he would be frozen and hungry by the time he was plucked from the sea. Condor crews had been down that hypothetical path often enough and they had no choice but to shrug off the risk they ran every time they hauled their big airliner-cum-bomber off the runway. Fortunately for them, German rescue dinghies stowed aboard aircraft were well-equipped to keep their occupants dry and fed for several hours.

Part of the expansion of KG 40 was that III./Gruppe could be partly based at Cognac and Bordeaux, giving the unit more flexibility and a marginally more direct flight to the patrol areas allocated in different sectors. III./KG 40's Kommandeur was (from September 1943) Major Robert Kowalewski, the former Fliegerführer Atlantik operations officer, who had been awarded the Ritterkreuz on 24 November 1940.

An Erganzungstaffel (training squadron) had been attached to KG 40 from October 1940 and this now provided the nucleus of Stab.IV./KG 40, itself established in July 1941. During that August, 10./, 11./ and 12./Staffeln were officially formed as subordinate units of IV./Gruppe, also to operate the Fw 200.

Numerous propaganda photographs of KG 40's aircraft were taken during the early months of the Battle of the Atlantic, the purpose being to demonstrate the power of the Luftwaffe in what became a vital struggle for control of Britain's trade routes. Awaiting inspection are machines of I./Gruppe at Bordeaux-Merignac in 1941.

FOCKE-WULF FW 200 CONDOR

Abortive tactic

Shipping attack techniques by Condors remained the tried and tested bombing and strafing, but during the course of the year the torpedo bombing experiment had been further explored. This had worked through to the point that crews trained in this form of attack had returned from Sicily to France, anticipating their first recorded success.

On 13 December 1941 KG 40 despatched a long-range torpedo-armed sortie from Bordeaux, comprising Fw 200C F8+KH under the command of Lt Gose and his crew, with Obfw Wall as radio operator. After more than twelve hours in the air Gose returned to Rennes. No details of his flight or any results were apparently released.

On 30 December a torpedo-carrying Condor was able to initiate an attack on a lone British steamer near the coast of Portugal. On this occasion three torpedoes were reportedly launched, but again no actual results were claimed. Despite the inherent drawbacks of attempting to turn such a large aircraft into an effective torpedo bomber, crews from KG 40 were still being seconded from France to take the torpedo course at Lecce as 1941 came to an end. Edgar Petersen was nothing if not optimistic about turning the Condor into a torpedo bomber.

Production pool

A further attempt – one of many aimed at a similar end result during the war – at rationalising the output of the German aircraft industry took place during 1941. On 15 August Erhard Milch announced formation of a Ring Organisation for the industry, this being a 'pooling' arrangement of all the leading firms, each controlling a network of smaller suppliers. This was not new: similar groupings of companies had been attempted before and in essence were well under way, but this latest version of the plan was to be made permanent. It was primarily aimed at speeding up the final assembly of aircraft, and Focke-Wulf AG became one of thirteen firms selected as a central controller with numerous smaller concerns supplying all manner of components. By then Focke-Wulf AG was running assembly plants under the aegis of Aero, AGO, Arado, Fiesler, Gotha and MIAG.

Production projections

Through all this behind-the-scenes upheaval, the one long-range aircraft the Luftwaffe had in service survived any culling that was found to be necessary with other types. This was primarily as a result of continual delays with the He 177, which, despite having made its maiden flight on 20 November 1939, was far from ready for full-scale Luftwaffe service. Months of tests lay ahead, many of them being of a 'troubleshooting' nature aimed at bringing the complex coupled DB 605 engines to a point of reliability, free of fires and in-flight malfunctions. As a result of these delays there was little choice but to keep the Condor in production and, according to the RLM GL/A Supply Programme 222 figures of 1 July 1942, 115 Fw 200C-3s had been delivered by 30 June of that year; two aircraft were then behind schedule – and the projected delivery total (to 30 September 1944) was put at 124 aircraft, with another production termination date quoted as March 1944.

Main assembly of the early Fw 200 airframes continued to take place in Bremen, the company having expanded rapidly once the war had begun.

Over the period 1940-42 completion of Condor airframes in terms of component sub-assembly was well dispersed, with sections of the Fw 200C-3, the first fully militarised variant, being built at five main plants: Tutow, Marienburg in West Prussia, Sorau in Silesia, Lubeck, and Johannisthal in Germany.

Final assembly was carried out at Posen-Cottbus in Saxonia and Bremen. In addition, wing sections were completed at Weser, with Blohm und Voss at Finkenwerder also participating in final assembly and Mecklenburg also supplying component parts – clearly Focke-Wulf had achieved dispersal of Fw 200 output to quite an impressive degree.

Plants attacked

Focke-Wulf's additional plant space in and around the city and port of Bremen was to prove a natural target for RAF bombers, mainly because sea-land contours showed up well, even without any electronic aids. Later, when RAF bombers were increasingly fitted with H2S radar, the port area stood out unmistakeably on their radar screens.

The first attack on the port facilities had taken place on 12 January 1941, by which time Focke-Wulf had, with the above-listed network, become the first German aviation manufacturer to achieve dispersion on such a scale. While the primary aim of putting the new plants beyond the range of British bombers was met for a short period, few industrialists could have envisaged the rapidity with which the air war would change and threaten their factories. When the Americans opened a long-range daylight offensive from Britain in mid-1942 and the RAF extended its reach at night with new and improved four-engined aircraft, the danger was crystal clear.

Airframe, engine and test centres came increasingly under attack, with the grim assumption by the German managers and factory workforce that they would most likely continue to be bombed until production capability was totally destroyed. Such pessimism was well founded. All the major aircraft and associated component manufacturers became subject to air raids to a greater or lesser degree, and the fact that Focke-Wulf's output included one of the deadliest fighters of the war put the company's plants at the top of the Allied target list.

The smoothly organised delivery of types such as the Fw 200 suffered – if only indirectly – from the enemy's air offensive. With the Fw 190 having become the company's top-priority aircraft type (as, for different reasons, it was for the 8th Army Air Force), fighter production plants were most at risk. The company took steps to ensure that minimum damage and disruption was caused by Allied bombing, and a programme of strengthening the most important buildings was initiated so that, despite the round-the-clock incursions by a burgeoning enemy bomber force, aircraft numbers were not too adversely affected. However, when USAAF heavies began to specifically target the dispersed plants, further steps had to be taken.

It soon became clear that it was Focke-Wulf's fighters that the Americans were after, not specifically the Condor or other types. Output of the Condor continued at a steady pace, to reach the eventual grand total of 268 aircraft. This figure was often quoted as too low for KG 40's requirements, and the company was indirectly criticised for its production rate, which was slow and unable to always keep abreast of operational losses, not to mention accidents that prevented individual Condors under repair from seeing action for weeks, if not months. Regular overhauls were also necessary to keep the Condors in good mechanical order and, unlike many other aircraft, they had to be kept free of the corrosive salt that is always present in seawater.

KG 40 could undoubtedly have been a more effective anti-shipping force had it had fifty to seventy-five machines on strength in 1939-41 when it faced far less enemy opposition than would materialise in 1942-43. Nevertheless, considering that the Fw 200 was one of the largest aircraft being built in Germany, the total number of machines completed represented an enormous effort on the part of the company workforce, not to mention the road and rail system that delivered raw materials and components to the various factories. And from late 1943 the German transport system was continually battered by Allied aircraft to further disrupt the smooth flow of new aircraft 'off the line'.

Most components fresh from the factories had to be loaded onto trains for shipment to the final assembly point and, despite the Allied air forces' attempt to disrupt such movement, production figures tend to confirm that most of the components arrived at their destination. In common with other manufacturers Focke-Wulf was building several different aircraft at the same time, although as the Fw 190/Ta 152 eventually took precedence over all other types, the company diverted relatively few resources into new projects. But for the unique nature of its operational deployment there is little doubt that the Condor would have been cancelled some months before the changing war situation forced this to happen. Other factors ensured that Fw 200 production was tailed off to terminate early in 1944, almost certainly without having compromised fighter production to any significant degree. In any event this would certainly have been ordered by the Jagerstab later in 1944, if only to better channel (as the High Command saw it) the raw materials used to build Condors and other bomber and night-fighter types into more urgent production.

Through no fault of its own Focke-Wulf had (ironically enough) reached something akin to the situation that Hitler and the High Command had envisaged before the war had even started. Insofar as the reasons were different and the decision to concentrate on building scores of twin-engine bombers prior to any military input from operational experience was almost fatally flawed, there were similarities. With the future progress of the war an unknown factor, OKL, via Führer directives, curtailed the building of nearly all four-engine aircraft to save on materials at a time when supply was adequate and running smoothly enough. In 1944 material supply was under dire threat and stocks had to be reserved for the one category of combat aircraft area that might save Germany at the eleventh hour – fighters, fighters and more fighters.

Prisoner input

As KG 40's exploits increased, the British were naturally curious to know more about the day-to-day activities of the unit, which seemed to be flying the only four-engine combat aircraft in the Luftwaffe. A sizeable dossier was compiled as the number of ships sunk by air attack steadily rose; practical counter-measures were few in the early days of the war and the Condor's deadly reputation continued to grow until more aggressive steps could be taken by the unit's seaborne targets to provide them with something with which to hit back. Available options to do so remained slim for many months, however, and the catalogue of ships sunk or damaged by the big aircraft showed little sign of decreasing.

Many individuals, including those who were responsible for the British mercantile marine and the Naval escort force, together with the officers of RAF Coastal Command and right up to Prime Minister Winston Churchill and the war cabinet, took the Condor threat very seriously indeed. Churchill knew that if a way could not be found to rein in KG 40 the already dangerous situation whereby shipping losses were exceeding the number of new ships rolling down the nation's slipways would continue. It was indeed fortunate for Britain that throughout most of the war she enjoyed the services of an excellent military intelligence organisation and vital inputs of data via the Ultra system.

By reading German military codes via their own Enigma decoding machines, the monitoring of Luftwaffe activity and that of the U-boat service took on a special importance.

Additional information on air force operations, personnel, aircraft and technical advances was derived from comprehensive interrogation of shot-down aircrew. When men who had served or were currently serving with KG 40 put their experiences in the hands of their captors, some strange anomalies were revealed. According to the meticulous post-interrogation reports that were compiled, prisoners understandably varied in the degree of data they were in a position to pass on. Much depended on the rank they held at the time and the degree or responsibility they had been given.

For obvious reasons the number of men recovered – mainly from the sea – from Fw 200s that had ditched were few in comparison with crews of the medium bomber units, a great many of which came down on land. Some of the observations they nevertheless made about the Condor were interesting and in one instance included the fact that the PoW's crew had never taken one to its maximum ceiling, so aircraft performance could not be commented upon. One reason given was that on some Condors, including the one this individual had flown, the high-altitude boost was sealed and could not be used. The booster (supercharger?) normally cut in at 3,000 metres. The rate of climb for the Fw 200 was quoted in the documents as 2-3 metres per second under 'general flight' conditions.

It was reported by some captured crews that the Condor had some technical restrictions that had to be adhered to: one example was that the high-altitude boost was sealed and could not be used, probably for a specific reason not transmitted to the crew who flew that individual aircraft. There could be several reasons for this situation, but it does appear that KG 40's crews were not always totally au fait with some aspects of performance.

Individual crew members did not shirk from sharing their doubts about flying in a Condor crew with their captors. Among the drawbacks they cited was the fact that, as the engines rotated in the same direction, a fully loaded Fw 200 was hard to hold in a straight line during the take-off run. They also felt the overall design to be poor – whether or not they were talking about the original civil configuration or the military compromise they were obliged to fly is unknown, but the degree of armour plate protection for the military Condor's crew positions was also felt to be inadequate. Those who had to fly it took a more sanguine view. Having experienced some of the detrimental results of trying to turn an airliner into a military weapon, the crews of KG 40 with less reverence and a lacing of typical aviators' black humour dubbed the Fw 200 the 'Stanniol Bomber' or 'tin-foil bomber'.

An implied superficial level of training was also detected in some aircrew interrogation reports; depending on the number of hours many of them spent in the air it was also surprising to learn that certain crews had not flown the aircraft to the limits, some to the point that they had never taken the Condor to its maximum ceiling. Although the Geschwader's first crews had numerous operational hours on the type, there were individual officers who joined KG 40 with less than three war flights to their credit; this appears to have been common at the mid-to-late period of the war, almost certainly following the loss of highly experienced pilots and a resultant influx of recently qualified trainees who would not have been allocated the time to gain much operational experience or build up their flying hours.

Captured aircrew of KG 40 also often expressed a frustration over the weakness of the military Condor conversion (with the implication that they would have preferred to have been flying something else), but most knew that there was nothing else. That was certainly true during the early part of the war – the Condor's anti-shipping heyday – but later, had they remained with KG 40, they would have converted to the He 177. A transfer may even have brought them into contact with the sturdy Ju 290. Neither aircraft was exactly trouble-free in a maritime role or a match for enemy fighters. In view of what happened to the Luftwaffe's maritime reconnaissance force through circumstance, these men may have adopted a different view had they not prematurely ended their careers in an Allied prison camp.

Comments as to how the crews viewed the Fw 200 as a combat aircraft were also revealing. Most views were tempered by personal preference, which in turn depended on how many different aircraft the individual had flown or crewed since the war began. If no comparison with other types could be made, the views expressed were perhaps more valuable vis-à-vis the unique role of the Fw 200. And the above-mentioned unfamiliarity with one aspect of the Condor's performance was not an isolated case, giving the impression that some crewmen, depending on rank and experience, were only informed about a given function aboard the aircraft on a 'need to know' basis. This usually applied to something that was not an integral part of the Condor's performance on a typical operational sortie.

Chapter 7

1942: Airlifts and convoy-hunting

January

Critical calls on construction priorities affecting the Condor were not being made on 4 January 1942 when Lt Gose undertook a further flight from Bordeaux in Condor F8+KH. Gose was flying an intended anti-shipping sortie, reportedly with torpedoes under the wings of his Condor, but after nine hours in the air he again returned without reporting any results. Similar training sorties continued at Lecce, and three days later an Fw 200C-3/U1 (0052/DE+OG) suffered 25 per cent damage during torpedo training, but whether this was while the machine was airborne or on the ground is unknown.

I./KG 40 persevered with the torpedo training programme throughout March and into April 1942, when the course at Lecce was finally wound up. It appears that no Condor crew was able to claim to have sunk anything with torpedoes, although the smaller German bombers used the weapon with some success a short time later.

Martin Harlinghausen, who had been wounded on operations during November 1941, was replaced as CO of Fliegerführer Atlantik by Generalleutnant Ulrich Kessler, effective from 5 January. An enthusiastic proponent of torpedo attack operations, Kessler had helped to devise the Lecce conversion course. However, like Harlinghausen he was ultimately forced to admit that not only was the Condor far from the ideal aircraft for the task, but also that targets warranting such a demanding and exacting approach with substantial crew risk had ideally to be worthwhile. Few such vessels appear to have been located to justify a torpedo or two when bombs were as effective and, in general, more accurate.

There is also some considerable doubt that the Condors belonging to IX./KG 40 seconded to the Italian front ever actually carried torpedoes, despite a definite intention to do so; no photographic evidence has yet come to light, and it is certainly possible that, while they were flying long-range reconnaissance sorties from a base closely involved with torpedo training of crews (flying He 111s and Ju 88s), someone confused the two separate operations.

Having a percentage of its crews absent from North Atlantic operations for several months' retraining in the Mediterranean did not adversely affect KG 40 at that time, for the unit's cooperation with submarines also tailed off significantly. With America a fully fledged combatant, Doenitz despatched the majority of his ocean-going U-boats to the eastern seaboard of the USA. Hard-bitten submarine crews could not at first believe their eyes and ears, for freighters were sailing into and out of American ports against a backdrop of fully illuminated buildings with their radio sets blaring out the latest popular tunes. It was no wonder that the U-boat men referred to this period as the second 'happy time' in terms of easy victims for their torpedoes and guns.

Of all the statistics compiled to cover the Battle of the Atlantic, a few stand out in their stark simplicity. They also cover such a catalogue of human and materiel loss that it is difficult to imagine how the situation was redressed in so short a time scale. Few would disagree that petrol and oil were among the most important commodities to all the combatants, so the fact that between January and June 1942 the Americans lost seventy-three tankers in the Atlantic and Caribbean Oceans (to all causes) with a further sixty-eight British-controlled vessels being sunk during the same period, is little short of staggering. To replace the capacity of 141 ships in this special category required an effort that almost defies belief. It was not surprising that a supply crisis loomed, leading the Admiralty to issue, on 8 November 1941, the document 'Western Approaches Convoy Instructions'. In part it stressed that 'Special Protection to Tankers' should be provided by all escort vessels whenever possible and that every effort should be made to disguise tankers as ordinary merchant ships with the aid of awnings and so forth. Small wonder that every effort was also made to neutralise the ability of the U-boats to sink Allied ships and that the Condors' contribution to the carnage was not taken lightly. It proved, somewhat surprisingly, marginally easier to sink U-boats than to destroy KG 40.

February

Since KG 40's formation its Condors had occasionally operated with the other aircraft types that equipped the Geschwader, and on 13 February 1942 Fw Kurt Hinze of 1./Staffel found himself assigned to fly a sortie in company with an He 111 of 8./Staffel to search for the crew of U-86. Neither Hinze's Fw 200 C-3 (0101/F8+FL) nor the Heinkel crew managed to spot their quarry that day, although a Do 24 flying boat of 1./Seenotstaffel did locate the submariners on the 15th.

Meanwhile, some seven months on from the launch of Operation 'Barbarossa' the German armies in Russia had made incredible progress and had taken thousands of prisoners. They did, however, come up against some stiff resistance from the huge Red Army, which brought about dangerous situations. One such had developed by mid-February when the Soviets, advancing from the Cholm area, had moved along the Lovat River in the direction of Lake Ilmen. By so doing they had breached the lines of the Sixteenth Army between Demyansk and Staraya, effectively encircling six German divisions with a total strength of around 100,000 men.

Having earlier managed to initiate the relief of the besieged German garrison at Cholm, which had, since 21 January, been encircled and threatened with annihilation by Soviet forces, the Luftwaffe's transport force was called upon once again to airlift supplies into the pocket. The garrison then held some 3,500 men who had resisted successive Russian attempts to destroy it. Lacking suitable airfields, the Ju 52/3ms, some of which towed DFS 230 gliders, together with KG 4's He 111s, which dropped supplies and also towed larger Go 242 gliders, embarked on a campaign that was to last for a total of 103 days.

Demyansk overlapped the Cholm operation and ran in parallel with it; with a far larger number of troops potentially at high risk, Oberst Franz Halder, chief of the Army General Staff, had no choice but to order (with Hitler's backing) a full-scale airlift. Luftflotte 1 promised 337 transports to fly in the 300 tons of food and materiel daily, and organised the seven air transport Gruppen assigned to it from 19 February. In addition there were four more transport Gruppen and elements of KGrzbV 105. Training units in Germany were brought together to constitute five further Gruppen, these including a number of Focke-Wulf Condors drawn from the instrument and blind-flying schools. In total there were eighteen Gruppen, or parts of them, to fly supplies, fuel and replacements into the pocket.

Although the Condor was updated, the older models operated for as long as they could be kept serviceable. This was because there were relatively few of them to equip KG 40, transport units and the flying training schools. Lack of visible armament would indicate that this example was indeed being used as a trainer. Note the requirement for a ladder for the fuselage door. *MAP*

Condors join in

Among the Condors flying east to boost the relief operation was Fw 200C-3 0037/SG+KM, then on the strength of Blindfliegerschule (B) 36. The aircraft had previously served in KG 40 as F8+CL of 3./Staffel, had crashed in bad visibility at Bordeaux on 11 January 1941, and had been transferred to 7./Staffel after repairs. The damage was put at 25 per cent, but while with the latter unit the aircraft had suffered a further 20 per cent damage to its undercarriage on 14 February 1942 when landing at Berlin-Staaken before transfer to the training school. These incidents notwithstanding, this particular Condor survived transport duty in Russia and went on to serve until 1945.

An excellent in-flight view of an Fw 200C-3 that has been updated by the addition of underwing bomb racks. *P. Jarrett*

In view of their load characteristics it would have been preferable to operate the Condors from different airfields from the Ju 52s, but at Demyansk there was no other. Peski was too far away and subject to strafing and bombing by Russian fighter bombers, although this did not appear to cause any problems and the airlift rolled on in the face of VVS interception, ground fire and at times adverse weather. The flow of supplies was not allowed to falter and the German garrison, sustained by the aerial supply service, survived to fight another day.

Airlift lessons

During the course of the airlift several valuable lessons were learned, including the need to establish stockpiles of supplies (at the two available airfields at Demyansk and Peski), the requirement for qualified personnel to direct loading of aircraft in the most economical and practical way, and ensuring that supplies arrived on time and were delivered to the areas for which they were intended.

A percentage of the 32,427 supply sorties and 659 sorties carrying replacement personnel flown into the Demyansk pocket were by Condors, the operation including the contribution of several different variants. These appear to have been mainly second-line C series machines, which had finished their operational flying with KG 40 and had been passed to training schools – but the urgency attached to the situation in Russia led to the mobilisation of most of the Luftwaffe's available transports irrespective of where they were based before the crisis in Russia manifested itself. Among the well-known figures who participated in the airlift was Hans Baur, Hitler's personal pilot. He flew an Fw 200C-3/U9 (0099/KE+IX) into the Demyansk pocket and brought out General von Brockdorff-Ahlefeldt, who was responsible for the overall defence of the area, and General Munoz Grande, commander of the Spanish Blue Division, soldiers of which had formed part of the German defence.

Demyansk's defenders were to rely on airlifted supplies, fresh troops and the evacuation of about 35,400 casualties until 19 May. The average daily tonnage reached 302, slightly more than the objective of 300 tons per day originally called for. This was an admirable achievement, but at a high cost in aircraft. Wastage of transports reached 265 Ju 52s lost to all causes, and while Demyansk/Cholm was an outstanding success for the Luftwaffe transport force, it masked a hidden and ultimately dangerous assumption. After two important relief operations had been completed without major hitches, it is easy to see how a false sense of security developed. Few individuals who ran the transport force seemed able to appreciate that a vastly more complex operation on a comparatively massive scale would be far harder if not impossible to carry out. This was especially true if the daily tonnage was far higher, the number of available transport aircraft was not doubled or trebled as was required – and the weather was as bad as it could get. That lesson would later be learned – at Stalingrad.

Lost for six decades

On 22 February Fw 200C-3/U4 0063/F8+BR of VII./KG 40 took off from Bordeaux for a routine flight that was not to end (in terms of the aircraft seeing the light of day again) for some fifty-seven years. When it crashed into the Stjordalsfjord in Norway and sank at a point not far short of the harbour at Hommelvik, this particular Condor had a subsequent history unlike most others, for the spot where it came down was to be the scene of a dramatic recovery attempt. The aircraft, which experienced engine and flap problems, was ditched in the fjord near Hommelvik (near Vaernes airfield) but did not break up on making contact with the water and the crew were able to abandon it in good order. The crew comprised Lt Werner Thieme, Lt Wolfgang Tonn, BM Obfw Leo Ludorf, 1BF Obfw Karl Kiessling, 2BF Obgfr Klaus Kappes and BS Gefr August Kaufmann. Decades later it appeared that the raising of a virtually complete example of the Focke-Wulf Fw 200 was feasible. More about what happened and some details surrounding this event may be found in the last chapter.

The aircraft in question had formerly been on the strength of 3./Staffel as F8+CL, the transfer to another Staffel being more or less standard practise to maintain numbers pending the delivery of replacement aircraft. While based at Cognac the Condor was involved in an action with a Whitley (Z6635/WL-Q) of No 612 Squadron on 17 July 1941. While in the act of attacking a convoy over the North Atlantic the Condor and Whitley had an exchange of fire in which Oblt Hans Jordens was killed and the Whitley, flown by Wg Cdr D. R. Shore, was shot down. Then passed to I./KG 40, the Condor was damaged when its tailwheel collapsed on 20 October 1941 before it was recoded and transferred to 7./Staffel; it was lost (albeit not totally) while on detachment to Vaernes, Norway.

March

While much Allied focus was at this time towards the Far East, where Japanese air, land and sea forces were continuing their offensive operations, Britain was sending convoys to assist the hard-pressed Soviets in their fight against Germany. Between 1 and 5 March convoys PQ.12 and PQ.8 sailed from Reykjavik and the Kola Inlet respectively. On the 5th an Fw 200 reported the sixteen vessels that made up PQ.12 some seventy nautical miles south of Jan Mayen Island. Four U-boats formed a patrol line and the battleship *Tirpitz* and three destroyers sortied from Trondheim in an attempt to destroy a high percentage of the merchant ships, but once again the elements intervened. The entire operation failed; elements of the British Home Fleet protecting the merchant ships made no contact in poor visibility and only one Soviet freighter was sunk, by a German destroyer. *Tirpitz* returned to Norwegian waters.

The wind of change was about to alter the composition of KG 40 when selected 8./Staffel crews were billeted at Fassberg to begin their ground school studies prior to re-equipment with the He 177. By the spring preparations were in place for the first training flights to commence in July.

April

By early April elements of KG 40's III./Gruppe, which had the previous year begun the transition from its original He 111H equipment to the Condor, had returned to Bordeaux-Merignac. This was the case with 8./Staffel, while 9./Staffel relocated to Rennes in north-western France, where it had a strength of nine Fw 200Cs by the end of the month. Not untypically, only two aircraft were then serviceable. This figure would, however, steadily improve by the early summer.

May

On 1 May 1942 Oblt Siegfried Gall, a veteran of the Condor Legion, attacked the well-armed boarding trawler HMS *Imperialist* about 60 miles off the coast of Cape San Vincente, Portugal. While running in on the ship, which had previously attacked and fatally damaged U-732 (Oberlt zur See Klaus Peter Carlson), Gall's aircraft, Fw 200C-4 0120/F8+AU of X./KG 40 IV (Erg), was hit by return fire and damaged. With little hope of reaching Bordeaux-Merignac, Gall set course for Spain and eventually crash-landed at 2140 on a beach at Apula, five miles south of Esponzende. Uffz Rudolf Melbig then activated the explosive device designed to destroy the aircraft, but it failed to detonate. Having extricated themselves from the wrecked Condor, the crew awaited events. They knew that a landing in Spain would not necessarily mean an end to their war flying but, in line with their orders not to let military equipment fall into the wrong hands, Uffz Ozud Abollig returned to the wreck armed with a pistol with which he intended to ignite the fuel. Whether he fired or not is uncertain but there was a sudden explosion, flying debris wounding him in the neck. As the Condor burned, with only the extreme nose and tail surviving the conflagration, Gall meanwhile used his local knowledge to guide rescuers to the location of his crew.

On 25 May, in ongoing operations against convoys QP.12 and PQ.16 in Arctic waters, a shadower aircraft was shot down by a Hurricane launched from the CAM ship *Empire Moon* sailing as part of the convoy. A phrase such as 'small unit action' does not really do justice to the tenacity of Norwegian patriots who, throughout most of the war, returned to areas of their country that had been abandoned by the Germans – and the Russians – earlier in the conflict. Their objective was primarily to re-establish contact with personnel who manned the vital radar stations in areas near the Arctic Circle. Additionally there was a vital need to service instruments that recorded weather conditions in a strategically important part of the world as far as the convoys to Russia were concerned, and to establish schools for Allied ski troops. On 14 May the icebreaker *Isbjorn* and the sealer *Selis* set out for Spitsbergen with a 100-man landing party. The 24-hour daylight assisted the passage of the ships to Ice Fjord where, true to its name, they were trapped by broken pack ice that needed be cleared before the ships could proceed. While the men were doing this they were attacked by what was identified as a Condor. This was indeed the case, as I./KG 40 had that day despatched three aircraft flown by Major Dazera, Bernard Jope (F8+EL) and Heinz Waterbeck (F8+FL) on a met/reconnaissance flight over that area of Norway.

As the Condors made their initial attack the Norwegians returned fire with Lewis gun and small arms, but the German aircraft had their targets firmly in their sights and, in four attempts, destroyed the small party and their vessels. The hour-long attack had been enough to sink the *Isbjorn* and set the *Selis* on fire. Survivors of the force moved up to the former Russian settlement at Barentsberg, finding food and shelter enough to tend the wounded.

Locally the Luftwaffe had established an airfield at Adventfjord near Spitsbergen, but this was abandoned in the summer of 1942, leaving a number of wrecked aircraft including at least one Ju 88. Norway itself was eventually abandoned by the German garrison troops to the bands of nationals whose tenacity enabled them to repair destroyed installations and re-establish weather and radio links with Allied forces.

Alarmed at the spiralling loss of ships and their vital cargoes to Condors, the British authorities improvised several counters including the CAM ship. Launching a Hurricane or Fulmar fighter from a merchant ship catapult took the German crews by surprise, but mid-ocean interceptions risked the loss of the British pilot, who had to ditch his aircraft. *RAF Museum*

To bear the weight of a Mk I Hurricane, the catapult had to be strong with enough length for the aircraft to retract its wheels and achieve flying speed. *IWM*

June

Early June saw the departure of convoy HG.84 with twenty-three ships under escort. A pro-German agent reported this on the 9th, whereupon aircraft of I./KG 40 were ordered to reconnoitre and one Condor duly confirmed the fact two days later. This aircraft escaped the attentions of a Hurricane from the CAM ship *Empire Moon*, and eight U-boats were ordered to form the Endrass group on the 14th. That same day a Condor crew sighted the ships and led U-552 (Lt Cdr Topp), followed by U-89 and U-132, to their target. Topp had the most success on the night of the 14/15th by sinking five ships. The other boats were driven off by the escort, both air and sea. Although on the morning of 16 June two Condors re-established contact, the weather had deteriorated such that the German submarine captains were concerned, with the sea running at Force 0 and with good visibility. The operation was therefore abandoned.

Having taken command of I./KG 40, Major Ernst Henkelmann directed numerous reconnaissance sorties over Iceland for several months. This remote British-occupied area had a number of 'weather stations' staffed mainly by Norwegian personnel whose job it was to log shipping movements, the number of which were increasing. The German aircrews made their own comprehensive maps of shipping movements, especially those in Hvalfjord and the vicinity of the Icelandic capital Reykjavik, and KG 40 was ideally placed to report an unusually large build-up of ships on 27 June. Generaloberst Stumpff and Fliegerführers Nord-Ost and Lofoten noted that convoy PQ.17 had put to sea, destination Soviet Russia.

A Condor crew of III./KG 40 reported that a convoy consisting of thirty-five merchant ships and two tankers was on a north-easterly heading. For several days the vessels were out of reach of the torpedo bombers of Luftflotte 5 based in Norway, but the Condor shadowers could keep them under almost continuous surveillance, aided by the Polar summer with its twenty-four hours of daylight. KG 40 also reported that PQ.17 had an unusually large escort force comprising twenty-four British and American warships. Based within range of Russian airfields, the aircraft of Luftflotte 5 came under attack from VVS fighters before they could strike at the convoy, but this skirmish met with only limited success. KG 40 lost contact with the convoy as it entered a fog bank between Iceland and Jan Mayen Island, but the Luftwaffe did not delay its opening attack for long, at which point the Condors, taking no active part in the ensuing action, merely kept a watching brief on unfolding events.

The attack on PQ.17 was a German victory that should never have taken place had Allied intelligence been more accurate as to the disposition of a perceived major threat from the battleship *Tirpitz*. The result was not only the loss of 143,977grt of vitally needed supplies but also the postponement of any further convoys to the beleaguered Soviets until later in 1942, when the days were shorter. As it was, the Allied cause was denied the use of 3,350 vehicles, 430 tanks, 210 aircraft and 99,316 tons of other war equipment carried by the ships that went down in the action.

During the month, KG 40's 9./Staffel returned to Germany to complete conversion training onto the Condor as a proportion of the unit's original crews had probably not flown so large an aircraft, particularly if they had joined in the days when the Staffel had been equipped with the He 111. Such men were not at a significant disadvantage as the work of the Staffel had, under the original raison d'être of a third Gruppe for KG 40, been that of anti-shipping attack. There were of course significant operational differences, not least the comparative size of the two aircraft and the larger crew complement of the Condor.

July

In mid-July 9./Staffel completed conversion training and moved to Cognac, taking charge of several Fw 200s formerly used by units of I./KG 40 when that Gruppe prepared to convert to the He 177 over a period lasting from the summer to the autumn of 1942. These diversions were not expected to interrupt operational commitments for any length of time, and Condors remained active during the summer months of 1942.

Despite having extra armament installed in the form of a cannon-armed dorsal turret, the Fw 200C-4 remained as vulnerable as before to well-aimed return fire from ships and/or aircraft, and on 8

July a 1./Staffel Condor, Fw 200C-4 0101/F8+EH, did not return from a patrol into the Arctic Ocean and Norwegian Sea area. With the Staffel Kapitän, Oblt Albert Gramkow, in command, the crew had taken off on reconnaissance sorties from Vaernes to additionally search for elements of PQ.17, which were assumed to still be inside the aircraft's patrol area. Garmkow and his crew – Obfw Anton Mohain, Obgfr Gerhard V. Stocki, Uffz Heinz Laxy, Obfw Rudiger Wedding, Uffz Franz Welters, Fw Gerhard Fischer and Lt Georg Libenau – were posted missing assumed killed when the aircraft ditched.

Another Condor was lost on 12 July when Obfw Richard Schongraf of IX./KG 40, flying Fw 200C-4 0135/F8+BT, failed to return from a reconnaissance sortie and was also posted as missing with his entire crew. It was determined that the Condor had crashed at Munros in Galicia, Spain, rather than coming down in the sea.

New war zone

By 1942 Iceland had became a focal point for increased Allied air activity against German submarines and reconnaissance flights, both British and US aircraft being based there. Several Condors were to fall to the enemy fighter strength in the area, one loss occurring on 23 July. An Fw 200 shot down off the east coast of Iceland that day was claimed to be the first victim of an Icelandic-based aircraft, and the war's only recorded combat victory for the Northrop N-3PB. Then being flown by a crew of No 330 (Norwegian) Squadron RAF, the American-built floatplane attacked the Condor successfully. However, despite other contacts, no others were claimed by the squadron, although in some two years of operations the little floatplanes did not shirk from firing on German intruders. Their presence dissuaded several German aircrews from spotting Allied convoys and reporting their position to the U-boats that patrolled the waters south of Iceland. To the submariners the area was cynically labelled the Rosengarten ('rose garden') because of the dangers they faced, both from ships and aircraft.

August

Not that many U-boat skippers bemoaned the fact that a few of their number had drawn the short straw and were ordered to patrol Arctic waters in search of an at times elusive quarry. The lucky crews had been sent across the Atlantic to reap the rewards of America becoming a full combatant on the Allied side following the Japanese attack on Pearl Harbor in December 1941. By early 1942 organised chaos reigned as the US service chiefs thrashed out plans to run the war most effectively, ultimately deciding that, of the two main Axis powers, it would aim to defeat 'Germany first'. The U-boats embarked on the second 'happy time' off the eastern seaboard of North America and, although the bulk of the fleet would not return to Germany for some six months, the war in Europe went on.

KG 40's lone patrols continued, now in the face of increasing danger from burgeoning Allied air power. Not only were enemy aircraft more plentiful, but they were also casting their net wider geographically. On 14 August Fw 200C-4 0125/F8+BB, flown by Obfw Fritz Kuhn, was the aircraft spotted by the N-3PB of No 330 Squadron as the German machine was shadowing a convoy south of the Grindavik peninsula. It then flew north before altering course to pass west of Reykjavik – whereupon it fell victim to United States Army Air Force fighters that were en route to England from the US to constitute the beginnings of the strategic Eighth Air Force. Iceland became a welcome stopping point on the long flight, particularly for the pilots of single-seat fighters.

Intercepting the Condor over Iceland, a P-39D Airacobra flown by Lt Joseph D. R. Shaffer of the 33rd Fighter Squadron was joined by Lt Elza K. Shahan of the 27th FS at the controls of a P-38F Lightning. Neither pilot was very experienced in air combat, and when they had the Condor cornered they pumped shell after shell into the German machine to the point where it was virtually ripped apart, with most of its crew reportedly dead before the wreckage fell into the sea. Both American pilots shared the Condor kill, which was recorded as the first AAF fighter victory in the European Theatre of Operations, and the victors received a Silver Star apiece for their efforts.

September

It was mainly to counter the lethal activity against RAF patrol aircraft over the Bay of Biscay by the Ju 88C-6 fighters of V./KG 40 that Coastal Command in its turn stepped up the defence in the form of the Beaufighters of Nos 235 and 248 Squadrons. On 17 September 1942 these fighters also demonstrated how effective they could be against the Condor. No 235 Squadron had sent eight Beaufighters to patrol the bay when they sighted an Fw 200 flying a mile to their starboard side, on a reciprocal course to a German armed trawler. The three leading Beaufighters attacked the German aircraft from the port side; one dived from 2,000 feet (610 metres) to press home a head-on attack, and four ran in on the Condor's starboard side. Notwithstanding the loss of one Beaufighter to fire from the trawler, the Fw 200 was doomed. In successive passes the Beaufighters set the big bomber on fire until it finally dived into the sea accompanied by a series of explosions. One member of the crew was observed climbing into a dinghy with three others floating in the water.

By 20 September 8./ and 9./Staffeln of KG 40 had a strength of seventeen Fw 200s, eleven of them serviceable; on the administrative side the Stab of III./Gruppe prepared to move from Rennes to Bordeaux-Merignac and was established there by the end of the month. Another move was in the wind when 9./Staffel was ordered to Lecce in southern Italy to assist in transporting fuel and supplies between German bases in North Africa.

October

October brought KG 40's aircraft into contact with enemy fighters. Even fairly 'clapped-out' Hurricanes and Fulmars were known to be lethal if they intercepted an Fw 200, and it goes without saying that more modern fighters were to be avoided by the German crews if at all possible. Understandably this was not always the case, and on 24 October a pair of Bell P-39D Airacobras from the 33rd Fighter Group, temporarily based at Reykjavik while en route to their base in North Africa, shot down Fw 200C-4/U3 0131/F8+EK.

Flown by 2nd Lts Michael J. Ingelido and Thurmann F. Morrison, the P-39s pumped enough lead into the hapless German bomber to bring down two or three aircraft. The Condor carried seven men, all of whom were killed. The German pilot had little hope of evading; the aircraft took fire and crashed in flames on a hill north of Kalmanstunga Farm in the Borgarfjordur area of Iceland. The crew – F Oblt Heinz Golde, 2F Fw Matthias Franzen, BF Obfw Horst Kroos, BF Uffz Manfred Unger, BS Uffz Alois Schwab and BM Uffz Helmut Engelmann – all perished in the crash together with an extra Bordmechanik, Uffz Hans Todtenhoefer. He was a member of 1.(F)/120, and there is some indication that the Condor, which incidentally had been fitted with Rostock radar, was on loan to the reconnaissance unit at the time.

Early metric wavelength radars required receive/transmit antennae arrays to provide port and starboard coverage to the aircraft's line of flight. A Condor fitted with a Rostock set has this arrangement above and below both wings. A. Price

To bring about the Condor's demise the intelligence officers who noted down details of the action elicited the fact that the American pilots had expended 1,715 rounds of 0.30in ammunition, forty-eight rounds of 0.50in and thirty-five rounds of 37mm cannon shells.

Four days later, on 28 October, Oblt Rudolf Feldt, flying a 3./Staffel Fw 200C-4 (0109/F8+KL) out of Vaernes, failed to return with his five-man crew. The aircraft may have collided with another Condor of the same Staffel and sub-type – Fw 200C-4 0162/F8+ML – flown by Obfw Herbert Fahje and a six-man crew, all of whom died in the ensuing crash after taking off from Orlandet in Norway. The exact circumstances of the incident are unclear, and loss records put the accident as occurring on the following day, 29 October, rather than the 28th.

By 25 October the Condors of 9./Staffel had completed the move to Lecce, where the unit would remain until the end of February 1943.

The odyssey of the *Omega*

A view of how the 'other side' viewed the activities of KG 40 unfolded in the autumn of 1942 with the voyage of the tramp steamer *Omega*, which, in the seesaw Battle of the Atlantic, had a surprising outcome.

Captain Douglas Grey stared in disbelief at the battered old steamer that he was asked to sail to England so that she could be used on convoy duty. Grey and the ship, the *Omega*, were in Gibraltar on 31 October 1942. Three times the *Omega* had put to sea only to return with faulty steering and leaking boilers, but so urgent was the need for freighters in England that Grey, with all the confidence of a twenty-six-year old, volunteered to undertake the voyage. However, his confidence was in no way boosted by the sight and sound of his charge, and he knew that he only held a Master's ticket because, as he put it, 'luck and survival were more important than experience'. He lacked much of the latter and had never previously commanded a vessel – and the one the powers that be had given him left much to be desired.

Built before the First World War, the *Omega* grossed 3,600 tons; she had sailed under five different names and four flags and had been captured by the Royal Navy early in the war. Troublesome boilers had stranded her in 'Gib' without a crew, although by the time Captain Grey came on the scene there were more than enough men, stranded by enemy submarine and air attack, who were keen to obtain a passage home to England. Grey had no difficulty in rounding up a forty-man crew, and the *Omega* duly sailed from the Rock, destination Glasgow, on 23 October. For defence she carried a pair of Lewis guns and as a last resort there were some parachute flares, which were not intended as weapons but they did make a spectacular explosion if used against low-flying aircraft and the operator managed to hit one. The escort for the small convoy consisted of an armed trawler and a freighter. Ahead of the ships lay a voyage of 1,800 miles (2,900km) through ocean waters frequented by U-boats and German aircraft and at the mercy of the weather in the Bay of Biscay. Grey had to resort to sail power to get him out of trouble during a 40-knot gale that battered the ship in the Bay. With her steering gear damaged by the storm, he and his crew somehow managed to keep the steamer from foundering, and when at last dawn broke the wind had abated.

The *Omega* had meanwhile been blown hundreds of miles off course and lost her escort, but there was no question of the captain breaking radio silence lest his signals were intercepted by a U-boat. The weather changed to a biting cold. Then, on the 31st, the ship's teenage third mate sighted an aircraft.

Grey recognised the Condor and gave orders not to expose the guns in the hope that the German aircrew would take the *Omega* for a neutral ship. But the Luftwaffe men were not fooled and lined up on the old tramp, flying down her port side and scrutinising her closely. Having decided that the ship was a legitimate target, the Condor captain banked and raked her decks with gunfire from stem to stern. The *Omega* promptly ran up the Red Ensign – Captain Grey decided that if his ship was to be sunk it would be under his own flag, and manned one of the Lewis guns. The fourth mate broke out the parachute flare. The Condor came in again, the scream of its engines drowning out all other sounds on the *Omega*. Grey blazed away with one Lewis gun, the flare was released and the bosun manned the second Lewis.

Detonation of the flare sparked off a chain reaction that doomed the Condor. The *Omega*'s crew saw the pilot fling an arm across his eyes as the dazzling light burst in front of him. Pulling back on the yoke to avoid the ship's rigging the Condor slowed, enough for the Lewis gun rounds to hit home and cause fatal damage. Bullets peppered the aircraft's belly and the port inner engine belched flame and smoke, the resulting fire streaming back across the wing. The Condor was some 500 yards (460 metres) from the ship when the latter's crew witnessed an explosion that tore the German aircraft apart. Eye-witnesses stated that it simply disintegrated. 'Thousands of pieces of twisted metal' fell into the sea, to the utter disbelief – and jubilation – of the seamen.

The *Omega* was subsequently found by her trawler escort – a minor miracle in the circumstances – and after overcoming further technical malfunctions she sailed into Glasgow on 7 November, having logged more than 3,000 miles. Patched up once more, she plied the sea lanes and survived to see out the end of the war.

The identity of the Condor lost in this action is open to some question. It may well have been that alternatively claimed as a kill by a Hurricane pilot operating from HMS *Empire Heath*; Fw 200C-3/U4 0057/F8+DS of VII./KG 40 was the aircraft reportedly involved in the action.

November

The latter part of 1942 saw much activity on the part of U-boat hunting groups – the wolf packs – which had, considering the massive effort usually involved to bring several U-boats into contact with merchant ships, achieved only mixed success. Although they had been improved, the reliability of German torpedoes still caused some concern.

Towards the end of 1942 the Battle of the Atlantic was reaching a crescendo. The Allies were growing stronger in terms of naval escort vessels, electronic aids such as automated HD/HF were more than proving their worth in action, the convoy system was well established on South as well as North Atlantic routes, and air cover was increasingly effective. German air reconnaissance, facing an increasing challenge, was not always required if the target convoy was located early and its course estimated accurately. The patrol areas of the U-boats were well defined, with individual submarines remaining on station for days waiting for the right conditions for a kill. Weather as ever played its part, and more than one promising tally of enemy ships had to be trimmed when the U-boats were hampered by high seas and bad visibility. Another factor was the amount of fuel each U-boat used and could conserve on a long patrol; the advent of the so-called Milch ('milk cows') to refuel the 'hunter-killer' teams in mid-ocean aided operations to a significant degree. These replenishment boats became in their turn prime targets for Allied attack once their purpose was known.

Meanwhile the fortunes of Kampfgeschwader 40 waxed and waned, with the Allies taking the initiative to render the unit's operations less effective. There was little if anything the Gruppenkommandeuren or Staffel Kapitäne could do about this situation, much less the crews, for the nature of their operations and the aircraft they flew could hardly be changed. Luck was to abandon the unit at various periods, and late 1942 proved to be a less than encouraging time, with portents of worse events that were to follow in the future.

Fighters on freighters

On 1 November 1942 Norman Taylor became one of the first pilots to go to sea with the Merchant Ship Fighter Unit (MSFU). An expedient measure introduced to counter the Condors out in the Atlantic far beyond the range of the fighters available at that time, RAF pilots volunteered for what was quite hazardous duty. But if the aircraft of KG 40 could at least be dissuaded from attacking at least some of the ships bringing in vital supplies to help sustain the British war effort, no sacrifice was believed to be too great. With Winston Churchill having put his weight behind any measure likely to reduce the threat posed by the Condors, the fighter-carrying merchant ships were quickly readied for service. They came as a nasty surprise to KG 40's crews.

December: mountain crash

On the last day of December 1942 KG 40 lost two more Condors – Fw 200C-4 0160/F8+FR, a machine from 7./Staffel that succumbed to aerial combat, and Fw 200C F8+CK, which came into contact with a Norwegian mountain near Voss. The first victim was intercepted by a Mosquito en route from a bombing raid on Casablanca. At a point near the Spanish island of Gran Canaria, the RAF fighter consigned Oblt Gunther Graber and his crew to a watery grave, none of the German airmen being known to have survived the encounter.

The second Condor, which crashed 5,000 feet (1525 metres) up, was not recovered but left to the elements. It was rediscovered in 1977 when a party of British troops taking part in Exercise Hardfall found aircraft wreckage buried under 4 feet (1.2 metres) of snow. Large sections of the Condor, badly battered but recognisable, were lifted from their resting place of more than sixty years.

Test vehicle

Several Fw 200s were utilised for experimental flying to test other new weapons, among them the Fieseler F 103, alias the ZFG 76 or V-1. There was an element of competition between the Luftwaffe's V-1 programme and the Wehrmacht-backed A-4 (V-2), both Vergeltung ('Vengeance') weapons needing funding that could only be authorised by Hitler. Testing of the simpler V-1 flying bomb proceeded without too many technical setbacks (unlike those initially suffered by the V-2 rocket), but its deployment was delayed by several factors. As the prime contractor for the weapon, the Fieseler Werke at Kassel needed proof that the V-1 would meet the specification. An aerodynamic test would provide convincing data and a Focke-Wulf Condor was modified to carry a dummy missile for release over Peenemunde.

On 10 October 1942 Gerhard Fieseler personally flew in an Fw 200C-4 (0156/CE+IU) carrying a single flying bomb airframe without the characteristic dorsal fuselage-mounted ram jet propulsion unit. A special rack enabling the bomb to be carried by the Condor had been fitted by the Fieseler Werke, after which it had returned to Peenemunde-West/Usedom Island for the actual test drop. The Condor was placed under the personal charge of Flugbaumeister Max Mayer, who flew the aircraft until April 1943.

The V1, configured as a small aeroplane complete with control surfaces, was dropped over the Baltic coast, first and foremost to verify its flight characteristics. This successful first flight preceded the initial launch of a V-1 from a ground ramp by a matter of weeks, the initial live ground test firing taking place on 24 December 1942. As with many innovative weapons, the aerial tests of the V-1 proved to be more useful than those undertaken on the ground, where technical malfunctions seemed to cause all manner of delays pending modifications and further test firings. All these problems were a blessing to the Allies, who were not plagued by a rain of flying bombs over the beaches during the D-Day invasion in June 1944. Had the problems been solved in time, the V-1 offensive would have dovetailed into Dietrich Peltz's conventional bomber operations against English cities under the general heading of Operation 'Steinbock'.

While the V-1 offensive more than succeeded in terrorising the citizens of London, it ultimately failed – but the early Condor tests presaged a later period of air-launching by the He 111s of KG 3 and KG 51, a pointless offensive that decimated the participating units when they were intercepted by RAF night-fighters. In retrospect the glossed-over ability of the British defences to react quickly seemed well in line with poor Luftwaffe intelligence, a random approach to targeting and the dubious estimated gains to be exploited by what appeared from the other side of the Channel to be an unprepared Allied 'Home Front'. Having missed the opening phase of Operation 'Overlord', the V-1 would have still been a massive threat to the bridgehead in Normandy. Instead, the flying bombs were sent winging across the Channel to subject the British civilian population to another ordeal of terror.

One of F des F Condors being refuelled on an Alpine airfield, possibly that serving Hitler's retreat at Berchtesgaden. The abbreviated ventral gondola, yellow spinner tips and outer wing panels are in evidence, the latter indicating that flights were being undertaken to areas of the Eastern Front, although the date of the photograph is unknown.

Engines being run up to full revolutions for take-off, a Condor pilot waits for his co-pilot and crew to board. In common with the majority of KG 40's aircraft, this Fw 200C-3 is fitted with the multi-branch engine exhaust flame dampers. *Author's collection*

Flight overalls and helmets in place, a KG 40 Condor crew sort out the straps to securely fasten their life jackets. Two men appear to be carrying side arms as part of their kit. *Author's collection*

Recording sorties together with successes against enemy shipping was in vogue with Condor crews while KG 40 enjoyed a run of good luck. The two earliest areas of operation were duly presented in white paint on the fins of individual aircraft. Some were flown regularly by the unit's leading pilots and crews, this example being attributed to Hermann Richter. *Author's collection*

The steady drone of BMW engines became second nature to KG 40's crews, who would be aboard their Condors for hours at a time on a typical maritime patrol. This machine, an Fw 200C-4, is fitted with the forward dorsal cupola housing a single 7.9mm machine-gun. Without much of a framework to create blind spots, the position offered a good field of fire. *F. Selinger*

Before the war few seamen had ever seen a large four-engine aircraft, and they were startled when the bombers they frequently misidentified as Allied were bent on attacking them. KG 40's F8+CH is an Fw 200C-4 of 1./Staffel. *F. Selinger*

Heading out across country, probably on a local training flight that gave far more identifiable features then the North Sea or Bay of Biscay ever could, the crews of a pair of KG 40's Fw 200C-4s from Bordeaux are probably enjoying the change of scene. *F. Selinger*

Focke-Wulf Fw 200 C-3 Condor aircraft on an airfield in the Bordeaux-Merignac region parked for arming after delivery from the factory at Bremen in 1941. *Edmund Daser via Franz Selinger*

1:144 Scale

This page and following two pages: A four-view drawing of Focke-Wulf Fw 200C-3 Condor, F8+FW, Stab.V./KG 40, Eastern Front, winter 1942-1943. RLM 72/73/65 finish RLM 04 yellow spinner tips, band around rear fuselage and undersides of wingtips; Black codes, with 'F' thinly outlined in yellow. Non-standard proportions on fuselage cross; unit badge on both sides of nose

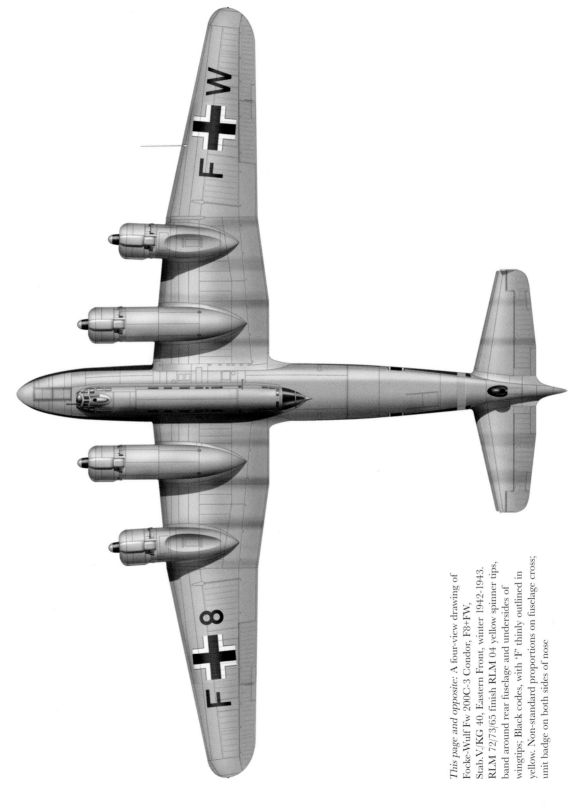

This page and opposite: A four-view drawing of Focke-Wulf Fw 200C-3 Condor, F8+FW, Stab.V./KG 40, Eastern Front, winter 1942-1943. RLM 72/73/65 finish RLM 04 yellow spinner tips, band around rear fuselage and undersides of wingtips; Black codes, with 'F' thinly outlined in yellow. Non-standard proportions on fuselage cross; unit badge on both sides of nose

Focke-Wulf Fw 200B-2
Condor, GF+GF, operated
in the transport role by
K.GrzbV.105. RLM
70/71/65 finish with all
codes in black; standard
national markings

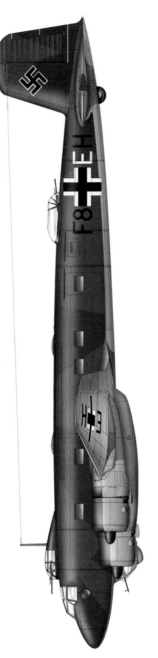

Focke-Wulf Fw 200C-0
Condor, F8+EH, 1./KG 40,
summer 1940. RLM
72/73/65 finish with black
codes and white individual
aircraft letter 'E' in white;
code repeated below wings

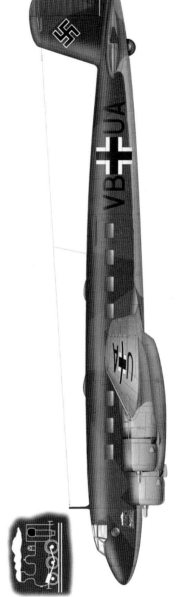

Focke-Wulf Fw 200D-1
Condor, W.Nr. 0010,
4./KGrzbV107, summer
1940. RLM 70/71/65 finish
with all black codes; white
unit badge on nose (both
sides)

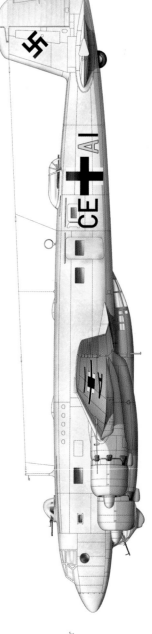

Focke-Wulf Fw 200C-3
Condor, W.Nr. 0034, ex-
F8+GW, captured at
Stalingrad and tested by the
N.I.I. of the V.V.S., Moscow,
spring 1943. RLM 72/73/65
finish with all German
markings overpainted in VVS
colours; red stars applied on
fuselage sides and below
wings (none above). KG 40
badge on nose and one sunk
vessel marking on rudder
retained. Yellow spinner tips

Focke-Wulf Fw 200C-3
Condor, A6+BH, 1 Staffel
(F) 120, Norway, 1942.
RLM 72/73/65 finish with
black codes and white
individual letter 'B'; note
unit badge below cockpit,
just aft of circular window

Focke-Wulf Fw 200C-3
Condor, CE+AI.
Temporary white distemper
applied over the standard
RLM 72/73 upper surface
finish; undersides in RLM
65. Code in black with 'A'
thinly outline in black

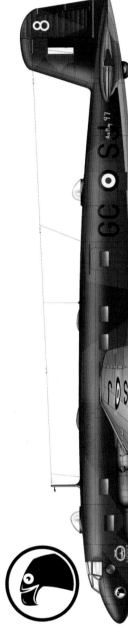

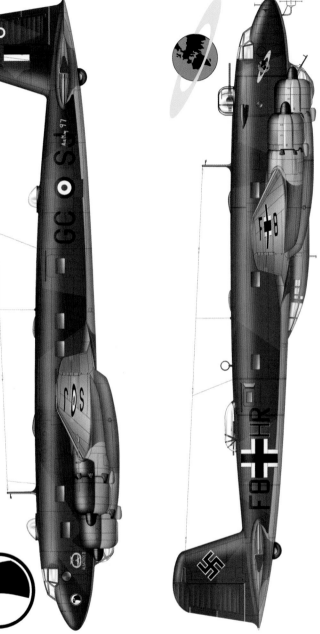

Focke-Wulf Fw 200C-3
Condor, B6+KM, B.F.S.36.
RLM 72/73/65 finish with
yellow rear fuselage band
and underside of wingtips;
code in black, with 'KM'
outlined in white. Unit
badge on nose; two white
naval vessels painted on
rudder, and a line of mission
markings below fin swastika

Focke-Wulf Fw 200C-4/U1
Condor, GC+SJ of F.d.F,
personal aircraft of
Großadmiral Dönitz,
captured and tested at
Farnborough as 'Air Ministry
97'. RLM 70/71/65 scheme
with all black codes; previous
Luftwaffe markings
overpainted and RAF
roundels applied to fuselage
and below wings, together
with flash on fin. White '8' on
rudder, F.d.F. marking and
U-Boat emblem 'Albatros III'
in gold on nose; 'Air Miny 97'
roughly hand-painted in
white on rear fuselage

Focke-Wulf Fw 200C-8
Condor, F8+HR, 3./KG 40.
RLM 72/73/65 finish with
black codes; 'H' thinly
outlined in Gelb 04. Unit
badge is carried on both
sides of the forward fuselage

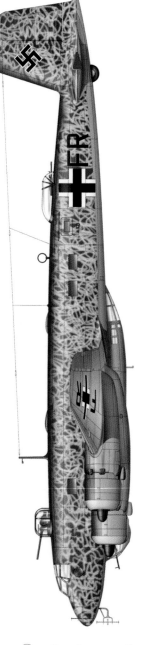

Focke-Wulf Fw 200C-8
Condor, F8+FR, 7./KG 40,
Norway, 1945. RLM
72/73/65 finish with a
'squiggle' pattern in (possibly)
pale grey applied to fuselage
and front of engine cowlings;
when captured by Allied
forces this pattern had began
to wear off the top of the
fuselage and leading edge of
fin. Codes in black, with 'F'
on fuselage thinly outlined in
white

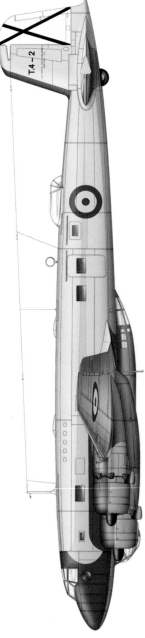

Focke-Wulf Fw 200C-4/U3
Condor, T.4-2 (W.Nr.0175,
ex-F8+AS) interned in
Spain, 31 December 1942,
served with Iberia Airlines
between January and June
1945 and then taken over
by Spanish Air Force. Dark
Green (possibly RLM 72)
fuselage front, cowlings,
wing and flying tail
surfaces' leading edges; light
grey uppersurfaces. Yellow
cheatline along fuselage;
national markings in six
positions. Fin white with
black cross. Fw 200C-4 ex-
F8+HS (W.Nr.0118) was also
interned (spring 1945) and
used as T.4-1

Chapter 8

1943: Stalingrad and the Hs 293

January

On 31 January 1943 Hitler promoted Admiral Doenitz to Commander in Chief of the Kriegsmarine in place of Gross (Grand) Admiral Raeder, who then retired. Doenitz was himself promoted to the rank of Gross Admiral with a staff that included Vice Admiral Ruge as Commander, Naval Defence Forces West. Doenitz himself continued as C-in-C U-boat operations, a position he retained until the end of hostilities, despite his elevation.

In a period of far-reaching discussions over the future progress of the war, the Allies decided that Germany would be forced to accept nothing less than unconditional surrender when she was finally defeated. At sea, among a list of immediate goals, top priority was given to the complete defeat of the U-boat; burgeoning Allied air and sea power virtually ensured that this would be achieved, although there would be bitter battles between German boats and surface units of the British, American and Soviet Navies together with French and Polish Naval units before the end. Almost all future victories for the U-boats were bought at higher cost than previously, despite the deployment of large hunting groups of ten or more submarines.

The danger of being caught on the surface increasingly drove U-boat skippers to run underwater during daylight hours and to surface only at night to attack or recharge their batteries. Fitted with increased anti-aircraft armament, the ocean-going boats resolved to fight it out on the surface if confronted by enemy aircraft. This tactic resulted in some successful shoot-downs of their aerial antagonists but also a rise in sinkings and heavy damage to some of the boats involved in such actions.

For their part the U-boats enjoyed valuable electronic assistance from the German 'B' service, which was able to decode W/T transmissions from the Allied side and thus enable the C-in-C U-boats to concentrate several submarines into patrol lines that would intercept a given convoy provided that it maintained its previously verified course. Luftwaffe air reconnaissance continued to play its part in such operations by confirming that the ships were indeed where they were estimated to be; KG 40 increasingly undertook such a support role while contact-keeper U-boats maintained a watch on operations, one or more boats taking station on most occasions when combats could be expected to last for several days and nights. Such actions were punctuated by hours of shadowing, attack and evading.

Casablanca diversion

A force not generally given to allowing its crews to undertake unauthorised combat missions, the Luftwaffe High Command was nevertheless known to view such transgressions with some leniency on the rare occasions when they occurred – if the effort involved brought results. One involving KG 40's Condors took place on 1 January 1943.

Condors had previously been flown on conventional bombing sorties, but on the first day of 1943 they created a furore out of all proportion to their efforts and number when they attacked Casablanca. A token force believed to have comprised no more than four aircraft (from 2./ and 7./Staffeln, plus possibly one from 8./Staffel), carried out the raid, which took place in the early hours. The aircraft dropped nothing more lethal then four standard 550lb (250 kg) bombs each, but it was enough to create a disproportionate furore on the ground. The reason was that the bombing appeared to Allied intelligence to indicate prior German knowledge of plans to hold an important international conference of Allied leaders in the town (starting on the 12th), although this was not actually the case as the Germans apparently had no advance knowledge of the talks.

This sequence of photographs shows the bombing-up of a Condor at Bordeaux, starting *(top left)* with the useful wooden blocks to give the height required to lift the bomb off the jack and attach it to one of the outboard underwing racks. *F. Selinger*

Bottom left: With the bomb positioned, the attachment lugs in the rack had to be connected to ensure a clean drop and arming of the detonation sequence. *F. Selinger*

Above: Smooth bomb loading involved correct angles and positioning of the loading cradle below the rack. Visible details of the Condor shown here include the 'fan' of flame damper exhaust pipes, the white-fronted spinner and the characteristically large box-like oil cooler intakes. *F. Selinger*

A diagram showing the Condor's oil system, including the prominent coolers below each engine, the L-shaped reservoir tanks, the feed lines and the control panel in the fuselage centre.

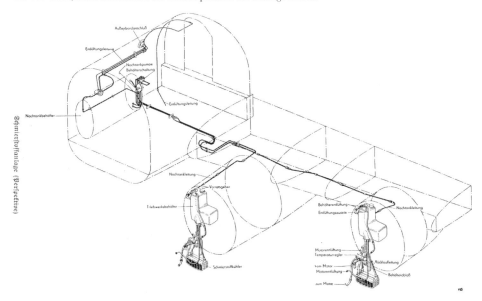

Fw 200C-4 F8+BR of 1./Staffel KG 40 being refuelled. The aircraft has a white-outlined individual letter and white spinner tips to denote its parent unit, while KG 40's badge was highly recognisable. *P. Jarrett*

Participants in the raid later admitted (albeit with a degree of tongue in cheek reticence) that the operation had not been officially sanctioned and was mounted more out of boredom than wartime necessity, but it turned out to be costly as two aircraft, an Fw 200C-3/U4 (0081/F8+CK) from 2./Staffel and a C-4/U3 (0175/F8+AS) from 7./Staffel, were obliged to land at San Pablo aerodrome near Seville in neutral Spain, where both aircraft were interned.

As indicated earlier, 9./Staffel returned to France in late February 1943 and 8./Staffel made a move to Fassberg, Germany, to begin conversion to the He 177. This was a dovetail operation involving both Focke-Wulf and Heinkel bombers, and the unit retained thirty-five (eighteen serviceable) Condors in France while elements of the Staffel were getting to grips with the intricacies of the more complex Heinkel Grief ('Griffon').

Eastern transports, 1942/43

Once again the wider war situation did not allow KG 40 to complete an important change in its operational order of battle, as conversion to the much-anticipated He 177 was interrupted by events thousands of miles from Germany. The gradually deteriorating situation faced by the German Army fighting on the central Russian front by the autumn of 1942 had worsened by December when the Sixth Army under von Paulus found itself engulfed by ever stronger Soviet forces. Battling the enemy and deteriorating weather conditions in the ruins of the city of Stalingrad, the situation rapidly deteriorated into crisis. As the Russians tenaciously held their positions and fed in replacements, the Wehrmacht was inexorably pushed into a pocket in and around the city. Stalin began to see the propaganda value of a city bearing his name withstanding the invader – and Hitler viewed the capture of Stalingrad as a massive coup for German arms.

Built as an airliner to serve international routes, the Condor was large enough to double as a military transport and the type flew thousands of miles not directly connected with anti-shipping work. Many examples flew under pre-service radio call signs as well as Luftwaffe military codes, as with this C-3 coded SG+KR. *MAP*

Bombed into a sea of rubble by the Luftwaffe, honeycombed with basements and dominated by shattered steel structures and towers of concrete, Stalingrad became a fortress. The city covered a massive area large enough to encompass three main airfields – Gumrak, Pitomnik and Kalatch – and gradually became the focus of a desperate fight for survival by the German Sixth Army and opposing Red Army units.

As the Russians sealed off the roads, supplies could only be airlifted to the beleaguered German troops. Scores of Ju 52s and He 111 bombers converted to the transport role embarked on an operation to relieve the soldiers; having flown hundreds of sorties since the start of Operation 'Barbarossa', the Luftwaffe transport force had performed well in earlier encirclement battles, air supply having been the key to the Wehrmacht breaking other such potentially deadly moves by the Red Army.

While the situation at Stalingrad was three times the size of any comparable previous operation, it did not on the face of it seem insurmountable. As noted previously, at Bryansk and Cholm the VVS had inflicted heavy but sustainable aircraft losses, although the Germans had been using more established airfields and the weather was reasonable despite the shortening autumn days. Now the call from the Sixth Army's troops was for more and more supplies of food, clothing and ammunition to be flown in by aircrews who had to brave the terrifying extremes of a deep Russian winter. Meeting those demands would require more aircraft – a lot more aircraft.

Stalingrad

In the meantime the weather simply got worse. With the Sixth Army in dire straits, the Luftwaffe airlift got under way. The Ju 52s and He 111s were manned by crews whose tenacity in the face of appalling difficulties set numerous aviation records, not least for courage. Earlier operations in the

East, together with commitments elsewhere, had sapped the transport force, which was hard put to rebuild quickly to meet the huge requirements of a military disaster. Von Richthofen cast around to obtain more aircraft, but his available options were slim. Even if bombers such as the He 111 were just about capable of carrying supplies equal in weight to their standard bomb loads, the same was not true of the Ju 88, and most of the Dorniers had been replaced. Lack of aircraft inevitably meant that supply delivery in the face of Soviet pressure and unbelievably cold weather dropped to a daily trickle compared to the true need for a non-stop shuttle flight service to bring in multiple tons of provisions and weapons and evacuate the spiralling number of wounded men.

To keep the ground troops alive and fighting, the only real option was a breakout of the pocket before the Russians were able to capture the Stalingrad airfields, but Hitler forbade this. Consequently when, on 10 January, the Red Army mounted an offensive to close off any escape routes and capture the remaining airfields inside the pocket, the last chance to do so was gone. The Russians pushed back the perimeter defence and captured Pitomnik on the 16th. There remained a slim chance that the remnants of the Sixth Army could attempt a 'last gasp' breakout, but Hitler's order for the troops to stand firm was obeyed by Paulus, who was made up to field-marshal. This cynical move was designed to set a precedent, as no individual officer of such high rank had previously surrendered. Hitler had every confidence that this 'tradition' would prevail once again. It did not. Intensive air supply operations had not of course been conducted without casualties.

One drawback to delivering the required daily tonnage was the limited internal freight capacity, particularly of the Heinkels, which were not configured as transports. Externally the He 111 could lift supply containers in place of bombs, but the total per aircraft could not equal that of the Ju 52. This meant that the basic tonnage of 550-600 tons of supplies required per day to sustain more than 250,000 men simply could not be met. To ease the situation the Luftwaffe cast around for aircraft with a larger freight capacity and sufficient range to reach the Russian city. The Condors of KG 40 were among the few aircraft that could be made available for the airlift at short notice, but it was early 1943 before they could be deployed in the East.

Accordingly, at 0930 on 9 January the first Fw 200C of 8./Staffel KG 40 (now under the designation KGrzbV 200) landed at Pitomnik. Throwing up showers of powdery snow, the Condor was packed with some 24 tons of supplies, a weight significantly above the aircraft's maximum payload of 19 tons. A few minutes later a second Condor touched down with Staffel Kapitän Schulte-Vogelheim at the controls.

In total eighteen Condors eventually arrived in Russia from Germany and the Atlantic coast to be formed into KGrzbV 200, which was placed under the command of Major Hans Jurgen Willers. The Condors were based at Stalino, some 300 miles (480km) from Pitomnik, which had better facilities for supporting the larger transports.

One of four smaller airfields inside the Stalingrad pocket itself (the others being Bassargino, Gorodischche and Gumrak), only Pitomnik was equipped with navigational and direction-finding equipment and a powerful radio beacon. Moreover, the guns of the 9th Flak Division were able to disrupt VVS ground attacks sufficiently to prevent serious damage to these vital installations. Should the Soviets avoid the flak barrages, two Gruppen of fighters from JG 3 were usually able to drive them off. While similar ground control facilities were not available at Bassargino, that airfield was chosen as one of the two to be used as logistical airheads for supply reception and, increasingly, casualty evacuation.

On 9 January seven Condors brought 4.5 tons of fuel, 9 tons of ammunition and 22.5 tons of provisions into Pitomnik. On the return flight to Stalino, 156 wounded men were evacuated. However, by this time another of the notorious Russian winters had really set in – proving to be the worst for many years – and the appalling conditions under which the aircrews were obliged to operate immediately brought about casualties in the Condor fleet. On the 10th Schulte-Vogelheim himself took off only to return to base with engine trouble, and a second machine was unable to take off from Pitomnik; a third landed with flak damage to one of its engines and the tail unit. A fourth Condor suffered a damaged airscrew, while a fifth was lost en route back to Stalino with twenty-one wounded men aboard.

Repairs were initiated without delay but it was almost inevitable that the groundcrews servicing the Condors would experience extreme difficulties in keeping their charges airworthy. Little material assistance had been provided to prepare for their arrival on the Eastern Front – and nothing on earth could have prepared the Luftwaffe 'black men', used to French base facilities, for the harshness of the conditions or the bleak, spartan surroundings. There was no undercover hangarage at Stalino and in temperatures as low as 20 to 30 degrees below zero Centigrade it was a miracle that any flying was possible. Open-air servicing was marginally improved by the use of collapsible maintenance huts, which could be erected in front of the Condor's wing to enclose each engine nacelle. Pushed into position and raised to the height of the wings like a giant Chinese lantern, these shelters enabled mechanics to remove cowlings and gain access to the radial engines without a howling gale and driving sleet hampering their demanding work.

Somehow the groundcrews managed to maintain a flight schedule despite the extreme difficulties of finger-numbing cold. The weather also created a 'knock-on' effect if some of the ground vehicles specifically designed to support aircraft failed to start. Petrol-driven portable heater units, which pumped warm air into the engines prior to most flights, were worth their weight in gold – when they could be made to start. These vehicles were doubly useful as they were regularly used to thaw out the mechanics themselves before they could work.

The one bright spot for those German aircrews who had to contend with the temperatures of a Russian winter was the procedure for starting engines. This was not the first occasion when such low temperatures had occurred and the Luftwaffe had since 1938 developed reliable cold-start procedures for the engines fitted into all the leading fighter, bomber and transport types. Every major engine manufacturer had also participated in the programme, which in broad terms was to refute the long-held mechanics' horror of diluting engine oil with petrol. This was proven to be a myth when the technicians at Rechlin demonstrated that a Kaltstart-Mischenlage (cold-start mixing unit) could solve the problem.

All Luftwaffe units had been trained to use the cold-start procedure but until the campaign against Russia began very few problems as a direct result of extremely low temperatures had been experienced. In the light of that fact it was almost inevitable that units forget how to initiate Kaltstart, even though regulations stated that groundcrews should remain fully conversant with the procedure. This some of them did in Russia and cold starts enabled numerous flights to be undertaken when the aircraft's engines and lubricants would otherwise have frozen solid. At Stalingrad it has been reliably estimated that only 30 per cent of the units engaged in the fighting, in whatever role, remembered or followed the procedure.

Popular mythology has it that only when captured Soviet flyers were willing to cooperate with their erstwhile opponents were German groundcrews aware of cold-start procedures.

An indifferent attitude to such a vital part of winter air operations was one of the factors that mitigated against the Luftwaffe being able to support the ground troops to a greater extent than the almost superhuman degree that it did. The reason was that, quite apart from the critical lack of enough transport aircraft, once winter had taken a hold there were so many other negative aspects to trying to operate an air transport service using the basic airfields that existed within the pocket. Wolfgang Späte, in his book *Test Pilots*, summed up the difficulties:

'The regrettably negative attitude of some units, as well as of their commanders, unfortunately persisted to the end [of the Stalingrad campaign]. But there were cases where cold-start preparations were not possible, such as when an aircraft had landed with a damaged engine, or was lying on the other side of the airfield with a collapsed undercarriage, or when the crew chief had been killed or wounded while performing his duties.'

Add to these woes occasions when mountains of snow covered wings and runways such that, when refuelling was required, neither tankers, other supply vehicles nor snowploughs were able to move an inch; when ice and drifting snow obscured visibility; and when nothing – no lorry, no weapon, no gun – worked properly: these were the things that made the difference. And they were never helped by the need for men who were half frozen, with empty stomachs and wearing poor clothing, to carry out their duties in temperatures of minus 40 degrees C or less.

When the German transports were able to take off, many captains forswore fighter escort on the grounds that groups of Me 109s or Fw 190s often served to attract Russian fighters. On their own, flying low and sporting a temporary white paint finish to cover their green camouflage, enough sorties went unmolested to maintain the airlift for several weeks.

Major Willers scoured the Luftwaffe for more large transport capacity and was able to obtain several Ju 90s, Ju 290s and He 177s, which were pressed into service without delay. The big Junkers transports were ideal, as each one could lift some 8-13,000lb (4-6,000kg), but they were not available in anywhere near the required numbers. And despite its large overall size, the He 177 had only a small bomb bay and a temporary external freight capacity even more modest than that of the He 111 – leaving the Fw 200, with its relatively spacious interior and top speed of 261mph (420kmph), as the champion of the 'four-engine' element of the airlift. KG 40's aircrews therefore kept flying into the pocket for as long as they had an airstrip near enough to Stalingrad on which to land.

When the Luftwaffe transports and several fighters were forced to use Gumrak, a pot-holed, wreck-strewn wasteland of a place quite unsuitable for sustained air operations, the end was in sight. But little else was available and on the night of 18/19 January Lt Hans Gilbert managed to land his Condor in a snowstorm with visibility down to 50 yards (46 metres). Although the aircraft's tailwheel assembly was damaged, Gilbert was able to take off and evacuate, among others, Gen Hans Hube, commanding XIV Panzer Corps. Transport flights continued and Gumrak held out until the night of 21/22 January when it too had to be abandoned. Thereafter German aircraft had nowhere to land, their crews resorting to dropping supply canisters by parachute. External pick-up points normally occupied by bombs were utilised to lift large supply canisters that were resilient enough to withstand the shock of parachute landings.

Each Condor was able to accommodate a single canister on each outer wing rack and/or the shallow bay in each outboard engine nacelle designed to accommodate a 500lb bomb. Scores of Vorsorgungsbomben (provisions bombs) were released to deliver dry mixed loads (Mischlast) or liquids (Flussigkeits-Abwurfbehalter). Even then, not all the supplies were delivered into Wehrmacht hands if they drifted off course and came to earth in the Russian lines or could not be retrieved from no man's land by exhausted, emaciated German troops.

The battle for Stalingrad was all but over by 31 January, and on 2 February 1943 the Luftwaffe recorded its last transport flights into the Sixth Army area. All airfields were then closed by increasingly frequent VVS operations and the Red Army advance, and it was clear that the survivors of the encircled army had to be left to their fate. Further sorties into the pocket were parachute drops or, in extremis, free drops from an altitude of no more than 50 feet (15 metres).

Of the 488 transport aircraft lost in the abortive airlift between 24 November 1942 and the end of January 1943, seven were Focke-Wulf Condors, a figure confirmed by several sources.

Table 6: Condors lost at Stalingrad

Condors known to have been destroyed or left behind after service in Russia were:

1 Fw 200C-3 (0034/F8+GW), KGrzbV 200; captured at Stalingrad (6 KIA), 31 January 1943

2 Fw 200D-2 (0018/NA+WK), KGrzbV 200, captured at Pitomnik (6 KIA), 10 January 1943

3 Fw 200C-3 (0046/SG+KV), KGrzbV 200, captured at Pitomnik (6 KIA), 16 January 1943

4 Fw 200C-4 (0151/F8+HW), KGrzbV 200, captured at Pitomnik (6 KIA), 10 January 1943

5 Fw 200C-3/U5 (0095/F8+DH), KGrzbV 200, abandoned at Gumrak, 19 January 1943

6 Fw 200A0/S8 (3098/NK+NM) Grenzmark, captured at Orel, 23 December 1941

7 Fw 200C-3 (V13) (0025/BS+AY), KGrzbV 200, damaged by bombs at Saporoschje, A/F and abandoned 29 January 1943

These were the survivors of the small force of Condors that helped to boost the ill-fated succour of the German Sixth Army. Others included most of the four-engine strength of KGrzbV 200: Fw 200A-0/S-8 (3098/D-ACVH/NK+NM Grenzmark); Fw 200C-3/U4 (0071/ KF+QK), which suffered 50 per cent damage at Novonikolepneko and was believed abandoned there; Fw 200C-4 (0179/KF+QK), similarly damaged at Vorochilovgrad and also believed abandoned. In addition, Fw 200C-3/U4 (0771/KF+QK) was damaged at Novonikolepnovo on 22 March 1943 but returned to Germany, and Fw 200A-01 (2893/D-ADHR), the exact fate of which is unknown. The aircraft is however, believed to have crashed at Pitomnik in January 1943.

When the Red Army combed the Stalingrad airfields to 'mop up', the haul of Luftwaffe aircraft included several Condors that were fit to fly again after fairly basic servicing had been carried out by their new owners. Initially, Soviet personnel were said to be duly impressed by the equipment and performance of the Condor, no comparable aircraft then being in the Red Air Force's inventory. At least one example was apparently test-flown by NII VVS (Air Forces Scientific Research Institute), and a single Fw 200C-4, most likely C-3 0034/F8+GW, was put on display in the Culture Park (Park Kultury), Moscow, in June 1943/44 as part of an exhibition of captured enemy equipment. Further Fw 200s were captured in the spring of 1945 and subsequently used as transports by the Russians in the early postwar period, as outlined in the final chapter of this book.

As Soviet technicians pored over the Condors that had fallen into their hands virtually intact at Stalingrad, so the resourceful Germans were deploying them elsewhere.

Before the Condors were finally pulled out of Russia, KGrzbV 200 participated in several more supply flights to support the withdrawal of German forces from the Caucasus. Continuing to come under the operational control of Luftflotte 4 with its highly capable commander Wolfram von Richthofen, this formation made an energetic recovery from the debacle of the Stalingrad airlift. KGrzbV 200 was able to boost supply flights to von Manstein's 17th Army so significantly that the Wehrmacht's spring 1943 counter-offensive was rarely short of supplies and met with outstanding success.

Richthofen deployed his transports, including the Condors, to supply the Gotenkopf (Goth's Head) bridgehead, one of several short-lived operational names allocated to identify various areas, under Fliegerkorps VIII control.

Air supply operations, admittedly on a much more modest scale than had been demanded at Stalingrad and using better-equipped airfields under improving weather conditions, amply demonstrated that the Luftwaffe's transport force was still more than equal to such a task, the ubiquitous Ju 52/3m continuing to be the backbone of the deployed units despite the recent losses. Heavier-capacity aircraft were still required for some operations, but by early February 1943 the remaining Fw 200s had to be withdrawn from the Eastern Front to resume their role in the Battle of the Atlantic. They flew back to Berlin-Staaken to be redesignated VIII./KG 40. It appears, however, that not all the Condors returned to Germany and, as noted above, it was early spring before the last airworthy machine had left with a German crew at the controls.

Atlantic losses

January 1943 had seen the attrition rate of the Condor force climb a little higher when, only three days into the month, Fw 200C-4 0170/CH+CK of I./Gruppe was 15 per cent damaged by, it is believed, an engine fire that occurred while being run up for take-off from Vaernes, a base that was clearly quite demanding for operating large aircraft such as the Fw 200. On 17 January another Condor was reported overdue on a reconnaissance sortie out of Norway when Fw 200C-5 0204/F8+CL of 3./Staffel apparently went down into the North Sea. With no further word on their fate, KG 40 had little choice but to post Oblt Ernst Rebensburg and six members of his crews as missing, believed lost.

February

Although February 1943 seems to have been relatively trouble-free for the Geschwader, further setbacks were always in the wind. The early weeks of the year continued with a not untypical additional workload for KG 40's hard-working groundcrews faced with repairing damage, much of it the result of accidents rather than combat. A spate of crashes plagued the Condor throughout its combat career, there being numerous incidents that resulted in a varying scale of damage as reported by Luftwaffe inspectors.

One of the greatest hazards to the Condor crews of KG 40 was to come into contact with rising ground in poor visibility. Viewed by a cameraman who also recorded an impromptu marker for one of its crewmen, this Condor may have come down in Ireland, the graveyard of several crews and aircraft. *F. Selinger*

March

On 18 March KG 40's I./Gruppe temporarily lost the striking power of yet another Condor when C-4 0173/F8+?? suffered 20 per cent damage in a hard landing at Vaernes. Repaired and back on operations, this particular aircraft would spend additional time in a hangar when, as part of III./Gruppe, it sustained 25 per cent damage at Cognac on 13 September 1943 while its engines were being run up. Again the cause of the damage was almost certainly fire.

Further unwelcome losses occurred in March. On the 24th Oberfeldwebel Werner Bock of 7./Staffel perished with his four crew members when Fw 200C-4 0192/F8+ER went down in the Bay of Biscay; the bodies of the German airmen were subsequently washed ashore in Spain. Three days later Lt Fritz Marschall's Fw 200C-4 (0168/F8+??) of III./Gruppe was apparently lost to German flak, which mistakenly opened fire on it west of Royan, France.

Reversal of fortune

From 14 to 20 March the Atlantic Ocean witnessed the largest convoy battle of the entire war when twenty-one ships totalling 140,842grt succumbed to U-boats. Four different convoys were attacked by several hunting groups and, although many skippers were frustrated in their endeavours by surface escorts and Allied aircraft, only one U-boat was sunk. Descriptions of such engagements state that on numerous occasions U-boats were 'driven off' rather than being sunk or damaged, which was a common enough occurrence. The heavy loss of freighters in this battle brought about some discussion of the convoy system being abandoned due to one fundamental disadvantage of grouping ships closely – if enough U-boats could attack en masse the toll was almost bound to be high, or so went the theory. Sound as it often was in planning its attacks, B du U found actual events were about to herald a reversal of fortunes for the German submarine fleet, so much so that the Allies marked mid-1943 as a turning point in the Battle of the Atlantic.

Early in the year KG 40 underwent a degree of reorganisation. I./Gruppe continued to be an all-Condor formation, but the attrition rate and the still slow output of new aircraft meant that it was impractical to fully equip a third Gruppe. Moves were therefore made to bring all Condors under the six Staffeln of I./ and III./Gruppen, still pending a degree of replacement by the He 177, which was also in short supply. Crew training on the new type had by then been under way for several months, but emergencies still arose far too regularly with the result that the Condor's intended replacement in KG 40 met further unexpected delays and protracted periods on the ground pending technical changes and modifications.

II./KG 40 had been additionally operating the He 111H-6, and in late 1942 the Do 217E-5 had been issued to part of the unit while it was based at Soeserberg in the Netherlands. Ju 88C-6 fighters had also been introduced into 13./Staffel, thus changing the composition of the Luftwaffe' s premier anti-shipping unit and broadening its operational commitments.

New weapons

It was then decided that all the Fw 200s would henceforth come under the control of III./KG 40 and to that end 8./Staffel replaced 2./Staffel, which had previously operated both Fw 200Cs and Heinkels. Training for the Condor crews now began to take in the additional demands of sighting and launching the Hs 293A glider bomb, a missile that was to be used by specially adapted models of the Do 217 and He 177 as well as the Fw 200C – at least, that appears to have been the original intention, but very few operational sorties seem to have been flown by the Condor.

One of the most promising of the advanced new aerial weapons developed by Germany in the second half of the war, the Henschel Hs 293A glider bomb was quite successful when used by aircraft other than the Condor. The degree of participation of the Condor in the programme is questionable, this being the only known view of the missiles attached to the aircraft.

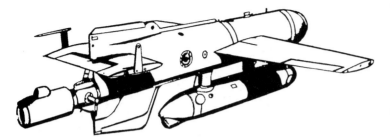

Trials with the Hs 293 began for Condor crews, probably at the Versuchsstelle Peenemunde West, when the programme took on tangible form with the initial flight-testing of dummy bomb rounds. Dipl. Ing Max Mayer was head of Department E2, which was responsible for 'automatically or remotely guided missiles and rocket-propelled aircraft'. He had previously worked with Focke-Wulf's wind tunnel department at Bremen and would have been fully conversant with the aerodynamic properties of the Condor and its suitability to carry the Hs 293. Mayer was a well-qualified pilot who in 1944 obtained his higher grade Luftwaffe licence for land-based aircraft, having completed some 3,500 flights and 2,500 flying hours. Together with the Condor, the Focke-Wulf 44, 58 and 190 appeared in his logbook. The Condor appears not to have been associated with 'proving' the only other German stand-off weapon that became operational, the so-called Fritz X, but was concentrated entirely around Henschel's remarkable missile.

Modifications

To enable the Fw 200 to better accommodate two missiles externally, Focke-Wulf engineers covered the shallow bomb-carrier recesses in the outer engine nacelles and thereby created deep fairings that formed a new aft section. This configuration change brought about the Fw 200C-6, which was used mainly to test the Hs 293's flight profile following launch. Few problems appear to have been encountered during this testing phase, the Henschel missile proving to be one of the most trouble-free new weapons that the Luftwaffe adopted for operational use. It was a relatively simple adaptation of a 500lb (225kg) bomb, which, with wing and tail surfaces, replicated a miniature aircraft, without a complex internal guidance system that was susceptible to failure.

Each Hs 293A had a 2,870lb (1,300kg) launching weight, a total extra payload of 5,740lb (2,600kg) to be lifted by the mother ship, which was not excessive. The one weakness of the system was its radio control; this could be affected by passive enemy action in the form of jamming, and Allied electronics experts were on the case immediately after the missile made its combat debut.

The modifications made to the Fw 200C-6 and later C-8 thus provided each aircraft with a dual missile carrier platform, enabling the Hs 293s to be firmly attached in a horizontal attitude. This was important to ensure a clean launch and subsequent 'straight and level' acceleration in the early stages of flight. En route to the target, the winged bomb was steered by an operator in the aircraft who sighted on a flare in the tail of the Henschel and used a small joystick to keep the missile on target.

Both the Fw 200C-6 and C-8 were conversions of existing airframes, but aircraft built as new accommodated the necessary internal wiring for the guidance system, the radar set and an operator. They were built in modest numbers, which may have coincided with an official order placing greater emphasis on training rather than an operational role for the C-6 and C-8, probably further evidence of a change in operational commitments.

A cleanly launched Hs 293A was designed to attain a maximum speed of 375mph (600kmph), its acceleration being such that the carrier aircraft needed to be held in level flight for a minimum time; this did not, however, instil much confidence in the Condor aircrew as the aircraft also had

Sliding in close to his wingman, a Condor pilot of 8./Staffel holds his aircraft steady while a crewman in the sister aircraft captures his F8+ES on film. Adopting a standard 'straight and level' attitude put less strain and reduced wear on the Focke-Wulf bomber, which would cover hundreds of miles throttled back at low engine revolutions. *F. Selinger*

to ideally maintain a steady climb, the operator keeping his eye on the flare. Any violent manoeuvre could easily result in an erratic bomb launch with no guarantee that the operator could keep sight of the flare in the missile's tail and regain control over its progress should this momentarily be lost. With a maximum range of 10 miles (16km) and good acceleration immediately after launch, the missile should have given the launch aircraft ample time to clear the area, were it not for the guidance requirement. The bomber could not simply execute a 180-degree turn and exit the area with all speed, as the bomb had to remain in sight of the operator. And if the missile 'mother ship' was an Fw 200C, flying steadily over the sea a few hundred feet above the waves risked imposing further stresses on an already weak airframe. The exact number of test launches made by Fw 200Cs to refine the weapon for its combat debut is unknown, although a total of 1,700 Hs 293As were completed, a percentage of which were expended in tests.

An anonymous Condor co-pilot photographs a second aircraft diving away towards a cloud bank during a sortie that was partly flown for publicity purposes, as this and other prints in the sequence were widely published. Although stress-inducing manoeuvres were frowned upon due to the Condor's weak structure, using cloud cover could make the difference between the element of surprise and alerting merchant shipping and escorts.

Among the Condors involved in testing the Hs 293 were:

Fw 200C-4 0106/NT+BF	Possibly served with KG 40 as F8+BH and was fitted with FuG 216 for trials.
Fw 200C-6 (0242/TK+CX)	Modified to accommodate the advanced FuG 242 Berlin radar, while testing at Tarnewittz and Rechlin was undertaken from October 1943 with Fw 200C-6/U2 0216/TA+MR; the fact that the latter aircraft was the first of the C-6 variants may indicate that the tests it carried out were also connected with the Hs 293 guidance system.
Fw 200C-8/U10 (0259/TO+XO)	Had the deepened nacelles for Hs 293 carriage and was one of only two C-/U10s (the suffix indicating longer range) to be built.

In all, fifteen Fw 200C-6s were completed. They were not allocated sequential Werke Nummern but were interspersed with C-4s, C-5s and C-8s at the end of Condor production.

The total number of C-8s to appear was twenty-two, Fw 200C-8 0268/TO+XX being the final example.

Purposeful

In Fw 200C-8 form the Focke-Wulf Condor reached its zenith as a warplane. With mounting points for revolutionary new weapons and radar to help locate it targets, the last of the Condors may have looked purposeful, even deadly, but in reality it had all but reached the end of its operational lifespan.

The C-8 was indeed more capable than preceding variants and in a more forgiving operational environment the last of the Condors could have achieved more realistic results with effective missile attacks. However, restricted in its deployment by opposing forces, the aircraft became an operational trials vehicle for the Hs 293's launch and guidance system; the few early operational anti-shipping sorties that were flown proved abortive, with the additional hazard that the crews encountered enemy patrol bombers, carrier fighters, escort ships and armed freighters when flying at the optimum low-altitude, straight-and-level approach required for a successful launch. Similar problems were experienced by KG 40's He 177 crews, who flew an aircraft that painted a substantial radar picture if it did not alert enemy pilots to its presence visually – and at a considerable distance from the intended target and missile launching point. Wasting trained crews to little or no purpose finally persuaded the Luftwaffe chiefs to stop using the larger bombers and hang the missiles on something a little more nimble, which had a greater chance of hitting the target. Consequently, for all its promise, the Hs 293's limited success was achieved only by several Do 217s of KG 40 and 100. A very small number of launches by He 177s were unsuccessful for the same reason that the Condors could not conduct an effective anti-shipping campaign with them.

The Condors that were modified to carry the Hs 293 became little more than attrition replacements for other units that used the glider bomb 'in anger', particularly their own parent unit, KG 40. Even then, risking the bombers was foolhardy.

When anti-shipping attacks resulted in the loss of a number of He 177s, the Fw 200 ostensibly 'replaced its replacement', although the aircraft's role became largely that of reconnaissance and perhaps as an operational trainer for crews flying more capable twin-engine aircraft who would use the Henschel-designed 'stand-off' bomb in combat with a marginally superior ability to survive.

That margin was very small indeed. Even so, the progress made by the Germans in developing effective 'stand-off' weapons proved superior to that of the Allies; several attempts were made, particularly by the US, which deployed them in a small number of B-17 Fortress raids in the European theatre and in the Pacific, where Navy PBY-2 Privateers successfully launched the BAT missile.

For the Condor the results achieved with glider bombs were similar to that of the aerial torpedo insofar as the Luftwaffe had limited call on alternative aircraft of comparable size with which to conduct realistic airborne trials. Unsurprisingly, the aircraft was relatively easily reconfigured to carry these unusual loads but – equally unsurprisingly – could not call upon non-existent residues of performance to really prove them in action.

How low can you get? Avoiding fire from four defensive guns by flying along the line of the target ship, a good Condor crew could start fires and release bombs while the gun crews' sights were masked by masts, davits, ventilators and deck houses. By the time their field of fire was clear, the German crew had probably inflicted fatal damage. *F. Selinger*

Target photos were valuable training aids for new crews, some of whom must have been impressed by the height at which KG 40's Condors usually attacked ships. If this freighter packed with deck cargo went down it would have been another serious loss to the Allies. *F. Selinger*

This dramatic view from a Condor, as an attack on a freighter develops, shows just how close the aircraft needed to get to carry out a damaging if not fatal bombing and strafing run. Ideally completed in one or two passes, the 'low and fast' strike gave the ship's company little time to man any weapons. *F. Selinger*

Radio guidance of air-launched missiles was a parallel development by the Germans, and this too largely achieved what the designers intended.

The Achilles heel of all such systems was enemy jamming on frequencies known to have been used to guide the bombs. Added to the performance limitations of the aircraft that the Luftwaffe was forced to deploy as missile mother ships, the concept was hard put to return comprehensive data. Most critically, even had this been possible the Germans no longer enjoyed the luxury of time in which to continue research. That the Hs 293 was susceptible to jamming had been proven in Italy by KG 100 at the time of the landings at Anzio in 1944, when numerous missile launchings were soon neutralised by passive Allied defence measures.

Other roles?

If being adapted to carry missiles was potentially the most sophisticated and technically demanding role for the wartime Condor, the aircraft also performed useful if more mundane 'maid of all work' duties behind the scenes.

Its size and load-carrying capability brought about a number of experiments, including that of glider tug. Little is known about the extent of flight testing of the necessary towing bars, cables and so forth (if any), but the Luftwaffe had maintained an interest in glider assault from the earliest days of the Second World War. Initial successes achieved by Fallschirmjager troops being borne into battle by gliders towed by Ju 52s were not overlooked when the relatively simple conversion of larger transport aircraft suggested more ambitious deployment for future operations. These latter focused on the Mediterranean, where Crete was successfully captured (albeit at a high cost in troops and Ju 52s), Stalingrad, where gliders were assembled but never used, and the far more strategically sound plan for an invasion of Malta. Notwithstanding the gradually increasing risk to almost any German aircraft being flown as a slow glider tug into a war zone after mid-1943, thought was given to the Fw 200 being converted to take towing gear to hook up a glider, most likely of the size and weight of the DFS 230. Nothing practical is believed to have come from this design study.

Condor versus Liberator

With Lend-Lease supplies of aircraft gathering pace, the RAF was finally able to close the 300-mile Atlantic gap, or 'black hole', by deploying long-range Liberators. Beginning in 1943 these and other Coastal Command aircraft, notably the Handley Page Halifax and B-17 Fortress, were occasionally proving to be deadly adversaries for KG 40's Condors over their hitherto sacrosanct hunting ground. That year the USAAF also began flying its own anti-submarine patrols from bases in England and North Africa.

Closer to the shore even more dangerous Allied combat aircraft could now confront the German maritime flyers, with the odds being heavily stacked against the Luftwaffe. Such an encounter took place on 12 March 1943 when Beaufighters of No 248 Squadron caught up with a III./KG 40 Condor over the Bay of Biscay.

In a three-minute running battle the Fw 200C-4 (0186/F8+ER) flown by Lt Ernst Rabolt tried frantically to shake off the well-armed British fighters but to no avail. The Beaufighters' cannon and machine-guns set alight both the Focke-Wulf's port engines and fire was also observed to have broken out in the fuselage. As the German machine made a long, flat glide towards the sea trailing smoke, two men were seen to jump from it but no dinghy and no survivors were observed after the aircraft ditched. Rabolt and his five-man crew were assumed lost.

The appearance of the Beaufighter was a traumatic event for KG 40's crews; fast and very heavily armed, the British twin could be a deadly adversary – so much so that even crews of the Condor Geschwader's sister V./Gruppe, flying the potent Ju 88, were advised to avoid contact whenever possible. An even more potent threat loomed for the Germans in the shape of the de Havilland Mosquito, which generally began to replace the Beaufighter in Fighter and Coastal Command squadrons in late 1944.

A sight of the final assembly line at Consolidated's plant at Fort Worth, Texas, would have given many a Condor crewman a heart attack, for it was the products of this and other plants across the US that would ultimately defeat the Germans, however long it took. Sea-search camouflage adorns these Liberators, colours similar to those adopted for the aircraft credited with shooting down a number of KG 40's aircraft in 1943. *USAF*

Should they suffer the misfortune of having to ditch, the fate of aircrew downed in the Atlantic and Bay of Biscay was grim indeed. If they did not manage to clamber into a dinghy their survival could be measured in minutes. Even a well-equipped dinghy offered scant protection from the bone-numbing cold even in ostensibly milder spring weather, and the chances of being picked was reliant on a tiny rubber boat being spotted in conditions that contrived to make it nearly invisible.

One of the grimmer aspects of the Battle of the Atlantic was that relatively few aircrew survived their aircraft being shot down, as demonstrated by the experiences of KG 40 since the opening of the anti-shipping campaign. Anther German crew was lost on 18 March when a Condor attacked the French sloop *Savorgnan de Brazza*. Engaged on convoy protection, the well-armed ship shot down an aircraft that could not be positively identified due to fog. Opinion differed as to whether

After carrier fighters, a very effective counter to the Condor turned out to be the Consolidated B-24 Liberator. Both RAF and USAAF squadrons flew it on Atlantic patrols and a number of spectacular combats ensued when the 'four-engine fighters' proceeded to dogfight! Identified by Coastal Command's short-lived single-letter code system, BZ877/2-Q was one of 86 Squadron's Liberator Vs. *IWM*

it was a Condor or a B-17 Fortress, but delay in opening fire could have resulted in the loss of the ship. For ten seconds all hell broke loose as thirty-seven guns of different calibres blasted into the sky. Fatally hit in the port wing, the aircraft caught fire and dived into the sea in an enormous fountain of spray. Still doubt remained as to its identity and it was only when a body was brought on deck that the sloop's crew could breath a sigh of relief. The victim had been the Condor flown by Walter Frohlich. As an indication of how serious a threat the Focke-Wulf bombers posed to Allied shipping, the ship's company were wildly congratulated on this success.

En route to Gibraltar, the crew of the *Savorgnan de Brazza* witnessed the curious spectacle of two Condors and two Fortresses patrolling much the same area of sky, the former to maintain a running commentary on the progress of potential maritime targets, the others to guard those same ships against

The other side of the Battle of the Atlantic for the Luftwaffe was the loss of its aircraft in actions that were sometimes dramatically caught on film. On 12 March 1943 Beaufighters caught a Condor and quickly curtailed its war career. None of the German crew survived the crash. *IWM*

attack. It was reckoned that the Fw 200 and B-17 more or less cancelled each other out in terms of performance and armament, and for that reason they left each other alone – most of the time. On 20 March one Condor crew decided to break the monotony and attack the *Brazza*. It was not a wise move. Coming in low over the sloop's bow the Condor met a barrage of heavy shellfire that blew away part of its fuselage. The bomber dived into the undercast and the ship's crew could not be absolutely certain they had destroyed it, but the kill (aircraft details unknown) was subsequently confirmed.

A curious rider to this saga was the fact that the *Brazza* crew later witnessed Luftwaffe aircraft attacking the rear of a convoy with what looked like 'bombs of unusual size'. They were reminded that the North Atlantic Convoy Instructions had stated that the Germans were beginning to use new weapons, which was a veiled reference to the Hs 293 missile. The instructions also suggested, seemingly in all seriousness, that: 'The radio guidance of flying bombs may easily be thrown into confusion by means of a small sparking station. A simple method is to set an electric razor in motion.'

April: recognition

In common with other first-line Luftwaffe units, KG 40's crews continued to receive their share of awards and decorations for operational milestones and achievements in combat. Those individuals awarded the Ritterkreuz are the subject of an Appendix, but by mid-1943 the picture regarding the vulnerability of Atlantic convoys had, from the German viewpoint, changed radically, and with it KG 40's future role. Faced with retaliatory Allied air and seaborne weapons that significantly reduced shipping losses and steadily decimated the U-boat fleet, the Condors themselves recorded fewer sinkings. It was clear that KG 40 might achieve greater success if operations were switched to a less dangerous theatre of war, particularly the Arctic Ocean and the convoy routes carrying war material to Russia. Such was their range and endurance that the Condors could support Luftwaffe anti-shipping strikes without a change of base, although the medium bombers were obliged to relocate to be nearer to their potential targets. Both bombs and torpedoes were deployed in an effort to prevent supplies reaching the Soviets, who were building their air and land armies for the decisive battles that lay ahead.

May

Severe weather also prevailed during the early spring of 1943 to blunt the effectiveness of KG 40's Condors, but on 3 May U-439 was alerted to the presence of a southbound convoy via radio signals transmitted by air reconnaissance. Some fifteen ships were sighted, escorted by only two armed trawlers. Oberleutnant sur See von Tippelskirch made all speed to rendezvous with the ships, Kapitän Leutnant Hans Stock commanding U-659 setting a similar course. Another Condor message then reported a second convoy of twenty-eight ships, also heading south. The same meagre escort force of two trawlers guarded the merchantmen, or so the Condor communication indicated.

May was developing into another grimly momentous month in the Battle of the Atlantic as, on the 24th, Karl Doenitz declared that, in view of recent heavy losses, his U-boats would not engage in protracted battles against Allied convoys. The C-in-C U-boats would, he said, resume such operations only when the situation had been clarified and new weapons had become available. The latter referred to equipment such as the Schnorkel system fitted to the much-anticipated Type XXI U-boat and other technical advances that promised to hand the initiative back to the German submarines. A new generation of advanced 'electric boats' had entered production and were reaching the force in small numbers; they would give Germany's submariners (as Doenitz believed) a welcome advantage, but realistically many knew that this could only be temporary. As to the future of the Kriegsmarine's primary striking force, that lay almost totally in the hands of the enemy: the initiative was slipping away and, once lost, would be all but impossible to regain.

Seafire combat

On 24 May 1943 another enemy fighter type, the Supermarine Seafire, was encountered by Condors for the first time when an Fw 200C shadowing a convoy en route to Gibraltar was intercepted by fighters from HMS *Unicorn*. A bitter combat ensued, ending with a damaged Condor and two chastened FAA pilots (flying Mk IICs MA975/L and NM917/A) of 887 Squadron, who waded into their potential target. In the event neither pilot managed to bring the German machine down despite using most of their ammunition. Due to the limited and rather late deployment of Seafires from carriers in the Atlantic, other skirmishes between KG 40 and navalised Spitfires were few, with only one Fw 200 being claimed as destroyed by Royal Navy pilots flying the type, on 22 June. On that occasion HMS *Battler* had launched a section of fighters over an area of the eastern Atlantic and Seafire Mk IIC MB302 of 808 Squadron flown by S/Lt A. G. Penney was credited with the demise of an Fw 200, the identity of which is uncertain.

A final encounter between a Seafire and an Fw 200 took place on 10 December 1943 when S/Lt Sachnovsky of 807 Squadron in Mk IB PA100/D launched from *Fencer*. The FAA pilot caught up with the Condor and 'chased it off'.

In developing the Spitfire for carrier deployment the Admiralty had conceded that the Grumman Wildcat possessed many of the qualities that the Seafire could not duplicate, such as a rugged landing gear, a cockpit roomy enough for a well-built pilot and general airframe strength. These and other advantages better tailored the F4F to the extreme conditions often prevailing in European waters – which eventually released the Seafire for extensive service in the Far East. Beforehand, several Royal Navy carrier cruises into the Atlantic with Seafires embarked helped to prove the point that Lend-Lease fighters had ably filled the gap between the deployment of fixed-wing Hurricanes and Fulmars and the appearance of 'folding' Seafires. All four types had countered Luftwaffe anti-shipping activity over many months when the danger posed by their mere presence had to be taken into account by Fliegerführer Atlantik.

The Condors also faced other airborne threats. On 9 July 1943 just how real the danger inherent in Beaufighter interception could be was brought home to Fw Nikolaus Gunther and his six-man crew. Flying Fw 200C-4/U3 0178/F8+NT of 9./Staffel in the vicinity of a convoy, Gunther was attacked by three Beaufighters from No 233 (or perhaps No 248) Squadron based on Gibraltar. Badly damaged, the Condor limped away, Gunther intending to reach dry land in Portugal and carry out a crash-landing. He almost made it but the cliffs near San Pedro du Cova proved too high for the damaged aircraft to clear and it crashed into them, taking the lives of everyone on board.

Condor crews had enjoyed a long and relatively safe hunting ground off Oporto in the Bay of Biscay west of Portugal, and 11 July opened with operations that aimed to repeat past successes, but this time an attack by two Condors did not to turn out to be quite so spectacular. The first intended victim of the German airmen was the liner *Duchess of York* (22,021grt), sailing as a troopship in a convoy that, they observed, was well armed against air attack in the form of an escorting corvette. Nevertheless Oblt Ludwig Progner primed his bombs and dived on the *Duchess*.

The liner failed to succumb to the big Focke-Wulf's weapons – insofar as it was not seen to sink – nor did the freighter *California* (16,792grt), which was part of the same westbound convoy and was also bombed. The vessel resisted the efforts of either or both Condor crews to send her to the bottom – a frustration and a blow to professional pride, but the fortunes of war have little regard for such things and, despite coordinating their attack runs, the pair of Condors were denied a confirmed sinking on this occasion. Both ships were, however, subsequently written off as a result of the air attacks: both had reportedly been set on fire and they burned to the point where they had to be abandoned. This final act would not have been witnessed by the Condor crews who were well on their way home by the time a rescue operation to pick up as many troops as possible was under way. Another act that went unseen by the German airmen was the British troopship *Port Fairey* (8,337grt) making for Casablanca escorted by a single Royal Navy destroyer, while two naval vessels picked up troops from the stricken vessels. Their combined efforts succeeded in the rescue of all but fifty-seven of the men who had been embarked in the transports.

American help

Having already encountered a number of different Allied aircraft during their Atlantic patrols, two of KG 40's Condor crews clashed with a pair of American PBY-5As on 12 July 1943. These machines were part of US Navy Patrol Squadron VPB-73 flying a convoy protection mission out of Agadir, French Morocco. The Condors had intercepted the tiny convoy consisting of the *Port Fairey* and the corvette HMS *Swale* just as the US amphibians appeared on the scene.

It was while climbing to provide top cover for the ships that the crew of Catalina 73P-2, commanded by Patrol Plane Captain Lt (j.g.) John W. Drew USNR, spotted what they initially took to be a pair of RAF Vickers Wellington bombers. The other Catalina headed off to initiate a standard patrol pattern at 800 feet (245 metres) above the ships. It was only when an object fell from one of the other aircraft that the Condors were recognised for what they were. Drew and his co-pilot, Lt (j.g.) Edward Bourgeault, another Naval Reservist, determined to block further attempts by the Focke-Wulfs to bomb the ships and manoeuvred accordingly, to literally get in the way of the German bomb-aimers. This the Catalina succeeded in doing by flying a collision course every time the Condor pilots made a renewed bombing run.

Having climbed to 13,000 feet (3,970 metres) during this passive turning match, Drew's machine came under heavy fire from the Condor's cannon and machine-guns. Responding with blasts from its 0.30-calibre bow gun, the 'Cat' crew additionally sprayed the German machine from its waist guns as it swept past.

Determined not to let their seaborne target slip away, the Condor pilots repeatedly attempted to evade the Catalinas and position themselves to attack the ships. One German skipper boldly tried to initiate a tail attack on the PBY but was forced to break away by return fire. Cloud cover briefly interrupted the combat, which then resumed with the Condors making a further attempt to attack the ships. Manning the Catalina's single bow gunner, Carl Adams, scored several hits on one of the Condors before he was presented with a perfect shot from 100 feet (30 metres) away, his pilot holding the aircraft in a steep bank. Adams, who later reported that he was 'working the machine-gun like a pump handle', raked the Focke-Wulf and saw smoke stream from one of its engines. As both the Condors turned away, Drew attempted to catch them but they appeared faster than his PBY. Flying over the ships he had protected so well, John Drew saw an Aldis lamp flash the message 'Thanks for the coverage'.

Part of the Allied airpower build-up to combat and ultimately neutralise the threat posed by U-boats, the Consolidated PBY Catalina was one of the capable and reliable US aircraft that re-equipped Coastal Command squadrons from 1941. The 'Cat' eventually served with eight RAF squadrons in Europe and its patrol area was vast, ranging from the North Atlantic west of Ireland to the North Sea, the Norwegian and Barents Seas and the White Sea out to Archangel in Russia. As the Catalina possessed a range of 2,000 miles (3,320km), it was not unusual for flights helping to close the Shetlands-Faeroes-Iceland gap to last eighteen hours or more. Such sorties were not only long but often tedious, the drone of the engines and the miles and miles of sea passing under the wings having a soporific effect on the crews, often without anything remotely hostile being sighted. Several spectacular attacks on U-boats were made by Catalinas, the results being in proportion to the fluctuating fortunes of the German submarines.

Fewer skirmishes with Condors seem to have been reported by Catalina crews than with other Allied aircraft, although it was inevitable that they would cross swords when they approached the same patrol area. No 240 Squadron had first recorded one such clash during 1941, the squadron having been the first RAF unit to receive the PBY-5 (Catalina Mk I) in March that year.

Cat fight

Condor crews had come into contact with a Coastal Command Catalina on 4 March 1942, when two of KG 40's aircraft, which had been about to attack Allied shipping, were intercepted by the aircraft (FP172/) flown by Dennis A. Briggs of No 202 Squadron. Known as 'Bismarck Briggs' ever since he and his crew had spotted the elusive German capital ship during the epic sea chase of May 1941, the pilot opened fire on the first Condor and both machines sustained superficial damage in the ensuing exchange. Briggs flew a 'blocking' pattern, getting between the Condor and its intended target and successfully shielding his seaborne charges. Both Condors were dissuaded from any further attempts to attack the ships and broke off. Briggs did the same and landed at base after a flight lasting eighteen hours.

With the patrol capabilities of the PBY Catalina, B-24 Liberator and Short Sunderland all matching that of the Condor, mid-1943 represented a definite change in fortune for the KG 40 crews. As before, when faced with a new Allied counter to their anti-shipping attacks, they had few options but to avoid areas where hostile aircraft were likely to be encountered and to vary their own surveillance patterns. It was not of course possible to anticipate all eventualities, as the Allied air forces had undergone gradual expansion since November 1942 when Operation 'Torch' had seen American forces land in North Africa.

The Germans henceforth had to face the danger of coastal bases being utilised by Allied (mainly US) patrol bombers. By early 1943 this threat had become a reality, although the build-up of long-range landplanes and flying boat units was slow at first. It would soon gather momentum.

For KG 40 trouble-free flights continued to be completed, often around Portugal, irrespective of the threat posed by Allied airpower. Single aircraft could be elusive in the vast area of the Atlantic and, flying low or high, the German aircrews could evade detection by the most alert Allied airmen. The Condors, many of which were by that time equipped with reliable ASV radar, continued to pose a threat to convoys, as did the U-boats.

However, attacks on ships by individual Condors drew urgent calls for air support, which was usually forthcoming and with admirable speed. For the Germans the probability of their own aircraft becoming a target was higher than ever before; sorties carried a much greater risk of detection and damage, if not destruction, by Allied air and sea units, so much so that such operations were almost a thing of the past. There were months in this middle phase of the war when KG 40's aircraft conducted little more than training flights, although the important weather reconnaissance sorties up into the Arctic Circle continued. And despite the heightened risks, the Condors achieved further success against Allied shipping. Numerous large-capacity passenger liners had been pressed into Allied service as troopships when large bodies of men needed to be landed on distant shores and, although the attrition rate exacted by the Germans on this traffic was not crippling, several liners were attacked and sunk.

More conventional interception of Condors by land-based RAF fighters also increased during 1943. In June Mosquitoes joined several squadrons engaged on Instep patrols, which were tailored specifically to intercept enemy aircraft over the Bay of Biscay, and although their numbers were small No 151 Squadron showed that no existing Luftwaffe aircraft was safe from a determined Mossie attack. Two aircraft, one flown by F/O Boyle and Sgt Freisner, with P/Os Humphreys and Lamb manning a second, found Fw 200C-4 0147/F8+CR some 250 miles (400km) west of Bordeaux. Both Mosquito pilots opened fire on the big German machine, which showed no sign of retaliating with its own guns. The combat ended with the Condor plunging into the sea with its tail blown off.

CAM swansong

Meanwhile the original convoy protection ships with their single Hurricane fighter, the Catapult Aircraft Merchantmen (CAM ships), continued to offer some protection to convoys well into 1943, although the scheme had about run its course with the commissioning of several more Royal Navy escort carriers. Guarding the forty-ship convoy SL.133 outbound from Sierra Leone with a stop at Gibraltar on 23 July 1943, the *Empire Tide* and *Empire Darwin* represented the last two CAM ships in service. The ships took station to guard eight columns of five vessels each – *Empire Tide* heading the extreme port column and *Empire Darwin* that on the port side. Despite the fact that their parent unit was due to be disbanded when they reached home, no complacency on the part of the CAM ship crews was evident, as it was common knowledge among merchant seamen that sailings from the Rock were regularly reported by German agents watching the sea traffic from the other side of the Bay of Algeciras. Therefore trouble from the Luftwaffe was not entirely unexpected. Sure enough, on 28 July an alert sent P/O James A. Stewart aloft from the *Empire Darwin* to seek out two reported Condors, one being the Fw 200C-4 (0132/F8+LL) of II./KG 40 captained by Fw Alfred Wolfrass. Making firing passes on the German aircraft, the Hurricane's guns jammed and Wolfrass left the scene in a hurry, setting a course for Vaernes. The other German machine had been shot down.

The *Empire Tide*'s Hurricane, flown by P/O P. J. R. Flynn, attacked what was reported to be a third Condor. Flynn's 'damaged' claim was confirmed at the time, but there were apparently no further losses for KG 40, at least to Hurricanes, on what had thus far been a less than successful day.

Unbeknown to the German aircrew, when the convoy passed roughly due west of Bordeaux some 800 miles (1,290km) distant, *Empire Tide* asked for assistance from a USAAF B-24D Liberator. The Hurricanes would be held back as other Condors (up to eight) had been reported, and these did materialise later on. In the meantime the B-24, flown by 1st Lt Elbert W. Hyde, obliged the British seamen and intercepted an Fw 200 that was attempting to attack a straggler from SL.133/MKS.18. Hyde dived practically to sea level to hit the Condor from astern. Closing up to make a firing run from 600 yards (550 metres), the Liberator gunners fired until the Condor went into the sea. During the action the German machine managed to put several 20mm cannon rounds into the B-24's top turret area, and T/Sgt James G. Kehoe was killed. The American aircraft also had its port outboard engine put out of action by the Condor's fire, and a prompt return to Port Lyautey was made, the Liberator being sent on its way by enthusiast watchers from the convoy ships, who were pleased to witness retribution for one of the hated Condors that had often plagued them. At the time it was feared that the Liberator had been lost.

Elated by the destruction of one Condor, *Empire Darwin* (*Empire Tide*'s catapult had developed a fault) turned 15 degrees off course in order to launch Jimmy Stewart to intercept a further two Condors, approaching the convoy at high altitude. Just before he was launched a third Condor was spotted flying at 500 feet (152 metres), 10 miles (160km) to the north-west; Stewart could see this aircraft clearly from the cockpit of his Hurricane and he was launched at 1938.

The Condor climbed to 1,000 feet (305 metres), turning south, then east. Stewart could not be contacted by radio from his parent ship but any further vectors were unnecessary as the Hurricane closed in on its quarry. Apparently the KG 40 crew took no evasive action as the British fighter closed in, the pilot opening fire at 300 yards (275 metres). The German crew retaliated with their guns but their fire was reported to be inaccurate as Stewart lined up for a second run before his guns jammed. Observers on the freighter *City of Exeter* kept the German aircraft in view and later reported that it crashed into the sea. On return Stewart noted that the ships' gunners were enthusiastically pumping shells into the sky, firing at a Condor flying at 7,000 feet (2,135 metres).

Meanwhile all was not well at the 1st Squadron's base at Craw Field as fog had rolled in and at sunset the area was completely 'socked in'. Elbert Hyde nursing the damaged Liberator but had little choice but to climb above the fog for his crew to bail out of the B-24. This all nine men did successfully.

Condors continued to patrol Atlantic waters to seek out Allied shipping, and on 31 July 1943 another air action involving two 'four-engine fighters' ended in the loss of an entire KG 40 crew. Surprised by another 480th Anti-Submarine Group B-24D Liberator, the Fw 200C-5 (0202/F8+AR) was flying at about 500 feet (150 metres) when the Germans were amazed to see that they were about to be attacked by an enemy bomber. The Condor was captained by Oblt Siegfried Gall of 7./Staffel.

Tenaciously following the wheeling, banking Condor, the American crew of Capt Gerald L. Mosier opened fire. Aboard the Condor the gunners shot back with equal determination, but the German captain soon realised that his aircraft was in mortal danger if he did not make a run for it. He firewalled the throttles in order to do just that. Little realising that his adversaries were low on ammunition, the German pilot made a last desperate effort to escape the big, white and olive drab enemy machine that stayed on his tail and was gaining fast. The race was a little unequal as the Condor could make only 240mph flat out, whereas a B-24D was capable of a top speed of almost 300mph. More importantly, despite being designed as a high-altitude, long-range day-bomber, the more robustly constructed Liberator proved to be surprisingly manoeuvrable, quite superior in this respect to the Condor at lower altitudes.

Overhauling his adversary, the American pilot accurately directed fire from the Liberator's heavy 0.50-inch machine-guns, which struck home in one of the Condor's wing roots and centre fuselage. An internal fire appeared to have doomed the German machine, although the pilot maintained control, going down and clearly aiming for a 'flat' angle for ditching. Then the port wing dipped and knifed into the swell and the Condor plunged, its racing engines carrying it forward in a huge ricochet. The nose dropped, it hit the sea and exploded. The location of the crash was off the coast of Portugal and the entire crew save one was posted as missing, including Oblt Gall (F), Uffz Paul Boller (F), Uffz Alfred Spender (B), Rudi Helbig and Obfw Hermann Peukert (BS), together with one other. Major Erich Adan was rescued.

In the third successful interception of a Condor by a USAAF B-24, Capt Mosier had picked up the enemy aircraft on his radar and tracked it for some distance before making his attack. Previously, on 18 July, pilot H. D. Maxwell had damaged an Fw 200, but subsequently had to report that it had made good its escape.

Further clashes

Other encounters took place between KG 40 and Liberators of the 480th ASG between July and October 1943, a series of combats resulting in the loss of at least three Fw 200s and three B-24s, although the adversaries met by the American crews were also other aircraft besides Condors. They may well, however, have been from the same unit, as V./KG 40's Ju 88s were very active at that time and several encounter reports filed by the 480th Group mentioned that type. However, in clashes with the Liberators the Fw 200 was really no match for its adversary apart from its comparable size – American 0.50in machine-gun rounds were significantly superior to those used in the rifle-calibre guns carried by most German aircraft and there were usually more guns for the Luftwaffe crews to contend with. If, on the other hand, the Condors could bring their 20mm cannon to bear, a contest between the two aircraft could prove more equal – as with most air combat situations, much depended on who fired first to gain an initial advantage. An additional factor was that the Liberator was structurally the stronger of the two types and could generally outperform the Condor in terms of speed and manoeuvrability, and, indeed, its ability to absorb battle damage.

August

KG 40's 7./Staffel inventory was less another Condor on 2 August, when Fw 200C-5 0215/F8+DR failed to return from a patrol. This was followed by the demise of another C-4 three days later. Aggressive enemy patrol bomber crews notwithstanding, it was Allied fighters that were rightly regarded by Condor aircrew as their most deadly adversary. The fact was rammed home forcibly on 5 August when another KG 40 machine fell foul of American fighters based in Iceland. This was a 3./Staffel Fw 200C-4 (0200/F8+FL) captained by Obfw Karl Holtrup and his six-man crew comprising Uffz Gunter Karte (F), Fw Josef Teufel (Bordfunker), Uffz Herbert Richter (Bordfunker), Obfw Emil Brandt (BM), Gefr Wilhelm Lehn (B) and Obgfr Siegfried Klinkmann (BS), all of whom were taken prisoner after the Condor came down about 6 miles (10km) south-east of Grimsey Island off the coast of Iceland. Victors over the Condor were the pilots of two P-38F Lightnings of the 50th FS flying from their base at Melgerdi airfield (alias Kassos Field), Lts Richard M. Holly and William M. Bethea, who made no mistake when catching up with their much slower quarry.

After being photographed with the American pilots at Melgerdi, the German airmen were flown by a USAAF Douglas B-18 to Reykjavik. In the meantime the wreck of their Condor was more or less claimed by the elements and, although it sank to a depth of 1,640 feet (500 metres), parts still tangle fishing nets put out by the trawlers that ply the area. As recently as 1990 engine cowling and fuel tank parts were brought up by the fishermen.

Another 'big fighter' dogfight

On 13 August 480th Group pilot Capt Frederick W. McKinnon realised that, despite the relative superiority of the B-24D over the big German patrol bomber, one tenacious Condor pilot flying a 9./Staffel Fw 200C-5/U1 (0221/F8+?T) from its temporary base at La Coruna simply had not read that particular book. Flying convoy escort, the AAF crew noted a Condor whose captain seemed determined to score hits on at least one ship. He tried three times but was forced back into cloud cover as the Liberator closed in. McKinnon gave chase and pursued the Condor from an altitude of 2,000 feet (610 metres) down to sea level, his gunners pumping out fire from their dorsal power turret and hand-held guns. No fewer than 1,790 rounds had been expended before any result was observed by the Americans, some of whom were by that time trying to clear jammed guns. None of the German aircraft's retaliatory fire made contact on the Liberator's airframe, but when its No 3 engine was seen to smoke the German captain prudently headed for home. The Condor apparently failed to make it and crashed near El Ferrol later that day.

A fatal incident removed Fw 200C-5 0218/F8+CD from the inventory of 8./Staffel on 14 August, the aircraft going down in the vicinity of Drontheim in Norway.

Five days after the McKinnon action, Capt Hugh D. Maxwell Jr and his crew participated in what was described at the time as the most spectacular air action experienced by the US anti-submarine squadrons in Europe. Having flown out of Craw Field on 17 August to provide convoy cover, Maxwell set course to pick up his charges in convoy MKS.21 some 300 miles (485km) west of Lisbon. He had previously received a warning that two Condors known to have departed from Bordeaux were likely to be heading for the same convoy and would rendezvous over the ships at much the same time as the Americans.

At an altitude of 1,500 feet (455 metres), Maxwell's radar operator picked up a contact at 15 miles (24km). When a second appeared on the 'scope there could be little doubt. Sure enough, when the Liberator emerged from the overcast at 1,000 feet (305 metres) the two Condors were about a mile ahead, preparing to make parallel runs on the columns of ships. One of the Condor skippers saw the Liberator, pulled off his bombing run to allow his gunners to open fire on it, and made a left turn. The German aircraft was out of range but fired anyway, probably to scare off the Americans. Maxwell closed on the Condor's tail whereupon the second latched onto his own tail. A three-ship line-astern procession formed with all guns blazing, which must have been an amazing sight.

Maxwell followed the leading Condor down to 50 feet (15 metres) above the sea, his own aircraft taking hits. The sound of machine-gun rounds thudding into metal would have been shared by German and American crewmen alike as all aircraft in the trio were taking fire. The Liberator, sandwiched between the Condors, had both its starboard engines knocked out, holes blown in the wing and numerous gashes torn in the fuselage skin. But then Maxwell saw that the leading Condor had come off even worse in the tail-chase combat and it promptly crashed into the sea. This aircraft was almost certainly Fw 200C-5 0211/F8+FK of II./KG 40, which was reported lost over the sea west of Portugal that day.

Damage to the B-24 included the dorsal turret's Plexiglas cover being blown away, leaving the gunner exposed to an icy blast of air as he fired on the second Condor. Preoccupied with preparing to ditch, a procedure that included jettisoning a bay-load of depth charges using the emergency release when hydraulic lines were severed, none of Maxwell's crew saw the second Condor depart. Witnesses aboard the convoy ships reported that it was last seen limping away just above the waves with its No 3 engine stopped. Those same observers believed that it had crashed, but this could not be confirmed.

The upshot of the action on the American side was that, with outstanding skill, Hugh Maxwell put the Liberator down in such an attitude that all but three men abandoned it successfully. The B-24 was a notorious aircraft to escape from in a ditching as the fuselage tended to flood before the high wing settled in the water to provide some buoyancy. Survivors from the Fw 200 and the B-24 were picked up by one of the ships in the convoy's escort. Four German airmen were hauled aboard but two badly burned men later died of their injuries.

A further August loss, to IX./KG 40, occurred on the 23rd when Fw 200C-5 0214/F8+NT was forced to ditch in Atlantic waters. Obfw Alfred Billing nevertheless handled the aircraft well in the emergency and the only crew casualty was Obfw Hans Gentsch. At Merignac yet another engine fire consumed part of Fw 200C-4 0191/F8+MS while it was running up its engines. The damage was put at 30 per cent by the Luftwaffe assessors, and after repairs this Condor, which had been converted to C-5/FK standard and fitted with FuG 203 radar for the reconnaissance role, served with 8./Staffel of KG 40. It was transferred to Transportstaffel Condor under Fliegerführer 4 after KG 400 was disbanded and served until virtually the end of the war. A final, quite unusual sortie was undertaken in May 1945.

On one of the 480th Group's final sorties out of French Morocco on 25 August (the AAF anti-submarine unit was withdrawn together with the 479th Air Support Group before the end of 1943), a clash with an Fw 200 involved the Liberator crew of Lt T. E. Kuenning. Some damage to the German machine was claimed, but the results were inconclusive and could not be verified.

Such aggressive reaction by Allied heavy bombers flying convoy protection sorties came as a shock to the Luftwaffe's maritime crews. The Focke-Wulf units were fully aware that the enemy had an impressive array of aircraft that could despatch a Condor with consummate ease, but the Atlantic Ocean covered a huge area and the inclement weather had often played into their hands to the point where two opposing aircraft could pass quite close to each other but not be recognised for what they were. Neither could 'flyers' luck' be discounted in an arena where something as fundamental as sound navigational skills could make the difference between survival and a watery grave. But the Allied fighter menace was looming ever larger: aircraft based on Gibraltar were able to range out into the Bay of Biscay far enough to create an added hazard to any German aircraft operating off the coast of Portugal, which had long been a profitable and relatively safe operational area for KG 40.

September

A similar situation prevailed in the Mediterranean, and although Condor operations in that area had been brief, German transport aircraft suffered appallingly heavy losses when North Africa had to be abandoned. Retreat into Italy was the only option open to the Germans; despite the surrender of their erstwhile ally, they decided to fight on in that ravaged country, bolstered to a modest degree by those pro-Fascist elements that had vowed to side with the Germans, come what may. The Luftwaffe was obliged to organise an air force contingent based in Northern Italy and manned by ex-members of the Regia Aeronautica. In the meantime the Fw 200 was deployed in small numbers both as a transport and maritime reconnaissance aircraft in a theatre of war that was increasingly dominated by Allied airpower.

Not that fighter-versus-Condor engagements were always a foregone conclusion, as two crews of Fleet Air Arm Beaufighter Mk IIs found to their cost on 7 September 1943. Attached to No 233 Squadron RAF, a Coastal Command unit charged with anti-U-boat operations from Agadir, the Beaufighters jumped the Condor (almost certainly F8+GT of IX./KG 40) off Cape Sardao in Portugal. The German crew reacted promptly and opened fire, forcing one Beaufighter (T3423) to ditch. The second (T3424) sustained enough damage for it to be good for little more than cannibalisation on its return to base, the result being that it was struck off charge.

Notwithstanding such isolated success against Allied fighters, Condors continued to be lost to KG 40's inventory through combat attrition and crew internment following forced landings in neutral as well as enemy territory. However, the duration of the German crews' stay as guests of a neutral country tended to depend on where they came down. The authorities in Spain, Portugal and Ireland were known to have released crews after only a short period of time, which hardly added up to incarceration 'for the duration'.

In mid-month U-boat group operations were resumed, the force having received boats equipped with up to eight 2cm AA guns, search receiver equipment and acoustic Zaunkonig T-5 torpedoes. Some initial success with the new torpedoes led the Germans to believe that previous poor reliability of the U-boats' principal weapon was at an end. That proved not always to be the case and the results continued to vary, although the T-5B was a considerable improvement over the older type of torpedoes. Fitting extra guns was a counter to attacking aircraft; Doenitz resolved to have his crews fight it out on the surface whenever possible. This new doctrine met with only mixed success.

October

By October Germany was experiencing reversals other than the loss of ships and aircraft directly involved in the struggle for control of the Atlantic. Coming soon after the surrender of Italy and the 13 October declaration of war on Germany by the new Badoglio Government was Operation 'Avalanche', the Allied landings at Salerno, which had taken place in September. That same month came news that Portugal, previously neutral, had granted Britain rights to operate aircraft from Fayal and Terceira airfields in the Azores, and on 19 October Norwegian troops were landed at Spitzbergen to re-establish bases. And that day the first RAF Coastal Command Fortresses operated out of the Azores to represent another thorn in the side of the U-boat fleet.

Late in October Kessler, C-in-C U-boats, working in conjunction with Fliegerführer Atlantik, devised a single, short-duration night operation to attack ships of convoy MKS.28, which was reported to have left Gibraltar on the 23rd. Two days later a Condor of III./KG 40 located the ships after they had joined those of SL.138. The main part of III./Gruppe was then based at Cognac-Chateau Bernard in south-western France, a small diversionary or secondary airfield near Partheney, some 120 miles (193km) due north of Bordeaux. In deference to increasing activity by

Allied aircraft, Fliegerführer Atlantik ruled that if hostiles approached within 75 miles (120km) of Cognac, the Condor crews had to take off and head for Bordeaux or Toulouse. A further attempt to reduce possible aircraft destruction and damage in the event of attack was dispersal, and at Cognac the rule was that aircraft be spaced at least 165 feet (50 metres) apart. Four to five crews of each Staffel remained on the airfield at all times, even when operations were not taking place. These men took up their crew stations ready to evacuate if attacked by enemy aircraft (the Eighth Air Force was KG 40's most likely antagonist, as was subsequently proved).

The flying personnel of I./KG 40 posed for a group photograph at Cognac airfield on 26 January 1942. *F. Selinger*

During this period the Condors received some welcome assistance from other Luftwaffe reconnaissance units, which included the Ju 290s of 1./FAGr 5, which had a range of 3,820 miles (6,150km) and the mighty Bv 222 flying boats belonging to 1.(F)/SAGr 129. The big boats were capable of a range of 3,788 miles (6,100km).

November

November 1943 saw the passing of maritime reconnaissance duty from III./KG 40 to FAGr 5, the change taking effect during October and December when sighting reports were passed not only to U-boats but KG 40's Condors.

Over the period 15 to 18 November these latter units became part of a major air-sea-submarine engagement that was centred around what appeared to be a prime target for U-boat attack, namely the ships of convoy MKS.30, which joined SL.139 to comprise sixty-six freighters, a massive concentration protected by the 40th Escort Group's frigates and sloops. More than two weeks would elapse before the two sides broke off the engagement; this was not an untypical period of time, marked as such actions often were by factors such as changes of course by the convoy(s) to elude the U-boats, loss of contact by aircraft and/or U-boats and the failure of several U-boats to make rendezvous. Above all, the battle was dictated by the speed of the merchant ships, around which the entire combat developed. Despite the assistance of radar and radio aids, this and numerous other engagements contained an element of guesswork by German submarine captains. Lastly, there was the decision of the shore-based Commanders-in-Chief to exercise the option to abandon the operation if it was deemed to have been too protracted without tangible results, or to carry a renewed element of risk due to the arrival of stronger hostile surface units.

A Ju 290 confirmed the initial reports from pro-German agents who had originally reported the departure of the ships of MKS.30 from Gibraltar on 13 November, the airborne message being transmitted two days later. The message was then passed to U-boat headquarters, which assembled a patrol line codenamed 'Schill 1' comprising eight submarines – U-262, U-306, U-333, U-466 and U-707, together with the AA boats U-211, U-441 and U-953 – on the night of 18-19 November, a Bv 222 having re-affirmed the position of the Allied convoy on the 16th. The Schill group had been positioned across the probable night route of the convoy by 29-30 October. Fw 200s had reported the Allied ships on 27 and 28 November as a group of fifty-six freighters with seven escorts.

British and Canadian Navy escort ships meanwhile engaged the U-boat force, with damage being sustained by both submarines and surface vessels. An RAF Wellington from 'the Rock' sank U-211 on the night of the 17th/18th.

Radar-equipped Condors of III./KG 40 flew regularly during the engagement, their radio operators transmitting bearings to the 'Schill 2' group (of nine U-boats), which was formed on the night of 20/21 November. Five boats received the messages while the force attacked the convoy with generally disappointing results from their T-5 torpedoes. U-536 was destroyed by a combination of depth charges and surface gunfire, while in the air the German shadowers were detected by Mosquitoes and Beaufighters that same night. The RAF fighters claimed the destruction of an Fw 200 and a Ju 290 near Cape Ortegal, effectively ending the Luftwaffe's passive but important role in the action, as the radar sets in the remaining two aircraft failed to function.

Further Luftwaffe sorties were ordered off by Fliegerführer Atlantik C-in-C Kessler, whose core force was twenty-five He 177s of II./KG 40 armed with missiles. Launching forty Hs 293As, the Heinkel force – twenty of which reached the target area – managed to sink the freighter *Marsa* and damage a second vessel for the loss of three aircraft shot down; two others turned back before making contact with the convoy. This was a typical large-scale North Atlantic engagement in late 1943, with both sides able to summon up reinforcements as necessary – but it is clear that the Condors of KG 40 had been sidelined into a secondary if still important operational role. The initiative had passed into other hands; while the U-boats ostensibly remained the most effective element on the German side, the Luftwaffe's power to mount a destructive strike was undeniably waning despite the potential of a new generation of 'stand-off' weapons.

Realistically, these weapons required far more performance-capable 'mother ships' than the Luftwaffe immediately had available; and although every effort was being made to introduce turbojet-powered aircraft into the inventory and arm some of them with missiles such as the X-4, all major efforts were geared towards fending off the ever more destructive air raids on Germany itself. Time was rapidly running out for anything comparable to be introduced into maritime operations apart from the Henschel missiles.

Missile carrier reshuffle

In the meantime training sorties by Condors to refine the technique of delivering the Hs 293A missile resulted in 8./Staffel KG 40, still then based at Fassberg, being confirmed as one of two Staffeln proficient in deploying the missile. To keep the Condor force together, 8./Staffel exchanged identity with II./KG 40, thus bringing it under the umbrella of I./Gruppe. This unit was seen as a stop-gap to the He 177 'main force'.

Fw 200C-3/U7 0226/DP+ON was among the Condors used to test the radio-guided bombs, the model suffix denoting special equipment. As the penultimate sub-types of the Fw 200, the following C-7 and C-8 variants were produced in very small numbers as more of them simply were no longer needed. However, despite early setbacks with deployment of the Hs 293 in north-western Europe, the German High Command wanted comprehensive reports on the in-flight characteristics of 'stand-off' weapons under the widest possible range of operational conditions.

There was no doubt that the guided bombs worked, as the launch of a few score of them had caused some anxious moments to Allied Naval commanders during the landings at Anzio several months previously, before American jamming of their radio links led to almost total neutralisation. Once the transmitting wavelength was an open secret, there was little the Germans could do to prevent jamming although every effort was made to obtain evidence of similar Allied counter-measures. Selected members of KG 40's crew complement were chosen to prove the new weapon, both the Condor and He 177 being modified to carry a pair of missiles. Numerous flight tests appear to have been undertaken by the Fw 200C-7, primarily to prove the reliability of each main phase of missile operation: release from the mother ship; en route guidance to the target; and destruction of the target. OKL was also interested to know how many Hs 293s it would take to sink a medium-sized cargo ship, or if one bomb striking a vital spot could send such a vessel to the bottom.

The Germans also hoped that production models of their 'stand-off' radio-guided bombs would bring about the dual advantage of reducing the crews' exposure to hostile reaction and result in further sinkings without the 'close proximity' risks always faced by anti-shipping aircraft by having to bomb from close range. Overflying the target vessel was often unavoidable, thus exposing the aircraft and crew to defensive fire. Using missiles this goal was largely achieved, but accuracy remained a grey area, one that, as with numerous new systems, required much further development time. This the Germans simply did not have.

First with missiles

What is believed to have been the initial Condor sortie on a war flight with the Hs 293A was flown by Fw 200C-4 0189/F8+MR of III./Gruppe on 28 December 1943. Fitted with FuG 217 Rostock radar, the aircraft was piloted by F Hptm Wilhelm Dette and a five-man crew comprising Fw Ernst Drabert (F), Uffz Kurt Lelwel (B), Bordfunker Obfw Johann Sewing, Bordfunker Uffz Walter Schmidt, Bordmechanik Obfw Friedrich Gunther and Uffz Wilhelm Hacker (BS). This special flight from Bordeaux consisting of four Condors (presumably not carrying missiles) completely ran out of luck as Dette's crew encountered a patrolling Short Sunderland – which promptly shot down the aircraft. Prematurely terminated by an enemy aircrew's quick reaction, the missile-armed Condor got nowhere near to its intended target ships and, although clashes with the RAF's mighty flying boat – an Atlantic campaigner that had been at the game longer than KG 40 – were relatively rare, the combat was significant.

It is doubtful whether the RAF crew even had an inkling of the coup they had achieved over their arch enemy, but this particular engagement seems to have severely set back the deployment of the Fw 200 in this new form of anti-shipping attack. It may, on the positive side, have helped prevent the pointless sacrifice of German aircrew (and Allied seamen), as the additional weight of the Henschel may well have impaired the Condor's speed and/or manoeuvrability, even against an aircraft that was itself heavier and slower than the German type. With little or no data from this flight the officers of KG 40 certainly repeated the same exercise if for no other reason than to obtain information on an important new weapon. However, no reports of how subsequent missile-equipped Fw 200s fared in a combat situation have yet come to light, nor for that matter has much photographic evidence.

Mishaps and accidents, part and parcel of operational flying anywhere, continued to occur. On 13 December Fw 200 F8+MR of III./Gruppe made a forced landing in County Tipperary, the entire crew extricating themselves from the aircraft without injury. The cause of the accident is unknown.

Condors usually came off worst when they encountered enemy fighters, and heavy bursts of fire often found a vulnerable spot. This crash on 28 December 1943 seems to be that of the III./KG 40 aircraft briefed to carry out the first 'live' Hs 293 attack, shot down by a Sunderland. Members of Wilhelm Dette's crew were rescued by a lifeboat from a British ship. *IWM*

On 28 December there was a report of an unidentified Condor being photographed from a British ship as it moved in to rescue survivors of the crew. Details of how many crewmen survived this incident, which left it burning on the sea, or why the aircraft came to ditch were not recorded.

It is to be assumed without very much evidence that other Condors were loaded with Hs 293s and the crews stood by awaiting suitable weather and worthwhile targets. Both were to prove quite elusive as the weather clamped down. Meteorologists duly recorded a fairly mild 1943/44 winter period with little portent of what was in store some twelve months hence, when one of the worst winters Europe had experienced for decades brought a virtual dead stop to air operations, for Axis and Allied alike.

Chapter 9

1944: Dangerous skies

January

Rapidly waning German fortunes on all war fronts coupled with burgeoning Allied airpower augured badly for the Luftwaffe as 1944 began. Also, in terms of comparable naval strength the Battle of the Atlantic, which had previously brought such major successes to the German U-boat arm, was entering its final phase. It was not a period that was likely to see much repeat of past glories for a force that Prime Minister Winston Churchill once feared could have proved disastrous to Britain's vital imports.

If the U-boat had passed its heyday, it did not necessarily mean that its aerial support in the shape of the Fw 200 Condor had completely waned in effectiveness despite being forced into a support role. However, unable to operate in anything like the near impunity it had enjoyed in 1940-42, KG 40 had to change its composition merely to survive in a much more demanding environment.

The number and quality of Allied aircraft made inshore and ocean patrols much more risky for large, slow and vulnerable bombers, despite an increase in single-seat fighter protection in the form of Fw 190s and Ju 88 fighters. Both types offered an escort force for short-range anti-shipping attack by Ar 196s, He 115s and Bv 138s as and when possible, but few fighters were available. Further afield the Condor and similar types would continue to be outnumbered and outgunned to the point where the wastage of crews (both actual and projected) outweighed any advantage that such aircraft could possibly bestow on patrolling submarines. That did not prevent Condors flying reconnaissance sorties and acting as shadowers for potential convoy attack by U-boats, although the early weeks of 1944 recorded a low level of activity by the Condor force. KG 40 had by that time become almost totally an He 177 unit, but, in common with the bulk of the Kampfgeschwader equipped with conventional bombers, an almost total eclipse was at hand.

February

The first two weeks of February 1944 saw a series of major engagements in the North Atlantic with a strong force of U-boats battling it out with Allied air and sea forces. The German submarines were bent on sinking ships from Arctic convoys RA.56, inbound to Lock Ewe, Ireland, SL.147/MKS.38, which was reported by Ju 290s of FAGr 5 on 5 February north of the Azores, HX.277 and the outward-bound ON.223. Such a large concentration of ships was a very tempting target for Doenitz's submarines and aircraft, and day and night actions ensued as the U-boats and escort groups sought the upper hand, both sides suffering casualties.

Final shipping attack

Allied opposition to German long-range anti-shipping aircraft was such that by 1944 KG 40's very future was in doubt. The last recorded attack on a ship by one of the unit's Fw 200s was during a separate action on 10 February when an aircraft of 3./Staffel flown by the Kapitän, Maly, found the British tanker *El Grillo* (7,264grt) in Seydisfjord, north-east of Iceland. If the results of the encounter were apparently successful for Maly, who claimed to have sunk the vessel, the final arbiters of such claims rested with the record-keepers who, on this occasion, could not confirm the tanker as a loss.

On 12 February a combined force of contact-keeping/shadower Condors and seven He 177s attacked convoy OS.67/KMS.41. The big Heinkels, some of which were armed with Hs 293 missiles, were intercepted by fighters from HMS *Pursuer*, which claimed one destroyed as well the destruction of a single Fw 200 from the shadowing force. From then on the Condors increasingly left reconnaissance and reporting to the Ju 290s, and anti-shipping attack sorties as such came all but to an end. Not that the big Junkers bombers were any less vulnerable than the Condor, two being lost on 16 February. Maritime patrols remained hazardous to all crews – who more often than not continued to work as a pair if not entirely alone, irrespective of the type they flew.

March: caught by Mustangs

That the Atlantic patrol areas of the Fw 200 were well enough known to the Allies was forcibly demonstrated on 5 March when three (four were initially claimed) unfortunate Condor crews fell victim to USAAF P-51B Mustangs at Cognac. Several Condors of KG 40 were using the base to avoid detection by the increasing number of USAAF and RAF fighters flying bomber escort and pre-D-Day 'softening up' sorties. American fighters were particularly deadly to the Luftwaffe as they were given carte blanche to shoot up anything that moved in north-western France, usually after shepherding their heavy bombers to more distant targets.

Three Condors, Fw 200C-4 0194/GC+SW, a C-5 (0244/TK+CZ) and a second C-4 (0248/TO+XD), took off from Chateau Bernard in the morning under a broken cloud layer. Unseen by the German aircrews and flying above the clouds was Gowdy Blue Flight of the 364th Fighter Squadron, 357th Fighter Group, comprising three P-51B Mustangs led by Capt Glendon Davis with Lt Morris Stanley and F/O Tom McKinney on his wing.

Stanley later noted in his encounter report that the large German aircraft were spotted through the proverbial hole in the cloud, and the three Mustangs initiated a steep dive in trail formation to catch up with the Condors. On the way down the American pilots apparently observed a pair of Bf 109s, but both kept their distance.

Overhauling their quarry at an altitude of around 200 feet (61 metres), Capt Davis had the Condor trio in his sights near the airfield boundary. He scored hits on one Condor before pulling up to avoid colliding with it, and Morris Stanley observed the German crew extending the landing gear, possibly in an attempt to land, but when he fired at the same aircraft (and observed no hits) the flight pulled up for a left-hand circuit of the aerodrome. In his attempt to make a landing the pilot of the first Condor lost control, and the American pilot witnessed a spectacular crash as the aircraft ground-looped after making hard contact with what the American pilots identified as the landing mat. It suddenly cartwheeled and tore itself apart.

Capt Davis then closed with a second Condor flying on the right of the runway and fired a long burst that struck the German machine's wing and engine cowlings. Flame and smoke billowed from the No 3 engine as Davis pulled up and Morris Stanley took his turn. Closing with the third Condor, Stanley began firing from dead astern at 250 yards (230 metres) out. Closing in to about 25 yards (23 metres) he too observed strikes on that big wing and long fuselage. Pulling away from the stricken Condor, Stanley witnessed the second aircraft that Capt Davis had fired at hit the ground and explode. His own victim began a similar death dive, a slow turn to the left into the ground, where it exploded.

According to their post-mission reports, the American pilots had downed three 'Fw 200Ks'. As with the He 111 before it, the Fw 200 had acquired the designation suffix 'K' in early Allied encounter reports. This was spurious in both cases, but the original British wartime recognition data was not always updated so 'Fw 200K' it remained. USAAF intelligence did not apparently question the designation.

Three Condors destroyed in the space of a few minutes together with – it is assumed – their entire crews was a terrible loss to KG 40, but the unit's commanders took some comfort in the fact that slaughter on the scale of 5 March had not previously occurred often enough to seriously curtail their operations. The writing was, however, on the wall, clear for all to see: it spelled out the undeniable fact that the Condor's heyday had irrevocably passed. By March there were no fewer than sixteen Merchant Aircraft Carriers available to cover the inbound/outbound convoys.

Ahead lay the very real threat not only of destruction of the Kampfgeschwader's aircraft in the air and on the ground but also the capture of its airfields if the Allies gained a firm foothold in France; if and when an invasion took place, airfields such as Merignac could eventually be captured by enemy troops. For these and other reasons the Luftwaffe bomber force underwent some drastic changes in 1944.

Incidental victim

Together with an increase in the number of convoy escort vessels and greater reliability of electronic aids to identify aircraft by IFF (Identification Friend or Foe) signal, on 25 March this Allied advantage turned sour when an assumption on the part of two Sea Hurricanes – or Seafires, according to the joint US-British intelligence journal *Impact* for May 1944 – of 824 Squadron from HMS *Striker* led to tragedy. Coming upon a four-engine aircraft that apparently had no IFF set fitted – at least it was not turned on or transmitting as the aircraft approached a convoy – the Royal Navy fighter pilots were immediately suspicious. Assuming the aircraft to be a Condor, they attacked and shot down the intruder.

What the RN pilots actually destroyed was not an Fw 200 but a Douglas C-54 (41-37274) en route from Stepenville in the Azores to Casablanca. There were no survivors from the American crew of six, all of whom were civilians. *Impact* ran the story under the heading 'Moral: Don't be Trigger Happy', citing this and other incidents of what is now termed 'friendly fire' as a constant and ongoing problem in wartime requiring extreme vigilance from aircrew who often had precious little time to make positive identification. It was also an object lesson in ensuring that trained personnel should use any and all available ID aids carried by their aircraft while they were in a war zone.

Three more to fighters

Fighters operating from escort carriers had now become the main protagonist of the Condors and a further major disaster for KG 40 occurred on 31 March 1944 when three were shot down by fighters from HMS *Tracker* and HMS *Activity*. Patrolling the waters some 250 miles (400km) north of the Lofoten Islands when they were intercepted, the Condor formation comprised an Fw 200C-3 (0063/F8+BL) flown by Walter Klomp, a C-6 (0060/F8+GL) captained by Alfred Weyer, and Uffz Alfred Gobel's C-8 (0224/F8+OL). Weyer's and Gobel's aircraft, members of III./KG 40, were lost with all personnel, seven men in the former case and six in the latter. The Allied fighters were again Grumman Wildcats.

It was a period of intense activity for the Axis and Allied air forces involved, the action centring on convoy JW.58 from Russia. These ships were threatened – if only indirectly – by *Tirpitz*, which was ready for sea. The German capital ship was subject to another Fleet Air Arm strike, this time spearheaded by Barracuda dive-bombers. *Activity* and *Tracker* were the designated escort carriers for JW.58, and on the 30th the first Luftwaffe shadower, a Ju 88, was shot down. A day later KG 40's Fw 200s from Norway appeared on the scene and after a long 'cat and mouse' wait the Wildcats shot down the first Condor at 0915. It was 1632 before the fighters from *Tracker* destroyed the second Condor, and at 1818 the aircraft that had replaced the one lost that afternoon was itself attacked by a section of *Activity*'s Wildcats, which put it into the sea.

April

A process of far-reaching change had already begun in the Luftwaffe with pressure from the Jagerstab (Fighter Staff) that led OKL to decree that the days of the conventional Kampfgeschwader were at an end: the chances of air strikes by Luftwaffe bombers meeting with strategic success on any front was now more remote than they had ever been. With air-testing of a new generation of turbojet fighters and bombers all but complete, it made economic sense to retrain combat crews to fly these potentially war-winning new aircraft. In addition Germany was increasingly running short of aviation fuel, thereby limiting the number of hours a complete novice would receive before being thrown into combat.

On the other hand, individuals with flight time at the controls of medium bombers – or indeed the Fw 200 – could be expected to master that much faster the higher speeds and different operating methods and overcome the fact that they were on their own without the support of navigators, bomb-aimers or gunners. Many bomber crewmen made the transition as the Luftwaffe strove to rise Phoenix-like from the ashes of its former glories. Few if any KG 40 Condor crewmen have been identified as having made the transition onto jet fighters, although some may have done so. It had been intended to re-muster KG 40 into a fully fledged Me 262 unit and, had there been time, the Luftwaffe would undoubtedly have had a KG 40 (J) as part of its last-ditch order of battle. In the event time prevented any such formation being created.

Despite the steady attrition rate it continued to suffer, Kampfgeschwader 40 had maintained a continuous service record (albeit in significantly changed form) since formation and was able to celebrate several operational milestones. One of these duly came around on 8 April 1944 when a crew of an Fw 200C-3 (believed to have flown aircraft F8+FL on that date) was photographed at Vaernes, Norway, bearing the traditional laurel wreath and placard to mark the 600th operational sortie by 3./Staffel ('war flight' in Luftwaffe terms) since the start of the conflict.

Following a Luftwaffe tradition of celebrating record numbers of sorties with a presentation plaque and a laurel wreath, a KG 40 crew has joined a select band of airmen who completed 600 war flights. Behind them is what was probably their regular aircraft, a Condor coded F8+FL of 3./Staffel, photographed at Vaernes, Norway, on 8 April 1944. *F. Selinger*

May

By 31 May only III./KG 40, then part of Luftflotte 3, retained the Fw 200, I./ and II./Gruppen having fully converted to the He 177. None of these Gruppen was to exist for much longer as the Luftwaffe's long-range anti-shipping force, together with most of the Kampfgeschwader, was being run down and/or disbanded. If conventional bombers were no longer operationally viable in airspace almost totally dominated by Allied aircraft, the vast wastes of ocean still offered potential targets for an air force that was not about to surrender.

Moreover, while pilots and crewmen with combat experience could be more effective in defence of the Reich if they were re-trained to fly fighters, particularly jets, units such as KG 40 had on its rolls men who also had a considerable number of flight hours, albeit as transport pilots. This experience would stand an individual in better stead than the complete novice, the raw student coming to an operational unit often lacking the skill even to fly his own machine, let alone handle combat with only an even chance of survival.

As a combat aircraft the Condor's value had undeniably diminished, but it remained in demand as a transport. Apart from an inherent weakness in defensive armament, one it shared with other transport types, it could fly further than many other bomber types in inventory. That fact alone would see it soldier on until the bitter end.

June

Pre-invasion activity on the part of KG 40 was hardly likely to make much impression on the mighty seaborne armada of ships being assembled in English ports, nor would the assembling troops give much thought to the appearance of a single enemy four-engine bomber. Had they been aware of the massive build-up of ships taking place in those South Coast ports, Condor crews might well have alerted OKL/K de U-boats that something big was about to take place. It seems improbable that a patrolling Condor would not have detected such a huge build-up of shipping in the Channel off the coast of Normandy in the days preceding D-Day – but even if it had done so, individual officers in the German High Command had convinced themselves that the 'real' invasion would take the shortest possible sea crossing and come ashore in the Pas de Calais area. The Allies did little to dissuade the Germans that what they believed was true, while the fact that the actual landing area was to be in Normandy was successfully kept from them.

Action with Seafires

It is not overstating the situation to record that the dwindling number of sorties flown by German bombers was partly the result of mass destruction and damage on their airfields. Conventional bombing raids by American and RAF medium and heavy bombers took a toll, but it was the rising tempo of strafing attacks that were often more effective in wrecking aircraft, destroying maintenance facilities and burning increasingly precious fuel supplies. Such an attack on Bordeaux-Merignac took place on 27 March, resulting in considerable damage to installations and the destruction of several aircraft. None of these were Fw 200s, however, as the French airfield was by then the exclusive province of KG 40's He 177s.

Invasion

The invasion of Europe at Normandy by Allied forces on 6 June 1944 was not an event that was in any way safe for German anti-shipping aircraft, despite the fact that they were not considered a direct threat. On the face of it there was a highly tempting plethora of targets in the English Channel, but Allied fighter superiority made any sorties in the vicinity of the landing beaches, and even many miles off those beaches, tantamount to suicide missions. Nevertheless, elements of KG 40 and KG 100 made some attempt on the nights of 6/7 and 7/8 June to attack invasion shipping. Missile-carrying aircraft of both Kampfgeschwader were used, there being a total of seventy sorties, but without any notable success. Partially trained crews largely failed to find their assigned targets, which lay a considerable distance from their coastal bases. Allied night-fighters were present en route to and from the landing beaches, and German flak gunners mistakenly opening fire on friendly aircraft did nothing to assist. After these two abortive night attacks the anti-shipping force was stood down until several days later, when even less was achieved in a final mission. What proportion of these forces was made up by Condors is unknown, but their departure from their traditional operational bases in France was imminent.

Led by Dr Lambert von Konschegg, the Condor Gruppe soldiered on into the post-Allied invasion period, and by 20 June twelve of the unit's twenty-six aircraft remained serviceable. But Allied air power, now impinging much closer to KG 40's main French bases than hitherto, meant that such slow and vulnerable aircraft as the Condors were unlikely to survive interception in an arena where Allied fighter-bombers were becoming almost a daily hazard. Despite this situation, few Condors appear to have been destroyed in the air or indeed on the ground, a fact surely attributable to their relatively small numbers.

July

It was as a transport that one of KG 40's Condors carried out an epic and dangerous sortie deep into the Arctic Circle on 1 July 1944. Under the code name Operation 'Schatzgräber' ('Treasure Hunter') a single Fw 200C-3 of 3./Staffel (F8+RL) flew some 2,000 miles to rescue the crew of a weather station. The flight was an outstanding success and a fine feat of flying on the part of the Condor's captain, Oblt Karl-Heinz Stahnke.

For the Condor force, losses since 1941 had been such that the 'old guard' of prewar Luft Hansa crews had largely gone, to be replaced by younger individuals, many of whom lacked the wide experience of their predecessors, the men who had become thoroughly familiar with the Focke-Wulf airliner's characteristics in both peace and war. Consequently, in July 1944 III./Gruppe was pulled out of France to return to Germany. There KG 40 was all but disbanded, at least as an anti-shipping unit operating the Fw 200.

The clean nose contours of an early C series Condor reflected its airliner origins and perhaps belied the fact that it was turned into an effective combat aircraft. The crew member on the left wears a Naval-style cap while he checks the paperwork with a more conventionally attired colleague in KG 40.

A pleasing view of an Fw 200C-4 of 8./Staffel KG 40, coded F8+LS. The clean finish indicates a recent arrival on the Geschwader's strength, as does the treatment of the Balkenkreuz. On an aircraft well known for its individualist rendering of the national insignia, such regulation markings were the exception. Paintwork would weather considerably after a few months on operations. *F. Selinger*

Eventually only 8./Staffel remained from III./KG 40, this subsequently becoming Transport Flieger Staffel Condor, a unit that reverted to using the Fw 200 in the role for which it had originally been designed. It will be recalled that during the previous year 8./Staffel had been reformed from a nucleus of crews who had flown transport sorties in Russia, and their experience was no doubt of great value to remaining operations with the Condor.

As a transport the Condor was stripped of most if not all of its armament, resulting in a lighter aircraft, more responsive on the controls, and less prone to overstraining of the main spar and breaking up upon landing. Its handling characteristics were therefore restored virtually to those of Luft Hansa's prewar transport heyday with a fast and useful long-range aircraft. This process took some time, however, and military Condors continued to be based at Merignac for the time being.

A proportion of Luftwaffe maritime sorties continued, these being undertaken mainly by the Ju 290s of FAGr 5 based at Mont de Marsan and the Bv 222 flying boat, which was on the strength of 1.(F)/129, together with a small number of other reconnaissance units. Still available for maritime patrol were KG 40's He 177s, which also continued to fly over-water patrols, mostly from bases in Norway and Germany, although their potential to hurt, let alone sink, Allied ships had dropped to virtually nil. The promise demonstrated by the 'stand-off' guided missile programme could not be exploited using large, ponderous aircraft that were often unable to survive in a theatre of war that had become highly dangerous for any aircraft that bore Luftwaffe markings.

Notwithstanding how critical the situation had become Junkers carried out conversion work on the Ju 290A-7, which was able to carry three Hs 293s or three Fritz X missiles. Thirteen examples of this variant were completed, but their deployment as anti-shipping missile platforms is believed to have been very limited.

Things hardly improved for the Luftwaffe's Condor force – nor would they unless the base at Bordeaux-Merignac was abandoned without delay. A further casualty accrued from the boosted USAAF presence over the continent when Fw 200C-3 0038/SG+KN fell foul of a 434th Fighter Squadron P-38 on 5 July. The Lightnings were out on a strafing mission in the vicinity of the Saintes/Nantes area, shooting up anything of use to the Germans. One of the pilots, Capt Arthur F. Jeffrey, came across what was again identified as an Fw 200K, taking off from Chateau Bernard airfield near Cognac – the same location that had seen the demise of three Condors at the hands of Mustang pilots earlier in the year. Once again the results were similar. Intercepted in the vicinity of the town, the Condor had little defence against the concentrated fire of the P-38J. It was observed to make a 180-degree turn and stay low, probably as the American fighters were seen.

Flak from the airfield and locations in Cognac tried to ward off the Lightnings but Arthur Jeffrey followed the Condor's manoeuvres and found himself in front of it. He made a 180-degree turn to the left, passed above the Condor and turned in for a stern attack. He opened fire at 350 yards (320 metres) and closed to about 50 yards (46 metres). The ten-second burst was enough to set the Condor's right inboard engine on fire and 'parts of it flew off', to quote Jeffrey's combat report. The American saw the German pilot execute a belly landing and skid along the ground with fire taking hold rapidly. One man, later identified as the Condor's radio operator, was seen to escape from the wreck, but by then the light and heavy flak was intense and Jeffrey left the scene in a hurry. One P-38 was shot down by flak.

The Condor was the first of fourteen victories credited to Jeffrey, who finished the war as the top ace of the 479th Group; fifty-six years later he was able to meet the sole survivor of the Condor crew.

Although enemy ground forces did not immediately threaten to capture that part of the west coast of France where Bordeaux-Merignac was located, every airfield in the area was bombed repeatedly before, during and after Operation 'Overlord' was launched. Even the few that were not touched awaited the almost inevitable bomb carpet as the Allies worked down their target list with impunity. Rather than wait for them to be bombed on the ground, OKW finally ordered the Luftwaffe's anti-shipping units to move. On 7 July the Fw 200s and He 177s remaining in the Marseilles area – some seventy aircraft – were withdrawn to airfields in Germany or Norway. This move had a secondary purpose, that of conserving fuel, stocks of which had been dangerously reduced as a result of Allied bombing.

Arctic venture

Condor crews had for some time been able to anticipate more successful sorties by supporting operations against Allied convoys in the Arctic, an area that had previously seen considerable Luftwaffe participation. I./KG 40 had provided six Condors under the command of Hptm Edmund Daser for reconnaissance missions in the patrol sector between Iceland and Spitzbergen, these initially being flown in conjunction with the Heinkel He 111 torpedo strike forces of KG 26 and KG 30.

Once a convoy was detected, the Condors, based at Trondheim, could shadow the ships for up to 850 miles (1,365km), flights usually deploying at least one aircraft fitted with radar. To give a typical example, on 1 July 1943 a crew from III./KG 40 had detected convoy PQ.17; the subsequent action, which has since become infamous, recorded the worst loss of ships from a single Allied convoy. The saga of PQ.17 has always been punctuated by a disastrous order for the component ships to scatter as the German attack developed. The participation of KG 40's Focke-Wulfs amounted to little more than token reconnaissance and shadower flights in the vicinity of the action.

Production reduction

By late 1943 Focke-Wulf had all but completed deliveries to the Luftwaffe of the main C series variants, with the last Fw 200C-6s and C-8s about to follow on in 1944. Externally these final examples represented a culmination of operational experience with earlier variants, combined with missile-launching capability and radar, which may have given the casual observer the impression of a new level of offensive capability. Operationally, however, the heavier C-8 was something of a retrograde step; it was the variant that proved least able to evade attention by the enemy in the role for which it had been created, although it was put to good use as an anti-shipping attack trainer. Few C-8s appear to have been used on anti-shipping operations; in the months following the disastrous debut of KG 40's anti-ship missile period, the aircraft was gradually withdrawn from front-line service to continue, it is believed, important test work. That being the case, the general retention of FuG 200 radar on the late-production Condors gave the impression that low-key transport flights had a greater importance, which was not always the case – radar was not an integral part of the Hs 293 programme.

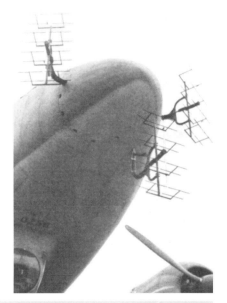

The late production Fw 200C-6 and C-8 variants were usually fitted with FuG 200 Hohentweil radar, which provided better target definition than the previous sets tested in Condors. The distinctive antennae array (on C-8 W Nr 0256), with its twelve-dipole arrangement, had a clear transmission field from its lofty perch on the nose.

This Hohentweil FuG 200 radar-equipped Fw 200 is probably a C-6, although the installation of the most efficient of the sea-search radars developed for the Luftwaffe was not an infallible guide to particular Condor variants. *F. Selinger*

August

August proved to be the swansong of KG 40, for on the 11th all flights by four-engine bombers in Germany were officially abandoned in a further attempt by OKL to save precious fuel. This meant that the Condor force was all but finished operationally, and on 21 August the unit, together with its sister Geschwader KG 100, was officially disbanded.

This unrealistic edict did not, of course, prevent a few further Condor flights under the guise of transport and liaison work, and fuel was found for several more, some of a clandestine nature, to take officials abroad. It is also believed that this order applied mainly to flights within the original boundaries of Germany, as it seems not to have been complied with by units based elsewhere.

September

Bad weather and waning German fortunes on all war fronts inevitably had a detrimental effect on the viability of Condor operations, and although by September III./KG 40 still had a strength of thirteen aircraft at Trondheim, strike forces were no longer in a position to simply go out and attack the ships reported by returning crews.

Now the Condors were increasingly deployed as shadowers, keeping well out of range of escort fighters to transmit the positions of Allied shipping to the U-boats. But the process that had begun with the disastrous losses of U-boats during the spring of 1943 had not improved some twelve months on; the submarine arm of the Kriegsmarine was meeting increasingly heavy opposition and sinkings as a direct result of Condor sightings were reduced. For its part, the Luftwaffe, with few other suitable aircraft available, was obliged to deploy KG 40's Fw 200s for several more reconnaissance sorties. Should enemy aircraft – be they Russian, American or Royal Navy carrier fighters – be reported, any hostile action against convoys, however tempting, had to be abandoned. Such flights were now far more potentially dangerous to the German crews – although on past evidence the outcome of an encounter with enemy interceptors was not always a foregone conclusion.

Night flights by Condors converted to civil configuration continued, the aircraft serving Oslo, Copenhagen and Barcelona from Berlin. One of DLH's originals (0021/D-AMHL *Pommern*) flew on these routes after overhaul, beginning in November 1943, and was scheduled on the Spanish run from April 1944. At 2015 on 27 September 1944 the Condor took off from Stuttgart-Echterdingen for another trip to Barcelona with Kapitän Helmut Liman at the controls. Over French territory at 0205 it was intercepted by a Beaufighter of the USAAF's 415th NFS. Pilot Capt Harold F. Augspurger and his radar operator, 2nd Lt Austin G. Petrey, on their first mission after their unit had moved into Dijon-Longvic, closed on the Condor and shot it down. It took a three-second burst of cannon and machine-gun fire to set the starboard engine and wing area of the Condor ablaze, the German aircraft falling away to crash at 2030. All occupants of what again went into US record books as an Fw 200K perished; beside the pilot, the aircraft had carried crew members Oberflugmaschinist Heinrich Papenhagen and Oberflugzeugfunker Leo Amphlett, as well as five passengers.

Chapter 10

1945: Surrender

Among the last operational formations that included Focke-Wulf Condors in their order of battle for 1945 were Transport Gruppen 2, 4 and 5. Having rationalised its transport force, the Luftwaffe High Command introduced a simplified designation system for units that were still largely built around a nucleus of the ubiquitous Ju 52/3m. There were in addition at least two Condors on the strength of the above units shortly before Germany capitulated. Other late-war formations were formed and provided with base facilities to give a semblance of order out of mounting chaos.

There is some evidence to suggest that Transport Gruppe 4 may have operated the last active Fw 200s in the entire Luftwaffe; equipped mainly with the Ju 52/3ms, TG 4 took two Condors on strength at an unknown date and they were still listed as part of the unit until the end of hostilities. These machines, in common with most Condors and numerous other types, including many transports, had their full identity markings reduced to a single individual letter, there being little time or indeed inclination to comply with any final instructions on the painting of aircraft. But such things had been normal during the war years and to ignore them would, to some observers, have reflected a total breakdown in the chain of command – the Luftwaffe reduced to anonymity. To emphasise the predicament, few unit badges, Staffel or Gruppe codes were worn – but until someone made an official announcement to alter things, the Luftwaffe would continue to fly.

April: fitting finale

By reverting to its origins as an unarmed transport, the Fw 200 was utilised by the Luftwaffe in a support role for the remaining months of the war. Lightened Condors had a useful load-carrying capacity; there were always cargoes that ideally needed to be packed into aircraft of substantial size rather than being loaded onto vulnerable trains or trucks, especially when roads and railways were primary interdiction targets for enemy aircraft. In addition, Condors had from the earliest days of Luftwaffe service been taken on the strength (albeit in small numbers) by several training schools, mostly those specialising in navigation, blind flying and reconnaissance. This process had continued as a low-key element of a training programme that was arguably too restricted in aircraft allocation. Diversions to gruelling albeit short-duration first-line operations such as the Russian airlifts had an adverse effect not only on aircraft but also on instructor crews. Any transfer of personnel, particularly experienced instructor pilots, to first-line units also brought detrimental results in the event that they were killed or wounded.

For a considerable period the Condor had been regularly deployed to the limit of its range up into the Arctic Circle, mainly on weather reconnaissance flights, and these continued with a degree of immunity from interception as they were often beyond the range of enemy aircraft.

Although no Fw 200s were directly assigned to Wekusta (Weather) units, KG 40 was usually able to fly such sorties to assist the Geschwader's own operations and, increasingly, those of other air and naval units. Condors were particularly useful in several support roles, among them the verification of convoy composition and direction. When the number of anti-shipping sorties was reduced and those Condors that remained in first-line service became more transport aircraft than maritime surface raiders, far-flung outposts manned by a few intrepid individuals who provided a weather monitoring and reporting service under less than ideal living conditions appreciated the contact with the outside world that the big Focke-Wulfs could provide.

May

With the Allied air forces having occupied an increasing number of former Luftwaffe airfields by the spring of 1945, each passing day brought the surrender of Germany that much closer; each of the former separate war fronts was gone and the final rounds of fighting were in Germany itself. Numerous units simply abandoned their arms and moved westwards, hoping to surrender to the Americans rather than the Russians. The USAAF announced that a number of designated airfields should be used by those Luftwaffe elements that wished to fly in from outlying areas and give themselves up; by this method, enemy aircraft would be assured of a safe passage without fear of being fired on.

When Germany capitulated on 8 May 1945 this safety net was even more important than it had been days before – nobody wanted to be killed or injured after hostilities had officially ceased. Allied ground troops consequently began to witness unique scenes as every conceivable type of German aircraft approached the airfields; some transports had high-ranking officers aboard while smaller types brought other flyers and/or ground personnel. Even single-seat fighters arrived with a second man crammed into the limited space in the fuselage.

But thousands of aircraft were simply left where they stood. There was an order that the enemy should be left only with wrecks, and numerous aircraft were indeed destroyed or damaged beyond repair by the detonation of explosive charges or simply a grenade thrown into the cockpit. This final act was also carried out if time permitted, but many aircraft escaped this fate.

Among the thousands of aircraft abandoned on European airfields after the German surrender in May 1945 were a number of Condors. Not all of them were deliberately wrecked and there were numerous eye-witnesses to the fact that enemy crews eagerly flew to designated airfields to surrender peaceably. American fighter pilots at Braunschweig in Germany were surprised when a machine, presumably of Transportstaffel Condor (+BD), put down there days after the capitulation. The code indicated a III./Gruppe Stab aircraft. *J. V. Crow*

Large transports such as the Condor could accommodate dozens of passengers, and a number of 'eleventh hour' flights were made to neutral countries with few questions asked, and even fewer answers being put forward. Some flights were tinged with drama, such as that on 8 May when Fw 200C-4 0191 was flown from Oslo-Gardermoen to Torslanda in Sweden. The Condor's captain was Oblt Albert Zepf with a crew from 1.(F)/22. The landing in Sweden was something of an emergency as Zepf decided to put down after a shooting incident aboard the aircraft. What happened after that is a mystery, but the story of the ruckus among the crew and/or passengers did garner some publicity at the time. All that is known is that the abandoned Condor remained on the airfield until 1948, when it was scrapped.

FOCKE-WULF FW 200 CONDOR

The single dipole radar antennae locating points are shown to advantage on the same aircraft. The purpose of the bulged fairing below the small gondola window is unknown, but as a non-standard item it may have been associated with the Hs 293 missile programme. An American pilot is taking a close look at the controls of what was formerly on the strength of a III./Gruppe Stab. *J. V. Crow*

Another Fw 200 to arrive at Braunschweig, a C-8 coded +CT, was believed to have been serving with a transport unit, the 'T' indicating a 9./Staffel aircraft. It has the individual letter repeated on the nose tip, and revealed its secrets to its captors including the FuG 200 radar, which has the three dipole mountings rather than the four seen on other aircraft. Also of interest is the waist gun with the wind deflector extended and the 'split' turret sections. *J. V. Crow*

Braunschweig mostly recorded the surrender of German fighters, so the arrival of a Condor impressed many of the onlookers, few of whom had ever seen one. *J. V. Crow*

On the port side the extended gondola of the surrendered Fw 200C-8 has been provided with additional windows, although they are a little hard to discern in the shadows. The aircraft is fitted with flame damper exhaust pipe fairings, not a feature on all Condors as some had a simple single pipe arrangement in six or eight locations protruding from the cut-outs in the cooling gills. *J. V. Crow*

FOCKE-WULF FW 200 CONDOR

Neatly parked alongside an Fw 190 and a flak pit, the surrendered Fw 200 awaits its fate at Braunschweig. Both aircraft apparently flew in from Norway in order to comply with the capitulation orders. *J. V. Crow*

This pleasing view of a late production Fw 200 C-6 or C-8 series Condor coded 'FR' shows salient details including the way disruptive light grey paint was applied in a dapple pattern over the top surfaces with some former markings obscured. This aircraft was abandoned at an airfield near Hamburg and the code would indicate that it belonged to 7./Staffel. *D. Howley via R. L. Ward*

Late Knights

As was not uncommon in both the Luftwaffe and other air forces, some awards for bravery were delayed and presented some time after the date(s) of service for which the medal was promulgated – in Germany a case of the paperwork not catching up within a system inexorably descending into a state of chaos. One such recipient who became a victim of the red tape tangle was Major Dr Lambert von Konschegg, whose Knight's Cross was not presented until 15 April 1945. The award was primarily to mark the Austrian-born officer's service as Gruppenkommandeur of III./KG 40.

Russian Condors

When the Sixth Army capitulated at Stalingrad, surviving German aircraft stranded for one reason or another on airfields inside the pocket fell into Russian hands as war booty. There had been insufficient time for the Luftwaffe groundcrews to systematically destroy the aircraft before they were forced to flee, and with proper servicing facilities to hand the Russians repaired those of most use to them. By all accounts their initial appreciation of the capabilities of such a large aircraft had dwindled and they were reportedly disappointed by the Condor after they had had a chance to examine several. Nevertheless, at least one of those that were captured virtually intact was put back in the air – Fw 200C-3/U2 0034/F8+OW, late of I./KG 40 – which had been abandoned at Pitomnik; it formed the focal point of a display of captured aircraft at Gorky Park near Moscow. By early 1943 the park was able to include examples of most of the first-line Luftwaffe types. As well as complete aircraft, a range of bombs was displayed, and when the public was allowed in to inspect the exhibits closely, the Condor had several stout wooden stakes to support its wings as a safety measure.

Despite their reservations regarding its capabilities as a warplane, the Russians were pleased to have the big Focke-Wulf transport flying under their colours as, together with some countries in Europe, such aircraft were far from common in the Soviet Union. The vast size of the country cried out for air links by four-engine aircraft, with the result that several Condors gained a further lease of life while 'under new management'. Reconnaissance flights were continued well into the early years of peace.

The Russian association with the Fw 200 had started early in the aircraft's career, albeit briefly and at a distance. On 23 August 1939 Fw 200A-0 3098/D-ACVH *Grenzmark* was used to bring foreign minister von Ribbentrop to Moscow for meetings with Stalin and Molotov. Hans Baur was the pilot and the Condor was the object of intense interest by the Russians during its stay at Moscow's international airport.

As one of Hitler's ploys to lull the Soviets into a false state of security and to foster a spirit of cooperation that he had no intention of honouring, the meeting did buy him time. By all accounts Josef Stalin was completely convinced that his country was safe from a German attack. However, not even a non-aggression pact, signed on 23 August 1939, could dissuade the Führer from his chosen course.

Some three years on, the result of the disastrous path taken by the Germans was reflected in the situation on the Volga – and the impending arrival of a Condor, this time bearing Russian markings, at the airfield near Moscow. Variously identified as several sub-types of the C series, this aircraft was most likely Fw 200C-3/U4 0034, discovered by Soviet troops at Stalingrad in virtually undamaged condition. Contemporary accounts stated that the Russians, having made W Nr 0034 airworthy, flew it to Moscow where members of the NII VVS (Air Forces Scientific Research Institute) waited with some anticipation to examine what they believed to be a fully fledged military transport. Among the personnel was engineer Major G. V. Gribakin and lead pilot Col A. I. Kabanov, who had carried out initial flight trials of the Condor soon after it was captured.

After the Condor landed and the Soviet team went aboard, it was noted that it bore some resemblance to the Douglas DC-3 in terms of cabin layout and internal compartments. There the similarity with the German machine ended, for the American aircraft, although of twin-engine configuration and considerably smaller, had been built as a transport from the ground up. The highly regarded Dakota became something of an icon, an international yardstick against which every contemporary airliner and transport was compared, despite the fact that on balance four engines were better than two on long-distance flights over the barren, sparsely populated terrain that constituted a huge area of the Russian hinterland.

The inescapable fact was that the Douglas Aircraft Company had built the DC series purely to carry passengers and/or freight, fully complying with the international air safety standards of the day. With their Condor, the Germans, the Russians soon realised, had not – they noted with some obvious surprise the fact that the cabin area was not much larger than that of the DC-3 and that the flight deck was surprisingly cramped for a large aircraft; they further observed the fact that the Condor's navigator would have been quite uncomfortable on a long flight.

A comprehensive report on the Fw 200's suitability as a bomber contained further unfavourable comments, few of which would have been refuted by Kurt Tank. The Russian team initially seemed unaware that the German aircraft was an expedient compromise and went on to analyse its shortcoming as though it had been designed as a bomber. Understandably not everything they found was negative. The Condor had good acceleration; was easy to control; trimmed well in flight; could be flown 'hands off' with confidence; and the landing was 'simple'. Adverse comments were made about the placement of some controls, which were stated to be out of the aircraft captain's reach when he was strapped in. He could not operate the backup electrical pumps or emergency brakes, and neither of the two pilots had any rearward view.

As a military aircraft the report listed a number of aerodynamic drawbacks resulting from the Condor's improvised configuration, among them the gondola, which carried the heaviest-calibre guns (an MG 151 cannon was installed in the forward position of this particular example); otherwise self-protection was poor due to the reliance on small-calibre 7.9mm machine-guns. Armour protection was inadequate for the crew positions, but both wing fuel tanks and the nacelle oil tanks were believed to be too vulnerable (to enemy fire) for safety.

One questionable comment was to the affect that the Russians believed that the Germans had been obliged to fit BMW-Bramo Fafnir powerplants (323R-2s in this case) in the Fw 200C due to a shortage of higher-powered engines, with the result that the overall performance was 'inferior'. Although this particular Condor was fitted with the MW-50 water/methanol injection system, which raised the take-off rating to 1,200hp, this was not apparently used in the Russian air tests.

A training film using the above-mentioned Condor was made during 1943 by NII VVS, the Soviet camera crew doing a thorough job of committing all details of the aircraft's interior and exterior features to celluloid.

With several German aircraft types at their disposal, the Russians could ostensibly make valid comparisons with indigenous types that could conceivably operate over the vast distances of the wartime Soviet Union. In reality, few comparable designs in the Condor's class actually existed in 1943; only the Petlyakov Pe-8 had entered production and seen front-line service as a heavy bomber. Perhaps surprisingly the Russians concluded that the Heinkel He 111 outperformed the Condor in terms of handling, powerplant reliability and build quality, and that visibility from the cockpit was better than that from the Condor. Much more closely comparable to the German machine, the Pe-8, powered by AM-35A engines, was also said to be superior to the Fw 200C in terms of maximum speed, service ceiling and the 'number and placement of weapons', as the report put it.

The Soviets gave the following performance figures for the Condor, based on first-hand flight test data:

Maximum speed (at normal engine power)	240mph (387kmph) at 13,750 feet (4,200 metres) 212mph (342kmph) at sea level
Time to 14,400 feet (4,400 metres)	11.6 minutes
Service ceiling	21,260 feet (6, 480 metres)
Take-off run from paved surface	2,070 feet (630 metres)
All-up weight	44,090lb (20,000kg)
Fuel capacity	9,040lb (4,100kg)

As can be seen by comparing the figures in Appendix III, the Russians came close to those published by Focke-Wulf, although a direct comparison was not really possible under such dissimilar circumstances.

The service ceiling of the Condor, as quoted above, was considered to be too low for military operations, particularly night sorties in areas where enemy flak was likely to be intense. Again this was a curious comment considering the primary use to which the Condor had been put by the Luftwaffe, and is assumed to have been a general rule of thumb as applied by the VVS to an aircraft in the heavy bomber class.

It has been suggested that the relative windfall of German four-engine aircraft for which the Soviets did not have to pay might nevertheless have still carried something akin to 'sour grapes', as they had previously tried to acquire the B-17 Fortress or B-24 Liberator and had been refused by the Americans. Desperate measures were called for and subsequently realised when a number of USAAF B-29 Superfortresses landed on Soviet soil and were copied to emerge as the Tu-4 bomber. Subsequently this amazing transformation was developed into the transport variants the Red Air Force had so crucially lacked in 1944-45.

As was often the case during the Great Patriotic War, the Russians, who were in a position to examine vast amounts of German equipment at their leisure, were invariably impressed at the quality of engineering and finish that went into many items. Regarding German aircraft in general and the Condor in particular, they commented favourably on electrical components, sights for low-altitude bombing, and the simplicity and reliability of the thermal de-icing equipment. All these, together with an EZ-2 radio compass, Lorenz blind-landing equipment, the Askania automatic course setting and homing device, the Bauer-Sperry artificial horizon indicator and a Patin remote-indicating electro-magnetic compass, were removed from the Focke-Wulf Condor and handed to the appropriate research institutes in 1943 for detailed analysis and, in some cases, eventual production for the VVS.

Grounded and destroyed

As already noted, relatively few Condors were lost in direct action with enemy fighters but a percentage of the surviving aircraft were destroyed on the ground as Allied fighters roamed the airfields of Germany and found the remnants of a once-effective Luftwaffe bomber force. On dozens of airfields the American 'Jabos' discovered bombers pushed under boundary trees, in hangars or grouped together in what had become in 1945 terms virtual scrapyards. These they systematically shot up, individual pilots running up high personal scores for ground victories. This category of kill applied primarily to fighter groups of the Eighth Air Force, the higher command of which reckoning that the risk in strafing defended airfields was worth an official credit. No similar credit was allowed for pilots of the tactical Ninth Air Force, who were equally likely to come across an airfield well stocked with German bombers. In any event the Germans had one last chore for scores of still serviceable bombers – that of flak bait. More than one unwary pilot was caught out by a seemingly juicy target when in reality the enemy aircraft, drained of precious fuel, was sighted exactly to catch ground fire when the strafing runs started. To be fair to them, Allied fighter pilots had mere seconds to sum up such situations and many paid the price by taking a few terminal hits in their vulnerable cooling systems should they be flying Spitfires or Mustangs.

The fact that numerous American aces were brought down by flak attested to the validity of ground victory claims by the Eighth – but the irony was that few of the German machines were going anywhere. Lack of fuel and the mere presence of enemy fighters tended to keep the bombers on the ground; in any event they had few remaining targets by the spring of 1945 and numerous pilots and other personnel of the former Kampfgeschwader were retraining to feed the Jagdwaffe. This policy, born out of dire necessity, was to have affected KG 40 insofar as the unit was to have become an Me 262 fighter formation in 1945. No jet aircraft were issued to the remnants of the unit, however, and although other bomber and Zerstorer variants did become part of an expanded Geschwader in 1943-44, all were powered by reciprocating engines.

While the foregoing comments applied to Luftwaffe bombers in general, it is a fact that less than a dozen Fw 200s were claimed by US pilots during the course of their war in Europe. The singular claim of three Condors by the 357th Fighter Group, as described in the narrative, was, much to the relief of KG 40, never surpassed. Neither did the RAF reduce the number of operational Condors by much; there were a handful of day and night combats that resulted in the demise of the German aircraft, but on the whole the Luftwaffe's primary maritime reconnaissance Geschwader led a charmed life in this respect.

November 1944: escape to Sweden

Given their widely recognised value as transports, few Condors were abandoned to their fate on virtually non-operational airfields. As related, courier flights were maintained virtually throughout hostilities. Several machines left Germany shortly before the surrender, including Fw 200A-0 2994/D-ARHW *Friesland*, which was flown to Sweden, there to disembark passengers who presumably wished to fade into the background suitably distant from the situation that prevailed as the Allied armies closed in to terminate the 'Thousand Year Reich'.

Exactly how that Fw 200 met its end is somewhat obscure as Swedish sources do not seem to have filed a comprehensive report. It is known that the aircraft took off from Berlin-Tempelhof airport at 0910 on 29 November 1944 en route to Stockholm. At 1025 it was reported to have been observed falling in flames into the Baltic off Falsterbo. All four crew members, Flugkapt Paul Gutschmidt, Flugkapt Ernst-Heinz Breitenbach, Oberfunkermaschinist Fritz Brauner and Flugzeugfunker Wolfgang Lenz, perished in the crash, together with six passengers. Recovery was difficult (from Maklappen, the aircraft's final resting place) but ten fatalities would suggest that the aircraft, flying under a Lufthansa directive, suffered catastrophic failure or that it was shot down either by aircraft or warships. The Swedish authorities did not rule out the latter possibility but recovery of one of the aircraft's wheel assemblies was not enough to clarify exactly what had occurred in the aircraft's final moments.

Condor profile

As *Friesland* was one of the original 'named' Condors, its history is interesting and some details follow. It should be noted that the changes in registration and military coding for one individual aircraft of this type was far from unusual; duplication of identity via revised code letters was also quite common.

Fw 200A-06 (S-5) Werke Nummer 2994 was manufactured at Bremen in 1938 and delivered to DLH on 13 January 1939. Operated as D-ARHW *Friesland* until the autumn of 1940, after civilian flying in Germany was generally suspended from 1 September it was passed to the Luftwaffe. The aircraft's early military service is unconfirmed as to the designation of its military unit, but it is understood to have been transferred to 10./KGrzbV 172 (the so-called Lufthansa Geschwader) that same month. Then its parent unit appears to have been 4./KGrzbV 172 when the code CB+TY was applied, in October 1940. Operating as part of 4./KGrzbV 107 from 16 April 1940, 2994 reverted temporarily to its old civil registration D-ARHW for one flight to the Canary Islands in December 1940. It possibly visited Algeria and Casablanca at the same time, and while the exact purpose of the visit is unknown, talks with high-ranking officials in the Franco Government are more than likely.

The Condor was flown to the DLH facility at Staaken in February 1941 to have extra fuel cells and camera equipment installed, and once again became CB+TY. It was back in Luftwaffe service from 9 February 1941 as a PR machine on the strength of Erg./KG 40 based in Germany rather than France. Having become a trainer from April 1941 the code F8+EU was adopted and the aircraft was taken onto strength of X./KG 40 from 26 May 1941.

On 1 August 1941 2994 flew to Athens-Eleusis in support of III./KG 40's Suez Canal operations the following month. Identified once again as CB+TY, the aircraft returned to Staaken for overhaul on 16 December, and by January 1942 the Condor had become part of IV./KG 40 and, as F8+NV, it was despatched to Russia to participate in the Demyansk airlift. Subsequent to this Wehrmacht support operation, 2994 reverted once again to its original civil registration and on 11 July 1944 work started to convert it back to full civil transport configuration to operate Spanish route services, which it did from 31 July. A switch to Swedish route operations was made on 30 October and it was, as recounted above, on such a flight that Condor 2994 met its end.

Final flights

Apart from numerous flights undertaken by the German Chancellor and his entourage, Luft Hansa had, as related, been able to complete a number of flights despite the war. These included the last schedules of the 'original' – ie. prewar – network, with a flight from Barcelona to Berlin taking place as late as 14 April 1945. This flight ended in a fatal crash on 20 April and the loss of the Condor in question while it was en route from Barcelona to Berlin via Munich-Riem. Flug Kapitän August Kunstle, who had seventeen passengers on board, took off from Berlin-Tempelhof and set course for Munich. He did not make it as the aircraft crashed at 2145, reportedly shot down by American fighters with no survivors. Officially no Condor figured in the only (shared) victory by two USAAF reconnaissance pilots that day, the only claim filed – which was little comfort to relatives of those on board. In addition, no wreckage was found. Then on 28 January 1952 came news that the remains of a Condor had been discovered on a mountain at Kreis Mulberg near Piesenkofen in Bavaria.

As the end of the war approached airfields throughout Germany fell silent as flying was curtailed, then halted. Fuel supplies had dwindled to the point that only specially authorised flights were undertaken, these usually being at the behest of high-ranking officers from the various services. Detailed flight plans were not given any priority and mystery surrounds the last flights from a country shattered by bombing, and all but deserted by its government. Condors and other four-engine transports remained in demand owing to the destinations they could reach on one full load of fuel (in many instances they were not planning to return to Germany), and although operating in Staffel rather than Gruppe numbers, individual machines such as Fw 200C-3 0191/F8+MS, belonging to Transport Staffel Condor, fled the funeral pyre of the Third Reich and set course, apparently for any neutral country within range, on the day Germany surrendered on 8 May 1945.

The ex-KG 40 Condor ended up at Torslanda in Sweden where its passengers were presumably disembarked without incident, but it is interesting to speculate as to exactly who they might have been, given the contacts the Third Reich had previously made with the neutral Scandinavian Government. Himmler was the highest-placed representative of the Nazi regime to make overtures to the Swedes some months before the surrender, although the Reichsführer SS remained in Germany to be captured by British troops shortly before taking his own life. Of the Condor little more is known, but it is said to have survived into the early postwar months before being scrapped in Sweden in 1947.

Wartime test Condors

On the military side at least one Fw 200C-3 was retained by Focke-Wulf for ongoing tests with torpedoes; in combat this weapon had proved more practical when carried by smaller aircraft, notably the Ju 88 and He 111, but neither could match the Condor in terms of range. For undetermined reasons (but almost certainly because it could fly so far) these flight trials continued at least as late as March 1945, according to documentation issued by the manufacturer. Exactly where they took place was not recorded, but it must be assumed that the sorties were carried out over a large expanse of water, which would strongly indicate the Baltic. This area remained relatively free of incursions by enemy aircraft until very late in the war and test-flying was able to continue for a remarkably long time. Despite this low-priority programme and the relatively straightforward airframe modifications to the aircraft itself, it is still doubtful that the Fw 200 was ever able to operate as a torpedo bomber. And it certainly appears that no photographic evidence of any modification carried out to that end has survived.

Chapter 11

VIP transports and projects

Personal transports

When Adolf Hitler came to power he saw to it that a suitable means of air transport was made available to him and his High Command entourage. As befitted his own position as head of state, Hitler directed that six Condors would constitute a permanent small unit variously identified in postwar references as 'Fliegerstaffel des Führers' (F des F), Kurierstaffel des Führers or Regierungstaffel.

A man quite averse to seafaring and probably impatient with the relative slowness and undeniable security risk inherent in rail or road transport, Hitler preferred to travel by air whenever practical. Consequently machines of the special Staffel were made available at short notice, around the clock.

Insofar as he required a multi-seat airliner virtually to himself, Hitler viewed the Condor as the ideal aircraft once it had been converted with special interior fittings complete with an early form of 'escape capsule' comprising an armoured seat and integral parachutes for use if his life was perceived to be in danger. There is no recorded incident when the capable hands of Hitler's personal pilot failed his chief, although the flight to Finland covered later in this chapter arguably came closest to a life-threatening emergency.

Fw 200s were the largest transport aircraft to serve the Fliegerstaffel des Führers, which in 1939 comprised twelve aircraft, the balance being made up by Ju 52s. Formed on 1 April 1936, the High Command Courier Staffel originally had twelve Ju 52/3ms; those used by Hitler included W Nr 4065 and 4053.

Both the early F des F Condors were the first to be powered by German engines, the 720hp BMW 132G-1 radial. While this engine had a lower horsepower rating than the American-derived motors that had powered the first Condors, this output was subsequently increased and, in any event, the nature of the High Command flights meant that a small reduction in power was of no great importance. The aircraft were taken over from DLH and became 'property of the Reich', but they continued to be maintained by the state airline, which also provided the aircrews. There were several other Kurierstaffeln, but none of them is believed to have been equipped with the Fw 200.

Hitler's Condors

The first Condor ordered for service with F des F was W Nr 3098/D-ACVH *Grenzmark*. It was accepted by the special Staffel on 30 June 1939 and used by Hitler while he awaited conversion of his own Condor, the V-3 3099 (D-2600); the prefix 'D' was subsequently dropped in line with changes in German international recognition codes, WL-2600 being substituted for a short period. This and other Fw 200s of the F des F were repainted a number of times, overall camouflage subsequently being applied as a security measure to comply with the schemes carried by other Luftwaffe aircraft. Depending on the war zone, the Condors also had 'theatre' markings, for example a yellow fuselage band to denote operational flights on the Eastern Front. On the ground concealing an aircraft the size of a Condor proved difficult at times and the prominent swastika on a red field emblazoned across the tailfin was also dropped in the unlikely event that enemy aircraft might spot it from above.

Grenzmark meanwhile bore the German leader on several occasions in 1939. Hitler usually boarded the aircraft at Berlin-Tempelhof Airport and on 20 September the aircraft touched down at Danzig. It arrived at Warsaw-Okecie on 5 October for a Führer review of troops; on this occasion it had acquired a 'new' identity with the Kennzeichen AC+VH. *Westfalen* was also seen at foreign airports, including Budapest, where it was noted on 25 May 1940, still wearing its black and silver DLH livery.

Condors reserved for Hitler's personal use were supported by standard service machines, these being available as back-up should they be required. All servicing was carried out by Luft Hansa, the aircraft nominally remaining on the strength of the airline for the duration of the war.

In one its many manifestations of colour scheme and registration for Condors belonging to the Fliegerstaffel des Führers, *Immelmann III* appeared as WL-2600 shortly before the war. These was no logical reason for these changes apart from the obvious desire to confuse would-be saboteurs and assassins as to the identity of the aircraft – and its passengers. *MAP*

The Fw 200 V-3 had the unique marking 26+00 shortly before it was given an overall camouflage scheme in 1939 in common with most other wartime Condors. The aircraft, seen here at Rhein-Main Airport near Frankfurt in 1940, was one of several Condors that were reserved for the personal use of Adolf Hitler and his staff. *J. V. Crow*

As indicated above, the Condors that carried Hitler had their markings periodically revised in line with changes made both to Luft Hansa livery and early Luftwaffe schemes. One of the best known was '26+00' applied to the Fw 200 V-3. Together with 70/71/65 camouflage, the fuselage marking denoted the city of Berlin and had been used previously on an F des F Ju 52.

When the Condor came into the Fliegerstaffel des Führers VIP service, Hitler's chief pilot was Hans Baur, who remained with the unit until the end of the war and was at the controls on most if not all flights undertaken by the Führer. These fell broadly into two categories – visits to front-line combat units, and conferences with general officers and those of a diplomatic nature whereby Hitler needed to meet foreign heads of state. Personnel of German combat units actually saw precious little of the man who had taken their country to a series of heady victories in 1940-41, although this was to be Baur's busiest period. While Germany's military fortunes were at their zenith, the Condors used by Hitler logged an impressive number of air miles. Christmas 1940, for example, saw the pilots of JG 26 entertaining their leader to lunch at the Chateau Bonnance at Abbeville on the French coast. The Führer's entourage arrived at the venue by road, although a Condor is assumed to have been on hand to fly him back to Germany.

On 4 June 1942 Hitler flew to Immola in Finland in Fw 200C-3/U-9 0099/KE+IX with Baur at the controls. The flight had several elements of farce about it as Hasse Wind, one of the Brewster Buffalo fighter pilots of LeLv 24 assigned to escort the Condor, later recounted. Wind and his colleagues were surprised to be ordered off to intercept and escort the German aircraft, but knowing that it was Marshal Mannerheim's birthday he guessed that the flight had something to do with it.

The flight ended in some drama when the Condor bearing the Führer burst a tyre on landing after narrowly missing a factory chimney. Poor visibility almost certainly caused the Condor's pilot to fly low over the Kauopaa factory on approach, a situation compounded by the fact that Hitler was apparently on a very tight schedule. So low was the cloud base that only two of the Finnish Air Force Brewster Buffalo fighters detailed as escort were able to keep track of the German machine in the gloom.

On touching down, heavy application of the Condor's brakes caused the port-side set to become red-hot and generate enough heat to set fire to one of the tyres, which caused a cloud of smoke to drift across the airfield as Hitler disembarked to meet his host. Both the Führer and members of his entourage ignored the acrid smoke given off by the burning rubber. Hans Baur immediately ordered the offending brake to be changed, the task being carried out with all speed under the chief pilot's supervision. Two groundcrew members extinguished the fire and changed the Condor's port wheel brake in time for the official party to leave later that afternoon.

Hitler had surely noticed the smell of burning rubber as the Condor touched down, but by all accounts he took no action against the flight crew over the incident. Baur almost certainly minimised the incident to the Führer's satisfaction.

Ostensibly the reason for the German Chancellor's visit to Finland was to celebrate the 75th birthday of the Marshal of Finland, Carl Gustaf Emil Mannerheim. In reality Hitler wanted to woo the Finns into continuing the war against Russia as an ally of Germany. A private dining-car conversation between the two leaders (which was subject to a clandestine recording by Finnish technicians) did not result in any guarantees and the German party left soon afterwards, at 6.10pm, Hitler having presented Mannerheim with a bullet-proof Mercedes sedan.

Incidentally, the illicit recording was seized, but Hitler's SS guards took no action against the Finns, instead ordering that the 'can' enclosing the tape be sealed. This was done, but when the Germans left the Finns broke the seals and listened to the spoken words, which are strongly believed to be those of Hitler, although some who were close to him are not totally convinced that the recording is indeed genuine.

That this was a heavyweight visit is shown by the passenger list. Occupying the Condor's seats were Keitel, Doenitz, Dietl, Jodel and other high-ranking German and Finnish officers. The talks were part of three attempts made to persuade the Finns that remaining a combatant on the German side was militarily sound, but the astute and highly respected Marshal Mannerheim was nobody's fool. He could see the way things were going on the Eastern Front, but courteously met with German delegations on two other occasions, besides the birthday visit by Hitler in 1942.

Hitler resumed his travels in July 1944 with a visit to Poltava in Russia on the 3rd. Soviet intelligence had enough advance warning of the event to lay on a bombing raid in an attempt to destroy the Condor and its occupants while it remained on the ground during the night of 3/4 June. This failed as *Immelmann III* had actually departed before the Soviet bombers arrived. The Condor headed for Stalino aerodrome outside Stalingrad where Hitler embarked briefly to inspect the aircrews and Heinkel IIIs of KG 27 the following day.

By June 1944 the Finns had become used to the elegant airliner bringing in other German VIPs, as on the 27th when Fw 200C-4/U1 CG+AE brought Generaloberst Lothar Rendulic, C-in-C of the 20./Gebirgsarmee into Helsinki-Malmi Airport.

A coat of winter camouflage helped hide the outline of the Führer's Condor when C-4/U1 CE+IB flew the German leader to staff conferences on the Russian Front. Such visits gradually tailed off as the war went badly for Germany.

The last known visit by a German military delegation to Finland took place on 15 August when a Condor carried members of the High Command to Malmi for a final round of talks. The officers, headed by Field Marshal Keitel, did their best to come away with something positive regarding the Finnish position. Realistically, it was a little late in the war to find much common ground and Finland's stance remained largely unchanged. The country signed an armistice with the Soviet Union on 4 September 1944.

Flights by Hitler tended to diminish in number after the bomb plot against his life at the 'Wolf's Lair' at Rastenburg in July 1944, the German leader becoming more of a recluse at Berchtesgaden, his mountain retreat in Bavaria, and finally the bunker in the centre of Berlin. The penultimate occasion when Hitler took a Condor flight was in late 1944, using Fw 200C-3/U1 0240/TK+CV, which flew from Berlin to land the Führer at Munchen-Riem, where a small convoy of limousines waited on the tarmac.

By the spring of 1945 the Red Army ring was closing around Berlin and the Third Reich's existence was measured in weeks. Due to its relative remoteness the Rechlin test centre housed a number of transport aircraft that were using the airfield and awaiting any final orders from Hitler and members of the High Command. On 23 April aircraft of the F des F were ordered to relocate to Rechlin-Roggentin, where they were to be dispersed in an area of cleared forest a short distance from the runway. Two days later Hitler's Condor (TK+CV) arrived, as did one of the Condor escorts (CE+IC), having made the hazardous flight from Berlin via Wittstock. Within hours the German capital had all but been sealed off by the Russians and the airports had been captured.

Someone then came up with a senseless scheme to carry out an air drop of troops into Berlin for the 'personal protection of the Führer'. These men were not crack SS troops but in the main poorly trained sailors who were unlikely to have achieved much against seasoned Soviet shock troops – but the flights went ahead. On the night of 26/27 April Fw 200 CE+IC took off from Rechlin accompanied by a Ju 352 and other aircraft and flew to Rerik to pick up the sailors. They were to return to Rechlin, presumably for a briefing, but not all of them made it, as the Condor was shot down by defensive flak during its approach and crashed south of Potsdam. Several men perished as a result. Further flights into the besieged city were made by light aircraft but no further sorties by Condors were recorded. A final hazard facing the last Condor flights had been friendly flak; the flak crews reverted to firing on anything that came into their sights on the grounds that there were so few German aircraft left that any they saw must be hostile. As a result of continuing to adhere to unnecessary radio silence rules and a general breakdown in communications (the flak units were part of the Luftwaffe), the ground guns claimed the lives of a good many German airmen when the outcome of the war must have been obvious even to the most dyed-in-the wool Nazi fanatic.

Other VIP Condors

While the Führer undertook tours of inspection and flew to meetings with foreign heads of state in his fleet of personal Condors, there appears to have been less usage by the other dignitaries afforded the honour of a specially outfitted Fw 200. A few flights are on record, however, including those associated with Himmler's involvement with the A-4 (V-2) rocket programme, which prompted him to arrange a surprise visit to Peenemunde on 10 December 1942. In the early days of the programme Himmler flew into the airfield at Peenemunde-West to inspect the establishment, which had, he stated, generated much talk in Hitler's inner circle.

The Reichsführer SS was there to offer what help he could to the scientists and technicians engaged on the army weapon, including Werner von Braun and Walter Dornberger. Although they had sought Himmler's assistance, the rocket chiefs noted with some apprehension his assurance that the SS would protect them from 'sabotage and treason'. With that Himmler returned to the aircraft (presumably his special Condor) and flew back to his headquarters. Such visits bore fruit, for on 22 December Hitler signed the decree authorising the mass-production of the A-4.

Himmler's Condor, Fw 200C-4/U1 0176/GC+AE, was the aircraft that had also been earmarked for Herman Goering's use although, as noted, the Luftwaffe chief did not travel by air as frequently as the other leaders of the Reich Government.

Probably because Himmler used GC+AE more frequently than Goering, another Condor was allocated to the Reichsmarschall carrying the code GC+SE. This aircraft was then allocated to Goering for his exclusive use, although it appears that – somewhat ironically – he still preferred to travel by rail whenever possible. His specially fitted-out train was used on many occasions when he had cause to visit Hitler or operational units of the Luftwaffe. While it may seem strange that the head of the air force would chose not to fly as a passenger or indeed to take the controls himself, Goering had a mountain of duties, at least for the first years of the war, which appear to have curtailed his flying. He retained his licence and did on occasion fly the Condor or one of three Ju 52s that had been allocated to him before the war, these aircraft also being put at the disposal of RLM officials.

As an expedient measure the Condors belonging to the F des F could be armed in similar fashion to their KG 40 counterparts, as and when this was a requirement. In addition, a number of Condors were detailed as escort aircraft, one being Fw 200C-4/U2 CE+IB. This particular aircraft was known to have been assigned to accompany the Führer's personal aircraft and would most likely have been fully armed on every flight it undertook.

When the war finished several Focke-Wulf Condors became 'spoils of war' and aviation journals of the period covered photographically what soon became the best-known representative of this converted airliner fleet, No 5 in the special Staffel's numerical sequence, and the machine placed at the disposal of Heinrich Himmler, Reichsführer and head of the Gestapo. This particularly aircraft was flown to the Royal Aircraft Establishment at Farnborough in Hampshire, where it was briefly flown. Further press coverage suitably awed (or outraged) its readers with the degree of luxury, including leather-upholstered chairs, that Himmler supposedly enjoyed while flying in it.

Although allocated an Air Ministry number, which indicated that selected German aircraft would be evaluated at the end of the war, little was seemingly done to preserve Fw 200C CG+AE, the specially modified machine allocated to Heinrich Himmler. Flown to Farnborough and put 'out to grass', there was no museum in which to house it – even if such an idea had been put forward at the time – and it was eventually scrapped. *Author's collection*

Perhaps because of its lavish internal furnishings, Himmler's personal Condor was more frequently photographed than the other VIP machines found at Flensburg. *D. Howley via R. L. Ward*

High Command transports

Individual Condors on the strength of the Fliegerstaffel des Führers were also allocated to such high-ranking Nazis as Grossadmiral (Grand Admiral) Karl Doenitz, head of the Kriegsmarine after 30 January 1943, head of the U-boat service and the man named as the last Führer of Nazi Germany, effective from 1 May 1945. This aircraft, an Fw 200C-4/U2 (0181/GC+SJ) named *Albatros III*, was usually captained by Hptm Paul Husslein, who became personal pilot to Doenitz. Both Husslein and the Condor's crew had previously served with KG 40.

While on the strength of the special Staffel, the aircraft was put at the disposal of the staff of the Naval High Command, and was frequently used for liaison flights to Lorient, the headquarters of MarineGruppe West and U-boat HQ. During 1944 the crew of *Albatros III* consisted of Hptm Paul Husslein (Captain), Fw Erwin Scheunemann (Radio operator), Obfw Karl-Heinz Hoemcke (Engineer), and Uffz Nikolaus Mau (Gunner). Whether or not this crew was able to stay together for the duration of the war is not known, but every effort would have been made for them to do so.

In common with several of the Condors used by the German High Command, the last Führer's personal example survived the war only to be scrapped after a heavy crash-landing at Schleswig on 28 February 1946. It had been planned that the machine would be presented to DDL as a replacement for *Wolf* when it was impounded in 1940, but this was not to be. At the time of the crash the Condor carried the British designator 'Air Min 97' on the fuselage.

Not so long-lived was the Fw 200C-6/U2 (F8+JH) allocated to Albert Speer as his personal aircraft. Previously coded TA+MR, the aircraft is understood to have been based at the Luftwaffe test centres at Tarnewitz and Rechlin in October 1943. The final spring of the war saw Allied aircraft carrying out air attacks on both centres, and one that took place on 20 March 1945 apparently destroyed Speer's Condor.

While most of the Nazi hierarchy with the rank to justify their own official aircraft were to survive the war, Reinhard Heydrich did not. A trained pilot, Obergruppenführer-SS (General) Heydrich was allocated an F des F Condor, probably upon his appointment as Deputy Reich Protector for Bohemia and Moravia in September 1941. He flew his own Condor on several occasions and was assassinated by Czech agents on 29 May 1942.

Several of these specially adapted High Command Condors were found by British troops on Flensburg-Weiche airfield at the end of war. The aircraft were drawn up along the runway together with D-ASVX of DLH and one of the German airline's Ju 52s. None of the aircraft had suffered obvious damage. In what is believed to have been the last markings change to a Condor used by Hitler, Fw 200 TK+CV had, in common with the others, been camouflaged and given the rudder code '1'. It was then parked alongside Himmler's No 5, and although the identities of the Condors with the intervening numbers are not confirmed there can be little doubt that TK+CV was indeed that last used by Hitler.

These Condors soon had RAF markings applied over their German national insignia and each was allocated an identity within a numerical Air Ministry (abbreviated to 'Air Min' on the aircraft) system designed to identify and log the more interesting examples of enemy types that were captured. Some were brought to England for evaluation, but beforehand the transports made an impressive line-up. Himmler's Condor, an exotic aircraft on several counts, should have been a prime candidate for preservation. Unfortunately, retaining such a machine for the edification of future generations was not a priority in the immediate postwar years; even a site for a suitable museum in which to house examples of the larger wartime aircraft would not be agreed for decades, and the erstwhile Reichsführer SS's Condor, together with numerous other intriguing and largely irreplaceable types, both Allied and Axis, was scrapped.

Spanish Condors

It is pertinent here to briefly mention the history of several Focke-Wulf Condors that served the Ejercito del Aire (Spanish Air Force) in the last years of and immediately following the Second World War. All aircraft were ex-Luftwaffe machines that had landed in the country during the war and had been impounded under Spanish neutrality laws, and the known examples are:

Fw 200C-4 (0103)	bel NO
Fw 200C-4 (0118)	T-4.1; broken up for spares after the war
Fw 200C-4 (0166/F8+HS)	T-4.2; to EdA in 1945 and used for spares
Fw 200C-4/U3 (0175/F8+AS)	To Spanish 12 January 1943; T-4.2; scrapped in 1948
Fw 200C-5/U1 (0221)	

As recorded earlier, the first two Condors arrived in Spain after KG 40's 1 January 1943 raid on Casablanca, these being subsequently followed by three more. Fw 200C-4/U3 0175 was assigned to the Spanish national airline Iberia, effective from 12 January 1943. It appeared, however, that nobody wanted this Condor; the Spanish authorities believed that it would be uneconomical to convert it to civil configuration and tried to present it back to DLH as payment for a number of Ju 52/3ms, but this offer was refused and the aircraft remained in Spain. In 1945 it was redesignated as T-4.2 in the Ejercito del Aire. Attached to the Escuela Superior de Vuclo (High Flying School), whose code it bore on the fin, the aircraft was damaged on 11 November 1947 and languished until the following year when it was scrapped as a result of general unserviceability of the brakes.

On 13 August 1943 Fw 200C-5/U1 0221/F8+IT of 9./KG 40, captained by Oblt Gunther Seide, put down at Arena de la Villa beach, near Seville, after being damaged by Allied fighters. Just two days later the fourth Condor arrived. This was a C-4 0166/F8+JR, which landed at Labacolla Airport near Santiago de Compostela, having sustained damage from naval gunfire. The fifth aircraft, another Fw 200C-4 (0103/F8+DT), was destroyed by Oblt Siegfried Gall's crew following a crash-landing at Apulia on 1 May 1943.

Of the surviving Fw 200s in Spain, C-4 0175/F8+AS, which had landed at Perello, north of Tortosa, probably garnered a record as one of the longest-serving Condors in western Europe. It survived retirement and subsequent scrapping until 1948. However, its Spanish service as a transport under the designation T-4.2 turned out to be brief.

The rather sad saga of the Spanish Condors would unfold after the war; of the five ex-KG 40 aircraft that were intact, four were repairable. As a country renowned for pressing into service any foreign aircraft that fell into its hands, Spain played up its neutrality and apparently made no move to return the Condors. With the country firmly under Franco's control, Spain was, however, unlikely

Internment in Spain was the lot of a number of Condors, those machines that were airworthy being impressed into Spanish service while spares lasted. This Fw 200C-4/U3 (0175/F8+AS) shared San Pablo airfield, Seville, with a Spanish aircraft marked with the characteristic black cross on a white field rudder marking. Similar identification would be applied to the Condors after their capture to serve into the postwar era of Franco's Nationalist regime. *F. Selinger*

Not so fortunate a fate awaited this Fw 200C-4 (0118/F8+HS), late of KG 40, which was abandoned at Rimbaud when the war ended. The camouflage paint has understandably deteriorated markedly. *F. Selinger*

　　　　　　　　　　　　　　　　　　　　　　　FOCKE-WULF FW 200 CONDOR

to create a diplomatic incident with the Germans who had helped secure control of the country during the civil war, especially as a tacit agreement with Hitler had resulted in the clandestine use of replenishment facilities for the U-boat fleet. On her part, Germany seemed prepared to write off the 'missing' Condors, there being no record of any demand to have them returned.

Postwar Condors

Postwar use of the Fw 200 has been touched upon elsewhere, and the Russians, despite their reservations about the aircraft, did press at least one into civil service. This C-4 was an example of several Condors models captured at Tempelhof, one of the main Berlin airports, in the spring of 1945. An ex-KG 40 aircraft complete with the 'world in a ring' insignia and a single merchant ship kill painted high on the fin, this Condor had Russian stars painted over the German national insignia when it was moved to NII VVS in 1945.

Four Condors captured in Berlin were overhauled and repaired at a factory in Krasnoyarsk before being assigned to the Polar Aviation. Mikhail A. Titlov of Polarnaya Aviatsiya was ordered to ferry a Condor to Moscow after undertaking two familiarisation flights. Titlov duly arrived in the Russian capital in a C-4 (presumably the one mentioned above) to prepare for a series of survey flights in the Soviet Far North regions; the task was mainly to log the movement of ice fields for the benefit of shipping using Arctic routes. For three months in 1946 Titlov piloted the Condor, which was civil-registered CCCP N-400 and retained the DLH colour scheme it was wearing when it changed sides.

Two other civil Condors were Russian-registered – N-401 and N-500 – these being used respectively at Igarka in northern Siberia during 1947 and in support of a Soviet Arctic research station in 1949. The latter was then attached to the Svernyy Polyus 4 (North Pole 4) district.

Utilisation of the Condor by Mikhail Titlov was extremely high, as he was at the controls for up to twenty hours in a single day. The aircraft's last flight took place on 13 December 1946 when Titlov was obliged to carry out a forced landing at Baydaratskaya Guba while en route from Khatanga to Moscow via Igarka. Apparently two of the Condor's engines stopped and the aircraft was badly damaged in the ensuing crash-landing; the pilot, the other crew members and twenty passengers were rescued by a C-47, the pilot of which put down on the ice close to the Condor, which was abandoned and left to its fate. As with other Condors that survived into the postwar period, the shortage of spares became critical, not least for the BMW engines. In 1948 the Russian aircraft registered H-500 was fitted with substitute Shvetsov Ash-621R radial engines in Plant No 23 at Moscow-Fili. In this configuration it was known as MK-200 (modifiteerovannyy Kondor, or 'modified Condor'). New engines did not, however, bestow longevity as the aircraft was damaged on 14 February 1950 while jacked up for landing gear checks at Zakharkovo airfield. The jacks collapsed, resulting in the aircraft's oil coolers being damaged. After repairs the Condor operated until 23 April 1950, when it crashed at Yakutsk while attempting to land in a high wind. Damage to the port-side undercarriage unit, wings and engine nacelles caused it to be declared a write-off, thus ending the career of the Fw 200 in Soviet service. Yet these particular machines lasted longer in actual operations than any of their Luftwaffe counterparts, thus creating another record for a remarkable workhorse.

Baur a traitor?

A curious incident – or non-incident – indirectly involving Hitler's personal Fw 200 has been aired in several places, notably the pages of the renowned British journal *Aeroplane Monthly*. That publication ran a story in February 2006 to the effect that Hans Baur became party to a plot that would ultimately deliver Adolf Hitler into British hands early in 1941. Details were vague and inaccurate to the point of giving Baur's nationality as Austrian and mistaking the names of several of his relatives. Probably following the tongue-in-cheek journalistic yardstick 'never let the facts spoil a good story', the crux was that an aircraft with Hitler aboard would be flown to England by Baur who would, using pre-arranged 'safe passage' signals, put down at Lympne airfield on the South Coast, where Hitler was to be escorted off the Condor – and by that action the Führer's pilot would have altered the course of world history. Contingency plans were outlined to the effect that RAF fighters would close in and as a last resort shoot down the VIP aircraft – assumed to be a Condor – if any deviation from the plan was evident. Baur was to make a steep approach to Lympne with undercarriage lowered and to fire off four red flares at thirty-second intervals if intercepted by fighters. Any evidence of German escort fighters, a failure to fire off the flares, a clear intention by Baur to fly further inland than Lympne, or any attempt to return to France, would have resulted in the German aircraft being attacked. The flight to England was originally to have taken place on or about 25 March 1941.

The plan, such as it was, involved the Deputy Chief of the Air Staff, Air Marshal Arthur Harris, and the AOC in C Fighter Command, AVM William Sholto Douglas, and although both men hoped that Hitler could be delivered into British hands, neither of them put great faith in it actually taking place. Other events caused the timetable to slip and eventually what records there were in the Public Record Office (now the UK National Archives) were opened in 1972; Hans Baur himself died in 1993.

In the event not even a small part of such a plan was initiated and even the fact that a Condor would have be used in the coup attempt (although this was the most logical aircraft) was only vaguely implied in the original story. One can only speculate on the relative ease at which the feat might have been accomplished with the full complicity of a handful of key German personnel.

Condor projects

Reliable references state that a total of 252 Focke-Wulf Condors, the majority being variants based on the original strengthened Fw 200C series, were delivered to the Luftwaffe between 1940 and 1944. Considering the tonnage of Allied ships they sank and damaged during the first three years of the war, their contribution to the German war effort was out of all proportion to the number of aircraft available to a single Geschwader at any one time. And as emphasised earlier in this narrative, it is undeniable that the Fw 200 could have greatly benefited from a complete re-strengthening to turn an airliner into a more effective warplane. As things stood, the results achieved by a compromise were remarkable.

In common with most designers, Kurt Tank had ideas to improve the Fw 200 Condor for both military and civil service, but to proceed with this venture he needed official backing. This came about in mid-1943 when the RLM requested design studies aimed principally at boosting the range of the existing Condor by adding extra fuel capacity, the weight of which would have raised its permissible take-off weight to 55,700lb (25,260kg) compared to 24,500 lb (50,000 kg) for a standard C-6 model. Under the paper designation Fw 200F, the ultra-long-range strategic reconnaissance model would have had both fore and aft ventral gun positions deleted to save weight. Ministry officials stressed that the configuration was to have minimum changes from the existing Condor, without, for example, any external fittings for the carriage of auxiliary fuel tanks – all fuel was to be carried internally. It was envisaged that cells for additional fuel tankage of 2,535 gallons (some 11,900 litres) could be installed by units in the field, as and when necessary.

By increasing the standard three fuselage fuel cells each containing 234 gallons (1,100 litres) to five to provide a total of 7,030 gallons (33,000 litres), the aircraft's centre of gravity would have been largely unaffected. This confirmed that the RLM was not looking for a major time-consuming re-design but an expedient measure that would not cause disruption to the existing assembly lines.

Focke-Wulf's conclusion was that the required range of 4,285 miles (6,900km) could only be achieved by a heavier airframe. Take-off weight at 55,700lb (25,260 kg) was to have been made possible either by the installation of Bramo 323R-2 engines fitted with water-methanol injection or by the use of specially hardened runways.

Some offensive capability would have been retained by the resulting Fw 200F, the proposed specification allowing 2,100lb (954kg) for weapons and ammunition, of which 1,100lb (500kg) was to be taken up by bombs. Maximum speed at 225mph (360kmph) was only 12mph (20kmph) less than the Fw 200C-6, and the service ceiling was estimated as 19,680 feet (6,000 metres) compared with the 21,650 feet (6,600 metres) attained by the C-6. This proposal was undoubtedly an early exercise to give Focke-Wulf a stake in the future Amerika-Bomber programme (see below) without the need for a full redesign. Alternatively, a more capable maritime reconnaissance/attack aircraft was urgently needed by the Luftwaffe.

In the event Germany's adverse war situation forced projects such as the Fw 200F to be cancelled, although Tank was interested in further developing designs based on the Condor and intended for civil service after the war. Lufthansa officials shared his optimism that international air services by German airlines would recommence at some future date, particularly those linking the USA with continental Europe. Tank and Dipl Ing Bansemir opened negotiations with the French company SNCASO to build what became known as the Fw 300. Visualised as a pressurised airliner powered by four DB 603 in-line engines each developing 1,950hp, a mock-up of the Fw 300 complete with an attractive interior was built shortly before the project was reworked as a bomber under the designation Fw 300A. Bansemir moved to Paris with a technical staff to work with French engineers who would build a prototype, the Fw 300 V-1. In the event there was no time to complete either the first Fw 300A or a further projected derivative, the Fw 300B, before the war ended.

The Amerika-Bomber

Further Focke-Wulf bomber projects were based only loosely on the Condor; the RLM continued to keep its collective options open in the event that Germany could somehow reverse or at least call a temporary halt to the tide of events engulfing the country by 1945. Had that happened, a bomber with enough range to strike the US mainland could have materialised and the idea remained alive. Ever since America had declared war on Germany in December 1941 the RLM had considered issuing a specification for the so-called Amerika-Bomber, an aircraft capable of attacking New York or blocking the Panama Canal after flying from airfields in Europe.

Focke-Wulf was one of three manufacturers with experience in the design of multi-engine military aircraft to undertake such a task, and Tank himself worked on a six-engine design that might well have achieved the required goal. This, the Ta 400, was a bomber with a wing span of 150ft 3.35in (45.80m) and a length of 94ft 2in (28.70m). Of twin-tail configuration, the aircraft, which had an estimated loaded weight of 132,300lb (60,000kg) and a range of 3,107 miles (5,000km), was in competition with Messerschmitt, which submitted the Me 264B, and Junkers, with the Ju 390.

Few German wartime aircraft did not have projected developments, which were either practical or mere flights of fancy. In the former category was the Ta 400, a serious contender for the dream goal explored by several manufacturers of bombing targets in the USA from Europe. General arrangement drawings and a wind-tunnel model were as far as the Focke-Wulf submission could be taken before the war ended. *E. J. Creek*

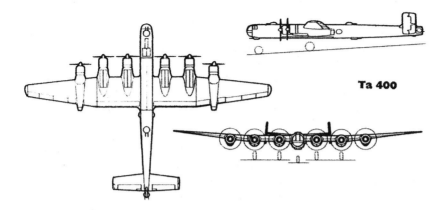

Ta 400

A three-view drawing of what the Ta 400 was intended to look like. Note that extended outer engine nacelles were included in a final six-engine version.

Focke-Wulf began detailed design work early in 1943 at Chatillon in France, a facility controlled by VFW. Contractors in Germany, France and Italy were brought into the programme to supply components. Of all-metal stressed-skin construction, the Ta 400 would have been powered by six fourteen-cylinder BMW 801D engines each developing 1,700hp for take-off. As a mid-winged design, the Ta 400 was to have a crew of six housed in two separate pressure cabins, the fuselage being a circular monocoque; it incorporated a heavy defensive armament of ten 20mm MG 151/20 cannon in five remotely controlled barbettes. A bomb load of 22,000lb (10,000kg) was proposed.

A number of design alternatives were envisaged for later versions of the Ta 400, including a smoothly contoured nose with extensive glazing in contrast to the original 'stepped' design for the crew stations, similar to that of the Ju 88 and Do 217. The installation of two Junkers Jumo 004B turbojets mounted below the outboard nacelles of the radial engines would have provided 1,980lb (900kg) of thrust.

Time was again very much against such advanced projects being brought even to the completion of a single prototype, and although the Messerschmitt and Junkers submissions did achieve that important milestone, Focke-Wulf did not. The Ta 400 consequently existed only in drawings and wind tunnel models before the entire project had to be abandoned at the behest of the RLM, which opted for the Junkers design. Eventually, however, only the Me 264 ever came close to mounting sorties across the Atlantic, its development having advanced to the point where several aircraft undertook a series of flight tests that resulted in considerable handling and performance details.

Up she rises…

Few tangible reminders of the Focke-Wulf Condor exist today, although in May 1999 an attempt was made to recover the virtually intact remains of Fw 200C-3/U4 0063/F8+BR from the waters of Stjordalsfjord in Norway. Slinging the sizeable section of the aircraft (the wing, engines and fuselage forward of the wing) to be lifted by barges went smoothly enough. Unfortunately the aircraft's wartime Achilles heel still proved dangerous when the main spar snapped during lifting operations. From what had been a virtually complete aircraft when it left the water, the resulting heaps of rusty wreckage were sobering to behold.

Closer examination confirmed, however, that there was enough of the original airframe for an aircraft to be rebuilt for static display, and the Deutsche Technical Museum in Berlin grew more confident that as complete a Condor as possible will eventually emerge for public viewing. At first the seemingly disastrous break-up of the Condor airframe appeared to indicate little hope that a complete museum exhibit could ever emerge. Examination of the remains did, however, give restorers confidence that such a goal could indeed be achieved, given ample time and sufficient funding. The fact that the Condor's wartime location was in Norway proved not to be a problem when the Norwegian Defence Ministry presented the aircraft to the German museum in return for work carried out by Lufthansa employees on a Ju 52 intended for display by the Forsvarsnuseet Flysamlingen at Gardermoen. Funds from the Berlin Lottery helped to launch an appeal to 'save the Condor', and although this endeavour was generously supported by several companies, public donations were – and still are at the time of writing – welcome.

Restoration of various components of the aircraft was placed with three organisations: Daimler Chrysler Aerospace Airbus at Bremen (tail unit and fuselage sections); Lufthansa in Hamburg (fuselage sections, rudder and flaps, etc) and Rolls-Royce at Dahlewitz (BMW engines). In due course work will be concentrated at two locations, one definitely being the Berlin museum and an as yet unspecified site in Bremen, the city where the aircraft was originally built. Apparently both locations will display parts of the Condor in due course. This plan will, however, depend on how well the damaged parts respond to being restored or, more realistically, copied.

In addition to the exciting prospect that Fw 200C-3 ex-F8+BR of KG 40 will eventually be put on display as a complete and unique exhibit, the Berlin Museum has in the meantime placed a main undercarriage unit on public view as a 'taster' for what is to come in due course. At the time of writing the process of restoration is continuing and, wisely with such a large-scale workload, no date had been announced for the public to see a genuine wartime Fw 200 on display.

Other Condor components have been recovered since the war. Among these are two intact engines, large sections of airframe and other items that, if not directly adaptable to a restoration, can provide patterns for a modern equivalent to be made by a dedicated team of highly skilled engineers.

Appendix I

Ritterkreuzträger of KG 40

Buchholz, Hans   Oberl II./KG 40: RK 19 May 1941

Daser, Edmund   Norway service; Hptm and StKap in I./KG 40; RK 21 February 1941

Fliegel, Fritz   Kap II./KG 40; later Kdr I./Gruppe; RK 25 March 1941

Harlinghausen, Martin   Eichenlaub 30 January 1941 (X Fl Kp)

Jope, Bernhard (ex-DLH)   RK 24 March 1944 (as Kdr KG 100)

Konschegg, Dr Lambert von   Kdr III./KG 40; RK 28 February 1945

Kowalewski, Robert   Gen staff X Fliegerk; RK 24 November 1940; Kdr II/KG 26 to July 1941, then Kdr III./KG 40 from September 1943

Kuntz, Herbert   StKap II./KG 40 at war's end; RK 14 March 1943

Mayr, Rudolf (ex DLH)   Flugzeugführer KG 40; award of EK 2 and I for ops at Narvik; Oberl and Staffel Kapitän IX./KG 40; RK 18 May 1943

Mons, Rudolf   Oberl I./KG 40; RK 18 September 1941

Petersen, Edgar   Kdore 1 March 1941; RK 21 October 1940

Schlosser, Heinrich   Oberl II./KG 40; RK 18 September 1941

Stahnke, Karl-Heinz   Flugzeugführer III./KG 40; RK 24 October 1944

Veith, Alfred   RK 16 May 1940

RK Ritterkreuz: Knight's Cross of the Iron Cross; Eichenlaub: Oak leaves

Appendix II

The Fw 200 in KG 40 service

Only units mainly equipped with the Fw 200 are listed.

Numbers refer to allocated aircraft on strength with those serviceable on the quoted dates shown in (brackets)

Stab./KG 40

Stab./KG 40	First formation (no contact with Fw 200)
Stab./KG 40	Second formation
c15 March 1941 to April 1941	Formed from Stabskette at Bordeaux-Merignac under Fliegerführer Atlantik within Luftflotte 3; also operated other aircraft types
1 April 1944	Transferred to X Fliegerkorps (Luftflotte 3)
26 June 1944	Stabskette with nine Fw 200s at Bordeaux-Merignac
July 1944	To Gardermoen, Norway, under Fliegerführer 4, Luftflotte 5
October 1944	Transferred to Lubeck-Blankensee, Germany
2 February 1945	Stab disbanded

I./KG 40

1939

23 September	I./Gruppe formed at Oldenburg, Germany
1 November	1./Staffel formed at Bremen-Neulanderfeld (with He 111); Fw 200C-0 received as available; personnel from Blindflugschulen and former Fernaufklarungstaffel Ob.d.l. among earliest crews

1940

Spring	I./Gruppe fully formed, equipped mainly with Fw 200C-1s; some elements at Luneberg for war operations over Denmark and Norway, April-June
9 April	Reconnaissance sorties for X Fliegerkorps from this date
11 April	Moved to Aalborg, Denmark; reconnaissance of Trondheim area
12 April	First Condor loss recorded near Namsos-Andalsnes
15 April	Reconnaissance of Narvik area
21-24 April	Further reconnaissance of Narvik and other areas
5 May	Ship reconnaissance flights
8 May	Four Fw 200Cs based in Denmark
17 and 25 May	Reconnaissance of shipping and Narvik area
29 May	Bombed Tromso
9 June	Unit's Condors sank *Vandyck*, believed first ship credited to KG 40
Mid-June	To Oldenburg, Germany; commences attacks on English coastal shipping
June	Minelaying sorties to East Coast of England from Oldenburg and Marx, Germany
July (early)	I./Gruppe fully re-equipped with Fw 200C-1
12 July (from)	Transferred to Bordeaux-Merignac, France. Daylight minelaying stops after loss of several Condors

Note: Bordeaux became permanent base until 1943, with diversions to other airfields as required. Limited night minelaying sorties stopped after short period due to further losses.

13 August	Based at Brest-Guipavas, Brittany, under 9 Flieger Division (Luftflotte 2) for operations against British Isles
1 May	I./Gruppe Stab formed
1 May	2./Staffel formed
1 June	3./Staffel formed; operations similar to other units of I./Gruppe but unit redesignated Ausbildungsstaffel/KG 40 in August; new 3./Staffel forms immediately
June-July	Moved to Bordeaux-Merignac
7 September	I./Gruppe has seven (four) Fw 200s at Bordeaux under IV Fliegerkorps
September (end)	Some 90,000 tons of shipping claimed sunk
26 October	I./KG 40 cripples liner *Empress of Britain*
23 November	Two Condors lost in RAF raid on Bordeaux-Merignac
22 December	Low-level attack on shipping in Loch Sunari, Scotland
December (end)	Average number of serviceable Fw 200s is eight
1941	
6 January	I./Gruppe removed from Luftwaffe control and placed under control of C in C U-boats with headquarters at Lorient, France; Gruppe remains at Bordeaux and continues armed reconnaissance over Atlantic, around British Isles, Iceland and Norway
January	Gruppe credited with fifteen ships sunk (63,000 tons)
9 February	Gruppe sinks five ships in single operation; total tonnage sunk to date is 363,000 tons
26 February	Seven ships from convoy OB.290 sunk off Ireland; total of twenty-two ships (84,000 tons) sunk during February
15 March	Unit placed under newly formed Fliegerführer Atlantik to support Kriegsmarine
March	Six Condors sent to Gardermoen to counter convoy re-routing
March (end)	I./Gruppe claims eighty-eight ships (390,000 tons) sunk but figure believed optimistically high
13 April	Merignac bombed by RAF; three Condors plus other aircraft lost
17 April	Three Condors lost off Shetland Islands
15 June	Attack on convoy off Iberian peninsula
26 July	Five of twenty-five Condors serviceable at Cognac; low in-commission rate of Fw 200Cs during summer months
3 August	First loss of Condor to CAM Hurricane
August (end)	Gruppe sends six Fw 200s to Athens-Eleusis, Greece, to fly night operations against ships in Suez Canal area, Gulf of Suez and northern Red Sea; nightly attacks on Suez area with aim of denying canal to Allied shipping
2-10 September	Phased withdrawal from Mediterranean area and return to France
18-19 December	Armed reconnaissance support of U-boat operations against convoy HG.76 off Spain and Portugal
1942	
14 February	Unit has twenty-six (nine) Fw 200s on strength
1 March	Unit complement remains unchanged at twenty-six Fw 200Cs based at Bordeaux-Merignac under Fliegerführer Atlantik

20 March	1./ and 3./Staffel transfer from Bordeaux to Trondheim-Vaernes, Norway, to patrol route of convoys sent to Murmansk, Russia; 2./Staffel remains in France
14 May	Four Fw 200s sink two ships in Esfjorden/Spitsbergen, thus preventing attempt to shut down German weather station in area
April-May	Condors shadow convoy PQ.16
June	2./Staffel exchanges identity with 7./Staffel (already based in Norway); its crews are first to detect convoy PQ.17
1 July	Crews maintain continuous contact with ships of PQ.17
August (mid to late)	Supports Operation 'Wunderland', German operation against Siberian sea route that includes sortie by battleship *Admiral Scheer* into Kara Sea, Arctic Ocean
8 September	1./Staffel returns to Fassberg, Germany, to begin conversion onto He 177
10 September	Condor operations against PQ.18 continue
1 December	1./Staffel inventory is four Fw 200C-3/U4s, fourteen Fw 200C-4s and seven He 177A-1s
December	Ten to eighteen Fw 200s of I./ and III./KG 40 transferred from Trondheim to Berlin-Staaken to become part of KGrzbV 200; flies to Stalino for Stalingrad airlift that starts that month; fewer aircraft than usually quoted believed actually arrive in Russia; 2./Staffel remains in Trondheim and loses at least seven Condors in last six months of 1942, mainly on reconnaissance sorties to Iceland, Jan Mayen and Bear Islands and Spitzbergen

1943

January	Elements of I./ and III./KG 40 fly Stalingrad airlift sorties in Russia until end February
2 February	2./Staffel returns to Germany to begin conversion onto He 177
February (end)	Elements of 1. and 3./Staffeln returned to Berlin-Staaken to be combined into VIII./KG 40; new 1./ and 3./Staffeln subsequently form, believed in March
1 July	Overlapping aircraft inventory of II./KG 40 shows two Fw 200C-3/U4s and ten Fw 200C-4s plus eleven He 177s
10 November	3./Staffel has sixteen Fw 200s in Norway; Stab./I transferred to Germany probably to convert onto He 177
November	2./Staffel at Bordeaux exchanges identity with 8./Staffel, then based at Fassberg
November-15 April 1944	New 2./Staffel remains in Germany training on Hs 293/Fritz X missiles, based at Fassberg, Schwabisch-Hall, Giebelstadt and Garz; unknown number of Fw 200s used during period
30 November	3./Staffel has sixteen Fw 200C-3s and C-4s at Trondheim-Vaernes
16-19 December	Stab./ and 1./Staffel transfer from Fassberg to Chateaudun, France

1944

17 January	3./Staffel loses Fw 200C-3 over northern North Sea
10 February	3./Staffel's Fw 200s still active out of Trondheim; sink tanker *El Grilla* off east coast of Ireland
31 March	3./Staffel losses three Fw 200s to Martlets from HMS *Tracker* north-west of Lofoten Islands
1 April	Main part of I./Gruppe transferred to Germany

15-26 May	Gruppe less 3./Staffel moves from Fassberg to Orleans-Bricy
3 June	Main part of Gruppe transferred from Orleans to Toulouse-Blagnac, southern France, to avoid Allied air attack
7-10 June	Hs 293 attacks (by He 177) result in heavy losses
26 June	Losses of eleven He 177s and ten crews at Toulouse
1 July	Inventory at Toulouse includes one Fw 200C-3, two Fw 200C-3/U4s, eight Fw 200B-4s, one Fw 200C-6 and five Fw 200 C-8s, plus thirteen He 177s
10 July	Main part of Gruppe transferred to Celle, Germany
July-September	3./Staffel based at Trondheim and Banak
3 August	Staffel continues Condor operations over Norway from Schwabisch-Hall, Germany
14 August	Some night operations by KG 40 against Normandy bridgehead, almost certainly all by He 177
7 September	3./Staffel flies what is probably last Arctic operation before its Condors are passed to Transportfliegerstaffel Condor

Other units equipped with Condors

With its range of more than 2,000 miles (approximately 3,200km), the Fw 200 was an asset acquired by two long-range reconnaissance Staffeln, although the aircraft did not completely equip any other Luftwaffe unit apart from KG 40. Those that numbered Condors among their aircraft inventory were 1.(F)/120 (identified by a badge depicting a black winged device on a white shield) and 1.(F)/122 (a white and black stork-like bird insignia superimposed on a vertical red shape like an artillery shell). In common with other reconnaissance units, these invariably operated several other types of aircraft, with the long-range Condors on hand for special duties.

'Temporary' transport units that operated Condors included 4./KGrzbV 107 (steam train insignia) and those that invariably included the number 200 in their designation, such as KGrzb 200 and Transportstaffel 200, both of which had their origins on the Eastern Front. All such units changed aircraft as a matter of expediency.

Several specialised training schools benefited from having one or more Condors on hand, as the aircraft's performance, size and handling qualities could not realistically be duplicated by other types. These schools included FFS (B) 36, which had as its insignia a white cow superimposed on a red-and-yellow-quartered circle, the bovine cartoon being blindfolded with a black saddle-like device in place.

The 'blind cow' symbol was widely used by the Luftwaffe to indicate the type of flying school where the curriculum placed great emphasis on students becoming thoroughly conversant in instrument flying under conditions of darkness or low visibility.

The special High Command courier unit adopted as its insignia the head of a hawk-like bird on a white circular background. This in turn had an outer black circle with fifteen white symbols and the letters FDF superimposed, but initially this outer circle was omitted from the insignia. At an unknown date the insignia was modified, the ring certainly appearing on Himmler's personal Condor and most probably other aircraft of the F des F unit.

Appendix III

Specifications

Fw 200V-1

Crew	Four plus twenty-six passengers
Powerplant	Four Pratt & Whitney SE1-G Hornet nine-cylinder air-cooled engines each rated at 760hp
Span	107ft 9.5in (32.84m)
Length	76ft 11.5in (23.85m)
Height	19.68ft (6.00m)
Wing area	127,000sq ft (11,800m2)
Weights	empty 20,290lb (9,200kg); 30,870lb (14,000kg) for take off; max 10,585lb (4,800kg)
Performance	
Maximum speed	235mph (375kmph); cruising speed 225mph (362kmph)
Service ceiling	20,000ft (6,100m)
Range	775 miles (1,250 km)
Endurance	4 hours

Fw 200C-3/U4

Crew	Five (pilot, engineer, navigator, radio operator and gunner)
Powerplant	Four BMW-Bramo 323R-2 Fafnir nine-cylinder radial air-cooled engines each rated at 1,200hp at 2,600rpm with water-methanol injection for take-off and emergency; 1,000hp at 2,500rpm at sea level; 940hp at 2,500rpm at 13,125ft (4,000m)
Span	107ft 9.5in (32.84m)
Length	76 ft 11.5in (23.85m)
Height	20ft 8in (6.3m)
Wing area	1,290sq ft (118m2)
Weights	empty 37,485lb (17,000kg); max loaded 50,053lb (22,700kg)
Performance	
Maximum speed	190mph (306kmph) at sea level; 224mph (360kmph) at 15,410ft (4,700m)
Cruising speed	208mph (335kmph) at 13,124ft (4,000m); maximum continuous cruise 172mph (277kmph) at sea level; economical cruise 158mph (255kmph)
Service ceiling	19,685ft (6,000m)
	Normal range at economical cruise with standard fuel (1,773 gallons (8,068 litres)) 2,211 miles (3,560km); with overload fuel (2,190 gallons (9,964 litres) 2,760 miles (4,440km)
	Endurance at economical cruising speed 14 hours
Armament	One 7.99mm MG 15 machine-gun with 1,000 rounds in hydraulically operated Fw 19 forward dorsal turret; one 13mm MG 131 machine-gun with 500 rounds on flexible mount in aft dorsal position; two 13mm MG 131 machine-guns each with 300 rounds firing from beam hatches; one 20mm MG 151 cannon on flexible mount with 500 rounds in forward ventral (gondola) position; one 7.9mm MG 15 machine-gun with 1,000 rounds in aft ventral (gondola) position.
	Maximum bomb load of 4,630lb (2,100kg) comprising two 1,102lb (500kg), two 551lb (250kg) and twelve 110lb (50kg) bombs on single racks outboard of outer engine nacelles, recessed into outer engine nacelles and in racks inside ventral fuselage gondola. Outer nacelle recess could alternatively accommodate one 66-gallon (300-litre) fuel tank

Note: German nomenclature identified gun positions simply as A Stand, B Stand, C Stand and D Stand. In the Fw 200 (and other types) the 'fixed' armament, ie. turret and rear dorsal positions, were the A and B Stands respectively, while the aft and forward gondola weapons were identified as the C and D Stand positions. In addition, identification names were applied to gun positions, but these were rarely used outside production and modification centres.

Appendix IV

Camouflage and markings

Civil Condors

The prewar Condors operated by DLH in the late 1930s were among the most colourful airliners that had ever entered service up to that period. The state airline adopted a black and silver company colour scheme for these early machines, although the overall orange of the Danish flag carrier was equally innovative and very different to what had gone before. On an airport apron the Condors in German and Dutch service stood out as highly impressive aeroplanes compared to the rather austere schemes representing other European airlines. Even the striking red band across the fin and rudder carrying a black Hakenkreuz seemed a very smart touch, instantly identifying the new National Socialist Government of Germany.

Blocks of black paint with their scalloped 'sweepbacks' applied to the DLH Condors made ideal backdrops for the company name, airline logo and individual aircraft names; a small detail was the addition of star names – such as *Aries*, *Wega* (Vega), *Mars* and *Polaris* – to the extreme tip of the nose, usually in white. These names endured into the Luftwaffe era and individual aircraft bore them until overhauls and repaints obscured them or the aircraft in question was lost in action.

Military Condors

On the outbreak of war Focke-Wulf Condors drafted into Luftwaffe service received an overall paint scheme in the standard upper surface colours of Green 70 and Black-Green 71 with light blue Hellblau 76 lower surfaces. Applied in a regulation straight-edged 'splinter' pattern, the demarcation lines between the two shades of green varied slightly from aircraft to aircraft and there were inevitably some variations. Division of the upper and lower surface paintwork was generally 'hard-edged', although once again such large aircraft would almost inevitably display some variation, often in the way the line from nose to tail was applied.

Weathering and strong sunlight effects tended to darken the colours to the point where some aircraft appeared, mostly in photographs, to have a single shade of very dark green over the fuselage, wings and tailplane. Black paint was substituted as a temporary measure for early night raids on England, this tactical paintwork being removed after a short period and the original Hellblau restored. The vast majority of Condors consequently flew all their war sorties in the 'standard' Luftwaffe colour scheme.

Another albeit temporary standard of paintwork was adopted by the Luftwaffe in the East when the long and deep Russian winters brought snow for weeks on end. It was prudent to mask aircraft that could easily be seen from above on snow-blanketed airfields and, in common with other types, several Condors were given a coat of white on the upper surfaces. One of the aircraft used by Adolf Hitler was painted white for flights on the Eastern Front, this also having a carefully applied yellow theatre band around the rear fuselage. This may well have served as a pattern for KG 40's Condors, but there is little evidence that front-line unit painters were quite so meticulous with their spray guns and masks. The white paint used on many aircraft weathered very unevenly, the finish often being doubly compromised by exhaust staining and sheer wear and tear of intensive day-to-day operations. Few if any other Condors were given a similar overall white scheme because, apart from the relatively brief Russian winters, the aircraft was never intended to operate on the Eastern Front for extended periods.

Gruppe and Staffel colours

Kampfgeschwader 40	A – blue
I./Gruppe:	
I./Stab	B – green (eg spinner tips)
1./Staffel	H – white
2./Staffel	K – white (eg 0003/F8+DK [Oblt Erich Adam])
3./Staffel	L – white (eg 0088/F8+LL [Oblt Herbert Fahje])
II./Gruppe:	
II./Stab	C – green
4./Staffel	M – red
5./Staffel	N – red
6./Staffel	P – red
III./Gruppe:	
III./Stab	D – green
7./Staffel	R – yellow (eg spinner tips, as on 0189/F8+MR and 0248/F8+IR)
8./Staffel	S – yellow (eg spinner tips, as on 0175/ F8+AS)
9./Staffel	T – yellow (eg 0221/F8+IT)
IV./Gruppe:	
IV./Stab	E – green
10./Staffel	U – blue
11./Staffel	V – blue
12./Staffel	W – blue

Standard colours

Additions to the standard camouflage schemes such as 70-71-65 were relatively rare on Condors, the exception being the yellow recognition markings denoting service on the Russian front. Some examples of rear fuselage bands in yellow were recorded, although these too were few, the aircraft's service in the East being brief. Underwing panels outboard of the Balkenkreuz were painted yellow, however.

White markings to denote the Mediterranean theatre seem to have been applied only to the handful of KG 40 Condors that served in that region, and individual aircraft appear to have been treated in a 'one-off' fashion. As an example, a photograph exists showing an Fw 200C-3 of I./Gruppe with narrow chordwise white bands on the underside of the wings. This does not appear to have been a very common practice but it was nevertheless used perhaps only for a brief period or for a specific operation.

These simple identification markings were surprisingly visible and highly effective in their primary purpose of identifying 'friend from foe', mainly to forces on the ground.

Considerable variation in the application of the fuselage Balkenkreuz may be noted from wartime photographs of Fw 200s. For an air force that generally abided by the guidelines officially laid down for the finish of military aircraft, complete with the size, location and style of the national insignia, the unit painters who marked the Condors of KG 40 and other units appear not to have been constrained by such orders and opted for an 'individual' approach. Many variations may be noted in photographs, as this book shows, and similar variations are quite apparent in photographs of KG 40's He 177s.

The 70/71/76 colour scheme was so universally applied to Luftwaffe aircraft throughout six years of war that there seemed only a remote possibility that it would be superseded by anything else. Some experiments were, however, conducted to determine if any colour(s) or pattern could more effectively be applied to aircraft used for specialised roles, particularly those that spent a good deal of their time flying over water. It was determined that a light colour Wellenmuster or 'wave mirror' scheme applied over the entire top surfaces of the Condor with the object of breaking up the original two greens had some merit in confusing the outline of the aircraft – indeed, making it blend into the background for those vital few seconds when an enemy interceptor might be about to open fire. As with many aircraft, the national insignia (particularly if it encompassed areas of white) tended to compromise any camouflage scheme, however carefully it was applied. The Germans overcame this problem by lightly overspraying the white areas of the Balkenkreuz and reducing the Hakenkreuz in the same way.

Apart from the treatment of several machines with black undersides for night bombing raids over Britain in 1940, Condors retained the Hellblau undersides throughout the war. The national insignia, most commonly the fuselage Balkenkreuz, underwent several changes aimed at reducing the areas of white in the cross in an attempt to 'hide' the marking, the result looking much like some presentations of the First World War period. This process led to several variations that were quite non-standard and rarely duplicated by other Luftwaffe aircraft, apart from the He 177, which often had its fuselage cross similarly adapted.

While it was true that the Condor had all but disappeared from maritime patrol and attack sorties by the time 'late-war' anti-shipping schemes were applied to Ju 88s and He 111s, some examples were so treated. Front-line Condors still flying in late 1944-45 generally had a single individual aircraft identification letter unless the Stammkirchen radio call letter code had been retained, which was not unusual. This made the ID letter even harder to read so that the cloak of anonymity officially adopted by the Luftwaffe as the war came to an end was all but complete.

Some colour trim was applied to the Condors of KG 40 from the earliest days of its existence, this generally being restricted to the propeller hubs and the fuselage identification letter, which was presented either in the Staffel colour or as a coloured outline to a single black fuselage letter flanking the Balkenkreuz. White paint was also used for a series of star and constellation names applied to the extreme tip of the nose on a number of early-production Condors. Those known included *Wega*, *Jupiter* (F8+BB), *Deneb* (F8+AH), *Polaris*, *Aries*, *Merkur* and so on, but their purpose, if any, has not been recorded.

Scoreboards

When anti-shipping sorties began in earnest the mission markers were accompanied by ship silhouettes if the crew had received credit for a sinking. Mainly during 1940-41 individual Condors flown regularly by pilots accumulated an impressive tonnage of ships sunk or damaged, and crews recorded these tallies by applying white 'sortie bars' or mission markers to the fin below the Hakenkreuz with the area of operations appearing as a name, such as 'Narvik' and 'England', preceding the totals. Silhouettes of ships, again mostly in solid white to contrast with the dark green camouflage, were applied to the Condor's rudder from the top downwards, denoting the earliest to the latest claims. These ship silhouettes were usually accompanied by the date of the attack. 'England' did not primarily denote bombing sorties against land targets in the British Isles but rather a record of coastal shipping strikes and mine-laying.

A few crews added a map indicating their operational area, but this was quite a rare embellishment as was at least one instance depicting an aerial engagement between a Condor and a defending fighter. Fin markings extending to other operational areas, namely 'Stalingrad' and 'Kaukusus', were applied to the small number of Condors seconded to transport duties on the Eastern Front.

Almost unique in applying KG 40's unmistakeable 'world in a ring' insignia, I./Gruppe painted the badge in two forms, with the ring presented above or below the equator. Against a circular light blue background, the globe was white with countries marked in solid black, while the Saturn-like ring was invariably rendered in yellow. A further variation of KG 40's insignia that appears in some wartime photographs shows the 'world' without the customary ring. This is almost certainly explained by the fact that the insignia was at the time of the photo in question incomplete pending more paintshop time. Second-line units, particularly blind flying and other types of training schools that operated Condors, also applied badges in much the same forward fuselage location as that of KG 40.

Together with its unit badge, KG 40 perpetuated standard Luftwaffe code letters on its aircraft virtually throughout its operational career, the code 'F8' extending to the He 177 Ju 88s, Do 217s and He 111s; because of their greater numbers the two four-engine bombers applied the code marking almost throughout hostilities. In 1944 bomber unit codes were drastically reduced in size, leaving only the two aircraft/Staffel letters; these were invariably painted aft of the fuselage Balkenkreuz on the port side and in front on the starboard side, although there were some departures from this general rule. The familiar letter/number unit code was subsequently reduced to a single aircraft and Staffel letter, and even the Staffel letter was dropped in many instances. This generally made it increasingly difficult to identify the parent unit but, in the Condor's case, when so few aircraft were issued to only a handful of units, the task was somewhat easier than it was with more numerous, smaller types such as twin-engine bombers and fighters.

Appendix V

Fw 200 Losses

Key:
- + = killed
- BS = Bordschütze (Gunner)
- Ac = Aircraft
- F = Flugzeugführer (Pilot)
- BF = Bordfunker (WOp)
- M = Missing
- BM = Bordmechaniker (Flt Eng)
- W = Wounded

Date	Unit / Aircraft	Crew	Remarks
06 Dec 38	Fw 200 V1 (2000) D-ACON	—	Force-landed in sea at Rosario Point, Manila due to fuel shortage and premature deployment of flaps.
23 Nov 39	Aufkl. Ob.d.L. Fw 200 V4, V10, 0001 (BS+AF)	—	Starboard engines seized, 50% damage at Jever, Germany.
22 Apr 40	1/KG 40 Fw 200	Oblt Karl August Beckhaus-F-M; Stfw Kurt Klann-F-M; Ofw Gerhard Krüger- -M; Fw Otto Schönthaler- -M; Uffz Karl Cloots- -M	Narvik area. Evening reconnaissance. Failed to return probably due to bad weather. (2 POWs)
22 Apr 40	4/KGrzbV 107 Fw 200 A-0 / S-10 (3324) D-ABOD Kurmark (CB+FB)	Oblt Alfred Henke-F-+; Gefr Helmut Rösel-BM-+; Gefr Josef Zieghaus-BM-+; Flg Wilhelm Fricke-BF-+	Written off in crash Berlin-Staaken.
25 May 40	I/KG 40 Fw 200 V 2/C-1 (2484) F8+GH (D-AETA Westfalen)	Oblt Hellmuth Schöpke-F-POW; Ofw Fritz Messer-F-safe; Fw Walter Börjesson-Bm-safe; Fw Eugen Fischer- POW; Ogefr Kurt Hartleben-Bf-+	Gladiator N5705 of 263 Sqn (Fg Off H F Grant-Ede). Near Dyroy Island (Overås Finnøy) c. 1030 hrs. Messer and Börjesson evaded Returning from a mission to Harstadt. Forced landed on shore and burned out.
28 May 40	I/KG 40 Fw 200 C-1	—	Crash-landing near Gardemoen, 30% dam.
29 May 40	I/KG 40 Fw 200 C-1	Lt Otto Freytag-F-+; Oblt Günther Thiel-B-+; Ofw Heinrich Ruthmann- -+; Ofw Willi Rieker- -+; Uffz Franz Seelbach- -+; Gefr Manfred Stephani- -+	Hurricane of 46 Sqn (Plt Off N L Banks). Shot down whilst bombing Tromsø, 1640 hrs. Crashed on Dyroy Island.

Date	Unit	Aircraft	Crew	Details
20 Jul 40	1/KG 40	Fw 200 C FE+EH	Hptm Roman Steszyn (Stkpt)-F-+ / Fw Herbert Külken- -POW / Fw Karl Nicolai- -POW / Fw Willi Meyer- -+ / Gefr Silverius Zraunig- -+ / Gefr Josef Perl- -+	Shot down by Flak during a mine laying sortie and crashed into the North Sea between Hartlepool and Sunderland 2355 hrs. The body of Fw Meyer was later washed ashore.
24 Jul 40	2/KG 40	Fw 200 C F8+BH	Hptm Volkmar Zenker-F-POW / Uffz Rudolf Wagner-F-+ / Uffz Heinz Höcker-BF-POW / Fw Willi Andreas-BM-+ / Gefr Leo Homann-BS-POW	Minelaying mission over Belfast Lough. Ditched 15 miles NE Belfast due to engine failure, 0340 hrs.
20 Aug 40	1/KG 40	Fw 200 C-1, F8+KH	Oblt Kurt-Heinrich Mollenhauer-F(I/40) / Reg Rat Dr Erich Krüger-Met / Ofw Robert Beumer / Uffz Hans Bell / Fw Ludwig Wochner / Gefr Kurt Kyck	Sortie over Northern Ireland. Damaged by Flak from cargo steamer early PM and crashed into Faha Mountain, Cloghane, Co. Kerry. 2 inj, crew interned.
29 Aug 40	I/KG 40	Fw 200 C-2 BS+AQ (0014)	crew unhurt	Fuel shortage. Crash-landing at Bordeaux. 10% dam.
21 Sep 40	1/KG 40	Fw 200 C-2 (0023) F8+EH	—	Fuel shortage. Crash-landed, Brest. 30% dam.
08 Oct 40	I/KG 40	Fw 200 C-2 (0022) F8+AK	Uffz Kurt Richard Schubert-w / Oblt Friedrich Burmeister & rest of crew uninj	Hit by Flak near Brest; 20% dam.
22 Oct 40	2/KG 40	Fw 200 C-2 (0024) BS+AX F8+OK	Oblt Theodor Schuldt-F-+ (Stellv Stfhr) / Fw Walter Berghaus-2 F-M / Fw Friedrich Gruber-1 BF-M / Gefr Walter Graessle-2 BF-M / Fw Friedrich Hoeger-BM-M / Reg Rat Dr Hans Sturm-Met-+	Missing from Weather reconnaissance, Irish Sea Schuldt & Sturm washed ashore and buried Eire.
23 Nov 40	I/KG 40	Fw 200 C-SG+KC (0027) / Fw 200 D-1 / V5 / KB-1 (0009) D-AEQP OH-CLA Kurmark	— / —	Destroyed in air attack at Mérignac. Destroyed in air attack at Mérignac.

Date	Unit	Aircraft	Crew	Remarks
14 Dec 40	2/KG zbV 108	Fw 200 (0010) (VB+UA) OH-CLB / D-AFST Westfalen	—	Crash-landed at Gardemoen due to icing, 70% dam.
10 Jan 41	Stab I/40	Fw 200 C-3 SG+KK (0035) F8+AB	Oblt Friedrich Burmeister-1 F-POW Ofw Walter Ibe-2 F-+ Fl.Hauptnautiker Heinz John-2 BF-+ Uffz Horst Kittner-1 BF-+ Ob Ing Bruno Gumpert-BM-POW Uffz Rudolf Steinmayer-BS-POW	Shot down by Mate Mr Reilly, tug *Seaman*, with Lewis gun during attack on the ship. 200 miles north-west of Ireland, 1350 hrs.
11 Jan 41	3/KG 40	Fw 200 C-3 (0037) SG+KM F8+CL	—	Landing accident at Mérignac. 25% dam.
11 Jan 41	I/KG 40	Fw 200 C-3 (0028)	crew safe	Damaged by Flak. Crash-landed, Ile-de-Ré; written off.
29 Jan 41	I/KG 40	Fw 200 C-3	Lt Alfred Winter-BF-+	Combat with Sunderland L2163/G. Fg Off Aikman of 210 Sqn near Ireland, 1137 hrs. Sgt R C Williamson, rear gunner, wounded.
05 Feb 41	I/KG 40	Fw 200 C-3 (0042) F8+AH (SG+KR)	Oblt Paul Gömmer-1 F-+ Ofw Willi Doose-2 F-+ Fw Max Hohaus-1 BF-inj. Fw Walter Clasen-2 BF-+ Ofw Werner Albrecht-BM-+ Reg Rat Dr Erich Herrström-Met & BS-+	Crashed into Hill between Durrus and Schull, Co. Cork, after being hit by gun-fire from SS *Major C*, 0800 hrs.
07 Feb 41	I/KG 40	Fw 200 C-3 SG+KE (0029)	Oblt Heinz Kreimeyer-1 F-+ Fw Hans Koppenhöfer-2 F-+ Lt Anton Schützendorf-B-+ Fw Heinz Claveri-1 BF-+ Uffz Heinz Kämpfe-2 BF-+ Fw Andreas Stingeder-BM-+	Destroyed in crash near Bordeaux airfield.
08 Feb 41	2/KG 40	Fw 200 C-1 (0003) F8+DK (BS+AH)	Oblt Erich Adam-F Fw Paul Hecht-F Ofw Dietrich Gropp-BF Uffz Kurt Dreyer-BF Ofw Erich Grasberger-BM Uffz Herbert Pluntke-BS	Shot down by Sloop *Deptford*. Crash-landed Moura, Portugal. Crew returned.

Date	Unit	Aircraft	Crew	Remarks
02 Mar 41	I/KG 40	Fw 200 C-3 (0031)	Reg Rat Karl Schwalb & crew safe	Crash-landing near Stavanger after sortie. 60% dam.
08 Mar 41	I/KG 40	Fw 200 C-3 (0040) (SG+KP)	Oblt Wilhelm Claussen-FF-+ / Oblt Gerhard Malitz-F-inj. (8/KG 51) / Lt Hans-Joachim Humbert-F-inj. / Uffz Erwin Rigwalski-BM-inj.	Crashed after take-off at Mérignac. 90% dam. Training flight.
18 Mar 41	I/KG 40	Fw 200 C-3 (0041) (SG+KQ) F8+AH	Lt Hans Winkler-F-+ / Oblt Helmut Nitsch-F-+ / Uffz Nikolaus Kleinert-BF-+ / Gefr Wilhelm Harding-BF-+ / Fw Anton Langner-BM-+ / Reg Rat Hermann Haller-Met-inj.	Crashed & burnt out at Plogoff nr Brest.
13 Apr 41	I/KG 40	Fw 200 C-1 (0004) (BS+AI)	—	Destroyed in ar attack Mérignac.
13 Apr 41	I/KG 40	Fw 200 C-3 SG+KI (0033)	—	Destroyed in ar attack Mérignac.
13 Apr 41	I/KG 40	Fw 200 D-2b / KC-1 (0020) (NA+WN) F8+GL *Holstein*	—	Destroyed in ar attack Mérignac.
16 Apr 41	I/KG 40	Fw 200 C (0039) F8+AH (SG+KO) F8+CT	Oblt Hermann Richter-2 F-M / Oblt Heinz Daerner-1 F-M / Lt Hans-Joachim Stein-BF-M / Uffz Günther Glöckner-BF-M / Uffz Martin Maier-BM-M / Gefr Rudolf Kunath-BS-M	Shot down by Flt Lt W Riley/WO Donaldson in Beaufighter T3237/K of 252 Sqn, Blacksod Bay, Scotland 1420 hrs.
17 Apr 41	1/KG 40	Fw 200 C-3/U2 (0051) F8+FH (DE+OF)	Oblt Paul Kalus-1 F-M / Ofw Edwin Schulze-2 F-+ / Uffz Walter Bittner-1 BF-M / Uffz Wilhelm Zeller-2 BF-+ / Fw Herbert Heidrich-BM-M / Ogefr Hubert Greschenz-BS-M	Off Shetland Isles. Uffz Zeller recovered from sea 21 May & buried Shetlands. Unknown cause.
18 Apr 41	3/KG 40	Fw 200 C-3 (0053) F8+GL (DE+OH)	Oblt Ernst Müller-1 F / Fw Karl Macht-2 F / Fw Georg Sigl-1 BF / Gefr Alfred Jäckel-2 BF / Uffz Wilhelm Salbenblatt-BM / Reg Rat Walter Habich-Met & BS	Ditched off Schull Island, 1215 hrs. Crew landed by boat in Éire and interned.

Date	Unit	Aircraft	Crew	Remarks
29 Apr 41	1/KG 40	Fw 200 C-3 (0054) F8+HH (DE+OI)	Oblt Roland Schelcher-F-+ / Uffz Josef Obergauling-F-+ / Ofw Otto Verpahl-BF-M / Ogefr Rudolf Renntrop-BF-+ / Uffz Josef Niklas-BM-M / Gefr Erwin Sengbusch-BS-+	Shot down by Flak (?), Shetland Is. Obergauling and Sengbusch recovered from sea.
19 May 41	1/KG 40	Fw 200 C-3 (0060) F8+DH (DE+OO)	Oblt Hans Buchholz-1 F-+ / Ofw Otto Friedrich Krocke-2 F-POW / Reg Rat Friedrich Karl Keller-Met-POW / Ofw Paul Schmidt-1 BF-+ / Uffz Meinhard Milde-2 BF-POW / Ofw Erich Kielke-BM-inj., POW / Fw Kurt Brattke-BS-POW	Shot down by a single 12-pdr shell fired from the SS *Umgeni* 300 miles (55.10 N / 17.10 W) west of Donegal Bay, Northern Ireland, 0715 hrs.
21 May 41	3/KG 40	Fw 200 C-3 (0061) F8+KL (KF+QA)	—	Take-off accident, Bordeaux. 20% dam.
24 May 41	3/KG 40	Fw 200 C-3/U2 (0050) (SG+KZ) later F8+CB	Oblt Heinz Braun-2 F-inj. / Ofw Lothar Cissarz-2 BF-inj. / Assistent Günter Schlarb-Met-+ (I/40) / Lt Paul Maly & remainder of crew uninj	5% Flak damage. North Atlantic (25W/5780).
15 Jun 41	10/KG 40	Fw 200 A-01 / S-1 (2893) F8+CU / GF+GF / D-ADHR *Saarland*	—	Aalborg-West airfield – engine fire, Ac destroyed.
15 Jun 41	1/KG 40	Fw 200 C-1 (0008) BS+AM/F8+FH	Lt Otto Gose-1F- & crew safe / Ogefr Oskar Meissner-BM-+	Damaged by Flak west of Gibraltar attacking Convoy HS 65. Emergency landing at Navia, Spain. Crew interned.
15 Jun 41	3/KG 40	Fw 200 C-3 (0061) F8+KL (KF+QA)	Oblt Erich Westermann-1F-+ / Gefr Günter Kunert-2 F-+ / Ofw Gerhard Singer-1 BF-+ / Gefr Erwin Hildenbrand-2 BF-+ / Ofw Walter Reiser-BM-+ / Uffz Fritz Grotstollen-BS-+	Broke up in mid-air and crashed at Amareleja, Portugal (Convoy HS 65).

Date	Unit	Aircraft	Crew	Remarks
15 Jun 41	3/KG 40	Fw 200 C-3 (0065) (KF+QE)	Ogefr Ignaz Widmann-1 BF-+	5% Flak damage. (Convoy HS 65, west of Portugal)
22 Jun 41	ErgSt/KG 40	Fw 200 C-3 (0068) F8+ST (KF+QH)	—	Accident due to damaged tyre, Lüneburg; 50% dam.
24 Jun 41	I/KG 40	Fw 200 C-3 (0067) (KF+QG)	Crew rescued	Ditched Bay of Biscay.
30 Jun 41	1/KG 40	Fw 200 C-3/U3 (0064) F8+HH (KF+QD)	Ofw Herbert Ohrbach-F-M / Uffz Hermann Nürberg-F-M / Fw Walter Scholz-BF-M / Gefr Willi Krossa-BF-+ / Uffz Georg Wirth-BM-M / Uffz Walter Neumann-BS-M	Missing Atlantic.
05 Jul 41	3/KG 40	Fw 200 C-3 F8+EL	Lt Rudolf Mayr crew safe	Emergency landing at Sevilla, Spain, 2245 hrs. Crew returned 6 Jul 41.
09 Jul 41	3/KG 40	Fw 200 C-3 (0046) F8+EL (SG+KV)	—	Crash-landing at Cognac due to technical defect, 30% dam.
09 Jul 41	3/KG 40	Fw 200 C-3/U2 (0055) F8+HK (DE+OJ)	—	Landing accident at Mérignac, 15% dam.
12 Jul 41		Fw 200 KA-1 / S-2 (2894) OY-DAM Dania / G-AGAY Wolf / DX177	—	Crash-landing at White Waltham; written off.
17 Jul 41	3/KG 40	Fw 200 C-3 (0063) F8+CL (KF+QC)	Ofw Hans Jordens-BF-+	Killed in combat west of Ireland with Whitley Z6635/Q of 502 Sqn. Whitley then ditched 0815 hrs, Wg Cdr D R Shore AFC-P, Plt Off J D McLeod wounded, Fg Off A T Brock, Sgt S Larmour & Sgt B C Hanson rescued by HMS Westcott.
18 Jul 41	Stab I/40	Fw 200 C-3/U2 (0043) F8+AB (SG+KS)	Hptm Fritz Fliegel (Grkdr)-F-M / Lt Wolf-Dietrich Kadelke-F-M / Fw Hans Tottke-BF-M / Gefr Karl Becker-BF-M / Uffz Johann Rottke-BM-M / Uffz Karl Mauerer-BS-M	Atlantic, Convoy OB 346. Possibly shot down by gunfire from Norman Prince or SS Pilar de Larrinaga.
19 Jul 41	IV/KG 40	Fw 200 C-3/U4 (0070) F8+DS (KF+QJ)	—	Crash-landing at Rechlin airfield, 25% dam.

Date	Unit	Aircraft	Crew	Remarks
23 Jul 41	Stab I/40	Fw 200 C-3 (0069) F8+BB (KF+QI)	Ofw Heinrich Bleichert-F-POW Ofw Josef Raczak-F-POW Fw Karl Übelhofer-BF-POW Gefr Josef Weid-BF-POW Ofw Heinrich Grube-BM-POW Ogefr Anton Rogenhofer-BS-POW Reg Rat Insp August Dollinger-Met-+	Shot down by Plt Off R Down/Plt Off Corken in Hudson AM536/J of 233 Sqn off west coast of Ireland (Achil Head), 54.00N/13.27W, 0815 hrs during attack on convoy OG69; survivors rescued by HMS *Begonia*.
24 Jul 41	1/KG 40	Fw 200 C-3 (0026) SG+KA F8+CH	Hptm Konrad Verlohr (Stkpt)-F-+ Lt Walter Gröner-F-M Ofw Henry Rasquin-BF-M Uffz Hans Zeitler-BM-M Fw Walter Drost-BS-M Oblt Paul Schlafke-F-M	Missing west of Ireland.
24 Jul 41	I/KG 40	Fw 200 C-3	—	Damaged by German fighters.
25 Jul 41	I/KG 40	Fw 200 C-3/U2 (0050) (SG+KZ)	—	Accident due to damaged tyre, Mérignac. 15% dam.
03 Aug 41	I/KG 40	Fw 200 C-3 (0066) (DE+OO)	Uffz Erwin Hauck-BF-+ Fw Franz Rudat-BS-+ Insp Werner Bibel-Met-inj.	Damaged by Lt R W H Everett of 804 Sqn, HMS *Maplin* in Hurricane W9277 during attack on convoy OG 70/SL 81, 50.33N/19.40W, 650kms SW Bantry Bay. Destroyed in crash-landing, PIQ 78/51. Hurricane ditched.
11 Aug 41	3/KG 40	Fw 200 C-3 (0037) F8+CL	Lt Hans Schuster-F-unhurt Uffz Philip Weppler-BS-+	Flak, 12% dam. BS died of wounds 15 Aug 1942.
15 Aug 41	3/KG 40	Fw 200 C-3 (0056) F8+AL (DE+OK)	Oblt Bruno Rose-1 F-M Lt Ingraban von Koerber-2 F-+ Ofw Willi Bettenhausen-1 BF-M Uffz Gerhard Komohs-2 BF-M Fw Werner Kuhwald-BM-M Gefr Hans Beutler-BS-+	Missing west of Portugal.

Date	Unit	Aircraft	Crew	Notes
05 Sep 41	1/KG 40	Fw 200 C-3/U4 (0074) F8+GH (KF+QN)	Oblt Horst Neumann-1 F-M Ofw Martin Heidenreich-2 F-M Ofw Willi Laufmann-1 BF-M Uffz Georg Johannes Schneider-2 BF-M Fw Willi Schilf-BM-M Uffz Franz Rabensteiner-BS-M	Crashed south of the Island of Fleves.
18 Sep 41	3/KG 40	Fw 200 C-3/U4 (0081) F8+CK (KE+IG)	–	Crash-landed at Cognac, 15% dam.
21 Sep 41	3/KG 40	Fw 200 C-3/U4 (0078) F8+EL (KE+IC)	Lt Georg Schaffranek-1 F-M Ogefr Adam Köhler-2 F-M Ofw Erich Junge-1 BF-M Uffz Willy Herse-2 BF-M Fw Karl Wetzel-BM-M Uffz Bruno Dröse-BS-M	Grumman Martlets of 802 Sqn, *HMS Audacity* (Sub-Lt N H Patterson & Sub-Lt G R P Fletcher). Convoy OG 74, 1400 kms west of Brest. Ac lost tail unit during first attack and crashed into the sea. 47.10N, 02.25W.
25 Sep 41	IV/KG 40	Fw 200 C-2 (0018)	–	Take-off accident at Rostock, 30% dam.
30 Sep 41	IV/KG 40	Fw 200 C-3/U2 (0055) F8+HK (DE+OJ)	–	Take-off accident at Bordeaux, 10% dam.
13 Oct 41	IV/KG 40	Fw 200 C-3 (0031) F8+BT	–	Accident at Lechfeld, 40% dam
21 Oct 41	IV/KG 40	Fw 200 C-2 (0023) F8+EH	Ofw Heinz Helleberg-F-+ Ogefr Manfred Bentzen-F-+ Gefr Hubert Smikalle-BF-+ Gefr Karl-Heinz Walter-BF-+ Fw Franz Psotta-BM-+ Ogefr Sebastian Huber-BS-+ Lt Hans Betschler-B-+ Ofw Erich Galler-?-unhurt	Destroyed in crash-landing, Oberkolkhofen.
02 Nov 41	1/KG 40	Fw 200 C-3 (0044) (SG+KT)	Oblt Herbert Dostlebe + 5 inj	Crash-landing due to engine fire at Nieulle-sur-Sudre near Rochfort & burnt out.
08 Nov 41	3/KG 40	Fw 200 C-3 (0083) F8+ZL (KE+IH)	Oblt Karl Krüger-1 F-M Fw Erich Kubsch-2 F-M Fw Franz Töhles-1 BF-M Uffz Ferdinand Oehme-2 BF-M Fw Gustav Kirstein-BM-M Fw Wilhelm Liebeler-BS-M	Shot down by Grumman Martlet of 802 Sqn, *HMS Audacity*; Sub-Lt Eric M Brown, Convoy OG 76/SL 91, 1426 hrs . 41.18N/15.28W. Sub Lt D A Hutchinson /Lt Cdr Wintour (latter shot down in BJ516) 41.09N 17.30 W.

Date	Unit	Aircraft	Crew	Remarks
04 Dec 41	I/KG 40	Fw 200 C-3 (0065) (KF+QE)	—	Undercarriage damage at Nellingen, 15% dam.
05 Dec 41	3/KG 40	Fw 200 C-3/U4 (0085) (KE+IJ)	Fw Ludwig Kögel-1 F-+ / Uffz Hans Kaspers-2 F-+ / Uffz Carl Reichl-1 BF-+ / Uffz Robert Skopek-2 BF-+ / Uffz Herbert Stritzel-BS-+ / Ogefr Walter Fetzer-BM-+	Destroyed at Cognac on training sortie.
06 Dec 41	I/KG 40	Fw 200 C-3 (0058) (DE+OM)	—	60% dam at Lecce due to obstacle on ground.
12 Dec 41	3/KG 40 & 7/KG 40	Fw 200 C-3/U2 (0055) F8+HK (DE+OJ)	Oblt Franz Vüllers-1 F-+ (3/40) / Lt Werner Striewisch-2 F-+ (7/40) / Ofw Lothar Cissarz-1 BF-inj. (3/40) / Gefr Roland Schmutz-2 BF-+ (7/40) / Ofw Willi Söchtig-BM-inj. (3/40)	Crashed destroyed during night-landing at Cognac on non-combat mission.
18 Dec 41	1/KG 40	Fw 200 C-3/U4 (0077) (KE+IB)	—	Technical problems at Cognac, 25% dam.
19 Dec 41	I/KG 40	Fw 200 C-3/U4 (0087) (KE+IL) later F8+FR	—	Undercarriage damage at Cognac, 20% dam.
19 Dec 41	3/KG 40	Fw 200 C-3/U4 (0086) F8+IH (KE+IK)	Oblt Hans-Joachim Hase-1 F-M / Ofw Karl Gendner-2 F-M / Ofw Karl Bock-BM-M / Uffz Wilhelm Müller-1 BF-M / Uffz Robert Cordes-2 BF-M / Gefr Raimund Steinke-BS-M	Shot down by Martlets of 802 Sqn, *HMS Audacity*. Convoy HG 76, off Portugal. Either S/Lt E M Brown or S/Lt J W Sleigh Sleigh noted the code F8+FH on his kill (collided with it).
21 Dec 41	1/KG 40	Fw 200 C-3/U4 (0073) F8+FH (KF+QM)	Oblt Herbert Schreyer-1 F-+ / Uffz Hans Scherer-2 F-+ / Fw Michael Obermeiers-1 BF-+ / Ogefr Wolfgang Watkinson-2 BF-+ / Fw Erwin Rigwalski-BM-+ / Ofw Albert Meesen-BS-+	Reconnaissance. Crashed at Soba, Ramales, Spain.
23 Dec 41		Fw 200 A-0 / S-8 (3098) D-ACVH / *Grenzmark* / NK+NM	—	Crashed, Orel / Russia.

Date	Unit	Aircraft	Crew	Remarks
02 Jan 42	3/KG 40	Fw 200 C-3/U4 (0088) F8+LL (KE+IM)	Ofw Herbert Fahje-F & crew-safe	Flak & force-landed Ria de Camarinas, Spain.
31 Jan 42	1/KG 40	Fw 200 C-3/U4 (0093) F8+MH (KE+IR)	Ofw Werner Bornefeld-1 F-+ Fw Rolf Wenkhaus-2 F-M Fw Walter Gasser-1 BF-M Uffz Willi Rosier-2 BF-M Ofw Walter Schlosser-BM-M Gefr Wolfgang Klocke-BS-M	Corvette Genistra, west of Ireland, Bloody Foreland. Ofw Bornefeld washed ashore 6 Mar 42.
13 Feb 42	3/KG 40	Fw 200 C-4 (0102) F8+FL (NT+BB)	Fw Kurt Hinze-1 F-+ Fw Heinz Dern-2 F-safe Ofw Fritz Andres-1 BF-safe Gefr Josef Langenbach-2 BF-safe Uffz Paul Müller-BM-safe Uffz Alfred Oletzki-BS-safe	Ditched in Atlantic, west of Ireland. Survivors rescued by U-Boat.
14 Feb 42	7/KG 40	Fw 200 C-3 (0037) SG+KM F8+GL	—	Ferrying flight, crash-landed at Berlin-Staaken due to undercarriage damage, 20% dam.
21 Feb 42	3/KG 40	Fw 200 C-3/U4 (0079) F8+EL (KE+ID) F8+BK	Lt Heinz Schwinkendorf-1 F-M Oblt Adolf Pfennigschmidt-2 F-M Uffz Kurt (Thomas ?) Schmidt-1 BF-M Ogefr Heinz Überwasser-2 BF-M Uffz Ernst Eckelt-BM-M Gefr Fritz Bobsin-BS-M	Missing Atlantic.
22 Feb 42	7/KG 40	Fw 200 C-3 (0063) F8+BR (KF+QC)	Oblt Werner Thiele-1 F Uffz Wilhelm Degand-2 F Stfw Jakob Weber-1 BF Ogefr Johann Baier-2 BF Fw Paul Maertins-BM Uffz Heinz Kirsch-BS	Ditched in sea at Hommelvik/Stordalsfjord due to malfunctioning of the flaps approaching Vaernes airfield.
25 Mar 42	III/KG 40	Fw 200 C-3 (0046) (SG+KV)	—	Taxying accident Rennes, 15% dam.
08 Apr 42	8/KG 40	Fw 200 C-3/U4 (0070) F8+DS (KF+QJ)	Crew safe, 2 ground crew injured	Technical problems, Rennes 5% dam.

Date	Unit	Aircraft	Crew	Remarks
11 Apr 42	8/KG 40	Fw 200 C-3 (0045) F8+HS (SG+KU)	Hptm Karl Kahra-1 F & Stkpt-+ Fl Hpt Ing Johannes Deutschmann-2 F-+ Fl Hpt Naut Herbert Burmeister-Nautiker-inj. Ofw Helmuth Peizsch-1 BF-inj. Uffz Heinz Thiele-2 BF-+ Ofw Ernst Schwarz-BS-+ Uffz Willi Hofrath-BM-inj.	Crashed on return from combat mission SE Rennes airfield, Armed reconnaissance along Spanish-Portuguese coast. Ac hit ground during approach.
12 Apr 42	7/KG 40	Fw 200 C-3/U4 (0075) (KF+QO)	—	Accident during take-off at Oslo Fornebu, 100% dam.
16 Apr 42	III/KG 40	Fw 200 C-3/U4 (0091) (KE+IP)	—	Damaged by German Flak & crash-landed near Lauveoc, 80% dam. Combat mission.
27 Apr 42	III/KG 40	Fw 200 C-3 (0025)	—	Taxiing accident Orleans-Bricy, 55% dam.
29 Apr 42	I/KG 40	Fw 200 C-3 (0065) (KF+QE)	—	Air attack Vaernes 15% dam.
29 Apr 42	I/KG 40	Fw 200 C-4 (0111) (NT+BK)	—	Air attack Vaernes 15% dam.
01 May 42	III/KG 40	Fw 200 C-4 (0120) F8+AU (NT+BT) C-1 (0012) F8+AD 0103?	Oblt Siegfried Gall-F Uffz Gerhard Harig-F Ofw Alfons Eisen-BF Ogefr Gerhard Hausdorf-BF Uffz Rudolf Melbig-BM Ogefr Alfred Spendler-BS	Shot down by HMS *Imperialist*, NW of Cape St Vincent. Crew returned.
05 May 42	IV/KG 40	Fw 200 C-3 SG+KH (0032)	—	20 %undercarriage dam, Orleans-Bricy
09 May 42	II/KG 40	Fw 200 C-3 (0082) (KE+IG)	Uffz August Müller-BM-inj.	Emergency landing at Neuendorf, due to engine problems, Ac destroyed.
09 May 42	7/KG 40	Fw 200 C-3/U4 (0087) F8+FR (KE+IL)	Oblt Karl Thiede-1 F-M Uffz Wilhelm Degand-2 F-M Stfw Jakob Weber-BF-M Ogefr Johann Baier-BF-M Fw Paul Märtins-BM-M Uffz Heinz Kirsch-BS-M	Lost between Iceland and Faeroe Islands. Probably shot down by SS *Duoro 60.41N 12.58W.*
25 May 42	3/KG 40	Fw 200 C-3/U4 (0080) KE+IE	Ofw Wilhelm Löhmann-1 F-+ Fw Bernhard Korber-2 F-inj. Uffz Josef Klüttgens-1 BF-inj. Ogefr Hans Trappe-2 BF-inj. Fw Erich Seifert-BM-+ Ogefr Georg Vogt-BS-inj.	Take-off accident at Vaernes. Ac destroyed by fire. Combat mission.

Date	Unit	Aircraft	Crew	Notes
27 May 42	I/KG 40	Fw 200 C	Ofw Friedrich Findeisen-BF-+	Killed by enemy gunfire, Iceland/Jan Mayen?
29 May 42	III/KG 40	Fw 200 C-3 (0031) F8+BT	—	Taxiing accident Mérignac airfield, 25% dam.
02 Jun 42	8/KG 40	Fw 200 D-2a / KC-1 (0019) F8+BU / F8+LV / D-AWSK *Rheinland*	Ofw Walter Riepold (3 crew +)	Ditched nr Zakynthos, Greece.
05 Jun 42	8/KG 40	Fw 200 C F8+IS	Uffz Kurt Hochmuth-2 F-+ Ofw Paul Zibull-1 F & rest of crew safe	Combat with Sunderland W3986/U of 10 Sqn RAAF 1933 hrs (F/Lt S R C Wood); Sunderland dam.
08 Jul 42	IV/KG 40	Fw 200 C-1 BS+AP (0013)	crew safe	Crash-landing at Orleans-Bricy, 25% dam.
08 Jul 42	1/KG 40	Fw 200 C-4 (0101) F8+EH (NT+BA)	Oblt Albert Gramkow (Stkpt)-F-M Ofw Anton Mohaim-F-M Ogefr Gerhard von Stocki-BF-M Uffz Heinz Laxy-BF-M Ofw Rüdiger Wedding-BM-M Uffz Franz Welters-BS-M Fw Gerhard Fischer-BM-M Lt Georg Liebenau-B-M	North Atlantic, convoy PQ 17/QP 13. 47 Ost/4270.
12 Jul 42	9/KG 40	Fw 200 C-4 (0135) F8+BT (VY+OI)	Ofw Richard Schöngraf-F-M Uffz Kurt Groneberg-F-M Uffz Helmuth Thiemann-BF-M Uffz Erich Althammer-BF-M Fw Rudolf Lätsch-BM-M Ogefr Ernst Thiel-BS-M	Crashed Ria de Muros, Spain.
14 Jul 42	7/KG 40	Fw 200 C-3 (0034) F8+GW (?)	—	Taxiing accident, Mérignac, 25% dam.
22 Jul 42	9/KG 40	Fw 200 C-4 (0136) (CE+IA)	Fw Alfred Praschl-1 F-+ Uffz Kurt Mayer-2 F-+ Uffz Herbert Gruber-BF-+ Uffz Fritz Pförtner-BM-+ Flg Anton Steinmetz-Waffenwart-+ Uffz Helmut Talke-BM-+ Gefr Alexander von Winkler-BS-+ Gefr Heinz Weihrauch-BS-+	Crashed 17 kms SW of Mérignac. Mid-air collision with Ju 88 C-6 (360017) of V/KG 40 (Hptm Weymar & crew killed). Air-combat training.

Date	Unit	Aircraft	Crew	Remarks
27 Jul 42	9/KG 40	Fw 200 C-4/U2 (0139) F8+FT (CE+IC)	—	Collision with Ju 88, 20 % dam.
31 Jul 42	IV/KG 40	Fw 200 C-3 (0031) SG+KG F8+BT	Oblt Helmut Krebs-1 F-+ / Uffz Walter Schwinge-2 F-+ / Uffz Ernst Röhl-1 BF-+ / Uffz Franz Linden-2 BF-+ / Uffz Georg Sturm-BS-+ / Fw Siegfried Meissner-1 BM-+ / Gefr Kurt Edler-2 BM-+	Crashed & destroyed at Royan.
31 Jul 42	IV/KG 40	Fw 200 C-3SG+KF (0030)	Oblt Hermann Frenzel-1 F-inj. / Uffz Paul Boller-2 F-inj.	Attacked by Wg Cdr B R O'B Hoare/Plt Off Cornes in Mosquito DD670/S, 23 Sqn, 0145 hrs. Ac crash-landed and burnt out, Orleans.
07 Aug 42	1/KG 40	Fw 200 C-4 (0104) F8+AB (NT+BD)	Ofw Alfons Kleinschnittger-F-+ / Fw Paul Lemke-F-+ / Uffz Werner Schelle-BF-+ / Uffz Oskar Walter-BF-+ / Ofw Karl Classow-BM-+ / Uffz Josef Kotzur-BS-+	Reconnaissance, Jan Mayen. Hit Mountain. at Danielenkrateret.
09 Aug 42	I/KG 40	Fw 200 C-3 (0084) (KE+II)	—	Technical problems, 30% dam, Vaernes.
14 Aug 42	2/KG 40	Fw 200 C-4 (0125) F8+BB (NT+BY)	Ofw Fritz Kühn-F-M / Ofw Philipp Haisch-F-M / Ofw Ottmar Ebener-BF-M / Uffz Wolfgang Schulze-BF-M / Obw Artur Wohlleben-BM-M / Ofw Albert Winkelmann-BS-M	Shot down by 1/Lt E Shahan 27th FS, 1 FG and Lt J D R Schaffer, 33rd FS, 1 FG off Grotta Point, Iceland.
18 Aug 42	IV/KG 40	Fw 200 C-2 (0018)	—	Take-off accident at Orleans-Bricy, 15% dam.
19 Aug 42	9/KG 40	Fw 200 C-4 (0146) F8+FT (CE+IK)	—	Undercarriage problems at Mérignac, 15% dam.
21 Aug 42	I/KG 40	Fw 200 C-4 (0141) F8+FW (CE+IF)	—	Take-off accident at Vaernes, 60% dam.
23 Aug 42	2/KG 40	Fw 200 C-4 (0111) (NT+BK)	—	Take-off accident at Vaernes, 60% dam.
24 Aug 42	3/KG 40	Fw 200 C-4 (0108) (NT+BH)	—	Landing-accident due to undercarriage dam, 10%. Vaernes.

Date	Unit	Aircraft	Crew	Remarks
25 Aug 42	2/KG 40	Fw 200 C-3 (0065) (KF+QE)	—	Crash-landing due to undercarriage damage at Vaernes, 10%. dam.
26 Aug 42	2/KG 40	Fw 200 C-6 (0133) (VY+OG)	—	Landing accident at Vaernes, 60% dam.
29 Aug 42	2/KG 40	Fw 200 C-3/U4 (0090) (KE+IO)	Oblt Theodor Jochimsen-1 F-+ / Fw Otto Schorer (Schörer ?)-2 F-+ / Fw Josef Hauk (Hauck)-1 BF-+ / Uffz Karl Vellmer-2 BF-+ / Fw Heinz Wagner-BM-+ / Uffz Felix Wiesner-BS-+ / San Fhr Lothar Schäfer-+	Crashed after take-off at Vaernes. Ac took-off burning and exploded. Combat mission. Killed on the ground.
04 Sep 42	3/KG 40	Fw 200 C-4 (0127) (VY+OA)	—	Take-off accident Vaernes, 25% dam.
04 Sep 42	IV/KG 40	Fw 200 C-3/U2 (0048) (SG+KX)		10% dam due to engine fire during landing at Orleans-Bricy.
08 Sep 42	2/KG 40	Fw 200 C-2 (0081) F8+CK (KE+IF)		Crash-landing due to technical defects when returning from sortie. 10% dam Vaernes.
08 Sep 42	3/KG 40	Fw 200 C-4 (0097) (KE+IV)	—	Damaged by low-level attack at Vaernes. 10% dam.
08 Sep 42	3/KG 40	Fw 200 C-4 (0132) F8+CK (VY+OF)		Damaged by low-level attack at Vaernes. 10% dam.
11 Sep 42	3/KG 40	Fw 200 C-4 (0110) (NT+BJ) captured becomes AIR MIN 96		Take-off accident at Vaernes, 15% dam. Combat mission.
14 Sep 42	IV/KG 40	Fw 200 C-3 (0036) SG+KL F8+FV		Taxying accident Orleans-Bricy, 15% dam.
17 Sep 42	8/KG 40	Fw 200 C-4 (0122) F8+AS (NT+BV)	Ofw Konrad Bär-1 F-inj. / Uffz Werner Siegle-2 F-inj. / Ogefr Karlheinz Graebig-B-inj. / Uffz Georg Herklotz-1 BF-+ / Uffz Alfred Böhmchen-2 BF-inj- / Uffz Johannes Linkert-BM-+ / Gefr Johann Neumann-BS-inj.	Shot down by Wg Cdr Hutchinson/Plt Off D S Gallimore, Sgt D Hill/Sgt K Yates, Plt Off G R Leahy/FS A D Ross, Lt R R Casparius/Sgt F Davies, Sqd Ldr A F Binks/Sgt J D Walters, FS G E Woodcock/Sgt W J Ginger, Sgt R H Payne/Sgt Ryan & Plt Off W D Hollis/Sgt H Taylor of 235 Sqn off Belle Isle, 1755 hrs; Beaufighter T5157/C (Sgt Hill) shot down. Crew rescued by French fishing-boat.

Date	Unit	Aircraft	Crew	Notes
17 Oct 42	3/KG 40	Fw 200 C-3 (0057) F8+EK (DE+OL)	—	Taxying accident at Vaernes. 35% dam.
18 Oct 42	2/KG 40	Fw 200 C-4 (0163) (CH+CD)	—	Take-off accident at Vaernes, 15%. dam.
24 Oct 42	2/KG 40	Fw 200 C-4/U3 (0131) F8+EK (VY+OE)	Oblt Heinz Godde-F-+ Fw Matthias Franzen-F-+ Ofw Horst Kroos-BF-+ Uffz Manfred Unger-BF-+ Uffz Alois Schwab-BS-+ Uffz Helmut Engelmann-BM-+ Uffz Hans Todtenhoefer-BM-+ [from unit 1(F)/120]	Shot down by 2/Lts M J Ingelido & T F Morrison, 33rd FS & crashed at Thingvallvatne, Iceland.
28 Oct 42	3/KG 40	Fw 200 C-4 (0109) F8+KL (NT+BI)	Oblt Rudolf Feldt-F-M Fw Bernhard Korber-F-M Lt Herbert Hachtmann-BF-M Uffz Georg Stiegler-BF-M Ofw Werner Sieth-BM-M Uffz Walter Schulze-BS-M	Missing Iceland.
29 Oct 42	3/KG 40	Fw 200 C-4 (0162) F8+ML (CH+CC)	Ofw Herbert Fahje-F-+ Uffz Siegfried Ramm-F-+ Fw Fritz Cordes-BF-+ Uffz Hermann Kraus-BF-+ Ofw Martin Laucks-BM-+ Ogefr Hermann Elpers-BS-+	Crashed after take-off for a sortie at Oerlandet airfield, probably due to pilot error.
31 Oct 42 01 Nov 42	7/KG 40	Fw 200 C-3/U4 (0070) F8+DS (KF+QJ)	Oblt Arno Gross-F-M Ofw Helmut Fischer-F-M Reg Rat Heinz Knothe-Met-M Fw Heinrich Wanniger-BF-M Uffz Ludwig Schön-BF-M Ofw Walter Pflugbeil-BM-M Uffz Willi Kuka-BS-M	Shot down by Flt Lt N Taylor DFM, MFSU, from *Empire Heath* off Gibraltar, 43.00N/15.24W. Combat possibly took place 1 Nov 42. (Flt Lt Heath DFM shot down a Condor on 1 Nov 42 at 43.00N/15.24W).
05 Nov 42	2/KG 40	Fw 200 C-4 (0124) F8+FK (NT+BX)	Fw Kurt Pieper-F-M Uffz Johannes Möckel-F-M Uffz Karl Wissner-BF-M Uffz Karl Kreft-BF-M Uffz Wilhelm Heck-BM-M Ogefr Hans Möller-BS-M	Missing reconnaissance, north of Iceland.

Date	Unit	Aircraft (WNr) / Code	Crew	Remarks
09 Nov 42	I/KG 40	Fw 200 C-4 (0096) F8+ER (KE+IU)	—	35% dam, take-off accident at Vaernes.
17 Nov 42	3/KG 40	Fw 200 C-4 (0105) F8+KL (NT+BE)	—	15% undercarriage dam. Returning from a sortie, Oerlandet.
18 Nov 42	8/KG 40	Fw 200 C-4 (0143) F8+KS (CE+IH)	Ofw Paul Zibull-F-M, Ofw Helmuth Knuth-F-M, Fw Wilhelm Ehmke-BF-M, Uffz Wilhelm Mehrens-BF-M, Ofw Helmuth Häse-BM-+, Uffz Franz Sehri-BS-M	Shot down by fighters, western Mediterranean Sea. Ditched 41.03N 02.56 E 1216 hrs 40 miles off Barcelona.
08 Dec 42	IV/KG 40	Fw 200 C-1 (0013)	Uffz Theobald Niebus-F-inj.	Crash-landed due to enemy fire nr Patay, 40% dam.
08 Dec 42	1/KG 40	Fw 200 C-3/U4 (0089) F8+JH (KE+IN)	—	Belly-landing at Vaernes due to undercarriage problems, 10% dam. Returning from sortie.
17 Dec 42	IV/KG 40	Fw 200 C-3 (0037) F8+CL	—	Hit obstacle at Chateaudun airfield, 10% dam.
24 Dec 42	7/KG 40	Fw 200 C-4 (0159) F8+BR (CE+IX)	—	Accident at Mérignac, 45% dam. Pilot error.
27 Dec 42	2/KG 40	Fw 200 C-4 (0140) F8+AK (CE+IE)	Oblt Waldemar Hackel-F-+, Uffz Adolf Liebscher-F-+, Fw Erwin Kopp-BF-+, Uffz Walter Schwarze-BF, Fw Fritz Albrecht-BM-inj., Gefr Karl Pech-BS-+	Hit mountain at Kvitanosi Stolsheimen Hordaland. Schwarze & Albrecht walked back to unit.
31 Dec 42	8/KG 40	Fw 200 C-4/U3 (0175) F8+AS (GC+SD)	Hptm Fritz Hoppe-1 F, Rank Unknown Werner Löffler	Attack on Casablanca. Crew interned. Emergency landing at San Pablo due to combat damage. Aircraft stayed in Spain and became Spanish T.4-2 .
	7/KG 40	Fw 200 C-4 (0160) F8+FR (CE+CY))	Oblt Günther Gräber-F-+, Uffz Rudolf Gerlach-F-M, Ofw Walter Jüttner-BF-M, Uffz Xaver Pappl-BF-M, Ogefr Karl Gräbig-B-M, Uffz Rudi Sureck-BM-+, Uffz Heinz Fröhling-BS-M	Attack on Casablanca. Crashed near Gran Canaria (?). Sureck washed ashore in June 1943. Einzelmeldung: '0805 hrs – PIQ 13W/7872 – 2 engines seized, ditching south of Spain. Believed south of Huelva.

Date	Unit	Type (Werk Nr.)	Crew	Remarks
31 Dec 42	III/KG 40	Fw 200 C	Uffz Günther Faller-BS-inj.	Flak, Casablanca.
31 Dec 42	2/KG 40	Fw 200 C-3/U4 (0081) F8+CK (KE+IF)	Oblt Dietrich Weber-F-M / Uffz Hans Wieser-F-M / Uffz Wolfgang Melzer-BF-M / Uffz Willi Nuss-BF-M / Fw Anton Lischke-BM-M / Ogefr Heinrich Köhl-BS-M	Between west coast of Norway and Iceland. Convoy JW 51 B.
01 Jan 43	8/KG 40	Fw 200 C-4 (0118) F8+HS (NT+BR)	—	Landed at San Pablo a/f, Sevilla, Spain. Became Spanish T.4-1.
02 Jan 43	11/KG 40	Fw 200 C-2 (0017)	Ofw August Brandt-BM-inj.	Landing accident, collided with a Fw 58 at Berlin-Staaken airfield, 40% dam.
03 Jan 43	I/KG 40	Fw 200 C-4 (0170) (CH+CK)	—	Take-off accident at Vaernes. 15% dam.
07 Jan 43	9/KG 40	Fw 200 C-3/U1 (0052) F8+PT (DE+OG)	—	Technical problems at Lecce. 25% dam.
10 Jan 43	KGr zbV 200	Fw 200 C-2 / KC-1 (0018)	Ofw Werner Brune-F-inj. / Ofw Berthold Hörning-F-inj. / Ofw Horst Ine-BF-inj. / Ofw Karl Slusarek-BM-inj. / Ofw Franz Surembsky-BS-inj.	Hit ground at Pitomnik airfield (Stalingrad), 90% dam.
10 Jan 43	KGr zbV 200	Fw 200 C-4 (0151) F8+HW (CE+IP)	Ofw Eugen Reck-F-M / Fw Kurt Menke-F-M / Uffz Fritz Elsenheimer-BF-M / Ogefr Jakob Bohnen-BF-M / Ogefr Heinz Engler-BM-M / Uffz Richard Schmidt-BS-M	Crashed on take off Pitomnik.
15 Jan 43	III/KG 40	Fw 200 C-4/U3 (0178) (GC+SG)	—	Taxying accident, Mérignac, 12% dam.
16 Jan 43	KGr zbV 200	Fw 200 C-3 (0046) (SG+KV)		Destroyed by German troops at Pitomnik airfield.
18 Jan 43	IV/KG 40	Fw 200 A-0 / S-3 (2895) (GF+GF – ex D-AMHC *Nordmark*) WL-AMHC / TK+BS / F8+HH / F8+DU / F8+MV	crew safe	Damaged by Bf 109 at Chateaudun airfield, 50% dam.

Date	Unit	Aircraft	Crew	Fate
Jan/Feb 43	1/KGr zbV 200	Fw 200 C-3 (0049)	Ofw Werner Boeck-F	Suffered fuselage break whilst taxying at Sslawjanskaja after flight from Saporoshje; overloaded plane.
19 Jan 43	KGr zbV 200	Fw 200 C-3/U5 (0095) F8+DH (KE+IT)	Ofw Karl Gruner-F-M, Uffz Fritz Neumann-F-M, Fw Heinrich Böhmlein-BF-M, Uffz Fritz Piehl-BF-M, Uffz Willi Haunero-BM-M, Flg Herbert Wallaschek-BS-M	Missing Gumrak airfield/Stalingrad.
22 Jan 43	KGr zbV 200	Fw 200 C-3/U4 (0071) (KF+QK)	–	50% combat dam, fighters. Nowonikolepneko.
23 Jan 43	KGr zbV 200	Fw 200 C-4 (0179) (GC+SH)	–	40% combat dam, fighters. Woroschilowgrad.
29 Jan 43	9/KG 40	Fw 200 C-4 (0149) F8+CT (CE+IN)	–	Landing accident at Elmas, 30% dam.
29 Jan 43	KGr zbV 200	Fw 200 C-3 / V13 (0025)	–	Accident due to lack of fuel, 15% dam. Saporoshje airfield.
30/31 Jan 43	KGr zbV 200	Fw 200 C-3 SG+KJ (0034) F8+GW	Ofw Karl Wittmann-F-M, Uffz Hubert Reder-F-M, Uffz Gerhard Karl-BF-M, Ogefr Erich Bohm-BF-M, Ofw Robert Röser-BM-M, Ogefr Karl Pulec-BS-M	Missing Stalingrad.
03 Feb 43	III/KG 40	Fw 200 C-3 (0058) (DE+OM)	crew safe	Damaged at Lecce airfield, 10% dam.
14 Feb 43	III/KG 40	Fw 200 C-4 (0164) (CH+CE)	Hptm Dr Lambert von Konschegg-F–Staffel Kapitän & crew safe	Bomb dropping training. Emergency landing due to engine fire, Toctoucau. destroyed.
22 Feb 43	KGr zbV 200	Fw 200 C-4 (0117) F8+JS (NT+BQ)	–	Crash-landing at Berlin-Staaken due to bad weather; 40% dam.
12 Mar 43	7/KG 40	Fw 200 C-4 (0186) F8+ER (GC+SO)	Lt Ernst Rabolt-F-M, Ofw Alfred Lauer-F-M, Ofw Hans Schmidt-BF-M, Ogefr Alfred Beier-BF-M, Ofw Hans Stöckl-BM-M, Ogefr Paul Florenkowski-BS-M	Shot down by Sgt P Wilkinson/Sgt S Bertram in X, Sgt C Goodwin/Sgt W J Perry in M, Fg Off C R Schofield/Sgt J A Mallinson in R & Fg Off R C Stringer/Plt Off S Hunter in U of 248 Sqn 45.16N/09.00W, 1001 hrs.

Date	Unit	Aircraft	Crew		Remarks
12 Mar 43	3/KG 40	Fw 200 C-4 (0127) (VY+OA)		—	Landing accident at Diepensee, 40% dam.
12 Mar 43	III/KG 40	Fw 200 C-4 (0133) (VY+OG)		—	Take-off accident at Mérignac, 60% dam.
16 Mar 43	I/KG 40	Fw 200 C-4 (0116) (NT+BP)	Ofw Wilhelm Pfitzenreuter-F-+ Uffz Georg Suchan-F-+ Uffz Werner Paulsen-BF-+ Uffz Helmut Gaiser-BF-+ Ogefr Horst Armighöfer-BM-+ Gefr Siegfried Klinkmann-BS-unhurt Uffz Wilhelm Reinhardt-?-unhurt		Crashed after taking off for a mission, Vaernes. Aircraft destroyed by fire.
18 Mar 43	I/KG 40	Fw 200 C-4 (0173) (GC+SB)		—	Crash-landing due to technical problems. 20% dam. Vaernes, returning from sortie.
19 Mar 43	KGr zbV 200 (III/KG 40)	Fw 200 C-4 (0128) F8+IK (VY+OB)	Oblt Erich Schlebach-F-M Fw Walter Fröhlich-F-+ Uffz Peter Schmitter-BF-M Uffz Anton Pammor-BF-M Fw Hans Müller-BM-M Uffz Ernst Sanner-BS-M		Shot down by destroyer *Savorgnan de Brazza*. One body (Fröhlich) recovered by ship's crew.
24 Mar 43	7/KG 40	Fw 200 C-4 (0192) F8+ER (GC+SU)	Ofw Werner Böck-F-M Fw Georg Markert-F-+ Uffz Hans Möller-BF-+ Uffz Harald Santler-BF-+ Ofw Hans Müller-BM-+ Ogefr Walter Rettke-BS-M		Missing Atlantic. Markert, Möller, Santler & Müller washed ashore Apr 43.
25 Mar 43	2/KG 40	Fw 200 C-4 (0144) (CE+II)		—	Crash-landing at Cognac due to engine failure, 70% dam.
27 Mar 43	7/KG 40	Fw 200 C-4 (0168) (CH+CI)	Lt Fritz Marschall-F-+ Ofw Heinrich Trumpfheller-F-+ Uffz Werner Heland-BF-+ Uffz Hans Sikoll-BF-+ Fw Richard Weber-BM-+ Ogefr Wilhelm Höcker-BS-M Ogefr Heinrich Schmidt-B-M		Friendly fire from German barrage-breaker, nr La Rochelle (west of Royan). Marschall & Heland washed ashore in April 1943. Trumpfheller washed ashore in June 1943.

Date	Unit	Aircraft	Crew	Remarks
29 Mar 43	III/KG 40	Fw 200 C-4 (0193) (GC+CV)	—	Crash-landed at Cognac due to pilot error, 25% dam.
27 Apr 43	IV/KG 40	Fw 200 C-4 (0121) (NT+BU)	Oblt Dietrich Melin-F-+ Ofw Klaus Timberg-F-+ Uffz Paul Zimmermann-BF-+ Uffz Willi Zelle-BM-+ Ogefr Gerhard Willmann-BM-+ Flg Werner Hoffmann-BS-+ Flg Albert Haak-BS-+	Crashed after take-off, Chateaudun. Ac destroyed by fire.
03 May 43	III/KG 40	Fw 200 C	—	Left wing damaged by Flak from convoy of landing ships & escorting vessels 0750 hrs, 24W/4656.
07 Jun 43	9/KG 40	Fw 200 C-3/U1 (0052) F8+PT (DE+OG)	Oblt Georg Ulrici-F-inj. Uffz Walter Drischner-B-inj. Uffz Günther Koch-BF-inj. Uffz Hans Kiebauer-BF-inj. Ofw Franz Ziegon-BM-inj.	Emergency-landing due to engine fire, Castanet near Toulouse, 90% dam. Ferrying flight. (1 civilian passenger +)
13 Jun 43	7/KG 40	Fw 200 C-4 (0147) F8+CR (CE+IL)	Stfw Rudolf Kensok-F-M Ofw Albert Breu-1 BF-M Uffz Gustav Brachmann-2 BF-M Ofw Artur Küssner-BM-M Uffz Heinz Harder-BS-M Uffz Heinrich Spemes-B-M	151 Sqn (Sqn Ldr Bodien/Fg Off R W Sampson – Fg Off L A D Boyle/Sgt H M Freisner – Plt Off J D Humphries/Plt Off Lumb) – Shot down 400 kms west of Bordeaux, 1020 hrs. Armed reconnaissance against northgoing convoy.
20 Jun 43	I/KG 40	Fw 200 C-5 (0205) (TA+MG)	—	Damaged due to engine problems. Vaernes, 40% dam.
24 Jun 43	7/KG 40	Fw 200 C-4 (0145) F8+DR (CE+IJ)	Ofw Georg Abel-F-M Fw Josef Steinbrunner-F-M Uffz Hans Heckmann-B-M Uffz Franz Haupt-BF-M Uffz Kurt Kosch-BF-M Fw Matthias Erhard-BM-M Uffz Florian Öhme-BS-M	Shot down by Lt P Constable & Sub Lt A G Penney, 808 (A) Sqn., *HMS Battler* in Seafires NM970 & MB 302 respectively; 40.25N/14.55W. A Fw 200 reported "2045 hrs combat with Lockheed. One engine hit by MG-fire and subsequently seized."
24 Jun 43	IV/KG 40	Fw 200 C-3 (0068) F8+ST (KF+QH)	—	Crash-landed due to pilot error, Chateaudun. 50% dam.

Date	Unit	Aircraft	Crew	Remarks
9 Jul 43	9/KG 40	Fw 200 C-4/U3 (0178) F8 + NT (GC+SG)	Fw Nicolaus Guenther-F-+ / Uffz Hans Weigert-F-+ / Uffz Werner Riecke-BF-+ / Uffz Walter Beck-BF-+ / Ogefr Ernst Herppich-B-+ / Uffz Martin Angermann-BM-+ / Fw Johann Bauer-BS-+	Shot down by Sgt J McLeod/Sgt N T Inglis of 248 Sqn and crashed into cliffs, Paredo, SW Aljezur(Portugal), 0852 hrs. Beaufighter. H (Sgt McLeod) & Beaufighter Y (Fg Off T R Buckley/FS E Swilcox) both damaged, claimed by Oblt Johannes Sacher in F8+IT, 0910 hrs, Cap Sardao. 5 Fw 200s and Hudson V/233 Sqn involved.
11 Jul 43	I/KG 40	Fw 200 C-5 (0217) (TA+MS)	Fw Willi Trautmannsberger-F & crew safe	Crash-landed and burnt at Drontheim airfield, 95% dam.
13 Jul 43	7/KG 40	Fw 200 C-4 (0142) F8+BR (CE+IG)	? (see below)	Crash-landed at Hourtin airfield due to engine problems, 10% dam.
13 Jul 43	III/KG 40	Fw 200 C ? (see above)	Ofw Hans Hauenstein-F-inj.	Flak.
15 Jul 43	III/KG 40	Fw 200 C-4 (0171) (CH+CL)	Ofw Hans Driedrichsen-BF-inj. / Fw Hans Kubach-BF-inj. / Ogefr Robert Kober-B-inj.	Ditched 0326 hrs in Gironde estuary due to lack of fuel. Combat mission.
20 Jul 43	III/KG 40	Fw 200 C-4 (0150) (CE+IO)	—	Broken undercarriage, 25% dam, Mérignac.
27 Jul 43	7/KG 40	Fw 200 C-4 (0141) F8+FW (CE+IF)	—	Take-off accident at Mérignac, 15% dam. Combat mission.
28 Jul 43	2/KG 40 (III/KG 40)	Fw 200 C-4/U3 (0177) F8+FK (GC+SF)	Uffz Heinz Meyer-F-POW / Ofw Rudolf Waschek-F-POW / Gefr Edgar Arnold-B-POW / Ofw Heinz Link-BF-POW / Fw Franz Hillebrandt-BF-POW / Stfw Hans Zacher-BM-+ / Uffz Georg Kiener-BS-POW	Shot down by B-24D of 1 Sqn/ 480th ASG (Lt E W Hyde), 1823 hrs (B-24 badly damaged and abandoned 15-20 miles ENE Sale, T/Sgt J E Kehoe+). Also claimed by Fg Off J Stewart MSFU, 1945 hrs, 43.03N, 16.06W.
29 Jul 43	2/KG 40 (III/KG 40)	Fw 200 C-4 (0132) F8-CK (VY+OF)	Ofw Alfred Bolfraß-F-+ / Uffz Hans Gnuechtel-F-POW / Gefr Siegfried Damm-B-POW / Uffz Rudolf Schöwe-BF-POW / Uffz Herbert Kalus-BF-POW / Ofw Wilhelm Holzhauer-BM-inj./POW / Uffz Wilhelm Hahnstadt-BS-+	Shot down by Fg Off P A S Payne/Fg Off A M Mc Nicholl in A, Fg Off G C Newman/Fg Off C C Cochrane in S, Fg Off F Lacy/WO G C Harker in J & Fg Off J K Thompson/Sgt G F Barnes in U of 248 Sqn, 45.30N/06.06W (75 Miles NW Cape Finisterre) 1219 hrs whilst attacking Convoy SL 133/MKS 18.
31 Jul 43	III/KG 40	Fw 200 C-4/U3 (0180) (GC+SI)	—	Landing accident at Cognac airfield, 30% dam.

Date	Unit	Aircraft	Crew	Remarks
31 Jul 43	7/KG 40	Fw 200 C-5 (0202) F8+AR (TA+MD)	Oblt Siegfried Gall-F-M Uffz Paul Boller-F-M Uffz Alfred Spendler-B-M Ofw Alfons Eisen-BF-M Uffz Markus Pippig-BF-M Fw Rudi Helbig-BM-M Ofw Hermann Peukert-BS-M	6 Fw 200 on armed reconnaissance; take-off 0353 –0455 hrs. Last radio signal: at 1242 hrs: "Luftkampf!". Shot down by B-24 coded 'C' of 2nd Aron, 480th ASG (Capt Mosier), 41.82N, 14.45W, 1145 hrs.
02 Aug 43	7/KG 40	Fw 200 C-5 (0215) F8+DR (TA+MQ)	Oblt Alois Pongratz-F-M Uffz Ernst Malik-F-M Uffz Rolf Devermann-B-M Fw Hans Hermann-BF-M Uffz Hans Stangel-BF-M Stfw Friedrich Kogler-BM-M Uffz Uwe Petersen-BS-M	Shot down by Flt Lt J C Newbery/Fg Off D Alcock in P, Plt Off P J McGarvey/Fg Off A M Barnard in W, Fg Off J F Green/Plt Off G B Forrest DFM in J & Plt Off V R Scheer/Fg Off R W Twallin in L of 248 Sqn, 46.36N/07.27W, 1045 hrs.
05 Aug 43	3/KG 40	Fw 200 C-4 (0200) F8+FL (TA+MB)	Ofw Karl Holtrup-F-POW Uffz Günter Karte-F(B)-POW Fw Josef Teufel-BF-POW Uffz Herbert Richter-BF-POW Ofw Emil Brand-BM-POW Ogefr Siegfried Klinkmann-BS-POW Gefr Wilhelm Lehn-BS-POW	Shot down by P-38s of 50th FS USAAF in sea about 50 miles N of Axar Fjord, Iceland. 66.30 N, 17.50 W – 1548 hrs. Lt Richard M Holly & Lt William Bethea.
10 Aug 43	III/KG 40	Fw 200 C-4 (0154) (CE+IS)	—	Undercarriage damage during landing at Mérignac airfield when returning from a sortie. 15% dam.
13 Aug 43	9/KG 43	Fw 200 C-7 [C-5/U1] (0221) F8+IT (TA+MW)	Oblt Günther Seide-1 F Fw Hans Greiwe-2 F Fw Gerhard Drews-1 BF Uffz Werner Zerrahn-2 BF Ofw Hans Böing-BM Ogefr Heinz Wagner-BS-inj. Uffz Kurt von Au-BO	Belly-landing Camarinas near La Coruna because of lack of fuel caused by combat damage with B-24 of 1st Sqn/480th ASG (Lt F W McKinnon) & force-landed on the beach at Arena de la Villa, Spain, 1830 hrs.
15 Aug 43	7/KG 40	Fw 200 C-4 (0166) F8+ER (CH+CG)	Oblt Bernhard Kunisch-1 F Uffz Otto Specht-F Uffz Horst Fleschsig-BF Uffz Fritz Oetker-BF Uffz Heinz Schatte-BM Uffz Gerhard Thielemann-BS Uffz Guenther Hellner-BO	Emergency landing Lavacolla, Santiago de Compostela (Santander). Caused by AA fire from HMS Stork. Convoy OS 53/KMS 23.

Date	Unit	Aircraft	Crew	Remarks
17 Aug 43	2/KG 40 (III/KG 40)	Fw 200 C-4 (0114) F8+EK (NT+BN)	Oblt Heinz Küchenmeister-F & crew safe	Crash-landing at Mérignac due to combat damage, engine fire. Aircraft burnt out. B-24D of 1st Sqn/480th ASG (Capt H D Maxwell).
17 Aug 43	2/KG 40 (III/KG 40)	Fw 200 C-5 (0211) F8+FK (TA+MM)	Ofw Karl Bauer-F-POW, Fw Georg Wenniger-F-POW, Ogefr Erich Gabein-B-+, Fw Alfred Wrana-BF-POW, Fw Hermann Jahn-BF-POW, Uffz Friedrich Dörter-BM-+, Uffz Friedrich Mangold-BS-+	Shot down in combat with B-24D of 1st Sqn/480th ASG (Capt H D Maxwell). Ditched near convoy MKS 21. B-24 also crashed, 3+, PIQ 24W/5036. (ex KGr zbV 200)
17 Aug 43	2/KG 40 (III/KG 40)	Fw 200 C F8+DK	Oblt/Hptm Riebesam, Vollrath & crew safe	Crash-landed and burnt out at Mérignac airfield. Non combat mission.
23 Aug 43	IV/KG 40	Fw 200 C-4/U2 (0139) F8+FT (CE+ID)	—	Taxiing accident at Chateaudun, 20% dam.
23 Aug 43	III/KG 40	Fw 200 C-4 (0190) (GC+SS)	—	Undercarriage damaged during take-off at Mérignac, 30% dam.
23 Aug 43	9/KG 40	Fw 200 C-6 (0214) F8+NT (TA+MP)	Ofw Alfred Billing-F, Uffz Kurt Lelewel-B, Uffz Otto Hirschfeld-BF, Uffz Gerhard Jacoby-BF, Ofw Hans Gentsch-BM-+, Uffz Josef Staniewski-BS	Ditched in Alantic. Except for Ofw Gentsch rest of crew rescued by U-boat.
24 Aug 43	IV/KG 40	Fw 200 C-4 (0134) F8+ES (VY+OH)	—	Broken undercarriage during landing at Chateaudun, 20% dam.
02 Sep 43	9/KG 40	Fw 200 C-5 (0201) F8+DT (TA+MC)	Oblt Hans Graul-F-M, Lt Max Händel-B-M, Fw Gustav Gold-F-M, Uffz Eckehard Lämmerhirt-BF-M, Uffz Hans Siegl-BF-M, Ofw Adolf Kamke-BM-M, Uffz Rudolf Böhm-BS-M	Shot down by Flak from Renee Paul during low-level attack off Cape St Vincent.
13 Sep 43	III/KG 40	Fw 200 C-4/U3 (0174) (GC+SC)	—	Undercarriage damaged during take-off at Cognac, 25% dam.

Date	Unit	Aircraft	Crew	Remarks
22 Sep 43	2/KG 40 (III/KG 40)	Fw 200 C-4 (0161) F8+IK (also F8+AA, F8+BB CH+CB, CE+IZ)	Fw Otto Ulfert(es)-F-M; Uffz Karl Richter-F-M; Gefr Adolf Betz-B-+; Uffz Helmut Rüger-BF-+; Uffz Walter Orschel-BF-M; Uffz Gerhard Oberthür-BM-M; Ogefr Helmuth Teiter-+; Hptm Gerhard Wacht-B-M	Missing from mission. Rüger, Teiter & Betz washed ashore in October 43.
24 Sep 43	III/KG 40	Fw 200 C-5 (0212) (TA+MN)	—	Broken undercarriage during landing at Bussac, 20% dam.
01 Oct 43	7/KG 40	Fw 200 C-4 (0159) F8+BR (CE+IX)	—	Technical problems, emergency landing at Yvrac nr Bordeaux, 85% dam.
14 Oct 43	1/KG 40	Fw 200 C-3/U4 (0089) F8+JH (KE+IN)	Oblt Walter Klomp-F-inj.; Reg Rat Brunner-B/Met-+; Uffz Heinz Heller-BM-inj.; Ogefr Reinhold Meyer-BS-unhurt	Crashed after take-off for a mission, Vaernes-West, 85% dam.
23 Oct 43	III/KG 40	Fw 200 C-5 (0203) (TA+ME)	—	Undercarriage damage at Cognac airfield, 25% dam.
27 Oct 43	III/KG 40	Fw 200 C-5 (0206) (TA+MH)	Fw Karl Blumenthal-BF-inj.; Fw Alfred Zander-BS-inj.	Engine failure 2 min after take-off and crashed at Cognac airfield, 100%. Combat mission.
28 Oct 43	III/KG 40	Fw 200 C-3 (0036) F8+FV	—	Take-off accident at Mérignac. Ac destroyed by fire.
02 Nov 43	3/KG 40	Fw 200 C-4/U3 (0130) (VY+OD)	—	Accident due to pilot error at Döberitz, 30% dam.
09 Nov 43	8/KG 40	Fw 200 C-4 (0100) F8+CS (KE+IY)	—	Emergency landing at LeVerdon due to lack of petrol. Returning from mission, 1850 hrs. 50% dam.
14 Nov 43	3/KG 40	Fw 200 C-4 (0105) F8+KL (NT+BT) NT+BE	Ofw Richard Liebe-F-M; Uffz Rolf Rühl-F-M; Uffz Herbert Noske-BF-M; Uffz Rudolf Barth-BF-M; Uffz Alfred Clavien-BM-M; Ogefr Friedrich Graser-BS-M	80 kms NW of Eidsa, Norway. Convoy reconnaissance.

Date	Unit	Aircraft	Crew	Details
20 Nov 43	7/KG 40	Fw 200 C-5 (0222) F8+AR (TA+MX)	Oblt Bernhard Kunisch-F-M Hptm Horst Lückstedt-F-M Uffz Günther Nellner-B-M Fw Hans Urbka-BF-M Uffz Fritz Ötker-BF-M Fw Heinz Schadde-BM-M Uffz Gerhard Theilmann-BS-M	Shot down by Fg Off/F Green/Fg Off G B Forrest DFM in N, FS A L Chisholm/WO G Phimster in K, FS G R Tomalin/Sgt B L Bennington in J & Fg Off B C Roberts/FS P Winsor in G of 248 Sqn. 43.40N/08.11W – west of Cape Ortegal, 1529 hrs.
21 Nov 43	/KG 40	Fw 200 C	—	Damaged by Ju 88 C-6 of I/ZG 1.
26 Nov 43	9/KG 40	Fw 200 C-8 (0233) (TK+CO)	Oblt Herbert Leuschner-F-+ Uffz Emil Grieshammer-F-+ Fw Walter Keller-BF-+ Uffz Richard Wagner-BF-+ Uffz Karl Lautenschläger-BM-+ Ogefr Robert Pöttinghaus-BS-+	Crashed nr Stuttgart. Ferrying flight from Garz to Cognac. Ac destroyed by fire. (& 5 passengers+ ?)
01 Dec 43	8/KG 40	Fw 200 C-5 (0207) F8+LS (TA+MI)	Oblt Joachim Knauthe-F-M Ofw Karl Gerhards-F-M Ogefr Gerd Vogel-B-M Lt Manfred Brieger-BF-M Uffz Karl Waltraum-BF-M Uffz Wilfried Wiederhöft-BF-M Ofw Kurt Schreiber-BM-M Uffz Ernst Eckel-BS-M	842 Sqn, H.M.S. Fencer (Lt [A.] L C Wort, R.N.V.R., & Sub-Lt [A.] E W Fleischmann-Allen, R.N.V.R.) Took off 0917 hrs for a reconnaissance over the Atlantic and Western Bay of Biscay. Declared missing since 0320 hrs, 02 Dec 43.
10 Dec 43	3/KG 40	Fw 200 C-4 (0126) (NT+BZ)	Ofw Mathias Esters & crew safe	60% dam due to technical problems. Vaernes.
11 Dec 43	8/KG 40	Fw 200 C-3 (0059) (DE+ON)	Ofw Kurt Metzmann-F-+ Uffz Hermann Blos-F-+ Uffz Horst Czerny-B-+ Gefr Karl Rademacher-B-+ Gefr Franz Pöhling-BF-+ Uffz Oswald Lukas-BF-+ Uffz Fritz Badenhopp-BM-+ Ogefr Karl Cedzick-BS-inj.	Hit high-power cable and crashed at St. Sulpice Limoges. 80% dam.

Date	Unit	Aircraft	Crew	Remarks
13 Dec 43	7/KG 40	Fw 200 C-6 (0237) F8+MR (TK+CS)	Oblt Egon Scherret-1 F Uffz Hans Meidel-2 F Uffz Karl-Heinz Schwarzkopf-B Fw Hans Rassek-1 BF Uffz Ulrich Winkler-2 BF Ofw Wilhelm Voll-BM Fw Alfred Thiemt-BS Uffz Bruno Arndt-BS	Landed at night at Dromineer, Co. Tipperary. Crew blew ac up and all were interned. Emergency-landing, two engines had been destroyed by Flak from Convoy ON 214, 1940 hrs.
28 Dec 43	9/KG 40	Fw 200 C-4 (0189) F8+MR (GC+SR) A/c of 7 Staffel	Hptm Wilhelm Dette-F-POW Fw Ernst Drabert-F-POW Uffz Kurt Lelewel-B-POW Ofw Johann Sewing-BF-+ Uffz Walter Schmidt-BF-POW Ofw Friedrich Günther-BM-POW Uffz Wilhelm Hackler-BS-POW	Take-off from Cognac at 0600 hrs. Outer starboard engine burst into flames at about 1100 hrs. Pilot ditched the aircraft at about 1110 hrs, 46.15 N, 13.14 W. Crew rescued by *Lord Nuffield* on 1 Jan 44. 0200 hrs. Ofw Sewing drowned.
29 Dec 43	7/KG 40	Fw 200 C-8/(C-5) (0246) F8+IR (TO+XB) TO+XD	Hptm Georg Schobert-B-M FljOfw Wilhelm Friedrichs-F-M Ofw Kurt Scheunert-B-M Fw Paul Böber-1 BF-M Uffz Erwin Pauli-2 BF-M Fw Johann Aixner-BM-M Uffz Fritz Lautenschläger-BS-M Uffz Siegfried Radauer-BS-+	Missing Atlantic.
05 Jan 44	III/KG 40	8 Fw 200 C destroyed 3 Fw 200 C damaged	–	Air attack on Mérignac.
07 Jan 44	12/KG 40	Fw 200 C-3/U2 (0048) F8+GW (SG+KX)	Uffz Werner Stolze-B-+ Ogefr Hans Fünkner-ground crew-inj.	Attacked by Bf 109 during bomb dropping practice. Landed at Orleans-Bricy.
17 Jan 44	3/KG 40	Fw 200 C-5 (0204) F8+CL (TA+MF)	Oblt Ernst Rebensburg-F-M Fw Georg Lothes-F-M Ofw Georg Bleier-1 BF-M Uffz Alfred Perina-2 BF-M Ofw Heinz Schneider-BM-M Ofw Johann Bauer-BS-M Ogefr Wilhelm Baxmann-BS-M	Missing on recce sortie northern North Sea.

Date	Unit	Type	Crew	Remarks
27 Jan 44	9/KG 40	Fw 200 C	Ofw Willy Schmidt-F-+ Uffz Wilhelm Reinhardt-B-+ Uffz Walter Schwarz-BF-+ Uffz Raimund Prettner-BF-+ Fw Karl Nothelfer-BM-+	Shot down by Flt Lt C C Scherf/Fg Off E A Brown, 418 Sqn, Vornay SE of Avord, 1630 hrs. Ferry flight to Bordeaux.
29 Jan 44	12/KG 40	Fw 200 C-4/U2 (0139) F8+HW (CE+ID), ex F8+FT	Fw Karl Miklas-F-trainee+ Uffz Karl Rau-F-+ Uffz Erhard Jaensch-Bf-+ Ogefr Benedikt Helmer-ground crew-+ Ofw Karl-Heinz Schwennicke-F-inj. Ofw Josef Haas-BM-inj. Fw Karl Sand-BM-inj. Fw Johann Nelles-ground crew-inj.	Shot down on a training flight by Wg Cdr E Haabjoern, Plt Off R S Colquhoun, Fg Off A S Aitcheson & Fg Off K B Sellick, 247 Sqn, Semerville, south of Chateaudun. Ofw Schwennicke instructor.
05 Feb 44	8/KG 40	Fw 200 C-4 (0170) (CH+CK)	Hpt Ing Anton Leder-F-+ Uffz Kurt Frosch-F-inj. Ofw Franz Krasemann-1 BF-+ Fw Josef Klütgens-2 BF-inj. Uffz Fritz Schimmel-BM-+ Ogefr Paul Stähler-BM-inj. Uffz Herbert Tücking-BS-+ Gefr Peter Möbus-Waffenwart+ Gefr Franz Hölter-Fugzeug-Elektriker-inj. Ogefr Artur Stieg-Flugzeug-Mechaniker-inj.	Ferrying flight. Shot down by P-38s nr St. Juest, 10 kms SW of Avord airfield. 20FG claimed 2, 55FG claimed 1 e/a. (Lt Col R P Montgomery with 2/Lt J E Davis & Capt P J Sabo, 77th FS / 20 FG, 1122 hrs, Bourges)
12 Feb 44	7/KG 40	Fw 200 C F8+CR	FljFw Karl-Heinz Schairer-F-M FljFw Horst Groschek-B-M Uffz Werner Desor-B-M Uffz Johann-Henning Jansen-1 BF-M (9/KG 40) Flg Hans Zdolsek-2 BF-M Uffz Franz Österreich-BM-M Uffz Horst Linde-BS-M Ogefr Gerhard Röthig-BS-M	Shot down by Flt Lt R D Doleman/Flt Lt Mc Allister, Flt Lt B M Whitlock/Fg Off Hull & Fg Off V H C Hannawin/Fg Off Tofts, 157 Sqn, Convoy OS 67/KMS 41 – 400 sea miles W of Cape Finisterre. Or fighters of escort carrier *HMS Pursuer.*
12 Feb 44	9/KG 40	Fw 200 C	Fw Günter Hickmann-BF-inj.	Possibly damaged in combat with Fg Off V H C Hannawin/Fg Off Tofts, 157 Sqn, PI.Q. 14W/7517 (see above).

Date	Unit	Aircraft (W.Nr / code)	Crew	Remarks
12 Feb 44	Stab III/40	Fw 200 C	Uffz Werner Zerrahn-BF-inj.	Probably damaged in combat with Fg Off V H C Hannawin/Fg Off Tofts, 157 Sqn, Pl.Q. 14W/7581 – 45.00N/07.22W. (see above)
19 Feb 44	12/KG 40	Fw 200 C-4/U4 (0152) F8+BW (CE+IQ)	Uffz Emil Kumpert-F-+ / Ogefr Ernst Selle-F-+ / Ogefr Hans Branscheid-B-+ / Ogefr Günter Gross-BF-+ / Gefr Lothar Wetzelt-BF-+ / Uffz Heinz Vogelmann-BM-+ / Gefr Arno Paul-ground crew-+ / Uffz Heinrich Beckmann-1. Wart-+ / Uffz Fritz Herting-Bildstelle-+	Crashed during training flight, probably due to pilot error. 100% dam. Unterbergen/Lech.
05 Mar 44	/KG 40	Fw 200 C-4 (0194) (GC+SW)	—	Enemy fighters, St Jean d'Angely. (see below)
05 Mar 44	7/KG 40	Fw 200 C-5 (0244) F8+_R (TK+CZ)	FhjFw Hermann Wesemann-F-+	Attacked by enemy fighters 15 kms east of St. Jean d'Angely airfield. (see below)
05 Mar 44	7/KG 40	Fw 200 C-4 (0248) F8+_R (TO+XD)	Lt Helmut Kütterer-F-inj. / Uffz Wilhelm Pohlmann-BF-+ / Uffz Wilhelm Schützek-BM-inj. / Ogefr Rudi Zeh-Flgz.-Mechaniker-+ / Gefr Herbert Winkler-Flgz.-Mechaniker-+	Shot down by enemy fighters 6 kms NE St.Jean d'Angely airfield. (see below) [Claims by Lt E P Freeburger & Capt K G Smith (Fw 200 shared), Capt K G Smith (destroyed), 355th FS/4th FG, Bergerac airfield, 1230 hrs, Capt K D Peterson, 336th FS/4th FG (destroyed Bordeaux, 1215-1220 hrs), Capt G V Davies 364th FS/357th FG (2 destroyed, Parthenay, 1200 hrs), 2/Lt M A Stanley, 364th FS/357th FG (destroyed Parthenay, 1200 hrs), Lt R A Peterson, 364th FS/357th FG (destroyed, Bordeaux, 1215 hrs)]
31 Mar 44	3/KG 40	Fw 200 C-3 (0062) F8+BL (KF+QB)	Oblt Walter Klomp-F-M / Fw Gotthilf Ackermann-F-M / Ofw Erich Karg-BF-M / Ogefr Reinhold Meier-BF-M / Uffz Wilhelm Sander-BM-M / Uffz Werner Böthling-BS-M	Convoy JW 58, N of Lofoten Islands. (see below)

Date	Unit	Aircraft	Crew	Remarks
31 Mar 44	3/KG 40	Fw 200 C-6 (0220) F8+GL (TA+MV)	Oblt Alfred Weyer-F-M Fw Hermann Kadow-F-M Ofw Erwin Löhr-BF-M Fw Albert Zielinski-BF-M Ofw Josef Glasstetter-BM-M Ogefr Rudolf Bringemeier-BS-M Fw Hans-Georg Drescher-B-M	Convoy JW 58, 400 kms NW of Lofoten Islands. (see below)
31 Mar 44	3/KG 40	Fw 200 C-8 (0224) F8+OL (TA+MZ)	Uffz Alfred Göbel-F-M Uffz Arthur Czychi-F-M Uffz Johann Göd-BF-M Uffz Albert Heil-BF-M Uffz Gerhard Henze-BM-M Ogefr Josef Straschek-BS-M Uffz Karl-Heinz Frink-B-M	Claims by S/Lt N M Simon in Wildcat JV601/Z & S/Lt L A S Swift in JV522/R of 819 Sqn, *HMS Tracker*, 69.29N/00.27E, 0920 hrs; S/Lt G B C Sangster in JV391/S & S/Lt B H Beeston in JV522/R of 819 Sqn, *HMS Tracker*, 70.20N /01.30W, 1819 hrs; S/Lt G C Debney in JV485 & S/Lt R H Meed in JV490 of 846 Sqn, *HMS Activity*, 70.18N/00.02E, 1627 hrs.
11 May 44	Stab III/40	Fw 200 C-5 (0203) (TA+ME)	Oblt Günter Seide-F-+ Uffz Helmut Jahn-BM-inj.	Ferrying flight. Gotenhafen-Schwerin. Both outer engines seized and crashed at Kunersdorf.
19 May 44	12/KG 40	Fw 200 C-4 (0113) F8+EW (NT+BM)	Uffz Karl Fick-F-+ Uffz Horst Kämpfe-F-+ Gefr Hans-Karl Freund-B-+ Uffz Anton Fröschl-BF-+ Gefr Walter Künzler-BF-+ Uffz Josef Holzbrecher-BM-+ Gefr Herbert Zahalke-ground crew-+	Crashed during training flight at Wormditt airfield/Eastern Prussia. Cause unknown.
21 May 44		Fw 200 C-2 (0016)	—	Destroyed by air-raid at Leipzig/Schkeuditz.

Date	Unit	Type	Crew	Remarks
14 Jun 44	9/KG 40	Fw 200 C-4 (0193) (GC+SV)	Ofw Hans Hauenstein-F-+ Fw Herbert Frei-B-+ Fw Heinz Schwarz-BF-+ Flg Hans Ahrens-BF-+ Fw Johann Leitenmeier-BM-+ Ogefr Herbert Daevel-BS-+ Ogefr Oswald Hauptfleisch-BS-+ Uffz Max Müssig-Flgz.-Motorenschlosser-+ Uffz Ludwig Haschke-Bodenpersonal-+ Ogefr Fritz Heisig-Fahrer-+ (Ln-Zug, III/KG 40) Ogefr Wilhelm Marcher-Bodenpersonal-inj. Ogefr Kurt Rössler-Fahrer-inj. (Stabskp. III/KG 40) Ofw Eckehard Roeder-BM-+ (Stabskp. III/KG 40)	Missed approach at Roth nr Nuremberg and hit tree. Ac carrying important technical equipment for the Invasion front.
17 Jun 44	7/KG 40	Fw 200 C-5 (0261) (TO+XQ)	Uffz Hans Liedtke-F-inj. Uffz Werner Krauss-B-+ Ogefr Kurt Meding-BM-inj.	Take-off accident at St. Jean d'Angely. No combat mission, destroyed.
22 Jun 44	Stab III/40	Fw 200 C	Fl Ing Anton Wagner-+	Attacked by Flt Lt L C Gregory/Fg Off R W Usher in MM437 & Fg Off B C Gray/Fg Off L T Gorvin in MM447 of 151 Sqn, 1445-1830 hrs, during landing at Cognac airfield. Ferry flight from Bordeaux. Less than 10% dam.
05 Jul 44	9/KG 40	Fw 200 C-3 (0038) (SG+KN)	Fw Otto Kipp-BF-inj. Uffz Siegfried Hoffmann-BM-inj. Gefr Fritz Meier-BS-inj. Uffz Otto Kiphut-1. Wart-+ Fw Heinz Graubner-F-& rest of crew uninj.	On the way to an auxiliary airfield and was attacked by P-38 Lightnings, Capt A F Jeffrey, 434th FS/479th FG & crashed at Cognac.
09 Jul 44	7/KG 40	Fw 200 C-4 (0183) (GC+SL)	Lt Helmut Kütterer-1 F-+ Fw Karl Novotny-2 F & B-+ Fw Horst Flechsig-1 BF-+ Fw Karl Greeb-2 BF-+ Uffz Kurt Schramm-BM-+ Uffz Ernst Kreigenfeld-BS-+ Ogefr Erhard Sumpf-BS-+ Ofw Siegfried Kalinowski-Oberwerkmeister-+ Uffz Bruno Greil-1. Wart-+ Uffz Georg Kunis-Funkwart-+ Uffz Ernst Lupp-Motoren Schlosser-+ Ogefr Walter Köbrich-K.Truppenführer-+	Crashed against a mountain (992 metres) due to fog, 100 kms NE Clermont-Ferrand. 0545 hrs. Crashed 90 metres below the mountain peak. Pl.Qu. 04Ost/37882. Ferrying flight, ac destroyed. St Nicholas des Biefs.

Date	Unit	Aircraft	Crew	Remarks
18 Jul 44		Fw 200 A-09/S9 (3099) *Ostmark* D-ARHU	—	Destroyed air attack.
17 Jul 44	III/KG 40	Fw 200 C-8 (0262) F8+IS (TO+XR)	FhjFw Willibald Schuster-B-inj.	Ferrying flight. Crashed after take-off at Werder/Havel. 85% dam.
18 Jul 44	12/KG 40	Fw 200 C-3/U7 (0227) F8+EW (DP+OO)	Oblt Eduard Zöchling-F-+ Oblt Ferdinand Schreithoffer-F-+ (7/40) Major Zipf-B-+ (Stab KG 40, Adj.) Fw Robert Brell-BF-+ Fw Walter Spenrath-BM-+ Ogefr Wilhelm Mathis-BS-+ Uffz Alfred Ehrfeld-ground crew-+ (KG 40) Uffz Manning-ground crew-+ (KG 40)	Crashed during ferrying flight 1 km east of Mirambeau (60 kms north of Bordeaux). Destroyed.
18 Jul 44		Fw 200 A-0 / V3 / S-9 (3099) D-ARHU *Ostmark* / D-2600 26+00 *Immelmann III*	?	Destroyed in air-raid.
14 Aug 44	8/KG 40	Fw 200 C-6 (0218) F8+CD (?) (TA+MT) F8+AD (?) on 15 Aug 43	Oblt Rudolf Biberger-F-+ Lt Karl Markert-BF-+ (3/KG 40) Uffz Helmut (Hellmut ?) Meyer-F-+ Uffz Erich Pfeifer-BF-+ Uffz Frido-Max Sander-BM-+ Gustav Walter (Walther ?)-Prüfmeister-+ Ogefr Horst Thelemann-B-inj. Ogefr Walter Küster--inj. Uffz Heinz Neubauer- -+	Crashed at Torp in Malvik nr Drontheim. Introducing a new crew. Probably hit ground during a turn due to air stream behind a mountain. (Circling at low altitude, wing suddenly touched ground.)
27 Sep 44	*Lufthansa*	Fw 200 D-2c / KC-1 (0021) F8+BU/D-AMHL *Pommern*, ex NA+WN)	Flug Kapitän Helmut Liman-F-+ Heinrich Papenhagen-Bm-+ Leo Armphlett-Bf-+ & 5 civilian passengers-+	2031 hrs, SE of Djion. Claim by Capt Harold F Augspurger & 2/Lt A G Petry, 415th NFS. Beaufighter. Crashed N of Saint Nicolas Les Citeaux.
11 Oct 44	7/KG 40	Fw 200 C-4 (0163) (CH+CD)	Lt Hans Gilbert-1 F-+ Ohfr Gert Jochums-2 F-+ Ofw Martin Hochmuth-BF-+ Fw Hubert Langguth-BM-+ Fw Hans Prahl-BS-+ Hptm Clement-?-+ Hptm Krenn-Kp.Chef 2. F.K.B.K.-+ Ob Ing Benecke & several *Luftwaffenhelferinnen*-+	Ferrying flight – crashed at Lavangerfjord south of Bardufoss, 1245 hrs. Destroyed.

Date	Unit	Aircraft	Crew	Fate
21 Oct 44	7./KG 40	Fw 200 C-8 (0257) F8+HR (TO+XM)	Ofw Wolfgang Liepe-F-+ / Fw Günter Mücke-F-+ / Ogefr Franz Nowak-BF-+ / Ofw Walter Fischer-BF-inj. / Ogefr Ernst Stroble-BM-inj. / Uffz Erwin Hedlich-BS-inj.	Take-off accident at Nautsi/Norway (Finl.), 98% dam. Transport flight.
09 Nov 44	7./KG 40	Fw 200 C-8 (0267) F8+HR (TO+XW)	—	Take-off accident.
29 Nov 44	KG 40	Fw 200 A-0 / S-5 (2994) D-ARHW *Friesland*/ CB+TY/F8+EU / F8+HH	Flugkapt Erns-Heinz Breitenbach-+ / Oberfunker-machinist Fritz Brauner-+ / Wolfgang Lenz-+ / + 6 pax-+	Shot down by *Kriegsmarine* at Falsterbo / Sweden. DHL-Linie Berlin-Stockholm.
22 Jan 45	Trans.St. Condor	Fw 200 C-4/U3 (0172) (GC+SA)	—	Undercarriage damage during landing at Aalborg-West airfield.
24 Mar 45		Fw 200 C-3 D-ASHG	—	Destroyed in air-raid Munich-Riem airfield.
01 Apr 45	Transp.St. Condor	Fw 200 C-1 G6+AY = 14./TG 4	Obfw Adalbert Schaffranek & crew – safe	Landing accident at Wien-Aspern.0620 hrs.
20 Apr 45		Fw 200 C-6/U2 (216) F8+JH (TA+MR)	—	Destroyed by air-raid at Berlin-Tempelhof airfield.
20/21 Apr 45		Fw 200 C-3 (0037) D-ASHH *Hessen*	Flugkapt August Kuenstle-+ / Oberflugmachinist Karl Felz-+ / Funkermachinist Fritz Hubrig-+ / Herbert Eschner-+ / 17 pax-+	Crashed at Piesenkof.
21 Apr 45		Fw 200 C-5 (0203) (TA+ME)	—	Destroyed by air-raid, Leipzig.
26 Apr 45	9./KG 40	Fw 200 C-4/U2 (0138) F8+IT (CE+IC)	—	Shot down by Flak, Wilhelmshorst.
05 May 45		Fw 200	—	Landed at Boellstein.
06 May 45		Fw 200 C-4 (0111) (NT+BK) D-ASVX *Thüringen*	?	Captured at Flensburg, RAF AM .96 – scrapped 29 Jul 47, Tastrup/Denmark.
06 May 45		Fw 200 C-4/U2 (0181) (GC+SJ) *Albatros III*	?	Captured at Flensburg, RAF AM 97 – scrapped 28 Feb 46.

Date	Unit	Aircraft type / code (W.Nr.)	Crew	Fate
08 May 45	8/KG 40 Transp.St. Condor	Fw 200 C-5/FK / C-3/U1 (0191) – F8+MS (GC+ST) = 14./TG 4		Crew from 1(F)/22: Schweitzer, Uffz Walter Träger, Uffz Harald Loseke, Ogefr Alois Bauer, Ogefr Eduard Schott & Lt Albert Zepf. Landed Torslanda near Göteborg.
17 May 45	Transp.St. Condor	Fw 200 C-3/U7 (0226) G6+FY = 14./TG 4 (DP+ON)	Haupt.Ing. Link-B & Kapt.-POW Fw Adalbert Schaffranek-1.FF-POW Fw Buthner-2.FF-POW Fw Hottlinger-1.BF-POW Fw Dehndel-2.BF-POW Fw Bohner-1.BM-POW Uffz Kuchinko-2.BM-POW	Captured at Calatos/Gadurra.
22 Jun 45	I/KG 40	Fw 200 C-5 (0205) (TA+MG) – Transp.St.Condor	–	Burnt at Gardemoen.
45/46		Fw 200 C-8 (0245) (TO+XA) – Transp.St.Condor	–	Cannibalized in Vaaler/Denmark.
Mai 46		Transp.St.Condor Fw 200 C-6 (0133) (VY+OG)	–	Burnt at Gardemoen.
04 Sep 46		Fw 200 KA-1 / S-4 (2993) OY-DEM *Jutlandia*	–	Damaged in landing Northolt. Not repaired.
8 Mar 47		Fw 200 A-0 / S-6 (2995) D-ASBK *Holstein* / PP-CBJ *Arumani*	–	Taxiing damage by DC-3, Rio de Janeiro. Scrapped.

Index

Other books in the Complete History series

The Lockheed Martin Hercules
Peter C Smith

The most versatile military transport aircraft ever built, the C-130 Hercules has been in continuous production for over half a century and has seen service with more than fifty different air forces around the world.

Originating in the 1950's when the USAF needed an aircraft with heavy cargo lifting ability, troop-carrying capacity and the ability to operate safely from the most primitive of runways the Hercules has appeared wherever there has been a crisis, war or emergency.

In combat, no matter whether in tropical jungle, desert landing strips or almost-impassable terrain, the C-130's homely and familiar profile has materialised where she was most needed. From the icy wastes of Antarctica to the earthquake-stricken island of Haiti in January 2010, the aircraft has arrived on the scene laden with medical and emergency supplies, aid teams and heavy lifting gear.

This is the full story of the Hercules and a faithful record of all her exploits in her many guises, from gunship in Vietnam, to flying hospital in Arabia, and is fully illustrated with many original colour and black-and-white photographs. All Hercules types and many foreign air forces and civilian operators are covered, including their varied uses and multiple roles.

This complete aircraft history also contains a type listing, details of sub-contractors, exhibits and museums together with colour aircraft profiles which combine to make the *Lockheed Martin Hercules* essential reading for the aviation enthusiast, modeller or historian.

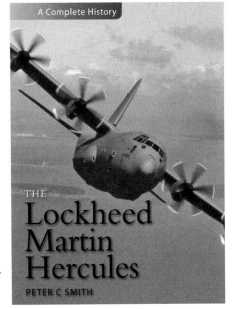

Over 300 pages, hardback
246mm x 189mm
Over 200 b&w and colour photographs
8 page colour section
9 780859 79153 3 £29.95

To order or for more information visit www.crecy.co.uk or telephone +44 (0)161 499 0024

The Hawker Hunter

Tim Mclelland

Tim McLelland's *Hawker Hunter* is both a comprehensive work of reference and an authoritative history. It covers the origins of the aircraft from both the P1040 and P1052 swept-wing versions and moves through design and development of the twin-seat dual-control Hunter T7 to the 'ultimate' FGA.Mk.9. The Hunters varied operational successes are noted with particular emphasis on major foreign users in Switzerland and India, and, amongst others, exports to Oman and Chile.

Extracts from the Hunter's original Aircrew Manual and appendices covering service histories, serial numbers and the fate of each Hunter constructed, combine to provide full details of this Cold War Interceptor and ground attack platform.

Colour profiles by Richard Caruana coupled with storied and anecdotes from former Hunter air and ground crew ensure the complete history of the aircraft is presented in a single volume and provides essential reading for the aviation enthusiast, modeller or historian.

384 pages, hardback
246mm x 189mm
Approx 250 b&w photographs + drawings and 27 colour drawings
9 780859 791236 £29.95

'An automatic addition to your bookshelf. Highly recommended.'
Model Aircraft Monthly

To order or for more information visit www.crecy.co.uk or telephone +44 (0)161 499 0024

The Avro Vulcan

Tim Mclelland

The story of the Avro Vulcan is as dramatic as the presence of the aircraft itself. Designed by a team led by Roy Chadwick, the man responsible for the legendary Lancaster, the Vulcan was one of the three bombers designed to carry Britain's nuclear deterrent in the 1950s and 1960's. But it was Avro's delta-winged colossus that became the backbone of the V-force, remaining poised to strike at the heart of the Soviet Union until the very end of the 1960's when the deterrent role passed from the RAF's manned bomber to the Navy's Polaris submarine fleet.

The Vulcan remained in RAF service as a tactical low-level bomber armed with conventional and nuclear weapons, and was only retired following the introduction of the Panavia Tornado. It was nonetheless able to write a spectacular epilogue to its operational career when in 1982 the aircraft was selected to undertake the longest bombing raid flown in British military history – to the Falklands.

This is Sheffield based Tim McLelland's brand new third book on the *Avro Vulcan* and is both a comprehensive work of reference and an authoritative history. It covers the origins of the Vulcan and delta-winged flight, details of every major production variant and also, using newly released information describes the aircraft's use as a test-bed for a variety of missile, engine and equipment technologies. The book reproduces extracts from the Vulcan's original Aircrew Manual together with appendices on both squadron disposal and the fate of every Vulcan built. Also included is a wealth of information and anecdotes from former Vulcan air and ground crews, describing from first-hand experience what it was like to live with the mighty aircraft.

This comprehensive coverage is completed with over 250 photographs, new scale drawings and colour profiles making the *Avro Vulcan* a vital read for historians, modellers and aviation enthusiasts alike.

368 pages, hardback
246mm x 189mm
250 b&w photographs + drawings
Over 20 colour drawings
9 780859 791274 £29.95

A Complete History

THE
Avro
Vulcan

TIM McLELLAND

To order or for more information visit www.crecy.co.uk or
telephone +44 (0)161 499 0024

The Bristol Blenheim
Graham Warner
2nd edition

An exhaustively researched narrative backed up by a wealth of photographs and illustrations cover the Blenheim's history from initial conception in the 1930's, through the outbreak of war to the Battle of Britain and beyond. *The Bristol Blenheim* details the aircraft's roles not just in the European and Far Eastern Theatres of War, the Middle East campaigns in the Western Desert and from Malta, but also the lesser-known air operations in Iraq, Syria and East Africa.

The aircraft's wide-ranging operational career as a day and night bomber, a low-level attack aircraft, night fighter, long-range day fighter, reconnaissance and training machine are examined in depth and over 400 photographs, some in colour plus a section of colour profiles highlight many of the aircraft's variants and liveries.

Informative appendices detail all Blenheim losses including aircraft serial numbers and crew members and provide an in-depth look into this remarkable and often overlooked aircraft.

654 pages, hardback
246mm x 189mm
Over 440 b&w photos and 2 x 8 page colour sections
9 780859 791014 £34.95

The Tiger Moth Story
Alan Bramson

The Tiger Moth is one of aviation's major success stories and Alan Bramson provides a comprehensive account of the aircraft origins and development as a trainer of Commonwealth pilots in times of peace and war, as a crop duster, glider tug, aerial advertiser, bomber, coastal patrol plane and aerial ambulance as well as its time in frontline service.

Technical narrative and drawings, handling ability and performance as seen through the eyes of the pilots including a fully updated world survey of existing aircraft combine to make *The Tiger Moth Story* the most comprehensive book of the aircraft. A bestseller since 1964, this edition is fully revised, updated, indexed and includes many new black and white photographs, plus a new colour section.

272 pages, hardback
246mm x 189mm
Over 100 b&w photographs
20 colour photographs, 7 maps and drawings
9 780859 791038 £24.95

'A must-read classic' **Pilot Magazine**

'as an account of the Tiger's evolution, it's second to none.' **Flyer**

de Havilland Mosquito
An Illustrated History
Volumes 1 and 2
Stuart Howe and Ian Thirsk

Both volumes of *de Havilland Mosquito An Illustrated History* trace the fascinating development of the Mosquito from its construction through to operational fighter and bomber. Human stories of RAF aircrew, ground crew and Commonwealth Air Forces are also detailed.

Volume 1 follows the history of the Mosquito from its first flight in November 1940 through to its production and many variants. The aircraft's varied post war uses are outlined in roles ranging from oil prospecting and air racing to aerial survey.

Volume 2 covers the Mosquito factory and the people who worked with and flew in her together with many of the Mosquito variants including fighter, bombers, sea Mosquitoes, target tugs and that operated by the Russians.

Extended captions in **both** volumes include aircraft numbers, specifications, dates, personalities, and background information coupled with over 1,000 black and white photographs which make the set a must for researchers and historians alike.

de Havilland Mosquito
An Illustrated History - Volume 1
Stuart Howe
176 pages, paperback
268mm x 198mm
Over 400 b&w + 18 colour photographs
9 780947 554767 £14.95

de Havilland Mosquito
An Illustrated History - Volume 2
Ian Thirsk
400 pages, paperback
268mm x 198mm
Approx 700 b&w + 22 colour photographs
9 780859 791021 £19.95

'Both books are a real treasure trove of pictures and complement each other as there is no duplication of photos. As usual with books from Crecy, they not only have quality content but 'feel' like quality books too!'
Catalina News

To order or for more information visit
www.crecy.co.uk or telephone +44 (0)161 499 0024